The Undivided Self

OXFORD ARISTOTLE STUDIES

General Editor
Lindsay Judson

PUBLISHED VOLUMES INCLUDE

Doing and Being
An Interpretation of Aristotle's Metaphysics *Theta*
Jonathan Beere

Aristotle on the Sources of the Ethical Life
Sylvia Berryman

Space, Time, Matter, and Form
Essays on Aristotle's Physics
David Bostock

Aristotle on Meaning and Essence
David Charles

Aristotle and the Eleatic One
Timothy Clarke

Time for Aristotle
Physics IV. 10–14
Ursula Coope

Passions and Persuasion in Aristotle's *Rhetoric*
Jamie Dow

Teleology, First Principles, and Scientific Method in Aristotle's Biology
Allan Gotthelf

Aristotle on the Common Sense
Pavel Gregoric

The Powers of Aristotle's Soul
Thomas Kjeller Johansen

Aristotle on Teleology
Monte Ransome Johnson

How Aristotle Gets by in *Metaphysics Zeta*
Frank A. Lewis

Aristotle on the Apparent Good
Perception, Phantasia, *Thought, and Desire*
Jessica Moss

Priority in Aristotle's *Metaphysics*
Michail Peramatzis

Aristotle's Theory of Bodies
Christian Pfeiffer

The Undivided Self

Aristotle and the 'Mind–Body Problem'

DAVID CHARLES

Great Clarendon Street, Oxford, OX2 6DP,
United Kingdom

Oxford University Press is a department of the University of Oxford.
It furthers the University's objective of excellence in research, scholarship,
and education by publishing worldwide. Oxford is a registered trade mark of
Oxford University Press in the UK and in certain other countries

© David Charles 2021

The moral rights of the author have been asserted

First published 2021
First published in paperback 2023

All rights reserved. No part of this publication may be reproduced, stored in
a retrieval system, or transmitted, in any form or by any means, without the
prior permission in writing of Oxford University Press, or as expressly permitted
by law, by licence or under terms agreed with the appropriate reprographics
rights organization. Enquiries concerning reproduction outside the scope of the
above should be sent to the Rights Department, Oxford University Press, at the
address above

You must not circulate this work in any other form
and you must impose this same condition on any acquirer

Published in the United States of America by Oxford University Press
198 Madison Avenue, New York, NY 10016, United States of America

British Library Cataloguing in Publication Data
Data available

Library of Congress Cataloging in Publication Data
Data available

ISBN 978–0–19–886956–6 (Hbk.)
ISBN 978–0–19–888245–9 (Pbk.)

DOI: 10.1093/oso/9780198869566.001.0001

Links to third party websites are provided by Oxford in good faith and
for information only. Oxford disclaims any responsibility for the materials
contained in any third party website referenced in this work.

To Sunny and Farooq Haroon

Preface

Aristotle undertook a systematic investigation of perception, the emotions, memory, desire, and action, developing his own account of these phenomena and their interconnection. My aim is to gain a philosophical understanding of his views and to examine how far they withstand critical scrutiny.

Aristotle's approach calls into question the way in which our, post-Cartesian, mind–body problem has been formulated. He was guided throughout by a conception of the psychological and of the material that was rejected by those who originally set up and subsequently sought to address our problem. His views constitute an alternative to basic elements of our conventional thinking about psychological phenomena and their place in a material world. They offer, in effect, the resources to dissolve, rather than solve, the mind–body problem we have inherited. Or so I shall argue.

Aristotle's account is not, as is sometimes suggested, a version of a standard post-Cartesian theory: dualism, materialism (whether reductionist or non-reductionist), functionalism, or neutral monism. But nor does it rest, as is sometimes claimed, on assumptions that we can no longer take seriously. Properly understood, it is a philosophically live alternative to standard thinking in this area of philosophy.

It is the task of historians of philosophy to grasp, and articulate, what is distinctive about the authors they study in a detailed, historically sensitive way. Doing so is, of course, a good in itself. But does twenty-first-century philosophy have anything to gain from their studies? Shouldn't contemporary philosophers simply tackle today's problems without considering the views of their predecessors?

One major benefit of the study of philosophy's history is that it provides the opportunity to look critically at the way in which contemporary problems have been formulated. Perhaps the manner in which this has been done sometimes leads us astray. It would, after all, be a piece of exceptional good fortune if they all had been ideally set up at just the time we came to study them. Consideration of Aristotle's views may suggest a way to 'deconstruct' major, seemingly irresoluble, questions in what we, but not he, would call the philosophy of mind.

Recognition of diversity is, of course, a good. So too is the possibility of experimenting with different ways of thinking. But it is also important for historians of Aristotle's philosophy to examine the extent to which his ideas, properly understood, withstand scrutiny, where they should be rejected and where retained and built on. Doing so may reveal ways to avoid apparently unsatisfactory orthodoxies in current thinking. Historians of philosophy need not, and perhaps should not, be narrow specialists confined to their own sub-branch of enquiry. Contemporary philosophy still has things to learn from a detailed study of its history.

The initial idea for this book emerged from discussions in a long-running reading group on *De Anima* held at Oriel College, Oxford. When we decided in 2004, after more than fifteen years spent on the second and third books, to read *De Anima* A.1, much fell into place. I vividly recall our lively meetings at that time in which Paolo Crivelli, Michael Frede, Edward Hussey, Benjamin Morison, Catherine Rowett, Annamaria Schiaparelli, and Cecilia Trifogli were actively engaged. As a result, I began to question and finally reject my earlier, non-reductionist materialist, interpretation of Aristotle's views. However, our work in 2004 was based on many earlier discussions, dating back to 1989, to which Jonathan Beere, Susanne Bobzien, Victor Caston, Stephen Everson, Katerina Ierodiakonou, Thomas Johansen, Lindsay Judson, Jean Louis Labarrière, Hendrik Lorenz, Michail Peramatzis, Frisbee Sheffield, Christopher Shields, and many others had contributed.

I have gained from the opportunity to give seminars on this material in Berlin, Brown, Oxford, Taipei, Tokyo, and Yale and from detailed discussions with, and comments from, Andreas Anagnostopoulos, Udit Bery, David Bronstein, Jason Carter, Kei Chiba, Alan Code, Daniel Devereux, Guus Eelink, Verity Harte, Devin Henry, Brad Inwood, Terry Irwin, Vassilis Karasmanis, Emily Katz, Emily Kress, James Lennox, Frank Lewis, Sam Meister, Giulia Mingucci, Scott O'Connor, Mika Perala, Oliver Primavesi, Diana Quarantotto, Bryan Reece, Jake Rohde, Richard Sorabji, Andrew Werner, Jennifer Whiting, Stephen Williams, and Chin-Mu Yang. I have been particularly fortunate to receive thoughtful and friendly criticism and advice from several experts with different views on these topics: Victor Caston, Klaus Corcilius, Mary Louise Gill, Thomas Johansen, Mark Johnstone, Marko Malink, Christof Rapp, and Christopher Shields. Our discussions have been a model of collaborative work: incisive and challenging but unfailingly constructive and good-humoured. I am greatly indebted to a formidable array of colleagues in ancient philosophy, only some of whom are mentioned in this paragraph, for their criticisms, suggestions, and encouragement.

I was helped in thinking about these issues by a second equally long-lasting group which also met in Oriel College. I owe most, in my present investigation, to those of its members who worked in the philosophy of mind and action, including at various times Bill Brewer, Justin Broackes, John Campbell, Quassim Cassam, Bill Child, Adrian Cussins, Naomi Eilan, Jennifer Hornsby, Michael Martin, Paul Snowdon, Helen Steward, and Rowland Stout. Our discussions were acute, enjoyable, and enlightening. On occasion, I found myself wondering how many comparable meetings of specialists in this area of philosophy there could have been since Aristotle and his friends discussed them long ago, in Assos, Lesbos, and Athens. Justin Broackes, Paul Snowdon, Rowland Stout, and Jonathan Westphal kindly read and commented on parts of the final version.

I am greatly indebted to Peter Momtchiloff for his support and advice, and to Lindsay Judson, Michail Peramatzis, and Howard Robinson for reading the penultimate draft, mixing criticism with encouragement in appropriate measure. Lindsay Judson has once again proved an exemplary critic and editor. Michail Peramatzis and I have discussed these topics in detail over the past fifteen years and I gratefully acknowledge his major role in their development. While I have sought to record his individual contributions on a point-by-point basis, my debt to him far exceeds these. I should also like to thank Paul Schilling for his generous help in preparing the final version for publication.

There are several people whose response to this book I would have valued and will greatly miss: John Ackrill, Myles Burnyeat, Michael Frede, Allan Gotthelf, and David Pears. Each of them discussed earlier versions of some of its ideas and contributed to their development. I am heavily indebted to all of them.

My immediate family, Zafra, Ilan, and Huw, has been an ever-present source of support, encouragement, and criticism. So familiar have they become with some of this book's philosophical and exegetical 'moves' that they have turned them into family jokes. I am very grateful to them for standing by me in the long years it has taken to complete this project.

It is a pleasure to dedicate this book to Sunny and Farooq Haroon, to whose constant friendship over more than fifty years I owe so much.

David Charles

New Haven, Connecticut
18 April 2020

Contents

	Introduction	1
1.	The Emotions	18
	1.1 Fear and anger in *De Anima* A.1	18
	1.2 The first moves	20
	1.3 Physics and mathematics	24
	1.4 The range of Aristotle's proposal in *De Anima* A.1	30
	1.5 The proper way to study anger: the role of matter	32
	1.6 The model of *De Anima* A.1	35
	1.7 Gaps and queries	40
2.	Enmattered Form: Aristotle's Hylomorphism	42
	2.1 Introduction	42
	2.2 Two Interpretations	45
	2.3 Snubness and S-structures	47
	2.4 Metaphysical basis (1): *Metaphysics* Z.10 and 11	53
	2.5 Metaphysical basis (2): *Metaphysics* H.2–4	65
	2.6 Forms and causation	68
	2.7 Is the matter of natural substances inseparable in definition from their forms?	79
	2.8 Interim conclusions: a problem	85
	2.9 Three ways of going (slightly) wrong	87
	2.10 Summary: surviving questions	92
3.	Desire and Action	94
	3.1 An unnerving silence	94
	3.2 How to fill the silence?	95
	3.3 The harmony theory: problems for the non-reductionist interpretation	97
	3.4 Desire in De Motu: Aristotle's four-stage account	102
	3.5 Desire, confidence, and the *connate pneuma*: their role in action	105
	3.6 Instruments, joints, etc.	110
	3.7 Desire and action: an overview of Aristotle's account	114
	3.8 Conclusions	115
4.	Taste and Smell: With Some Remarks on Touch	118
	4.1 Introduction	118
	4.2 Some reminders	119
	4.3 Perceiving: ontology refined	120
	4.4 Perceiving: a 'mere Cambridge change'?	130

4.5   Perceiving: the issue   133
4.6   Tasting: an inextricably psycho-physical completion   136
4.7   Tasting: problems for the spiritualist interpretation   138
4.8   Tasting: problems for the non-reductionist materialist
      interpretation   144
4.9   Tasting and smelling: a summary   152
4.10 The case of touch   153
4.11 Taking on the form without the matter   155
4.12 Interim conclusions   162

5. Hearing, Seeing, and Hylomorphism   163
   5.1   Hearing: the issue   163
   5.2   Hearing: what is the sound in the medium?   165
   5.3   Sounds, sounding, and hearing: the message   168
   5.4   Hearing: interim conclusions   171
   5.5   A spiritualist argument concerning seeing   172
   5.6   What happens in the medium?   174
   5.7   The medium (1)   179
   5.8   The medium (2): the 'illuminable', fire, and the colours
         in the 'illuminable' (*diaphanes*)   182
   5.9   The sense organ: seeing   185
   5.10 Seeing: a more general perspective   188

6. Perception, Desire, and Action: Inextricably Embodied Subjects   194
   6.1   Introduction: further extensions?   194
   6.2   The perception of moving objects: 'common sensibles'   195
   6.3   Perception, pain, pleasure, and desire: the basic model   205
   6.4   Imagination and desire: the basic model extended   210
   6.5   The human subject: the unity of our soul   213
   6.6   Practical thought: an essentially enmattered type of thought?   217
   6.7   Thought and subjects of thought   220
   6.8   Summary   223

7. Aristotle's Viewpoint   225
   7.1   Common to body and soul   225
   7.2   A first comparison: non-reductionist materialism   229
   7.3   Partial overview   232
   7.4   Aristotle and functionalism   234
   7.5   Ackrill's problem: different perspectives   239
   7.6   Aristotle and neo-Aristotelian hylomorphism   246
   7.7   No longer credible?   253

8. Aristotle's Undivided Self   254
   8.1   Two inextricability theses   254
   8.2   The first inextricability thesis: the search for the purely
         psychological   259
   8.3   The search for the purely psychological continued:
         subjectivity revisited   264

8.4 Further arguments against essential embodiment 269
8.5 The second inextricability thesis: the role of the purely physical 272
8.6 Isn't Aristotle's view a 'notational variant' of non-reductionist
materialism? 276
8.7 Diagnosis, resolution, and remaining problems 281

Bibliography 287
Index Locorum 295
General Index 299
Index Nominum 302

Introduction

Aristotle developed a way of understanding psychological phenomena, such as the emotions, desire, and perception, that differs in important ways from those favoured by nearly all post-Cartesian philosophers. He did not accept the assumptions that we make in setting up and addressing our mind–body problem. If his viewpoint is defensible, it is Descartes' problem—and not Aristotle's account—that should be taken off the philosophical agenda.

Our mind–body problem can be expressed, at first approximation, as follows: how can the physical, defined without any explicit reference in its definition to the psychological, give rise to the psychological with its distinctive features, where the psychological is defined (in part or in whole) without any explicit reference in its definition to the physical?

In articulating this problem, the psychological is defined in terms of features such as consciousness, rationality, or certain phenomenal properties, themselves defined (in whole or in part) without reference (in their definition) to any physical properties. Psychological events and states are ones defined in terms of their possession of these distinctive properties. The physical, in turn, is defined in terms of features of events or states, such as being spatio-temporal or being studied by physics, themselves defined without any reference to the psychological. Our mind–body problem is: how does the physical, so defined, give rise to the psychological, so defined? How, for example, does our conscious experience of colour, the painfulness of our grief, what it is like to experience the pleasures of touch or taste and our commitment to principles of rationality arise out of the states, events, and properties studied by physics?

For some, like Descartes himself, this problem, once stated, is insoluble: the psychological, when properly understood, cannot arise from the physical because physical and psychological features belong to fundamentally different types of subject. Subjects of conscious experience are not, and cannot emerge from, purely physical phenomena. The world is made up of two fundamentally different types of substance. Later philosophers, dissatisfied with Descartes' substance dualism, have searched for ways to solve his problem. Here, in barest outline, are five of their suggestions:

(a) Reductionist materialism: the psychological, properly understood, can be fully explained in terms of the physical, so defined. Psychological events, states and their properties are reducible to physical events, states, and properties.

(b) Non-reductionist materialism: the psychological, so defined, 'arises out' of the physical but is not fully explicable in terms of it. Even if particular psychological events are identical with physical events, their psychological properties are not reducible to physical properties but rest on, or emerge out of, them. (Non-reductionist materialism.)[1]

(c) The psychological itself, phenomenal consciousness and rational commitments alike, can be fully defined in terms of their causal roles (as in various versions of functionalism) or dispositions to behaviour. So understood, all psychological phenomena can be unproblematically realized in physical events or states. (Hostile critics sometimes refer to this view as 'consciousness denial'.)

(d) Pan-psychism or spiritualism: the physical is understood in terms which make its connection with the psychological readily intelligible. It, or some parts of it, is redefined as alive with consciousness or proto-consciousness, primitively disposed to have conscious experience.

(e) Neutral monism: the physical and the psychological, defined as above, are each to be understood as emerging from a more basic type of stuff which is neither physical nor psychological but neutral between them.

Aristotle, I shall suggest, did not adopt any of these approaches. Instead, he developed a way of thinking about psychological and physical phenomena which, once properly set out, dissolves the mind–body problem that these proposals are designed to address. More specifically, he did not accept:

(1) the definitions of the psychological or of the physical later used to formulate it

or

(2) the ontology of events and states generally presupposed in doing so.

Our perception of colour, experiences of pain and pleasure, desires and the rest are, in his view, inextricably psycho-physical activities whose essential properties are inextricably psycho-physical.[2] Neither these activities nor their properties can be adequately defined without reference in their definition to types of physical

---

[1] Some non-reductionists (like Colin McGinn 1990) argue that while the psychological arises out of the physical, we cannot understand or render intelligible to ourselves how this happens. Most seek to render these connections intelligible.
[2] Aristotle, as we shall see, carefully distinguished processes and activities of various types. The formulations in this chapter are a first approximation to a fuller interpretation of the relevant ontology.

activities, capacities, and properties. Nor, in his view, can the latter be adequately defined without essential reference in their definition to psychological activities, such as perception or conscious experience of the world. The phenomena at issue cannot be defined by decomposition into two definitionally separable components, one purely psychological (defined without explicit reference to the physical), the other purely physical (defined without reference to the psychological). From his perspective, the two assumptions (1) and (2), which drive nearly all post-Cartesian philosophy of mind, spring from mistaken ways of thinking about the psychological and the physical. Nor does his approach rest on analysing out, still less denying, the problematic features of the psychological or on redefining the physical in the radical way pan-psychists require.

Aristotle's views have been the subject of scholarly debate. He has, in fact, regularly been interpreted as an advocate of one or other of the options just outlined. For some, he was a dualist.[3] For others, a precursor of a version of functionalism or of non-reductionist materialism, options that have become fashionable in recent years.[4] For still others, he avoided Descartes' challenge but only at the cost of embracing an account of the physical which it is difficult, if not impossible, for anyone today to take seriously. This is because, in their view, he adopted a 'spiritualist' view of matter as 'pregnant with consciousness' or 'essentially alive and capable of awareness', a form of pan-psychism which was, many think, rightly 'junked' in the seventeenth century.[5]

Aristotle's views are not, I shall argue, accurately captured by these interpretations. Their proponents are, or so I shall suggest, led astray by shared, deeply rooted, post-Cartesian assumptions. His account, in fact, offers an interesting and defensible alternative precisely because it does not share the preconceptions that we, and most since Descartes, unreflectively use in thinking about this problem. It merits and repays philosophical scrutiny even though,

---

[3] See, for example, Robert Heinaman (1990: 83–102).

[4] For one example of a functionalist interpretation: see Hilary Putnam and Martha Nussbaum (1995: 27–76), for another, see Christopher Shields (1990: 19–33). For an example of a non-reductionist materialist account, see my earlier attempts to understand these matters (1984: 197–250 and 1988: 1–53), for another see Victor Caston (2005: 245–320). In the present study, I shall discuss functionalist and non-reductive materialist interpretations separately. For some non-reductionist interpreters, the psychological is defined in terms of goal-directed rationality which, to use Davidson's phrase, 'finds no echo' in physical theory. Functionalist interpreters, by contrast, define psychological states in terms of their physical causes and effects without essential reference to specific types of internal physical states. This is true of materialist functionalists: while, in their view, the states that realize psychological states must be (generically) physical, there is no specific type of internal physical state referred to in defining them. To do so would be to violate the constraints of generality and autonomy from (internal) physical states of this type which they see as constitutive of the psychological.

[5] Myles Burnyeat and Thomas Johansen developed this line of interpretation. I shall sometimes label their view 'spiritualist', following Burnyeat's use of the term 'spiritual change' to capture what he intended (see Myles Burnyeat 1992: 15–26, 1995: 422–34, 2001: 129–53 and 2002: 28–90 and Thomas Johansen 1998). In recent years, pan-psychism, a close relative of the view Burnyeat thought should have been 'junked' in the seventeenth century, has undergone a cautious revival in the writings of David Chalmers (1995: 200–19, 1996) and Galen Strawson (2006).

indeed in no small measure because, its assumptions are fundamentally different from those with which we are now familiar.

To make the issues somewhat more determinate, it may be helpful to focus on Aristotle's account of visual perception. For non-reductive materialist interpreters, this runs (in outline) as follows: in any case of visual perception, there is a particular event of a given physical type which 'underlies' or 'grounds' the subject's (particular) conscious awareness of, for example, red.[6] Psychological (or phenomenal) awareness is itself defined without reference to any underlying, internal, specific type of physical event or property and is not reducible to such events and property. What makes the underlying (or grounding) type of event physical is that it is of the same general type as occurs in objects which lack awareness or perception.

There is a lively debate among non-reductionist interpreters as to (i) how 'underlying' (or 'grounding') is best understood and (ii) what physical event is involved.[7] But most agree that Aristotle understood particular acts of perception as constituted by (i) a particular physical event (of a type defined without essential reference to anything psychological) and (ii) some psychological feature, such as phenomenal awareness, defined without essential reference to any specific type of internal physical event, where the physical event and its physical properties (in some way or other) 'underlie' or (in some way) 'ground' the relevant psychological features. Aristotle, so interpreted, engages directly with our mind–body question: how do these purely psychological features arise out of purely physical ones?

According to the spiritualist interpreters, by contrast, Aristotle did not accept that there is a distinct particular physical event, as just defined, essentially present in perception. All that is essential to seeing red (in their view) is a subject's becoming aware of, or attending to, redness: an activity that does not itself essentially involve any underlying or 'grounding' physical event (of the type just specified) in the sense organ (even if it may require the presence of certain physical necessary conditions). Aristotle, in their view, thought of perceptual awareness as a purely psychological phenomenon because he took the underlying matter in the sense organ to be primitively endowed with capacities for phenomenal awareness.[8] He did not, so

---

[6] There is debate about the relevant type of physical process: for some, the eye jelly literally turns red, for others the type of physical change involved is exemplified by (e.g.) water turning red when red light is played on it, for others the process is one of being affected by the ratio of the relevant colour. The first view was set out by Richard Sorabji (1974: 63–89) and Stephen Everson (1997), the second by Sorabji (2001: 49–61). The third view was developed by Victor Caston (2005: 267ff.).

[7] Some take Aristotle to hold a token identity theory in which psychological properties 'supervene on' or 'emerge from' physical ones. Others have denied that he held a token identity thesis.

[8] Two further points of clarification are required. (i) Burnyeat noted that a material organ's act of awareness could itself be described (by Aristotle) as a *physical* change (since it is the act of a physical body with material preconditions) even if it involved no change in its matter (and so would not have been counted as a material change). This is a different use of the term 'physical' from the one used in the debate between modern physicalists and their opponents. I shall use the term '*physical*' in the way

understood, engage with the Cartesian question of how an essentially physical event can be related to purely psychological features because in his account there is (incredibly as it now seems) no physical event essentially involved in perception.

These opposed schools of interpreters share two assumptions. They agree that, for Aristotle, individual cases of perception are instances of some purely psychological type, such as awareness of redness, which can be fully defined without explicit reference to any internal type of physical event defined as such.[9] They also both accept that the only types of event we can seriously entertain (as contemporary philosophers) are either purely psychological (in the sense just defined) or purely physical (defined without reference to the psychological) or else a combination of one purely physical and another purely psychological type.[10]

Aristotle, I shall argue, did not share these assumptions. More specifically, in his account:

[A] The psychological activities involved in emotions, desire and perception (and their essential properties) are defined as inextricably psycho-physical, not definable by decomposition into two separately defined types of phenomena, one purely psychological, the other purely physical. Being psycho-physical is (in a way to be explicated) an essential aspect of their nature.[11]

[B] The relevant specific type of physical activity cannot be defined without explicit reference in their definition to some psycho-physical activity. It too is an essentially psycho-physical activity, even though the relevant matter is not itself primitively endowed with consciousness.

Both schools of interpreters err in claiming to find in Aristotle's discussions a purely psychological feature or activity essential to, for example, perceiving or desiring. They also go astray in assuming that his views can only make philosophical sense today if they contain a purely physical event which 'grounds' the relevant purely psychological feature. Non-reductionist materialist interpreters seek to find, or make room for, a determinate purely physical grounding event of this type in his writings. Spiritualists, finding little sign of, or space for, any such thing,

---

defined above (in note 4) and reserve the term '*physikal*' (if needed) for the sense Burnyeat notes. (ii) Burnyeat allows (2001) that concomitant processes (of a type congenial to the physicalist interpreter) may occur when we perceive (in Aristotle's account) but denies that these processes are essential elements in perceiving (or stand to perceiving as matter to form).

[9] I discuss further aspects of functionalist interpretations in Chapter 1, Section 6 and Chapter 7, Section 4.

[10] 'Combination', as I use the term, allows for the possibility of psychological events or their properties supervening on, or being in some other way determined by, physical events and their properties.

[11] I use the terms 'psychological' and 'mental' to indicate (in general terms to the modern reader) the type of process at issue. For Aristotle, it should be noted, nutrition is also an inextricably psycho-physical activity of the soul (*psuchē*).

conclude that his view must be rejected by anyone who seriously accepts the view of matter which drove the scientific revolution of the seventeenth century.

Aristotle, by contrast, in committing himself to [A] and [B], presents the relevant phenomena as, in their very essence, inextricably psycho-physical. It is not just that we choose to describe them in inextricably psycho-physical terms. It is because they are psycho-physical in this way that they are the very phenomena they are. In what follows, I shall call this suggestion the 'inextricabilist' interpretation.

[A] and [B] are independent exegetical claims: Aristotle might have accepted one and not the other. In holding [A], he sets himself apart from what might be described as the 'philosophical idea of the psychological as purely psychological'. Emotions, desire, and perception are, in his view, inextricably psycho-physical. However, he could have held [A] while thinking that these states rest on, or emerge from, purely physical states. Conversely, he could have accepted [B] but nonetheless understood emotions and the rest as defined solely in purely psychological terms.

[A] will be, for many scholars, the more controversial exegetical claim. Indeed, [B] has, in some version, been widely (if not universally) accepted in recent years. A major part of my interpretative task is to argue that Aristotle did not accept 'the philosophical idea of the psychological' and had good reasons, based on his more general views concerning enmattered essences (or forms), not to do so. However, for many philosophers, [B] will be the more unsettling claim, apparently committing Aristotle to a disturbingly anti-modern conception of matter. In response, I shall suggest that he held an intelligible, if distinctive, metaphysical view of the relation between matter and the psycho-physical in natural organisms. Rightly understood, his viewpoint did not commit him (or his supporters) to rejecting the view of matter which took hold in the seventeenth century. That said, when in the final chapter I assess both aspects of Aristotle's account, [B] may well remain the more controversial.

Aristotle's account of fear and anger provides a model for his treatment of other 'passions common to body and soul', such as perception and desire. The type of desire for revenge which defines anger is, in his view, an essentially embodied, 'hot' type of desire, defined in terms which explicitly refer to its being a specific type of bodily activity. Its form, in Aristotle's terminology, is captured in this definition. One cannot define its form simply as the desire for revenge without referring to it as an embodied-in-heat type of desire. The type of desire for revenge which defines anger, and constitutes its form, is, in his account, an inextricably psycho-physical, enmattered, activity with essential properties of the same type. Its form itself is, in Aristotelian terms, definitionally enmattered.[12] This is his way of expressing claim [A].

---

[12] In the Introduction, the terms 'embodied' and 'enmattered' are used interchangeably. This is a first approximation to a fuller interpretation, developed later, in which these terms are distinguished. Forms can be enmattered other than in bodies.

We can grasp somewhat more precisely what is involved in Aristotle's claim [A] by considering his discussion of snubness, which he defined, I shall suggest, as nasal-concavity: a type of concavity which cannot be defined without essential reference to the nose. Snubness is not, in his view, a type of concavity, defined independently of noses, which is realized by or related (in some way) to noses. It is, instead, an essential (*de re*) aspect of the nature of the relevant type of concavity that it is nasal-concavity. This type of concavity is, we might say, in itself or intrinsically, nasal. The form in question contains, in Aristotle's own terminology, being nasal 'as a part'. While these terms may require further elucidation, snubness is to be defined in ways which explicitly refer in its definition to a distinctively nasal way of being concave. It is because snubness is, in its nature, this specific type of concavity that it can only be realized in noses.

In the case of anger: the distinctive type of desire for revenge (that defines anger) is, if like snubness, in its nature a type of essentially bodily phenomenon. It is not that the relevant type of desire for revenge, defined independently of a specific type of bodily activity (such as boiling of the blood), is only a case of anger if it is accompanied by, realized by or otherwise related to that very type of bodily process. On the contrary, to be the relevant type of desire is to be in itself an embodied-in-heat type of desire, one whose nature is defined as a specifically embodied way of desiring revenge. One cannot define this type of desire, or capture its form, without explicit reference in its definition to specific types of bodily capacities or activities. The relevant type of desire must be, in its own nature, inextricably psycho-physical in this specific way to play the role required of it.

In accepting [B], Aristotle commits himself to the view that the relevant specific type of physical activity cannot be defined without explicit reference in its definition to some psycho-physical activity. [B], however, immediately strikes us as problematic. We think that the very same type of physical activity—such as boiling of the blood—could occur in a variety of different cases, not just when we are angry. It might occur, for example, when we are in a fever or simply disgusted or perhaps when blood is heated by some mechanical means without any psychological state being present. Indeed, when we think in terms of *events* of physical heating, this seems correct. However, Aristotle employed a different ontology, focusing on the unfolding *activity* (or process) at issue, understood as a type of phenomenon which develops and stops in the way it does in, for example, an angry person, when confronted with reason, pity, changed circumstances, or the recognition of some previously unnoticed fact (e.g. that one has not been insulted). This is why he defines the relevant type of heating as one which results from the psycho-physical capacity to desire revenge. It is because the heating in question is the realization of this goal-directed capacity that it develops and wanes as it does, why it is responsive to some considerations and not others. Remove reference to the relevant psycho-physical capacity and one will have, in Aristotle's view, no account of the way the specific kind of heating unfolds as it does in cases of anger. In his model, there will be as many types of heating as there are distinct psycho-physical capacities exercised. These types will differ even if they are all cases of heating at the same temperature in the same area of the body, provided that they realize different capacities of the organism in question. While, at a given moment, two distinct types of heating may appear indistinguishable, they will differ (in type) if they are the realizations of different psycho-physical capacities.

There is, in Aristotle's view, just one essentially psycho-physical capacity realized in anger. There is no need to postulate the existence of a further separate determinate purely physical capacity which underlies it. Indeed, were there to be such a capacity, given its lack of sensitivity to reason or pity, there would be no guarantee (short of a successful reduction—of which Aristotle despaired) that the resulting physical activity would 'march in step' with that of the psycho-physical capacity for anger. In that eventuality, the organism in question, Achilles (to take the case of a famously angry person) would not be a properly unified subject, endowed with an integrated capacity to respond appropriately when wronged. In Aristotle's view, by contrast, Achilles' capacity for anger is an inextricably psycho-physical capacity of an inextricably psycho-physical subject, an essentially integrated organism with its own unified teleological goals. A capacity of this specific type is required to generate the one unified activity that ensued before the walls of Troy.

Another example may serve to make Aristotle's idea more vivid. Consider weaving and the skill of Penelope the weaver. In Aristotle's account, one cannot define her activity of weaving without essential reference to her hands, the loom, and the wool on which she operates. But equally, one cannot define which physical movements are essential to weaving without reference to her skill and know-how. It is the latter that controls the developing movements that are essential to the weaving. Further, since the weaver's skill is defined as that which guides skilled bodily movements of this type, it too must be an inextricably psycho-physical capacity: a type of inextricably embodied phenomenon which can be the per se cause of our skilled bodily activity.[13]

My investigation has three stages. At first, in Chapters 1, 3, 4, and 5, I focus on Aristotle's discussion in *De Anima* and *De Motu Animalium* of emotions, desire, and perception. I suggest that they are all, in his account, inextricably psycho-physical. They are, as I argue in Chapter 6, together with imagination and certain

---

[13] One might also, consistently with Aristotle's viewpoint, succeed in capturing the causal profile of the state that realizes Penelope's skill in purely physical terms. Perhaps, with great ingenuity, one might even isolate a physical property P* such that whatever has P* has some purely psychological feature (Q). But, if one were to succeed, the ground for the claim that whatever has P* has Q would be, in Aristotle's view, the inextricably psycho-physical skill—from which P* and Q would be abstractions. There is, in his picture, one such psycho-physical capacity, the unified cause of the resulting bodily movements. This is why the latter are not over-determined by two distinct properties: P* and Q.

aspects of human thought, the activities of inextricably psycho-physical subjects. The resulting picture exemplifies (what I shall call) his 'simple theory' of the relevant phenomena. At the second stage, in Chapter 2 and parts of Chapter 7, I shall consider those features of Aristotle's general theory of hylomorphism which parallel his account of these psychological activities. My aim is to show that his discussions in the *Metaphysics* and *Physics* of form, matter, definition, and causation provide the background for his distinctive account of essentially embodied psychological activities in *De Anima*. These chapters contain a progressive elucidation of his key concepts: form and matter. The forms of natural substances, I argue in Chapter 2, cannot be defined without reference to matter in the way indicated because they are (at first approximation) inextricably material (or bodily) capacities. Subsequently, in Chapter 7, I suggest that Aristotle's forms are best understood not strictly as capacities but as distinctive 'activities' (*energeiai*): those of being capable of acting or suffering in a variety of ways. Being capable of acting is not to be identified either with the capacity to act or with the acting that results. It might be better described as the way an object is when it possesses the capacity to act. In these sections of Chapters 6 and 7 my aim is to formulate, defend and motivate what is sometimes called 'an impure form' interpretation: the relevant forms cannot be defined without explicit reference in their definition to matter because they are inextricably material ways of being capable of varying actions. At the third stage, beginning in Chapter 7 and continuing into Chapter 8, Aristotle's own account, as interpreted in Chapters 1–6, is contrasted with some contemporary theories and tested by considering criticisms that might be thought to refute it. If his distinctive viewpoint withstands these objections, as I suggest it does, it offers a credible way to dissolve the mind–body problem that we have inherited from Descartes.

The first two stages of enquiry call for careful reading of complex and difficult texts. Detailed exegesis of this type will appeal more to some than to others. But there is, it seems, no other way to secure a firm, historically sensitive, grasp on what is distinctive of Aristotle's approach. In developing my interpretation, I have aimed to understand continuous passages in his argument (in, for example, *De Anima* A.1 and *Metaphysics* Z.10–11), not to take smaller pieces of texts in isolation from their extended context. I have also attempted to show the extent to which he employs the general approach sketched in these and other passages in his detailed discussion of specific psychological phenomena. Further, I have sought to articulate the philosophical motivations which led him to hold these views: to explain why he held them. All three ingredients are required if one is seriously to challenge now standard interpretations, sometimes based on a few isolated texts (or even fragments of such texts) studied in isolation from the overall flow of Aristotle's argument in those passages with little concern for the theoretical considerations about form, matter, and causation that underlie them. However, it must be ceded, the resulting exegetical journey is long, arduous, and in constant danger of being overwhelmed by interesting if peripheral detail.[14] It may be helpful for those faced by this somewhat daunting prospect, if I offer a brief sketch of the interpretative arguments developed in Chapters 1–6. Those interested in the philosophical 'pay-off' may choose to rest content with this overview and Chapter 1, skip the exegesis and move directly to Chapters 7 and 8.

In Chapter 1, I shall suggest that Aristotle's account of 'passions common to body and soul', such as the emotions and perception, in *De Anima* A.1. (i) is consistent with the inextricabilist interpretation just sketched and (ii) on balance supports it over its closest competitors. Since the form of anger is defined as an embodied desire for revenge, it is (what I shall call) an impure, essentially enmattered, form: one which cannot be defined without explicit reference to its being material. Aristotle's discussion of anger and fear provides an intuitive introduction to his 'simple theory' of a wider range of psychological phenomena. However, partly because *De Anima* A.1 is introductory, it does not provide conclusive evidence for the inextricabilist interpretation of these emotions or the other passions at issue. Perhaps, even as a whole, it can be read, albeit with some difficulty, consistently with other interpretations. Or perhaps it does not give Aristotle's final view of these or other passions, such as desire or perception. This chapter leaves important questions unresolved.

In Chapter 2, I suggest that Aristotle understood the forms of natural substances in the *Metaphysics* and elsewhere as impure, inextricably enmattered, forms (on the model of snubness already mentioned). I argue that he was motivated to do so because he saw them as efficient and teleological causes. Forms of this type are required as the direct and specific (per se) causes of bodily or, more generally, material phenomena. They are, at least at first approximation, inextricably material capacities. His general account of hylomorphic substances, based on his views of definition and of causation, both efficient and teleological, provides the theoretical background for his views of passions 'common to body and soul' in *De Anima* A.1. In the final sections of Chapter 2, I outline the view of matter which guides this account and compare my interpretation of Aristotle's views of form and matter with some influential alternatives.

In Chapter 3, in considering Aristotle's account in *De Anima* and *De Motu* of how desire leads to action, I offer further considerations in favour of the inextricabilist interpretation of the relevant phenomena. More specifically, I suggest that this account

---

[14] I am painfully aware of many important detailed interpretive issues which will be not pursued (or not pursued fully) in this investigation. However, my aim is a narrow one: to formulate, and argue for, a distinctive, inextricabilist, overview of Aristotle's account and to engage in questions of exegetical detail only to the extent that they are required to achieve this goal. If the resulting interpretation is correct, it will need to be supplemented, and refined, by careful analysis of many specific points and of other areas of his thought, especially his biological thought. Conversely, if it is mistaken, it cannot be rescued by the accumulation of further scholarly detail.

(a) offers a simple and complete account of how desire, in Aristotle's view, leads to action, while its competitors are confronted with an unnerving silence at points where a theory is most needed; and

(b) enables us to understand what was, in Aristotle's view, mistaken in the other accounts, including the 'harmony' theory which, in certain crucial respects, resembles that offered by the non-reductionist materialist.

Both arguments rest on a further claim:

(c) In the case of anger, desire for revenge, the relevant form, is, for Aristotle, the direct and specific (per se) efficient cause of action and, as such, has to be an enmattered, impure, form. Since the form of such desires (defined in part in terms of what they are for: revenge in the case of anger) is the specific cause of bodily movement, it must be an enmattered or impure form. This is, I suggest, an application to the case of desire of his general theory of hylomorphism and causation developed for natural substances, sketched in Chapter 2.

In Chapters 4 and 5, I argue that Aristotle's discussion of perception of flavours, odours, sounds, and colours follows, in general outline, his account of anger and desire. In the case of taste and sight, for example, the relevant types of awareness and responsiveness are defined as inextricably embodied, the realization of distinct enmattered goal-directed capacities. Capacities of this kind allow us to discriminate flavours and colours, defined as enmattered properties of water or light, which impact on our senses in water- and light-based ways. The connections that Aristotle envisaged between enmattered forms and per se efficient causation, outlined in Chapter 2, are at work in this account of the distinctive capacities, processes, and activities essential to perception. Inextricably embodied capacities and activities are required as the relevant effects of essentially enmattered causal processes originating in appropriately enmattered causes. His relatively simple and intuitive theories of tasting, seeing, and the rest are underwritten by a more general understanding of definition and causation and of the ontology of forms, activities and processes they require. As in the case of desire, the inextricabilist interpretation offers a simple, complete, and theoretically based account of Aristotle's views at points where other interpreters see (and struggle to fill) unnerving gaps and silences.

In Chapter 6, in considering other aspects of Aristotle's discussions of perception, desire, and action, I suggest that the inextricabilist interpretation offers a convincing account of how these are integrated as the activities of essentially and inextricably embodied and unified subjects. I also consider, somewhat more briefly, the extent to which this style of interpretation is applicable to Aristotle's view of human thinking and of the soul more generally. My main aim in this chapter, as in Chapters 1–5, is to formulate and defend an inextricabilist interpretation of

Aristotle's view of the emotions, desire, perception, and imagination, 'passions common to body and soul', and to show its basis in his account of the essentially enmattered, 'impure', forms of hylomorphic natural substances. This interpretation offers a textually secure and properly grounded reading of Aristotle's discussion of the relevant psychological phenomena which enjoys major advantages over its main competitors, spiritualist, functionalist, non-reductionist alike. Or so I argue. Chapters 1–6 provide the exegetical basis for my attempt in the final two chapters to capture, in somewhat more general terms, what is distinctive about Aristotle's account and to test the extent to which it is still philosophically defensible.

In Chapter 7, I seek to confirm that Aristotle's viewpoint is not a version, or notational variant, of two options with which it has recently been associated: functionalism (in its various guises) and non-reductionist materialism. Further, I suggest that it differs, in somewhat parallel respects, from several prominent neo-Aristotelian versions of hylomorphism. In commenting on these differences, I further develop the interpretation of the form of natural substances set out in Chapter 2, focusing on its intrinsic nature as an inextricably material way of being capable of various activities, on the type of unity it possesses, and on the way in which it is prior to matter. My aim in this chapter is not to argue for the superiority of Aristotle's conception of form or of the psychological but to isolate its distinctive commitments.

In the final chapter, I examine some considerations that challenge, and might be taken to refute, Aristotle's account, as interpreted in Chapters 1–6. In doing so, I shall focus on those aspects of our psychological lives that seem to exemplify a purely psychological domain, defined without any reference to physical processes or properties. I also consider, and reject, the suggestion that Aristotle's viewpoint is committed to a wholly unacceptable view of matter. My aim, building on the detailed exegetical work undertaken in the earlier chapters, is to offer an overview of his position and to seek, in some measure, to defend it.

What are the philosophical attractions of Aristotle's account, as interpreted here? First, the descriptions it offers of anger and other emotions have intuitive appeal. When angry, we are tense, pained, anxious, and excited. We become agitated and distressed. The pain and tension influence how we speak and distort our facial expressions. Anger, as we experience it, is not just any type of desire for revenge, but one which, in its nature, is permeated with physical and psycho-physical features. One cannot, it seems, define the tension, anxiety, or excitement essential to this type of desire without reference to specific bodily states. It is, in its nature, an embodied response to what befalls us.[15] It was, I suspect, because he shared this intuition that Aristotle began his discussion in *De Anima* A.1 by focusing on fear and anger, which he saw as clear cases of inextricably psycho-physical phenomena.

---

[15] It is instructive to compare Aristotle's account with Damasio's description of the role of the body in emotional responses. See, for example, his (2000: chapter 9).

Aristotle, however, had a more theoretical motivation for his position. He wished to account for the causal role, especially the efficient causal role, of the relevant type of desire for revenge. It is because it is an embodied type of desire that it affects our bodies and bodily movements in the way it does. Thus, Achilles' anger led him not merely to kill Hector but to desecrate his corpse and leave it to rot outside the walls of Troy. The bodily pain and tension he experienced at the death of his friend Patroclus, modified, and in some measure controlled, his subsequent actions. Anger has to be a distinctive bodily type of desire for revenge, itself possessed of an impure form, to account for these consequences. In fact, as he suggested in *De Anima* A.1, it is because it is defined as a bodily type of desire of this type that anger sometimes arises and sometimes does not. If one is calm, relaxed, at ease, he argued, one may not be provoked by phenomena which would spark anger if one was initially tense, excited, or agitated. Sometimes, in the latter states, one can become angry when there is nothing to merit it. Indeed, in some cases, one's pathology alone, in the absence of any external stimulus, explains the onset of anger. It is because, Aristotle thought, the type of desire involved is, in its nature, bodily that anger arises in the way it does. It must be defined as an essentially bodily type of desire to have as its specific direct causes (and effects) bodily states.

Aristotle's line of thought rests on two specific features of his account of efficient causation.[16] First, the cause and the effect in question have to be of the same general type, possessed of matter of the same general type. Only something which is in its nature bodily can be the direct and specific (per se) cause of bodily changes, one which is adequate to bring them about. Such causes are not only necessary for their effects but adequate to account for their occurrence. If the effect is bodily, the relevant cause must also be and, similarly, if the cause is bodily, so too must be the effect. More generally, if either the cause or the effect is material, the other must be also. There has to be, at some generic level, a type of matter which both share. It is only in virtue of being enmattered in this way that the type of desire for revenge which defines anger can be a per se cause of certain bodily changes and the per se effect of others. Its form, the basic cause, must be inextricably psycho-physical to be a per se cause and per se effect of this type.

Second, to be a per se cause the type of desire in question has not only to initiate the activities that ensue but also to guide and control them. Thus, it was because Achilles desired revenge in this way that he not only fought Hector but killed him in the brutal way he did. This was why he was not easily swayed by pity or by Priam's tears. It was in virtue of the specific nature of his desire that he acted throughout as he did, relenting only when it was satisfied or modified by entreaty from others or his own sense of justice. His action was an activity directed by, as

---

[16] For further discussion of Aristotle's activity/process-based view of per se causation, see Chapter 2, Section 6.

well as arising from, this specific type of desire. It is not just that had he not been angry, he would not have killed Hector. Instead, his anger made a difference to how his actions unfolded, determining their order, many of their properties and when they ended. Achilles' anger was—in the ways described—the controlling cause of what he did, when and how he did it, and of when he stopped doing it. Per se causes, the forms at issue, are not only the starting points of the processes or activities they initiate: they are also, in the ways indicated, their controllers.

Before the walls of Troy, the per se cause of the unfolding drama was the realization, or actualization, of Achilles' relevant capacity to desire revenge. This capacity must be an essentially material, embodied, capacity to generate bodily results of the type just specified. Its actualization is also sensitive, as the story develops, to reason and pity. Indeed, it is because the capacity is responsive to reason that the resulting bodily activities unfold as they do. This goal-directed capacity is, in its nature, inextricably psycho-physical. It has to be such to be a per se cause of bodily activity which is responsive to reason and pity in the ways indicated.

Aristotle's account has several distinguishing features. First, what is caused is an activity (or process) that stretches through time, developing and being modified as it develops. The effect is not an event, such as the movement of one's hand (or the crossing of the road or even the killing of Hector), but rather an activity, such as Achilles' moving his hand (road-crossing or killing Hector), which continues through time and (if all goes to plan) achieves its goal. Correspondingly, the per se cause is understood as the embodied capacity to be angry: for it is this capacity that, when Achilles decided to act, guided his developing action. The per se cause was not, for example, simply his decision to strike Hector, which initiated the event or chain of events in question. The per se cause, in Aristotle's account, is that in virtue of which the resulting activity began, continued and ended in the way it did.

The per se causal role of anger will be lost if one takes it to be a purely psychological phenomenon, defined without reference to the physical, which happens to be realized in a purely physical state or capacity that is the per se cause of the resulting bodily movement. In the latter model, the resulting action would not follow in virtue of the presence of a desire for revenge, sensitive to reason and pity in the way just noted. Equally, a purely material or physical capacity, defined without reference to these factors, could not account for why Achilles' anger developed or ceased in the way it did. A purely material capacity of this type, when actualized, would not be, in the sense explained, the cause of the specific type of action that resulted. The cause needs to be an inextricably psycho-physical, embodied, capacity to account for what unfolded in the way it did. It is this view of causation that underpins, and motivates, Aristotle's discussion. If the form is to be identified with being capable of acting in these ways, it too must be essentially embodied if it is to play the required causal role. If the capacity for action is essentially embodied, so too will be being capable of so acting.

Aristotle had a further motivation. The emotions, desire, and perception are defined as the inextricably psycho-physical activities (and capacities) of unified, essentially psycho-physical subjects. This is one part of his organism-based account of a wider range of biological and (in his sense) physical phenomena. In his model, the matter involved is defined as the matter of specific psycho-physical organisms, not in terms of a general science of matter, which accounts for all change in terms of universal laws that apply to all matter, whether in animate or inanimate substances. It is the latter, with the distinctive view of the physical it entails, that helped to generate Descartes' mind–body problem. How do the states defined by a universal and complete physics of this type give rise to psychological activities?

There is a major shift in perspective from Aristotle's organism-based account to one defined by a physics of the type just described. But are they fundamentally incompatible? Did the development of a modern view of the physical render Aristotle's viewpoint obsolete? Or can they be seen as consistent, indeed complementary?

One might characterize parts of our post-Cartesian perspective, in rough outline, as follows:

1) There is, or will hopefully eventually be, a general and complete physical theory taking as its starting point matter defined without reference to sentience (or life more generally).

2) The general theory is expressed in terms of events and the physical laws covering such events.

3) There are, above the most fundamental physical level, a series of other levels, including the biological and the psychological, which—in some way—rest on, or are grounded in, it.

Is the Aristotelian viewpoint, in which inextricably psycho-physical processes and capacities are taken as basic, inconsistent with this perspective? Do we have to choose between them?

Although I shall discuss these questions in the final chapter, it may be helpful to offer a preliminary overview of the issue at stake. If one begins with inextricably psycho-physical activities and capacities, it is possible to view these (in a given way) as physical events or states with purely physical features, as it is possible to see snubness as a case of geometrical concavity (not as nasal-concavity). We can achieve this viewpoint by isolating certain aspects of the relevant activities and characterizing them in a purely physical way. (Aristotle describes this as a type of 'abstraction'.) We may then be able to construct, on this basis, a general theory of matter applicable to all physical events (so understood), wherever they occur. In this way, we can re-describe the psycho-physical activities in terms of purely physical events and properties and seek laws that apply to them, wherever they are found.

The perspective just sketched becomes available if we are able, in good philosophical conscience, to take as basic the inextricabilist viewpoint and see physical theory as—in a sense to be explained—an abstraction. If we do so, we might even accept as a constraint on an adequate universal physics that it be consistent with the organism-based laws and regularities that Aristotle took as his starting point. Problems arise only when we reverse this order of explanation and take the basic physical level thus abstracted (whatever it may turn out in the end to be) as the starting point for our account of everything psychological or biological. When we do so, we are faced with some well-known problems:

(a) The danger of unexplained gaps between the different levels (of which our mind–body problem is a striking example),
(b) The difficulty of accommodating the causal role of the entities at the higher level, and
(c) The loss of explanatory power provided by talk of organisms, their capacities and the goods they are set up to achieve.

These problems arise when we take what is physically, or compositionally, basic (whatever that turns out to be) as metaphysically basic and attempt to account for all else in terms of it. They can be avoided if we can construe inextricably psycho-physical activities and capacities as the metaphysically basic starting point and separate what is metaphysically basic from what is compositionally basic. From this viewpoint, it is not the scientific picture, as defined by (1)–(3) above, that needs to be rejected, only a form of 'scientism' that requires us to take what is compositionally basic (whatever that may be) as metaphysically basic. It is the order of explanation that is at issue.

Aristotle's perspective has three complementary aspects: (i) his simple theory of the relevant psychological phenomena and their role as causes and effects of enmattered processes, (ii) his general view of the matter and form of natural substances (and their analogues for natural processes) and their central role in definition and causation, and (iii) his conception of what should be taken as basic in a good metaphysical account of natural substances and their processes and activities. (ii) enabled him to integrate his simple theory of the emotions, desire, and perception as inextricably psycho-physical with his understanding of form, definition, and causation. (iii) provided the resources to justify taking as metaphysically basic aspects of his simple theory, now supported by and expressed in terms of the considerations assembled in (ii).

Aristotle's viewpoint, if adopted, has its advantages.

(a) It avoids the seemingly insoluble problems of post-Cartesian picture: the attempt to account for the psychological on the basis of the purely physical. In recent years, as the reductionist project has stalled, we have been left with brute, unexplained supervenience claims linking the various levels. Aristotle himself compared a similar picture to a badly constructed, episodic, tragedy!

By contrast, if one takes as metaphysically basic the inextricably psycho-physical, while there may well be supervenience conditionals linking the purely physical and the purely psychological (understood as abstractions from the psycho-physical), these will be grounded in, and made intelligible by, the metaphysically more fundamental psycho-physical. While no true claim made in the post-Cartesian picture will be denied, these will be seen as the result of sophisticated and coherent abstraction from what is metaphysically more basic.

(b) avoids the intractable, possibly insoluble, difficulties of accounting for the causal powers of purely psychological phenomena because it offers a view of emotions, perception, and desire as fundamentally psycho-physical capacities which issue in psycho-physical activities (and processes).

(c) avoids the loss of explanatory power which ensues when talk of the psycho-physical activities and capacities of organisms is replaced with that of physical events and their law-like connections.

When we abstract in the way envisaged, we lose our grasp on the organism as an essentially unified subject, with its biological needs and coherence as a continuing unified entity. It is a mistake, from the Aristotelian viewpoint, to treat the purely physical description as the metaphysical basis for an account of all the features of such processes and organisms, not as something abstracted from a metaphysically more basic set of psycho-physical processes and capacities of organisms. To take the latter option is not to turn one's back on any aspects of our favoured scientific model. It is only to reject the 'scientistic' claim to account for everything on its basis. Or so I argue in the final chapter.

Aristotle's account, so understood, need not have been rejected in the attempt to develop a universal physics in the seventeenth century. The costs of accepting his starting point were, and continue to be, seriously exaggerated. It could have been retained as the basis for an intelligible metaphysical account of mind and its place in nature fully consistent with the 'new science' and its characteristic focus on purely physical events and properties, studied in isolation from the essentially psycho-physical activities, capacities, and properties of essentially psycho-physical organisms.

If it can be shown that Aristotle's picture, as interpreted in the exegetical Chapters 1–6, withstands several immediate and serious criticisms, we will have good reason to take it seriously as offering a coherent and convincing account of many psychological phenomena, firmly grounded in a philosophically plausible general theory of hylomorphic substances. In fact, it enjoys major advantages over its post-Cartesian competitors and offers a fresh starting point for future work in an area which we (but not he) would describe as the 'philosophy of mind'. Or so I shall suggest.

1
The Emotions

1.1 Fear and anger in *De Anima* A.1

In *De Anima* A.1, Aristotle develops his account of certain 'affections of the soul' such as anger and fear, his model for other 'affections and actions common to the body and soul' such as sensual desire and sense perception (403a5–8).[1]

Aristotle describes anger and fear as 'enmattered formulae' (*logoi*) with definitions of the following type: 'to be angry is a certain type of process of this kind of body (either of one of its parts or capacities) caused by this for the sake of that' (403a25–7). In the immediately preceding lines, he had offered some considerations in favour of this suggestion, which he takes to explain why 'it is the task of the physicist to enquire about the soul, either as a whole or as a soul of this type' (403a27–8). In the remainder of the chapter, he attempts to clarify his viewpoint and concludes by emphasizing the way in which the affections of the soul are inseparable, reverting to fear and anger as his examples:

> We have said [or sought to say] that the affections of the soul are inseparable from the physical matter of living beings in the way in which anger and fear are inseparable and not in the way in which line and plane are.   (403b17–19)[2]

In this remark, he seeks to encapsulate what is distinctive about the physicists' project (rightly conceived) and to distinguish their accounts from those given by a mathematician.

There are two ways to understand Aristotle's remarks in this chapter. Take anger as an example:

> [A] *The Pure Form Interpretation*: anger is, in this account, essentially a compound made up of two distinct features, one purely psychological (a desire for revenge) and the other physical (the boiling of the blood), where the latter in

---

[1] Thought appears to be treated as somewhat different from desire and perception (403a8–10). I shall return to his discussion of thought in Chapter 6.

[2] I read the MSS text of 403b18–19 without Ross's addition of *hoia* (such as) in 403b18, taking anger (*thumos*) and fear (*phobos*) as the subject of belong (*huparchei*). This sentence, so understood, contrasts the way in which the passions of the soul are inseparable from matter from that in which mathematical objects are. The phrase 'phenomena of this type' (*toiauata* in 403b18) refers back to what are inseparable (*achoristsa* or *ou chorista* in 403b17).

some way 'underlies' the former.[3] The purely psychological aspect is separable, definable without explicit reference in its definition to any physical or material feature. Even though anger (the compound) may be essentially enmattered and inseparable in definition (and not abstractable) from the physical process, it is defined in part in terms of a pure psychological component (desire for revenge) defined without explicit reference to any physical feature. If this psychological component is the form of anger, anger has a pure form.

This interpretation yields a picture with which we, as post-Cartesians, are readily familiar: there is a purely psychological phenomenon (such as the desire for revenge) which some physical process or event underlies. Psychological phenomena are defined without reference (in their definition) to anything physical or material, even if the composite (of which the psychological is a component) cannot be defined without explicit reference to that further physical component. What makes the relevant desire that of an angry person is that it is accompanied by, or grounded in, a distinctive physical process. However, the type of desire itself is abstractable from, and definable without, explicit reference to such processes.

[B] *The Impure Form Interpretation*: the type of desire for revenge mentioned in the definition of anger is, in this view, inseparable in definition from (and not abstractable from) physical features such as the boiling blood. The type of desire which defines anger might be defined as a boiling-of-the-blood-desire for revenge. Being thus enmattered is an intrinsic feature of this type of desire. Anger, the compound, is essentially and inextricably enmattered because its form is itself essentially and inextricably enmattered. Anger has an impure form whose identity as the form it is is (partially) constituted by its being psycho-physical in the specific way it is.

This picture may seem less familiar. In it, part of what makes the relevant desire for revenge that very desire is that it is a hot (boiling-of-the-blood) type of desire. One cannot define this type of desire without explicitly referring to it as a type of bodily desire—for example, as a physically stressful and tense or 'hot' type of desire. It is, in its very nature, different from any desire, even one targeted at obtaining revenge, which is not a physically stressful, tense, 'hot' desire. There is not, as in the first account, a purely psychological desire for revenge which is—as it happens—enmattered, in angry people, in certain physical processes or states. Instead, the desire itself is an inextricably psycho-physical type of desire.

The second picture, however, has some intuitive appeal. Many think that there is a distinctive form of tense or stressful desire for revenge which can be distinguished phenomenologically (as a type of desire) from the cold calculating

---

[3] I shall use the term 'physical' in its modern sense to refer to whatever falls within the domain of the physicist or is covered by physical laws.

20 1.2 THE FIRST MOVES

desire to get one's own back. It was the latter, and not anger, that Maupassant described as aiming at 'a dish best served cold'. Today, neuroscientists, building on this distinction, represent anger as a distinctive form of stress or excitement, understood as an essentially bodily involving process or state.[4] Philosophers, relying on thought experiments, might distinguish anger from fool's anger, not itself a genuine case of anger. They would imagine people desiring revenge in the cool and calculating way described by Maupassant while at the same time suffering from boiling blood. Perhaps, their (unfortunate) subjects have been rigged up (by a skilled neuroscientist) so that the very same antecedent event triggers both a cold desire for revenge and a boiling of their blood (which the patients regard as an unwelcome distraction from their calculated and dispassionate desire for revenge). They are not, or so the intuition goes, angry because they lack the right type of desire for revenge, one which is its very nature 'hot', stressful, and tense. There is not the right kind of unity in their experience. Even if all the components for anger are present, they are not unified in the right way to yield the required type of desire.[5]

Which view did Aristotle himself adopt in his discussion of anger and fear in *De Anima* A.1? I shall argue in favour of the impure form interpretation by providing in Sections 1.2–1.5 an account of his argument as it develops through the chapter.

1.2 The first moves

Aristotle offers several considerations in favour of the view that the definition of anger must involve explicit reference to certain specific bodily parts or capacities (403a25–7). He begins by suggesting that the presence of such bodily features is necessary if anger and fear are to occur (403a19–20):

> Sometimes one is not stimulated or made afraid by great external misfortunes. But sometimes one is moved by small and insignificant things, when the body is stirred up (*orgai*) and is in the type of condition one is in when angry. Sometimes, even when nothing frightening happens, one is in the emotional states of one afraid.[6]

---

[4] For this view, see Damasio (1999).

[5] The components would be, to use Davidson's phrase, connected by 'deviant' causal chains. An account is needed of how the differing components present in genuine cases of anger are related to each other. Similar concerns are relevant to the conditions of genuine grounding: under what conditions does a physical process ground a psychological type, rather than being (in some deviant way) a causally necessary condition for its occurrence?

[6] I take this sentence as providing a further proof of the claim made at 403a18–19: the body suffers at the same time as the *pathē* of the soul (just listed) occur. That is, '*touto*' in 403a23 refers back to the claim in 403a18–19 as further evidence (along with the claims made in 403a19–21). It seems

He notes that certain bodily states play a major role in the occurrence of anger or fear. Sometimes, he remarks, one is moved to anger by small or insignificant events, when the body is stirred up. Presumably in his final case, one experiences fear (largely or wholly) because of the presence of some bodily state in the absence of an external cause (403a23–4).

What do these remarks show? In the last two examples, the body's state is part of what accounts for the person's being angry (or afraid). Omit reference to it and one fails to state the conditions under which someone is (or comes to be) in these emotional states. In the first example the presence of some bodily state or other is necessary if one is to be afraid. Indeed, its absence explains why one is not afraid in certain situations. From these considerations, Aristotle concludes that anger and fear are 'enmattered formulae' which capture, it seems, the conditions under which someone is (and comes to be) angry. It is because anger comes about in these ways that it is itself to be defined as an enmattered process: the realization of a specifically bodily capacity.

Aristotle states his conclusion in the following terms:

> If this is so, it is clear that the affections are *enmattered* formulae (*logoi*). It follows that their definitions will be of this type: to be angry is a certain kind of process of a body of this type (or a part or a capacity of it) brought about by this for this goal. For this reason it falls to the physicist (*physikos*) to think about the soul, whether this is the soul as a whole or a soul of this type.

According to the pure form interpretation, Aristotle is suggesting here that while the definition of anger (the compound) includes reference both to form and to matter, its form, like a mathematical form, is to be defined independently of matter. It is a pure form exemplified by the desire for revenge (403a30–1), which is enmattered in a physical process (such as the boiling of the blood) when anger occurs. According to the impure form interpretation, by contrast, the definition of anger is a 'form in matter' style of definition: the form itself, desire for revenge, cannot be defined except as an enmattered type of desire. Its form is a hot-type-of-desire-for-revenge (an impure form). Its being hot is part of the very type of desire it is.

These interpretations generate different accounts of the definitions Aristotle offers: the pure form interpreter, the purist, understands the defining phrase: 'a process of this kind of body or part or capacity of the body caused by this for the sake of that' to be decomposable into two separate components:

(i) a psychological process (desiring revenge) caused by this for the sake of that [Form defined independently of the body], and
(ii) this type of body or part or capacity [matter]

---

implausible to take this sentence as making clear the quite different situation mentioned in the previous sentence: 'being moved by small occurrences'.

where this is subsequently spelled out as

(ii)* a bodily process (such as boiling of the blood).

The impurist, by contrast, takes the defining phrase as a non-decomposable unit, yielding a definition of the form: anger is a process of this type of body caused by this for the sake of that. In this account, the type of process, desire for revenge, is itself defined as (*inter alia*) a bodily process: a process of this body (or part or capacity).

Which alternative did Aristotle adopt? The purist interpretation of his views has its difficulties: it removes the phrases 'of this type of body' and 'bodily capacity' from the definition of the form, while retaining in the form reference to the causal origin and consequence. However, it will be said, these remarks may simply serve as an initial formulation of the definition of the compound which will later be broken up, under further analysis, into two separate components corresponding to (i) and (ii) or (ii)*.[7] The psychological aspect of the original definition (suggested by (i)) will later be abstracted from and then separated from talk of the body.

Is this how the next stages in Aristotle's discussion unfold? He continues:

The physicist and the dialectician might [be inclined to] seek to define each of these (affections) differently. Take the case of anger. The dialectician might say that this is a desire for revenge or something like that, the physicist might say that it is seething of the blood around the heart and the hot. Of these one talks of the matter, the other the form, that is the definition [or formula captured in the definition].[8]

To resume:[9] the definition is the definition of the thing in question [in this case: anger] and must be *enmattered* if it is to be the definition [of this thing]. For the

---

[7] An alternative would be to take Aristotle to be talking only about human anger in this context. If so, the addition of boiling of the blood would be specific to the definition of anger in the human case. Although the examples used (403a20–4) may refer to human subjects, there is no reason to take Aristotle's definition of anger in 403a26 as limited to the human case. Indeed, his concern throughout this section seems to be with psychological phenomena (quite generally) and their subjects, not simply with human subjects. In the present context his focus seems to be on (all) souls capable of being angry ('such a soul': 403a28). Although in every case, anger has to be associated with the hot, it need not be associated with specifically human physical characteristics (such as blood boiling around the heart).

[8] Taking 'and the hot' as indicating a possible clarification of the phrase 'the blood around the heart'. These phrases refer, I shall assume, to the best account of the relevant type of specific physical process, whatever that turns out to be. Aristotle's theory does not require commitment to, for example, calorific fluid!

[9] The connective '*men gar*' standardly is used resumptively to indicate a back reference: *N.E.* 1147a26ff.: See J.D. Denniston (1966: 67). I take '*touton*' in 403b3 to refer to '*logos*' in the preceding line, the nearest relevant masculine subject, not to '*eidos*' (wrong gender, further away and clarified by '*logos*' in 403b2). The next sentence shows that Aristotle is focusing on what is required for an adequate definitional account, not on the existence of the form in question.

house, one account would be: the covering which prevents destruction from wind, rain, and heat. Another account will specify the stones and timbers, yet another speaks of the form in these (stones and timbers) for the sake of those things (viz. preventing destruction).

Which of these is [the one offered by] the physicist? Is he concerned with the matter while ignoring the formula, or concerned with the formula alone, or does he rather take [his account] from both? (403a29–b9)

According to the purist, the physicist takes the dialectical definition (given independently of matter) and adds to it an account of the matter. On this view, the dialectician gives a complete account of the form of anger. The physicist adds talk of matter because anger, the compound, is defined as a combination of pure form and matter. This is how the latter 'takes the account from both'.

There is, however, a problem. Dialectical definitions, if understood in the way suggested, are not, it seems, adequate for the role required of them in Aristotle's account. They are said earlier to be 'empty' (403a1–2) because one cannot derive from them the other necessary features of the phenomenon in question (402b25ff.). One would not be able to derive the other, bodily, features of anger already mentioned from a dialectical definition (403a20ff.). It does not provide the resources to explain why people are angry in certain bodily conditions and not in others. It also fails to explain the bodily consequences of anger. To provide the required explanation, the impurist claims, Aristotle needs to define the form explicitly in an impure way as a hot-boiling-of-blood type of desire for revenge. He could not explain the presence of the relevant bodily features on the basis of a pure form alone.

In the parallel case of a house, one could not, according to impurist interpreters, derive the other features of a house from a dialectical definition: being a covering designed to prevent destruction from the wind, heat, and rain. This is because, for example, tents, caves, and canopies of branches, as well as houses, meet this condition. A pure form could not be used as the basis of the explanation of why houses are made from stones and wood or how they resist wind and heat in the way they do. This is why, in their view, Aristotle's preferred definition is the third one offered: 'the form in these things (stones…) for the sake of safety' (403b6–7), mirroring the parts of the definition offered of anger in 403a27 (although without reference to the efficient cause). The relevant type of covering is defined as one made from stones, logs, and the rest: it is a made-from-these-materials type of covering. This is why it successfully keeps out rain and heat in the way it does. The dialectical definition does not by itself fully capture the nature of the thing or how it explains the other necessary features of a house.

There is a further difficulty for the purist interpretation. In the present passage, Aristotle explicitly identifies the form with the definition or defining formula (403b2). The latter formula itself, he says, has to be enmattered to be the defining formula of this thing: it must refer to the matter. If so, the form must itself be enmattered: a matter-involving form. The definition, the defining formula, of anger, the composite, is to be given in terms of the form alone. There are, it seems, no other ingredients in that definition. If definition and form are identified in this way, the definition of the composite, anger, will not include anything beyond the form. It will not contain (*pace* the purist reading) reference to material parts of the composite in addition to the form.[10]

These considerations suggest the relevant type of account (*logos*) refers to a distinctive type of essentially enmattered form (as suggested in 403b2–3):

The definition is the definition of the thing in question [in this case: anger] and must be *enmattered* if it is to be the definition [of this thing].

The original dialectical definition of anger needs to be enriched in this way to refer to an enmattered form of this type. So understood, 'the account from both matter and formula' (403b8–9) will refer to an impure form. The dialectician initially attempted to define anger in terms which did not refer to the bodily states involved. If pain, for example, is involved in their account, as is to be expected given that the desire in question (*orexis antilupēseōs*) is characterized as a 'repaying of pain for pain', it will not be defined as an essentially bodily state. Even if the dialectical definition were to succeed in marking out the correct extension of 'anger', it would not provide the resources to explain why anger has the bodily causes, concomitants, and consequences it does. It will be, in Aristotle's terms, 'empty and vain' (403a2). It is only if one defines the latter as the impurist interpreter does, with explicit reference to an enmattered form, that one can explain the relevant bodily features on the basis of the form itself. The dialectician cannot fully capture what is distinctive of the bodily pain-driven desire at issue. To do so, one must, in Aristotle's view, define the form of anger as itself enmattered.[11]

1.3 Physics and mathematics

The impurist interpretation is further supported by what follows. Or so I shall argue.

Throughout his discussion Aristotle compares (and contrasts) anger and fear with geometrical entities, such as lines and planes. Lines and planes are, in his

---

[10] For an acute discussion of these problems, see Stephen Everson (1997: 286ff.).
[11] These remarks offer an implicit challenge to the purist account of the form: specify the kind of desire for revenge at issue without reference to pain understood as a body-state in such a way that it (i) marks out anger as a distinctive state, (ii) explains why it is enmattered in the way it is, and (iii) accounts for the causal role of this desire in producing bodily states. Aristotle, I shall argue, thought that this could not be done. However, in the present context, his approach may be: it is best to avoid all these problems by beginning with impure forms. Either way, there is no sign of his attempting in this context to meet the three challenges that confront the pure form theorist.

view, separable and distinguishable from physical (or perceptual) matter in two related ways: they are grasped by successful abstraction from the specific perceptual matter in which they are realized (403b15). When grasped in this way, they are not considered as properties of perceptual matter. Features can be abstracted in this way from perceptual matter, even if they cannot exist except as enmattered in such matter. Second, because they can be abstracted in this way, it becomes possible to define lines and planes without reference to their being perceptually enmattered.[12] This is why Aristotle claims elsewhere that the definition of mathematical objects does not involve (perceptual) matter at all (*Physics* B.2, 193b35ff.). Unlike man, bone, and the snub, they can be defined without explicit reference to (perceptual) matter, of the type mentioned in 403b10ff. The mathematician is able to separate his objects from all perceptual matter in thought, and define them accordingly, without error arising as a result (see also *Metaphysics* M.3, 1078a17).[13]

Affections of the soul, such as fear and anger, are, by contrast, neither abstractable from (perceptual) matter nor separable in definition from such matter. What is the basis of the disanalogy? In the case of mathematical entities, Aristotle distinguishes three objects of investigation:

(i) the straight ruler (a compound with physical, perceptual, matter),
(ii) the straight line—which is physically enmattered in the ruler—but not seen as so enmattered, and
(iii) the straight line defined independently of any physical, perceptual, matter.

(i) is the compound, (ii) the line not seen as enmattered (seen in abstraction), (iii) the geometric pure line defined in separation from such matter. In considering (ii), Aristotle envisages a way of looking at the line of the ruler (that is, not seeing it as enmattered) which is the basis for the account of the mathematical form

---

[12] Separation, so understood, is distinct from abstraction. One can envisage the mathematician proceeding as follows:

Stage 1: abstract away certain features from the object in thought (e.g. perceptual matter): see *Metaphysics* K.3, 1061a27ff. This involves not thinking about the perceptual matter of material objects but considering only their mathematical aspects.

Stage 2: check that it is OK to proceed with the results of this abstraction: does error occur in one's relevant reasoning as a result of (Stage 1) abstraction?

Stage 3: separation occurs when one moves from *not* thinking of the line as perceptually enmattered to thinking of it as *not* being perceptually enmattered. (Note the distinction in scope!)

At Stage 3, one might attempt a definition of mathematical entities which does not involve any reference to perceptual matter. I am indebted at this point to advice from Edward Hussey.

[13] Aristotle seems to be relying on an intuitive distinction between (1) what is essential to mathematical reasoning and (2) what are external claims about mathematical reasoning. The latter might include claims about (e.g.) the metaphysical status of numbers. This distinction allows a mathematician to make a true mathematical claim (e.g.: 2 + 2 = 4) even when he (or she) holds a false (e.g.: Platonist) view about the ontological status of numbers.

invoked at stage (iii). The compound, on this view, is a combination of perceptual matter and a definitionally separated form. If it is defined at all, it is defined as a combination of this type.

Aristotle claims that one cannot—in the case of anger or fear—advance to stage (ii), let alone to stage (iii). Had the relevant type of desire for revenge been a pure feature (defined independently of perceptual matter), this step would have been possible. Indeed, it would have been required. One would have to be able to abstract to a state in which one did not see the desire for revenge, which like the straight is necessarily enmattered, as itself enmattered. Only on this basis could one arrive at a pure form at stage (iii): a desire for revenge defined independently of perceptual matter. Had his discussion of fear and anger followed the pattern set by his geometrical examples, these emotions would—contrary to his explicit view—have been separable in just the way the line and the square are. However, since their forms cannot even be abstracted from matter, they are not separable in this way. They are essentially enmattered forms.

We can arrive at the same interpretative conclusion by a somewhat different route: had the definition of anger—like that of a compound ruler or a brazen square—been made up of two separable parts (a desire for revenge and the boiling of the blood), the former would have been graspable in abstraction from the latter. There would have been no difference (in this respect) between the form of anger and the form of the line: both would have to be enmattered to exist and both could be grasped by abstraction from perceptual matter. However, the two cases, Aristotle notes, differ at precisely this point. In the case of the line, one can abstract and, on this basis, define the form without explicit reference to perceptual matter. But the case of anger is different. Since one cannot abstract the form of anger from the relevant perceptual matter, it is not possible to define the relevant form except as a (perceptually) enmattered form.

These remarks suggest the basis for Aristotle's distinction between the two cases described at 403b17ff.:

anger and fear: their form is existentially inseparable and inseparable in thought from perceptual matter

geometrical objects: their form is existentially inseparable from but separable in thought (and definition) from perceptual matter.

Since the form of anger (desire for revenge) cannot be thought of or defined in abstraction from matter, it must be defined in ways which essentially are matter-involving. Being so enmattered is essential to its being the type of desiring it is.[14]

---

[14] While this formulation is in terms of separation, an alternative might be in terms of abstraction: leave out (in thought) what makes something a case of being angry (its being the in-certain-matter-desiring-revenge) and one has also left out (in thought) what makes it a case of the relevant type of desiring revenge.

The form of anger, so understood, is inseparable in thought (and in definition) from physical movements or changes of a certain specific type (processes-in-the-heart). More precisely, the type of desire for revenge which defines anger is a boiling-blood-type of desire. It is a matter-involving form. In the final stage of his discussion, Aristotle shows that the original dialectical definition of anger is incomplete in that it does not fully capture its distinctively material form.[15]

How should a purist interpreter respond to these considerations? There are several possibilities:

(a) It might be suggested that Aristotle (in 403b17ff.) is comparing the account of the compound anger with that of the pure geometrical line defined by the mathematician. While the former involves matter as a separable component, the latter does not. He is not, in this account, comparing the *form* of anger with the *form* of the line. For all that he says, both can be equally matter-free. Both accounts of the compound may involve matter, which is essential to the account of the relevant compound, and a pure form which can be abstracted and (for all that has so far been said) defined separately from any such matter.

However, so interpreted, Aristotle fails to compare like with like. He should surely have compared his accounts of the two compounds (the ruler and anger), not his account of the abstracted geometrical line and that of the whole compound, anger. However, had he proceeded in the way suggested, he would not have discerned any significant difference between the two cases. Since he is clearly seeking, in the passages discussed, to contrast and not to assimilate them, this purist reply undermines the point he is trying to establish.

The purist interpreter faces a further difficulty. Aristotle refers (at 403b17: 'we were saying...') to an earlier passage which discussed these two cases. Previously, in considering the compound, straight ruler, he had written:

> But if there is nothing specific to the soul, it would not be separate [from the body], but the situation would be as it is with that which is straight in so far as it is straight. For many things belong to the latter [the straight in so far as it is straight], such as touching the brazen sphere at a point.[16] But the straight separated from this [viz. body] would touch nothing.[17] For the straight [the straight in so far as it is straight] is inseparable since it always is found with some body. (403a11–16)

---

[15] We shall consider Aristotle's grounds for this distinction between the definition of mathematical and natural objects more generally (in *Phys.* B.2, 193b32ff.) in Chapter 2.

[16] 403a13: Ross deletes the word for 'bronze' against all the MSS. I prefer to retain it for the reasons discussed below.

[17] 403a14: Ross adds *houtōs*. I retain *toutou* with majority of MSS, taking it to refer to the straight line.

1.3 PHYSICS AND MATHEMATICS

In this passage, he offered as an example a straight object (such as a ruler), which touches a bronze sphere at a physical point (403a12–13). This object interacts with and touches other objects. It is a compound object (with an enmattered type of straightness). By contrast, he notes that, if something straight were separated, it would not touch the bronze sphere in this—or any—way. The separated object—the geometrical line—cannot touch the bronze sphere at all. This is an instance of a more general claim: geometrical forms cannot interact with physical objects. Even if (in 403a11–16) Aristotle had been considering a parallel treatment for two compound objects (the ruler, passions such as anger or fear), his subsequent discussion would have shown that these cases differ. Abstraction, and subsequently separation, is possible in one case, not the other. Further, his remark suggests an explanation of why they differ. The straight—as a purely geometrical line—cannot touch, or interact causally with, physical bodies. When we see the line of the ruler in abstraction, we err if we think of its straightness (so understood) as causally interacting with other objects (even though the compound ruler does so in virtue of its physical (non-abstracted) straightness). Of course, this will not trouble us as geometers since, as such, we are not concerned with causal relations between the straightness of the ruler (so understood) and other objects. In the case of fear and anger, by contrast, Aristotle focuses on:

(i) the specific bodily states necessary if one is to be angry/afraid [Case (1): 403a20]
(ii) the specific bodily states that are part of what accounts for someone's being angry/afraid [Cases (2) and (3): 403a21–4].

These specific types of bodily states causally interact with the desire for revenge. Its onset is dependent on specific bodily states in this way. If one were to abstract, as we do in the case of the line (not seeing desire for revenge as enmattered), one could not account for the causal origins or consequences of the desire for revenge. Since these causal origins and consequences are bodily, Aristotle concludes that we should think of the form of anger (the specific type of desire for revenge) as itself enmattered (and non-abstractable from matter). It is because of these causal considerations that we cannot, without loss of explanatory power, abstract the form of anger from the body. By contrast, in the geometrical case, where there are no such causal considerations, we can—without error—abstract from the physical features of the ruler when defining straightness.[18]

(b) There is a second purist reply to consider: some may agree that bodily causal origins and consequences are not abstractable parts of the proposed definition of anger but suggest that reference to the boiling of the blood is abstractable.

---

[18] I shall return to this issue in Chapters 2 and 3.

Aristotle, so understood, would agree that we can think of anger in abstraction from its specific material basis. If so, he must be able to define and think about the form of anger without defining it as an essentially enmattered type of desire. Or so it might be argued.[19]

Aristotle's reference to the 'boiling of the blood and the hot' may suggest, as was noted above, that the form is to be defined in terms of physical features more generic than boiling blood. Indeed, his talk of 'the hot' may indicate a physical genus of which blood boiling is a species. If so, reference to the boiling of the blood will not be essential, even though it remains true that when many, or even all, animals are angry, their blood boils. However, the crucial claim remains: the relevant type of desire for revenge has to be enmattered in some generic type of material state. If so, even if one can think of, and define, anger in abstraction from the boiling of the blood, one cannot do so in abstraction from this more generic physical feature which he labels 'the hot'. Anger, so understood, is to be defined as a hot-desire for revenge where 'hot' refers to the generic type of physical feature required for this type of desire. While anger may be variably realized in different types of heat, anger is essentially a hot desire for revenge.

Nor should this result surprise us: Aristotle is concerned to distinguish anger from other states that resemble it. He himself mentions, in the *Rhetoric* 1390a15ff., the cool, calculating, desire to repay evil for evil of the elderly which is not said to be anger. (Remember Maupassant!) If one thinks of anger as essentially involving bodily pain (or stress), the type of desire characteristic of anger will itself be a bodily involving, enmattered, one. Since Aristotle thought of pain, like anger, as common to the body and soul, it too will be enmattered in the same non-abstractable way. The relevant type of pain is a bodily pain: one that afflicts, and can be located, in specific parts of the body.[20] It is not an abstractable, purely psychological, feature oasis in a series of non-abstractable states.[21]

There is a further, more theoretical, point: Aristotle is attempting to account for the presence of the consequences of anger in terms of its own nature. How, one might reasonably ask, could a purely mental nature (or essence) have this causal impact? If one cannot explain these physical consequences on the basis of the form (or essence) of anger, one will have failed to give a genuinely explanatory definition (in the *Analytics* style required).[22]

---

[19] This approach will commend itself to functionalist interpreters.
[20] Pain is said to be a bodily affection (*Ethics* 1173b7ff.), sometimes, in the human case, identified with a type of cooling of the area around the chest (see [*Prob.*] XI, 900a27f.). This is why pain is described as 'common to the body and the soul' (*De Sensu* 436a10).
[21] Compare Damasio's discussion of stressful conditions (1999).
[22] Aristotle invokes *Analytics*-style definitions in *De Anima* A.1, 402b22ff. In them the basic feature, often identified as 'what it is to be the thing' in question, should be the 'starting point' of the account of the consequential features of the phenomenon. For further discussion of this style of definition, see my (2000: 197–220).

This more general point depends on understanding Aristotle's view of the role of the relevant form as the (efficient) cause of bodily effects. Physical forms, it will be suggested, differ from mathematical forms in that they are, *inter alia*, efficient causes of bodily changes. They must be enmattered, impure, forms to play this causal role. Pure forms, like mathematical forms, are incapable of being efficient causes of bodily changes. I shall return to, and defend, this more general point in Chapter 2. However, before doing so, it is important to consider the range of Aristotle's account: how far did he mean it to extend beyond fear and anger?

1.4 The range of Aristotle's proposal in *De Anima* A.1

In *De Anima* A.1 Aristotle, it seems, aims to apply the model he has devised for anger and fear to a wide range of cases, including sensual desire and perception. He begins his discussion as follows:

> It appears that most of the affections of the soul cannot be suffered or acted out without the body: take for example anger, confidence, sensual desire, and perception generally.   (403a5–7)

He continues in a similar vein, talking generally of 'items of the soul' with their affections and things they do (403a10–16). Finally, at the end of the chapter, he returns to his previous discussion (*epaniteon*: 403b16) noting that the affections of the soul are inseparable from physical matter in the way in which anger and fear are (not in the way mathematical entities are), presumably referring back to the items previously contrasted with mathematical entities: 403a10ff. It appears that he has in mind the same division as earlier between affections (*pathē*) of the soul (including perception and desire) and mathematical entities. If so, he is saying (in effect) that all the affections of the soul so far mentioned (apart from possibly thought) are inseparable in the way that the passions are (such as anger and being confident). By the end of the chapter his remark has greater point because he has spelled out—in the intervening sections—the specific way in which fear and anger are inseparable.

Aristotle's overall strategy seems clear. In 403a16, he turns to examine one subset of the general class of the affections (*pathē*) mentioned in 403a5–7: the passions of anger and fear (among the *pathē* listed in 403a15ff.), interestingly using a different phrase to do so. (Contrast *ta tēs psuchēs pathē* 403a16 with *ta pathē tēs psuchēs* in 403a3.) He proceeds to clarify how anger and fear are inseparable (403a19–24), spelling out the type of bodily process involved in more detail in terms of boiling of the blood (403a31–b1). When he notes that the physicist will give the type of account he has just offered of anger 'either for all the soul or for this type of soul' (403a28), he is considering how far to generalize his account of fear and anger. The answer to that question emerges in 403b10ff. when he says that the physicist will give an account of the type in question 'for all the deeds and affections of such bodies and matter'. Aristotle is extending his specific account of the passions of the soul (understood as in the narrower list 403a16) to all inseparable affections and doings of bodies of a given kind. Affections of the latter kind will include all members of the original list (as given in 403a5ff.), which were shown to be inseparable prior to 403a16 (as well as other such phenomena as nutrition). He can now return (in 403b16ff.) to his earlier point: the account devised for anger and fear will apply to the affections (*pathē*) of the soul in their full generality (*ta pathē tēs psuchēs*), all of which (with the possible exception of thought) are to be contrasted with mathematical entities. All these affections of the soul (including desire and perception) will essentially be inextricably psycho-physical processes of the type exemplified by the cases of anger and fear.

It is correspondingly difficult to take Aristotle's conclusion in 403b16ff. to apply only to the narrower list of passions (*pathē*) mentioned in 403a16–18: anger, gentleness, fear, pity, confidence, joy, friendship, and hatred. Here are some reasons why:

i. There is no explicit reference to a contrast between passions (narrowly defined) and mathematical entities in 403a17–18. That contrast was made earlier and with a wider range of affections in mind.

ii. It was assumed in 403a16–18 that all the passions (*pathē*: narrowly construed: 403a17f.) work in the same way. Little would be gained by making explicit what has already been taken for granted. What we want to know (at the end of the chapter) is whether the account of anger and fear is, in Aristotle's view, to be extended to perception and desire.

iii. Given that Aristotle is seeking to generalize his account of passions such as anger and fear to the whole of the soul (403a29), it would have been extremely strange if he had restricted his final account in 403b17–18 to the narrow list of passions (mentioned in 403a17–18), especially after he had mentioned the even wider class of phenomena in 403b10–12 (actions and affections of a given type of body: e.g. one exemplified by houses). He would have needed, at the very least, some further argument for restricting his claim in this way.

Nor should it surprise that Aristotle generalizes in this way at the end of *De Anima* A.1. He is, it seems, attempting to develop a model which can apply to all the (so-called) affections of the soul, not just to the special case of passions such as fear, confidence, and anger.[23] His discussion, in effect, sets the agenda for the

---

[23] In 403a3, the affections (*pathē*) of the soul include things we suffer and things we do (*paschein* and *poiein*: 403a6–7). It is possible that perception, desiring and thinking, in the present context, fall in the latter category of things done (*erga*: 402b12), fear and anger into the former (things we suffer). But, if so, in 403b12, when Aristotle speaks of '*pathē* and *erga*', he is generalizing his account of things we suffer to apply to the whole range of affections (*pathē*) mentioned earlier in the chapter at 403a3

remainder of *De Anima*. Perception and desire will also be inseparable affections of the soul in the way anger and fear are if they too are defined as inextricably psycho-physical processes of a given type of body (403a26f.). Had Aristotle, by contrast, intended to confine his model only to emotions such as fear and anger, he would have needed to signal this explicitly (as he did in the case of thought: 403a8, 413b24f.).[24]

I shall argue in Chapters 3–5 that Aristotle did, in fact, extend this model to desire and perception. The case of anger and fear provided him with an intuitive example of what he took to be distinctive of the physical, as opposed to mathematical, forms required to define the broader set of psychological phenomena he investigated.

1.5 The proper way to study anger: the role of matter

Aristotle points to his generalizing aim when he raises the question: what type of account should the physicist give (403b7ff.)? His own answer is clear: the one that combines both form and matter, specifying an enmattered formula like the one of house just sketched: the in-stone-and-wood-covering designed for a given goal (403b8–9). Nor should this surprise us: when he first introduced the idea of the body as suffering something when one is angry, he described the body as 'angry, that is in the state one is in when one is angry' (403a21–2).[25] This condition, perhaps one in which one's blood is up, is explicated as the one which one is in when angry, using a description which involves the psychological (as in 403a24: 'the affected states of the person afraid'). In a similar fashion he defined the relevant process of the body as one which has a given goal, such as revenge (403a26–7, see a30–1) using a psychological (or psycho-physical) feature (desiring revenge) to define the relevant physical process. No purely physical account was offered in this case. The relevant type of material process (in the case of anger) is one which is essentially directed towards revenge. It is the presence of this goal that makes the relevant material process the one it is.[26]

(using '*erga*' to pick up the earlier reference to what we do: 403a6–7). Given this context, it is implausible to take Aristotle as suggesting in 403a12ff. that his account of what we suffer (such as anger) does not apply to things we do (such as perceive). A major move of the latter type would require explicit preparation and a very different context.

[24] This would be so if perception or desire were either not processes at all or not inextricably psycho-physical processes of the type anger and fear are.

[25] I take the phrase 'and is in just such a condition as it is in whenever the person is angry' (403a22–3) as explicative of the phrase 'the body is angry', taking the '*kai*' as epexegetic and the emphatic phrases 'in such a way…as it is whenever' as indicating an attempt to specify more precisely what it is for the body to be angry. The body is in ferment, one's blood is up, in that very way it is when one is angry.

[26] Similar concerns are relevant at the level of particular processes. See note 35.

Aristotle's adherence to this perspective explains why his physicists work as they do. It is only by grasping the goals in question that they can grasp the affections or activities of the soul of this kind of body (403b9–10, 11–12). Thus, he writes:

> There is no one who studies the affections of matter which are inseparable from these bodies, not that is as if they were separable from them. (403b9–10)[27]

One who attempted to do so would fail to grasp what the relevant affections and processes are. This is because they essentially serve certain goals in the specific organisms involved, such as revenge in the case of anger. Omit reference to these goals and one no longer has the relevant material process or affection. This is why one cannot, in Aristotle's view, define the specific type of material process without reference to its relevant teleological (here, psychology-involving) goal. Aristotle's physicists are concerned 'with everything which are actions and affections of this type of body and this type of matter' (403b11–12) because their subject matter is material processes of this specific type: ones directed towards the goals of the organisms in question (such as, in the case under consideration, revenge).[28] From their perspective, there can be no specific purely physical process, defined in purely physical terms, which enmatters anger. The relevant processes are essentially directed towards a higher (psychological) goal such as revenge. Those who specify in more detail the type of material processes involved are not referring to a distinct purely physical process, defined in its own terms, which 'underlies'

---

[27] I take the phrase '*mēd' hēi' chōrista*' to mean 'not that is as separable'. The phrase 'there is one who studies the inseparable properties of matter as separable' when negated yields 'there is no one who studies the inseparable properties of matter as separable'. But Aristotle needs to pinpoint what precisely is being negated and so adds 'not that is as separable'. One might regard the use of '*mēd*' in this context as epexegetic: not that it is. (Bonitz suggested a somewhat similar interpretation of this use of '*mēde*': *Index Aristotelicus*: 539a37f.)

[28] The physicist is concerned with all the actions and affections which are inseparable from this type of body (perceptual body) *as* inseparable actions and affections of this type of body. Aristotle contrasts the physicist with three others who are not concerned with all these affections in this way:

(i) The craftworker is concerned with only some of the inseparable affections of this type of body (403b12–13) [as inseparable affections of this type of body].

(ii) The mathematician is concerned with those affections which are inseparable from this type of body but not as affections of this type of (perceptual) body, that is in abstraction (403b14–15). Unlike the physicist, the mathematician does not think of such affections as (inseparable) affections of perceptual matter. So, for example, he (or she) does not think of the straight line as an entity which is made up of perceptual matter.

(iii) The first philosopher studies affections of this type of body 'in so far as they are separated' (403b15–16).

Of these (i) and (ii) are concerned with inseparable affections of this type of body but either (i) not with all of them or (ii) not with them *as* inseparable (but *as* abstractable). (iii), by contrast, is not concerned with inseparable affections of this type of body but with its separable ones. It follows that no one is concerned with the inseparable affections of this type of body as separable. The mathematicians come nearest but they (here) are only concerned with the inseparable affections of the body in abstraction (not as truly separable).

being (or getting) angry. They are simply spelling out the material features of the relevant psycho-physical process in more detail.

For Aristotle's physicist, anger is essentially a certain type of bodily process: one directed towards a given goal, such as revenge. It is because it is directed at this goal that the type of material process is the one it is. The form makes the material process the type it is. Had blood boiled around the heart for the sake of some different psychological goal, the type of material process would have been different. In this account, the specific material process is itself inextricably psycho-physical, inseparable in thought from the formal features characteristic of anger. One cannot decompose anger into two processes, one of which is purely physical (definable without reference to some psychological goal), if the relevant bodily processes are essentially directed towards some higher order goal.

Aristotle, so understood, advanced two distinct inextricability theses in *De Anima* A.1:

[A] Psychological activities, such as are involved in the emotions, desire, and perception, are defined as inextricably psycho-physical, not definable by decomposition into two separate types of activity or feature, one purely psychological, the other purely physical.[29] Their form is inextricably psycho-physical.

[B] The relevant specific type of physical activity cannot be defined without explicit reference in the definition to some psycho-physical activity. It is an inextricably physico-psychic activity.

These two theses are independent. One could accept [A] but not [B], taking the basis for essentially psycho-physical forms to be purely physical. However, Aristotle could not do so if he made one, substantial, further assumption. If he held that:

(1) The type of desire used to define being angry is (a boiling-of-the-blood type of desire for revenge). (Premise: Inextricability Thesis [A])

and added that:

(2) There is one and only one specific type of physical/material process that occurs in cases of anger, which is made the one it is by the inextricably psycho-physical type of desire referred to in (1), (Unifying Assumption),

he would have been committed to:

---

[29] I use the term 'mental' to indicate (in general terms to the modern reader) the type of process at issue. For Aristotle, our nutrition is also inextricably psycho-physical.

(3) The relevant specific type of physical/material process that occurs (boiling of the blood) is itself essentially and inextricably psycho-physical: one which is essentially a desire for revenge. (From (2) and (3): Inextricability Thesis [B])

The Unifying Assumption may be spelled out as follows: there is one specific type of boiling blood found in angry people, which is made the one it is by its being a desire-for-revenge-type of boiling of the blood. This one (non-accidentally) unified type of process exemplifies a distinctive type of boiling of the blood: a for-revenge-type of blood-boiling. A psycho-physical form determines the specific type of boiling involved. It makes the matter be the matter it is. This is why in talking of anger there is reference to the (one) process, 'a certain type of process' (403a26), not to several.

Had the type of desire for revenge which characterized anger been defined in purely psychological terms, the Unifying Assumption would have been unmotivated. Why should being of a given purely psychological type be an essential feature of a purely physical process? The latter should, it would seem, be definable in purely physical terms. It would seem ad hoc to insist that the physical process be made what it is by the purely psychological type it enmatters.

Aristotle, I shall argue in subsequent chapters, held both [A] and [B] and connected them in the way just suggested. Indeed, what is distinctive about his approach is that his acceptance of these two theses forms part of his theoretically driven account of animals and their distinctive souls as properly unified entities.[30]

1.6 The model of *De Anima* A.1

It may be helpful, at this point, to position Aristotle's claims on a broader conceptual map.

1. Aristotle's account of anger and fear in *De Anima* A.1, as understood here, is not the model a non-reductionist materialist philosopher would propose. They would understand being angry as follows:

[1] There is a relevant type of physical process (or aspect) involved which is to be defined without reference to any psychological activity or description.
[2] Being angry involves a purely psychological type of process or aspect (desiring revenge), defined as the one it is (desiring revenge) without reference to any internal physical process or description.
[3] This instance of desiring revenge is realized by or grounded in a particular process of the physical type (or types) mentioned in [1].

---

[30] I shall argue further against the suggestion that he held [B] but rejected [A].

Aristotle (I have argued) accepted neither [1] nor [2] and hence would not accept [3]. In his account, the relevant specific type of 'physical' process (boiling of the blood) cannot be defined as the one it is without reference to some psychological process (or aspect). Nor can the apparently purely 'psychological' process (or aspect) be defined as the one it is (desiring revenge) without reference to it as a hot-type of desire: as an enmattered form.

2. Aristotle's account of anger also differs from the one spiritualists would offer, were they to seek to define anger in accordance with the model they favour as follows:

[1] Being angry is desiring revenge and this does not essentially involve any distinct physical change in the subject at all.
[2] Aristotle did not require the presence of any concurrent physical process because he understood the relevant matter (that in the sense organ) as primitively endowed with capacities for ungrounded psychological activity: matter as 'pregnant with anger'.

Aristotle, it seems, rejected [1] without regarding the relevant matter as mysteriously 'pregnant with anger,' ready to deliver a purely psychological process. For while there is no concurrent (or underlying) physical process (as in the materialist account), anger is nonetheless an essentially psycho-physical process.

An analogy that Aristotle subsequently draws between being angry and weaving or building may prove helpful (408b1–13). Weaving, as was noted in the Introduction, is a clear example of a process (or activity) which essentially involves bodily movement. One cannot, it seems, define it (in a purely psychological way) without reference to the hands, fingers, and loom of the weaver. There is no pure form to be abstracted from the process. But the bodily movements at issue are precisely those which are directed towards the goal of making some garment and are correctly described in terms of that goal (moving the shuttle, tying the wool, etc.). One cannot, it seems, define the relevant bodily movements without reference to this goal. (The weaver may make other bodily movements as she weaves—moving from foot to foot, whistling, or crossing her legs—but these are not parts of her weaving.) Weaving, like being angry, is an inextricably psycho-physical process.

3. According to *De Anima* A.1 being angry, perceiving, and desiring (if they follow the same model) will be '*common* to body and soul' in a particularly demanding way. The processes involved will be inseparable in definition into two separate components. There is not one (definitionally) separable purely formal process to which can be added another definitionally distinct physical (or bodily) process, both making (definitionally) separable but individually necessary

contributions to the outcome. The process involved is indissoluble in definition into two such components.[31] Even when considered as a 'formal' process, it cannot be defined except in terms which essentially involve matter.[32]

If this line of argument is correct, the following cannot be an adequate definition of anger (by Aristotle's lights):

[C]*   desiring revenge caused by an insult,

since it does not refer to the distinctively material features at issue.[33] In an adequate Aristotelian definition one must specify the relevant desire in a matter-involving way. However, [C]* is an example of what Hilary Putnam once called a 'logical description' of the relevant phenomenon, one which does not essentially include any specification of the physical nature of the realizing 'states'.[34] Indeed, it is just the type of definition of anger favoured by most functionalist interpreters. If Aristotle rejected [C]*-style definitions of anger in favour of one explicitly involving matter, he rejected a key assumption shared by functionalists, non-reductive materialists, and spiritualists alike: one cannot, in his view, define anger as a given type of desire which is fully determinate without explicit reference to specific types of matter internal to the organism. The type of desire involved is essentially a psycho-physical phenomenon, not itself further decomposable into a combination of purely psychological and purely physical phenomena. Nor is this point only about *types* of activity. Individual cases of hot (or angry) desiring revenge will essentially be instances of the psycho-physical type

---

[31] Contrast *Philebus* 34a3ff. where the soul and the body are described as jointly (*koine*) in one single passion and jointly (*koine*) moved when the body suffers in a given way which reaches through to the soul (in contrast with cases where the body suffers and the soul is oblivious). In this case the soul suffers a passion (*pathos*) 'together with the body' which it can later recall without the body. The passion in question belongs to the soul even if the body has also to be moved at the same time and in the same way if the soul is to perceive. The relevant movement of the soul (when it perceives) and that of the body are, in Plato's account here, separable in thought even if the former cannot happen without the other.

[32] In particular, it will not follow from the fact that perception is a formal change, that it is 'at the level of form alone', understood as not essentially involving any material change. Contrast Thomas Johansen (1998: 290, n. 10) quoting Myles Burnyeat (1995: 431).

[33] In such an account the efficient causal connection would need to be specified in an abstract (non-essentially physical) way: e.g. in terms of necessary and sufficient conditions.

[34] 'Minds and Machine', in his (1975, vol II: 371). Functionalists note that the relevant grounding physical states must be such as to sustain the causal role of the psychological states they realize. Some may even think that the realizing states need to share those intrinsic features required for them to sustain such causal roles. (Kim noted this possibility in his 1996: 86–7). However, crucially, they do not think that reference to the physical is required in the definition of the relevant psychological states. In their view, the physical plays no role in determining the identity of the psychological states themselves. Indeed, this is the basis for their 'autonomy of the mental' thesis. Rae Langton challenges the functionalist reading of Aristotle at just this point in her 'The Musical, the Magical and the Mathematical Soul', in Crane and Patterson (2000: 13–31).

just specified. Being an instance of this type is essential to its identity as the individual activity it is.[35]

4. Aristotle's account, as we have seen, is not (so understood) the one generally attributed to him by recent friends or critics. In their view (but not in his) there are two distinct psychological and physical 'components' or 'parts' of anger, which are definitionally separable even if not separable in existence. Indeed, this is precisely the view he was rejecting.

From this perspective, we can diagnose the precise point at which the exegetical debate between Aristotle's materialist and spiritualist interpreters (as sketched in the Introduction) went awry. Important consequences flowed from their shared assumption that, in the affections of the soul, there is a type of psychological process (or aspect), defined in purely psychological terms—such as awareness or discrimination (in the case of perception) or desiring revenge (in the case of anger). The materialists (correctly) saw that there was more than this to Aristotle's account of perception: there were also, they insisted, bodily changes with physical features. Then they made their crucial move: they added a distinct physical type of process, instances of which 'underlie' the psychological activity of perceiving. This was their way of accounting for Aristotle's insistence on the role of the boiling of the blood (with its physical features) in the case of desire and the operation of the material sense organ in the case of perception.

To some, the key materialist move seemed so obvious that they saw Aristotle as making it even in contexts when he did not appear to be doing so. Thus, Martha Nussbaum and Hilary Putnam once suggested his claim in *De Motu* that perceptions *are* quality changes in shape, size, and temperature as equivalent to the claim that 'perceptions are, *are realised in,* quality changes of this type'.[36] They were led to this view (for which there is no genuine warrant in the text) because they did not consider the possibility that Aristotle could have taken perception to be one activity which is (essentially) inextricably both physical and psychological. There was simply no space on their conceptual map for such a radically non-Cartesian position. Others were led astray by (what I have argued is) an incomplete and faulty analysis of the argument of *De Anima* A.1, mistakenly thinking that Aristotle was proposing his own two-component definition of anger in the few lines in which he surveys the views of others (403a30–b1), while ignoring the importance of the following lines and the flow of argument of the chapter as a whole.

The spiritualists, for their part, developed one important criticism of both functionalist and non-reductionist materialist interpretations. They denied

---

[35] See the view of process individuation set out in my (1984: 6ff.). (I take desire for revenge to be a psycho-physical, not a non psycho-physical, purely biological activity.)

[36] See 'Changing Aristotle's Mind', in Nussbaum and Rorty (1992: 39).

(correctly, as I am now inclined to think) that in, for example, Aristotle's account of perception there is a separate underlying physical process type distinct from the purely psychological one.[37] However, they shared with their opponents the Cartesian assumption that there must be, in Aristotle's picture, a purely psychological (formal) activity of perceiving (or desiring). As a result, they were led to their highly paradoxical, not to say disastrous, conclusion, regarding:

(a) perceiving as (for Aristotle) simply a purely psychological (formal) process not (essentially) involving any material change at all, and
(b) the physical organs (in Aristotle's account) as mysteriously issuing in (formal) psychological processes without any material change occurring at all.

Since there was, in their view, no separate physical change, Aristotle must (they concluded) have thought that all that essentially occurs in perception is a purely formal change, the purely psychological (or spiritual) act of attending to redness. There was simply no space in their Cartesian conceptual map for thinking of perception as inextricably psycho-physical.

Aristotle (as I understand him) developed in *De Anima* A.1 the basis of an account which accepted the starting points of these materialist and spiritualist interpreters while rejecting their conclusions. In his view:

(1) recognizing (or being aware of) A and desiring revenge essentially involve a bodily change involving changes in shape, size, temperature or spatial position [the materialist starting point];
(2) recognizing (or being aware of) A and desire for revenge essentially involve certain aspects which are irreducible to purely physical ones [common assumption];
(3) there is no distinct physical process underlying the psychological process of recognizing (or being aware of) A and desiring revenge [the spiritualist starting point].

Aristotle could accept (1)–(3) because he took desiring revenge (in the way required for being angry) and recognizing (or being aware of) A to be essentially inextricably psycho-physical phenomena. In developing his picture, he was (in effect) offering an alternative to any picture in which perceiving involves a purely psychological process (or aspect) separable in definition (or, indeed, abstractable from) from all material processes (even if not separable in existence).[38] In his

---

[37] This claim will be defended in some detail in the case of desire and perception in Chapters 3–6.
[38] Plato appears to have thought that certain human mental activities (e.g. those of the intellect) were separable from matter in both thought and in existence. I shall return to this issue in Chapter 6.

intuitive and simple theory of the relevant emotions, this is the way in which anger and fear are to be defined. Indeed, they must be defined as inextricably psycho-physical in this way if their forms are to be causes and effects of the bodily processes which follow from their natures (or forms).

It may seem ironic that both materialist and spiritualist interpreters alike (guided by the Cartesian assumptions set out in the Introduction) have presented Aristotle as trapped by the very assumptions he was, in fact, struggling to undermine. It remains to be seen whether he succeeded in finding a way to do so in a credible fashion.

1.7 Gaps and queries

In this chapter, I have developed an impure form reading of a central section of *De Anima* A.1 and noted some of its consequences. I have also suggested that this model, his simple theory of the emotions, sets the agenda for subsequent discussions of desire and perception in *De Anima*.

In Chapters 3–6, I suggest that Aristotle followed this model in these cases. This is important exegetically. Even those inclined to accept the interpretation just sketched of *De Anima* A.1 may suspect that his remarks there are introductory, put forward without commitment to their truth, perhaps to be revised as the discussion proceeds. It is important, in any event, to confirm whether, and to what extent, Aristotle sought to deploy the inextricabilist model developed in *De Anima* A.1 to a wider range of psychological phenomena.

There are more general issues at stake. In this chapter I have mentioned several of Aristotle's views about definition, form, and causation which require further elucidation. In Chapter 2, I shall support the impure form reading of *De Anima* A.1 by considering his more general view of the form of natural substances and the philosophical motivations that led him to adopt it. His account of the form of natural substances parallels, or so I shall suggest, the one offered for the inextricably psycho-physical processes studied in *De Anima*. His remarks on anger, fear, desire, and perception exemplify a more general conception of the type of form which, in its central application, natural substances must have if they are to be unified (efficient) causes of natural changes. This is why they have to be defined in terms of impure, inextricably material, forms.

Both tasks are important. It may be possible to maintain, albeit with considerable ingenuity, that the relevant sections of *De Anima* A.1 can, taken by themselves, be understood in a manner consistent with a pure form interpretation. Perhaps, for example, the relevant forms require (or 'hypothetically necessitate') the presence of specific material changes but are not defined in terms which refer (in the definition) to matter.[39] To counter this and other concerns, Aristotle's discussion of the emotions and other phenomena needs to be placed in the wider context of his views on related issues and of his own philosophical motivations for adopting them.[40]

---

[39] Thomas Johansen suggested this approach in his discussion of *De Anima* A.1 (2012: 168) and developed a similar account of taste, smell, vision, and hearing (2012: 166–8). His approach requires Aristotle to hold that the relevant purely psychological ingredient (such as the desire for revenge) requires the presence of a specific kind of material process (such as boiling of the blood) *because* of the nature of the psychological ingredient itself. That is: one must have reason to think (in his account) that this psychological ingredient, so understood, can only be present in matter so organized (see *De Anima* A.3, 407b16 for his statement of this requirement). This is clearly a non-trivial task. Why cannot the desire for revenge be found in the aged, or Maupassant's cool, calculator, without any boiling blood at all? Or, as Putnam once suggested, realized in 'soul stuff'? It is far from clear that the task Johansen envisages can be successfully accomplished. Nor is there evidence in *De Anima* A.1 to suggest that Aristotle himself undertook it or thought it could be done. For further concerns about the general approach Johansen commends (pure forms which hypothetically necessitate matter) see Chapter 2, Section 6 and Chapter 3, Section 6. (It should be noted that it is not enough for a proponent of this approach to say that anger (defined as the combination of desire for revenge *and* boiling of the blood) requires the presence of boiling of the blood. For this would be to trivialize Aristotle's demand that one derives from the essence of the phenomenon its other necessary features (A.1, 402b21–5). Nor, for similar reasons, is it enough to suggest that desire for revenge, defined relationally as the form of a given type of matter, requires the presence of that matter.)

[40] I am particularly indebted, at this point, to discussions with Victor Caston. In his comments on an earlier paper of mine, he offered a different construal of *De Anima* A.1 which rested, in part, on presenting the relevant forms as one (pure) part of the (impure) definition of the composite state (which involved in addition reference to matter). ('Commentary on Charles', 2008: 30–47). To make further progress, it will be important, as Caston and I predicted then, to assess the broader issues at stake, especially those concerning form and definition, which are the subject matter of Chapter 2.

2
Enmattered Form
Aristotle's Hylomorphism

2.1 Introduction

In *De Anima* A.1, Aristotle suggested that:

[1] The psychological activities involved in the emotions, desire, and perception are inextricably psycho-physical. They cannot be defined without explicit reference to some physical activity or physical feature. Their form, the sole object captured in their definition, is inextricably psycho-physical.

[2] The physical activities involved in the emotions, desire, and perception are inextricably psycho-physical. They cannot be defined without explicit reference in their definition to some psychological activity or psychological feature (understood as in [1]).

If Aristotle is committed to [1] and [2], anger, fear, desire, and perception will not be, in his account, definable by decomposition into two definitionally separate components, one of which is purely psychological (defined without explicit reference to the physical), the other purely physical (defined without explicit reference to the psychological). Or so I argued in Chapter 1.

Aristotle accepted [1] and [2], I shall now suggest, as a reflection of a more general hylomorphic theory he developed in thinking about natural objects. More specifically, he held that:

[A] The forms of natural objects are inextricably enmattered, inseparable in definition from material features or material activities,

and

[B] The matter of natural objects is inextricable in definition from such forms.

Further, he held [A] because he believed that

[C] The forms of natural objects have to be inextricably enmattered to play the causal roles required of them.

His key distinction in *De Anima* A.1 between the definitions of mathematical and natural objects follows, I shall argue, the pattern of his general account of the form and matter of natural objects developed (at least in part) to capture their role in causing change. In arguing for these claims, my aim to arrive at a more precise understanding of Aristotle's position and his motivations for adopting it.

In *Physics* B.2 Aristotle wrote:

> nature is said in two ways, both as matter and as form. We should investigate as if we were investigating what snubness is. Such things, that is natural objects, are neither independent of matter nor are determined by matter. (194a13–15)

At this point, as in *De Anima* 403b11–19, he is concerned to contrast the forms of natural with those of mathematical objects. Earlier in the chapter he had written:

> the mathematician is concerned with such things as the shape of the sun and the moon and whether the earth and the cosmos are spherical or not. But he does not consider them as a boundary of natural bodies; nor does he consider such things to be accidents of natural bodies as belonging to such things. This is because he separates them. They are separate in thought from change and it makes no difference nor does any error result from their separating them. Those who speak of Ideas fail to notice that they're doing this; for they separate natural entities even though these are less separable than mathematical entities. This would be clear if one tried to give a definition of both cases and of what follows them. For the odd, the even, the straight and the curved, even number, line and shape, are defined without reference to change while flesh, bone, and man are not. But these are defined, as snub nose is defined, and not like the curve.
> (193b31–194a7)

In order to define the snub nose, Aristotle introduces snubness (in 194a13–15: as the *definiens*).[1] When he says that we should investigate nature 'as if we were investigating snubness', he is suggesting that the feature which defines natural objects, like that which defines snub noses, 'is neither independent of matter nor determined by matter'. The feature cited in the definition of snub noses cannot simply be concavity: that is common to many objects besides noses. It must be a type of concavity which is, in some way, specific to noses. If this feature is nasal-concavity, defined as a distinctively nasal, or enmattered, type of concavity, and

---

[1] In 194a6 Aristotle refers to *snub nose*, which he treats as an entity like man or bone, whose definition he is seeking. In 194a12–14, he talks of *snubness*, a feature *(pathos)* of snub noses, such as nasal-concavity, which would be cited in defining them. Knowledge of this feature, which is their form and referred to in their definition, will involve some knowledge of their matter (194b9–12). It is because they possess this feature that snub noses 'are neither without matter nor determined solely by matter' (194a14–15). In fact, their matter is understood as relative to their form (194b7–9).

the form and essence is what is cited in the definition, natural objects will be defined in terms of enmattered forms. In this, they will differ from mathematical forms which are to be defined independently of (perceptual) matter and its features, even if they can only exist when such matter exists.

Aristotle's remarks are suggestive. In the final sections of *Physics* B.2, he enquires how much of the matter students of nature should know in grasping the definition of the relevant objects (194b9–10). Should they, he asks, like doctors, grasp just as much of the objects they study as is required to understand how those objects (such as sinews or bines) achieve their goals in the body?[2] At the end of *Physics* B.9 he indicates that definitions of certain objects contain matter within them: they are, in some way, matter-involving (200b4–8). Since in *Physics* B.2 (194b9–10) and B.3 (194b25–7) he identifies the essence (as captured in the definition) with the relevant form, the latter will be an enmattered form. Taken together, these passages suggest that the definitions of natural objects, in referring to their forms, refer explicitly to some of their material features.

Aristotle's remarks in *Physics* B suggest a possible motivation for this view. In *Physics* B.1, the forms of natural objects are identified with the starting points of change and rest, the causes of the relevant changes (193b4ff.).[3] In *Physics* B.7, they are identified with the final causes of natural objects and said to be efficient causes of the coming to be of objects of the same kind (198a23–5).[4] If the relevant causes are essentially enmattered, the forms of natural objects will themselves have to be defined as essentially enmattered. Perhaps this is why, if we construe them as mathematical forms, error results (193b35): they are not, *inter alia*, capable of playing the causal roles required of them.[5]

Aristotle did not, however, specify in *Physics* B the exact way in which the forms of natural substances are enmattered. Nor did he spell out what is involved

---

[2] Smiths, Aristotle's other example, presumably need to know a lot about the material nature of bronze to understand how it is to be used for their purposes in (e.g.) making instruments. In these cases, the objects studied are said (somewhat telegrammatically) to be 'separable in form' but themselves to be 'in matter' (194b12–3). If the material nature of bronze or bone is part of the form, this may need to be distinguished from the matter in which the objects are. But Aristotle does not give any indication here as to how this is to be done. We will return to this issue in considering *Metaphysics* Z.10–11.

[3] *Physics* B.1 develops further his suggestion in *Physics* A.7 that the principles of being are to be identified with the principles of becoming (190b17–18), where the latter involve that which underlies (later identified with matter) and the relevant contraries (one of which may be with form). While these claims may commit Aristotle to thinking that form, as the endpoint of becoming, is necessarily enmattered, they do not show that the form itself is essentially enmattered. The form, for all that is said in *Physics* A, could be (in the terminology of *Physics* B.2) a mathematical, not a physical, form. This latter distinction is required, I shall suggest, to account for the efficient and teleological causal role of physical forms highlighted in *Physics* B. I discuss some relevant issues in my '*Physics* 1.7', in Diana Quarantotto, ed. (2018: 178–205) and am indebted to her for subsequent discussion of these questions.

[4] In 198b1–3, essence and shape (*morphē*), which presumably includes form, are described as unmoved efficient causes (movers). I am indebted to Emily Katz for discussion of this passage.

[5] These considerations provide the background, I shall argue, for the causal claims about anger and fear in Chapter 1.

in examining them 'as if one were investigating snubness' or state explicitly how the forms of natural objects have to be if they are to play the causal roles required of them.[6] Even if his remarks suggest that the definitions (and forms) of natural substances are, in some way, enmattered, we have to look elsewhere for a fuller understanding, and clearer articulation, of his position. Indeed, he himself suggests as much when he concludes *Physics* B.2 by noting that it is the task of metaphysics (first philosophy), another study, to work out what is separable and what is to be revealed in the definitions of natural objects (*the definiens*: 194b14–15).

In the next four sections (Sections 2.3–2.6), I shall examine two ways to interpret Aristotle's background metaphysical account: one in terms of pure, the other of impure, forms (paralleling the two styles of interpretation of *De Anima* A.1 discussed in Chapter 1). In Section 2.7, I shall consider his account of the matter of composite objects. While his remark that 'matter is in the class of relatives—for different forms there is different matter' (194b8–9) suggests the view of matter expressed in [B] above, it is not developed in detail in *Physics* B. It too requires elucidation. My aim is to arrive at a more precise statement of Aristotle's understanding of impure forms and a better grasp of his motivations for adopting such a view.

2.2 Two Interpretations

One style of interpretation sees the forms of natural objects as being, like those of mathematical objects, what I shall call '*pure*'. A pure form can be fully defined without containing as a part any term that refers explicitly to perceptual matter, understood as specific types of concurrent internal bodily features or processes. The definition of the form of man would not contain any term which refers to man's body, its parts (such as hands, nose, or flesh) or its bodily capacities: the matter present in men. While the existence of this form may (in some way) require (or 'hypothetically necessitate') the existence of a body of this type, the form is not itself defined as a form-of-this-type-of-body. A pure form of this type is enmattered in a different way from a mathematical form in that its existence requires the presence of some specific type of matter. However, both mathematical and natural forms are pure, defined without any term which refers explicitly to them as perceptually enmattered. (This interpretation parallels the Pure Form account of anger in Chapter 1.)

---

[6] It is not clear, for example, in *Physics* B whether natural forms are essentially or only necessarily enmattered. James Lennox (2008) does not take a clear stand on this issue: he refers to snubness sometimes as a feature that is 'necessarily concave flesh and bone' (p. 173), sometimes as one invoked in the definition (p. 171). For further discussion of this question, see Michail Peramatzis (2011: 122ff.).

This interpretation, initially developed by some ancient commentators, has been central in much modern work.[7] I shall call it the '*Pure Form interpretation*' and contrast it with an alternative, '*Impure Form interpretation*': the view that the relevant form cannot be fully defined without terms which refer explicitly to it as enmattered in some specific way in perceptual matter.[8] An impure form definition of man will contain expressions which refer to, for example, a human's bodily capacities or activities. This is because the form itself is, in its own nature, an essentially bodily (or enmattered) form.[9] (This interpretation, too, parallels the Impure Form account of anger developed in Chapter 1.)

Some pure form interpreters see man as a compound defined in terms of two distinct components: a pure form, defined without explicit reference to any concurrent internal material bodily processes, and matter.[10] In their view, the definition of the compound contains more than the pure form. They see Aristotle's apparent identification of form with *definiens* (and essence) in *De Anima* A.1 and *Physics* B.2–3 as infelicitous, corrected in his more considered discussion in the *Metaphysics*. For the impure form interpreter, by contrast, the compound man is to be defined in terms of an impure form, one defined in terms which explicitly refer to man's bodily activities or capacities: the matter of the man. It will, as such, parallel the definition of the form of anger as a hot type of desire for revenge. There will be nothing misleading, or merely introductory, about the identification of form with *definiens* (or essence) in either *De Anima* A or *Physics* B.

Since Aristotle says that we should investigate in studying nature 'as if we were investigating what snubness is', (*Physics* B.2, 194a13–14), we can best begin by examining:

(i) his account of snubness, and
(ii) how, and why, the forms of natural substances, in his view, resemble snubness.

---

[7] It was developed by, for example, Philoponus and pseudo-Simplicius (possibly Priscian). In current discussions it has been advanced by a variety of authors, notably Mary Louise Gill (1989), Michael Frede (1990), James Lennox (2008), Victor Caston (2008/9), and Daniel Devereux (2010/11).

[8] This is a *de re* claim about the nature of the form itself. I advanced this suggestion in my 'Aristotle's Psychological Theory' (2008). Michail Peramatzis developed a similar view in considerably more detail and over a wider range in his (2011) and has defended it in a series of subsequent essays: (2014), (2015: 195–216), and (2018: 12–32). Remarks made by Alan Code (2010b) and Stephen Menn (2002) reflect some sympathy for an interpretation of this general type. David Balme was an earlier proponent (1987: 306–12) but the view has, I believe, ancient roots. The full history of early Aristotelian hylomorphism has yet to be written.

[9] This is, it should be noted, a *de re* claim about the nature of the entity which is the form. It is not a *de dicto* claim about that object, relative to some ways of describing it.

[10] On this account, the essence of a natural object, what is captured in the definition, is made up of its form and its matter. Not all pure form interpreters take this view. Some, like Michael Frede, see Aristotle as taking forms alone to be the essences of natural objects. In his view: even if such forms necessitate the presence of matter, there is no reference to matter in the definition of the compound object.

Aristotle's answers to these questions show him to be committed to impure, essentially enmattered, forms. They also serve to show more precisely how he understood the forms in question. Or so I shall suggest.

2.3 Snubness and S-structures

Aristotle offers his most detailed account of snubness in *Sophistici Elenchi*, Chapter 31. He remarks:

> In the case of predicates predicated of things through which they have the reference they do, we should say the following: what is referred to (*to dēloumenon*) is not the same when the predicate is used by itself and when combined in the phrase in question.[11] For 'concave' signifies (*sēmainei*) the same thing when used commonly of the snub and of the bandy (a type of leg). However, when added to the nose and the leg it can signify different things. In the former case it signifies the snub, in the latter the bandy; and, in this case, there is no difference between saying snub nose and concave nose. Further, we should not permit this expression ('the snub') to be used as a subject term: for this is a mistake. For the snub is not a concave nose but this, for example, affection of the nose. Hence there is nothing strange if the snub nose is the nose having nasal-concavity.
> (*Sophistici Elenchi* (S.E.) 181b34–182a6)

In the earlier parts of this chapter, Aristotle had discussed relative terms, such as 'double or half', which, in his view, 'either signify nothing when used separately or do not signify the same thing as when part of a complex phrase'. He now applies this idea to the term 'the snub', which he understands as signifying a quality: snubness. He suggests that while 'concavity' may signify something when used separately, it does not signify the same entity when used as a part of the phrases 'concavity of the nose' ('snubness') and 'concavity of the leg' ('bandiness'). 'Snubness' signifies a distinctive type of feature, nasal-concavity, which cannot be defined as a combination of concavity (defined independently of the nose) and the nose. Could it have been defined in the latter way, 'concavity' would have signified the same thing when used by itself and when 'added to the nose'. Instead, 'snubness' signifies a distinctively nasal type of concavity: concavity-of-[or-for-]the-nose.[12]

---

[11] I take the verb 'to signify' as indicating reference (rather than definition) in the context of S.E. 1.31. While issues concerning essence and definition underwrite his relevant discussion of per se predication in the *Posterior Analytics,* they are not explicitly invoked in S.E. 1.31.

[12] I am indebted to, and in general agreement with, Michail Peramatzis' discussion of S.E. 1.31 in (2011: 122ff.). We differ only in that I take Aristotle's discussion in S.E. 1.31 to focus solely on the inextricability of snubness (or nasal-concavity) from noses. It does not, in my view, suggest that noses are similarly inextricable from snubness. Nor should it: noses, it seems, can be defined independently of their varying shapes.

By contrast, 'being spherical' has the same signification when used separately and when predicated of, or instantiated in, differing types of object. This is because there is, in Aristotle's view, a common type of sphericity present in, for example, bronze and gold spheres.[13] Although we could choose to describe the type of sphericity present in bronze as 'brazen sphericity', there is no distinctive, non-decomposable, feature, being brazenly spherical, to parallel the non-decomposable feature: being nasally concave.[14] Snubness is an inextricably nasal type of concavity.[15]

We might capture Aristotle's idea by distinguishing between 'independent' and 'dependent' components.[16] 'Independent components' can be defined as follows:

A is an independent component in a compound (AB) if and only if A can correctly be compounded with some C to yield a new compound [AC].

'Spherical' would be an independent component in the sentence 'the bronze is spherical'. It can be used to describe both bronze and golden balls as spherical in the same way. Dependent components behave differently. 'Being snub' is a dependent component in 'the nose is snub' because it cannot be used to describe legs or yield a new compound phrase ('snub leg'). However, from Aristotle's perspective this distinction is grounded in the fact that 'snubness' signifies a distinctive, inextricably nasal, way of being concave different from the way in which bandy legs are concave. (This is, *de re*, the nature of the relevant type of concavity.) 'Brazen sphericity', by contrast, does not signify a distinctive way of being spherical which is inextricably tied to bronze objects. There is one way of being spherical shared by bronze and golden spheres.

---

[13] The shared property, sphericity, is not the essentially non-(perceptually) material sphericity used to define geometrical spheres because this cannot be instantiated by (perceptually) material objects. If the type of sphericity is shared by both geometrical and brazen spheres, it will be an abstracted type of sphericity: one which is not essentially (perceptually) enmattered. This type of sphericity is to be distinguished from the essentially non-perceptual sphericity which is the sole prerogative of geometrical spheres. (This distinction matches that between abstraction and separation noted in Chapter 1.) For a somewhat contrasting account, see Peramatzis (2011: 127).

[14] Aristotle's claim is not that snub noses and bandy legs cannot also instantiate a shared property of concavity. Indeed, he suggests that they do (181b37–9). His point is only that snubness is not to be understood, or defined, as that shared property when present in noses. When reference to the nose is added to form the complex expression 'snubness', what is signified is not the shared property added to the nose but a distinctive type of concavity: nasal-concavity. For a contrasting, but less detailed, reading of these lines, see Victor Caston's remarks (2008: 46).

[15] One can, as Aristotle notes, describe both snub noses and bandy legs as concave (*S.E.* 181b36f.). Just don't think, he adds, that 'snubness' is composed of this common element added to the nose or that 'snubness' is decomposable into this common element and something else. The way in which concavity is combined with the nose to form 'snubness' signifies a distinctive type of concavity which is not decomposable in that way. If it were, concavity would, contrary to his hypothesis, signify the very same thing in snubness and in bandiness.

[16] To follow a suggestion made by Timothy Williamson (2000: 32–3).

Aristotle elsewhere describes flesh as *part* of snubness (*Metaphysics* 1035a5–6), taking flesh as a 'stand in' for nose (which he uses later in 1037a32f.).[17] In talking of flesh as a 'part' of snubness, he is thinking of it as in some way part of the type of concavity that snubness is. There is, he suggests, a definitional connection between snubness and the nose grounded in the fact that being nasal is a 'part' of, or ingredient in, the definition of snubness: it defines the kind of feature snubness is. The nose and snubness are in this way per se connected.[18] While one well-defined common feature, or nature (being spherical), is used to define both bronze and wax spheres, there is no such common feature, or nature (being concave), used in the definition of snubness and bandiness.[19]

Aristotle's account of the signification of 'snubness' rests on two claims:

(i) it is defined as an inextricably nasal way of being concave
(ii) there is no one well-defined common feature, or nature, being concave, referred to in the definitions of snubness and bandiness.

Being bandy and being snub are defined as respectively inextricably 'leggy' and nasal ways of being concave. While being snub entails being concave, this is because being snub is defined as a distinctive, inextricably nasal, way of being concave.[20]

This account can be generalized to apply to any term which refers to a property (P) defined as:

(i) a distinctive way of being a more general property (Q) but
(ii) not one defined by decomposition into two or more terms, one of which refers to a general well-defined property shared with other cases.

I shall call this the S-structure (S for snubness!). In an S-structure, a term signifies a property P where:

---

[17] It is striking that in Z.10 Aristotle talks of flesh (1035a5 see also 19, 33), in Z.11 of nose (1037a31f.) as the matter involved.

[18] It is described as a per se $_2$ connection: *Posterior Analytics* 73a10ff. Aristotle also discusses snubness briefly in *S.E.* 10 and more fully in *Metaphysics* Z.5 and 11. Some aspects of the latter chapter are discussed below. For an interpretation of the puzzles of *Metaphysics* Z.5 fully consistent with the interpretation offered here, see Peramatzis and Charles (forthcoming).

[19] This is not, of course, to deny that concavity can be understood as an independent feature found in many objects, including snub noses. It is simply to claim that snubness itself is not to be defined in terms of a combination of that independent common feature and noses.

[20] There may be a limited number of ways of being concave: snubness, bandiness, ... But, nonetheless, while being snub entails being concave, being concave does not entail being snub (and is not defined as a way of being snub). Aristotle, I believe, uses this point in his discussion of colour in *De Sensu* Γ, 440a25ff.: while being red entails being coloured, and being coloured entails being either black or white (or on the spectrum between them), it does not entail being red. In both cases, the relevant asymmetry is maintained. I am indebted to Fred Miller for discussion of this point.

(i)* being P is defined as a distinctive way of being Q and
(ii)* being P is not defined by decomposition into two or more terms, one of which refers to a more general well-defined property or nature (Q*) shared by other properties.

'Being red', for example, will exemplify the S-structure when redness is defined as a distinctive way of being coloured, not in terms that refer to one well-defined common property, being coloured, shared by many different colours. Features such as being red or being snub cannot be defined by decomposition into one shared well-defined property (being concave or being coloured) which is, as it happens, instantiated in different types of cases.

Aristotle's goal in S.E. 31 is to point to cases that are not adequately defined by decomposition in terms of a well-defined separable feature (Q*) to which something else is added, not to develop a general theory of the phenomenon at issue. However, it may prove helpful to introduce some terminology to refer to the features found in S-structures. I shall (following long-standing tradition) call the Q property in an S-structure the *determinable*, the P property a *determinate* way of being Q, and the feature which generates being P from being Q (the R feature) the *determinant*.[21] (Since these terms have been understood in a variety of different ways, it is important to emphasize that I shall use them solely to refer to the ingredients of an S-structure as here defined.)

There are, it should be noted, several types of S-structure, as we can see if we contrast the case of snubness with that of redness. In the former, the general feature (being concave: the determinable) is defined independently of the determinate (snubness) or the determinant (nasal). In the latter, this would not be the case if being coloured (the determinable) were to be defined as being red or blue or green. There would be no well-defined, common non-disjunctive property or nature: being coloured. By contrast, there may be a well-defined common property (being concave), but it is not referred to in the definition of snubness. Further, the determinant (being nasal) is also a determinant of other determinables (such as straightness in the case of aquiline noses). In the case of redness, the determinant (being redness-generating) is a determinant only of being coloured. This determinant is essentially a determinant of this determinable, defined as a differentiator of this determinable. Finally, while in this case, one cannot define the determinant (being red-generating) without reference to the determinate itself

---

[21] See W.E. Johnson (1921, pt 1: 175–6). In this view, it is not that red and yellow both share some distinct quality (colour) which is conjoined with their specific colour to yield redness and yellowness. There is no more general quality which they share once their distinctive yellowness or redness has been subtracted. While red and yellow objects are both coloured, there is no one common feature, being coloured, which they share (see A.N. Prior's essay (1949: 5 and 13)). Johnson's distinction was employed earlier by J. Cook Wilson and later developed in a quite different way by J. Searle. The correct characterization of determinable-determinate relation is still a controversial issue: see E. Funkhouser (2006: 548–69).

(redness), in others one can (as being nasal can be defined without reference to snubness).

That said, in all S-structures there are:

(i) determinate (P) types defined in terms of R-ways (e.g. nasal or red-generating way) of being a more general determinable (Q) and
(ii) no independent well-defined common property or shared nature referred to in the definition of this (and other) determinate types.

These two conditions are connected. If the determinate type (such as being snub) is defined in this way as an *inextricably R-way of being Q*, there will be no more general common property (or shared nature) used to define it. Equally, if there is no more general well-defined common property referred to in defining P, R (if defined by appeal to any more general feature) will be an inextricably R-way (such as nasal) of being that feature.[22] Although there are several types of S-structure, all will, in my terminology, involve *determinables*, *determinants*, and *determinates* (as here defined).[23]

So far so good: but what possible connection can there be, in Aristotle's view, between these reflections on the signification of 'snubness' and his account of the forms of natural objects? Why is isolating the S-structure more than a proposal about semantic restrictions on certain linguistic expressions? What does it have to do with the metaphysics of forms? How close is the parallel between snubness and the forms of natural substances?

The impurist interpreter has a ready answer: the forms of natural objects are to be defined, in Aristotle's account, as inextricably matter-involving. Just as snubness, the form of snub noses, is defined as an inextricably nasal type of concavity, the forms of natural objects are to be defined as distinctively bodily or material forms. These will be inextricably enmattered, impure forms,[24] not pure forms defined independently of matter, which could be shared by natural and mathematical objects.[25] There is no one common well-defined feature (such as shape or form) referred to in the definition of both natural and mathematical

---

[22] By contrast, if a genus is defined in terms of a common feature or nature, definition by reference to this genus and a further differentia will not be a case of an S-structure: it will not fulfil condition (i). For further discussion of this distinction, see James Lennox's essay 'Genera, Species and the More and the Less' (1980: 340–4).

[23] This is a 'broad church' characterization of determinants, determinables, and determinates. Others prefer narrower definitions of these terms using one of the features of one of the species of S-structure as definitive. For the latter approach, see Caston (2008: 42–3).

[24] If one traced the line of a snub nose on a piece of paper, the line would not instantiate snubness because it would lack the causal powers that snubness has. At best, one would have the geometrical shape that snub noses have: a geometrical abstraction from snubness. I am indebted at this point to discussion with Catherine Rowett and Mark Gasser-Wingate.

[25] This will be true even if the shape so defined is necessarily realized in one type of matter. That matter would still not be part of the form.

objects. Natural objects, like anger and fear, are inextricably enmattered, not definable by decomposition into a pure form (whether shape or activity) and the varying types of matter present in natural objects. An impure form [F] of a natural object [c], if it is precisely like snubness, would be defined as follows:

[I.F.] F_c = df one specific material way of being a more general feature Q

where Q is a determinable which could (in principle) be made determinate in some other way.[26]

However, an impure form could also be *like* snubness in a less precise fashion: Q might be a feature which is only present in this one material way, not in any other. Such cases (if there are any) would resemble snubness in not being decomposable in definition into a pure formal element to which something else is added. They too will be inextricably enmattered, non-decomposable, forms.[27] The more general account, which will cover both types of case, would be:

[I.FF.] F_c = df one specific material way of being Q

where Q might, but need not, be a determinable made determinate in other ways (whether material or not). Unlike [I.FF.], [I.F.] allows that the feature Q may be variably realized in several ways. If Aristotle held [I.FF.], the forms of natural objects will be impure. They cannot be defined without explicit reference in their definitions to matter because they are essentially material. Being material will be, *de re*, an essential part of their nature.[28]

---

[26] Michail Peramatzis defines enmattered forms somewhat differently in (2011: 96ff.). In his account of forms of natural objects:

[D] F_c = df $F_1 \ldots F_n$ enmattered in $M_1 \ldots M_n$

where $F_1 \ldots F_n$ are the formal parts and $M_1 \ldots M_n$ are material parts of its essence. In his account, enmattered forms are themselves hylomorphic compounds made up of formal and material parts. There are two salient differences between these formulations:
(a) [I.F.], unlike [D], distinguishes enmattered forms (e.g. as akin to nasal ways of being concave) from the forms of bronze circles (if the forms of the latter are understood as circularity enmattered in bronze even though being brazen is not a way of being circular).
(b) In [I.F.], unlike [D], there can be no one well-defined general feature (or features) [$F_1 \ldots F_n$] which can, in principle, be added to a distinct set of components (whether material or immaterial).
While [I.F.] does not preclude talk of 'parts', the parts in question cannot be added to each other in the way two independently defined entities are added together.

[27] For example: the pain-driven desire for revenge might be an essentially enmattered form even if there is no determinable desire for revenge invoked in this and other (non-angry) types of desire for revenge.

[28] There is also a question of whether Aristotle subscribed to [I.F.] or [I.FF.]. Did he, perhaps, always favour one? Or did he define some impure forms using [I.F.], others using [I.FF.]? Although this question is not central to the present study, which aims only to establish that Aristotle regarded the relevant as impure, I shall note (as the discussion proceeds) some passages which bear on it. The impure form view is consistent with, but does not require, the possibility that Q be 'variably realized' in several material ways.

Did Aristotle hold this general view? His discussion of the forms of natural objects in *Metaphysics* Z.10–11 and H.2–6 suggests that he did. He thought that:

[A] The forms of natural objects are inextricably enmattered, inseparable in definition from material features or activities

and he held [A] because, in his view, impure forms of the type just specified are required as causes of certain types of change. If this is correct, he had strong theoretical reasons for taking the forms of natural objects to be impure. Or so I shall argue in the next sections.

2.4 Metaphysical basis (1): *Metaphysics* Z.10 and 11

Aristotle writes in a famous passage:

> to reduce everything in this way by getting rid of matter is wasted labour (*periergon*): for some things are this (sc. this form) in that (sc. that matter), or those things in such and such condition. The comparison which Socrates the younger used in the case of animal is not well drawn: for it leads away from the truth and makes one suppose that the human can exist without its parts as the circle can be defined without the bronze. The cases are not similar. The animal (in question: human) is a type of perceptible (*aistheton*), which cannot be defined without movement; nor, for this reason, without parts in a given condition.[29] For it is not in any state that the hand is part of the human but only when capable of performing its task in such a way as to be alive. If it is not alive, it is not a part of a human. (*Metaphysics* 1036b21–32)

In his view, it appears, certain definitions refer explicitly to movement and to parts of the body in a given condition. A human, for example, could be defined as a walking animal and, as such, as one with two feet in a given condition (perhaps as capable of walking). If this is correct, one cannot define a human except in terms (*inter alia*) of our mode of movement which cannot be defined except in terms which refer to the body in a given condition. While several of these expressions need further explication, the definition of human, so understood, will be an inextricably matter-involving definition: its form will be an inextricably enmattered form.

This passage follows one in which Aristotle rejected definitions offered by those who regarded some forms as pure. Some Platonists had defined the form of

---

[29] I follow the MSS reading here, as defended by Peramatzis (2011: Appendix 1).

a line as the form of two (the dyad), others identified the dyad with the line itself, still others took the dyad as the form of the line (without identifying the dyad with the line: 1036b14–16). In these views, the relevant forms could be defined without any expression which refers explicitly to the relevant matter. (Definition is taken to be of the form in these passages: 1036a29.)[30] Aristotle rejects their style of account in the case of man because it cannot be defined without explicit reference to hands or flesh in some condition.[31] One cannot, he says, get rid of matter in the way Socrates the younger suggested: by driving all reference to matter out of the definition and suggesting that while flesh and hands are material parts of the compound on which the form rests, they are not referred to in specifying the form itself. Indeed, Socrates' suggestion would encourage us to think, mistakenly, that we can survive without flesh and bones (or indeed any material parts)—on the assumption, one supposes, that we could lose any feature that is not a part of our form (or essence) and still survive. For Aristotle, by contrast, one cannot define man without explicit reference to movements (such as walking) which in turn cannot be defined without explicit reference to some bodily condition (such as that of our feet when capable of walking).[32] The definitional account of man will contain an account of bodily movements and, as a consequence, an account of hands. The form of the human, defined in this way, appears to be impure, essentially body-involving.[33]

Is this Aristotle's settled view? Later in the same chapter he wrote:

> the account of the essence (*ousia*) will not contain those parts that are parts *as matter*, for they are not part of the essence but of the composite—of which there is in some way an account and in some way not. For there is no account of it

---

[30] The Platonists mentioned in 1036b7ff. thought that there were compound lines made of pure form and some kind of matter. Their aim was to define such compounds in terms of their pure forms alone. It is their and other parallel views about definition, which exclude all reference to matter in the definition, that are at issue in 1036b21–4.

[31] This will also be true of geometrical objects if their definitions refer (as Aristotle thinks they should) to 'lines and the continuous' (1036b9–10). Their proper Aristotelian definitions will, as Whiting (1991: 626) points out, refer to matter (albeit intelligible matter), as predicted by the impurist interpreter. The Platonists go wrong in excluding from their relevant definitions reference to the continuous (a genuine type of matter from Aristotle's viewpoint). Their error is not, as Devereux suggests (2010: 180), that they have a wrong view about what the relevant matter would be. They rightly take it to be lines and the continuous but err in excluding this type of matter from their definitions. However, in the immediate context, Aristotle does not press this point, focusing on the clearer case of the definition of man.

[32] As Aristotle notes in *De Generatione Animalium* 736b22ff., one cannot define walking without reference to the legs.

[33] This passage adds a further important point: Aristotle, in commenting on the type of form at issue, writes: 'some [viz. the forms at issue] are this in that or these things in such a condition' (1036b23–4). Take the case of snubness: this can be defined *either* as concavity-in-the-nose (nasal-concavity) or as noses-being-concave (concave-nasality). Aristotle is, it seems, offering two ways of defining snubness, which, at this stage, he regards as interchangeable (in the present context). Bodily conditions or capacities can, in a similar way, be defined as capacities-in-the-body or as bodies-being-in-given-conditions (being-capable). I shall use the phrase 'bodily condition' and 'bodily capacity' (at this stage) to cover both.

together with the matter; for this is indeterminate. But there is an account of it in accordance with the first substance (the *ousia*) of the compound (viz its essence), such as the account of the soul in the case of man. The essence (*ousia*) is the form present in the composite, from which and the matter the composite substance is said to be. Similarly, in the case of concavity: for from this and the nose there is snub nose and snubness (in which the nose is present twice). But in the compound, such as snub nose or Kallias, the matter will be present. (1037a24–34)

This passage is often, and not unreasonably, taken to suggest a different account. Aristotle, it appears, now insists that reference to matter, such as to nose or flesh and bone, is not to be included in the definition of the compound. The latter, it appears, is to be defined in terms of a pure form, defined without any reference to perceptual matter at all. However, this remark, so interpreted, is clearly inconsistent with his earlier comments, as understood above.

How best to address this apparent inconsistency? *Either* we were wrong to interpret the earlier passages as requiring impure, essentially enmattered, forms *or* the parts excluded *as matter* from the account of the form (or essence) at the end of *Metaphysics* Z.11 are different from the matter included in the impure form of man mentioned earlier in the chapter.[34]

Aristotle, I shall suggest, adopted the second approach, using a distinction drawn in Z.10 between flesh *as matter* and flesh *as a principle of form*. While flesh *as matter* is not present in the definition of the compound, flesh *as a principle of form* is. Aristotle avoided inconsistency at the end of Z.11 because he was deploying in this passage a distinction he had developed in Z.10.

Aristotle needed just this distinction in the previous chapter. In Z.10, he noted that:

(a) Flesh is part of snubness (1035a5–6)[35]
(b) Snubness is the form (or *logos*) of the snub

but also claimed:

---

[34] There is no sign that Aristotle revoked his remarks in 1036b30ff. in the intervening sections of the chapter (1036b32–1037a20). This problem is discussed by Michael Frede (1990: 113–29) and Michail Peramatzis (2011: 52–3). While I am in general agreement with Peramatzis' interpretation, my aim is to ground an account of the concluding remarks in Z.11, 1037a21–34 on the conceptual resources introduced in Z.10. So understood, the flow of argument in Z.10 and 11 as a whole supports the impure form interpretation.

[35] While I have taken flesh as part of snubness (the form of the snub), Frede and Patzig suggested that in 1035a5–6 'snubness' refers not to the form of snub noses but to the snub nose (as a type). However, in the immediate context snubness should be the form since concavity, with which it is compared, is clearly a form as it is described as present in matter. Further, when 'snubness' is used to refer to the snub nose (as in Z.11, 1037a31), the context indicates that this is the case. Indeed, there 'snubness' is used to explicate the phrase 'the snub nose'. Since in 1035a5–6 there are no such indicators, the phrase is best taken, correlatively with 'concavity', as indicating the relevant form.

(c) The flesh into which the snub is destroyed is not part of the form (*logos*) of the snub. (1035a25–7).

While (a) and (b) imply that flesh is part of snubness, the form of the snub, (c) states that it is not. Aristotle's position will only be consistent if the flesh that is part of the form, snubness, referred to in (a), is not the same as the flesh into which the snub is destroyed, referred to in (c). The required distinction appears to be this: in (a) the flesh (or elsewhere nose) which is part of snubness is a principle of the form, to be understood as a distinctively enfleshed (or nasal) way of being concave (a *pathos* in the terminology of *Sophistici Elenchi* 182a4). This is different from the flesh into which a snub nose is destroyed in (c): bits of flesh understood simply as spatially divisible objects or quantities of matter. It is from the latter that particular compound objects are formed and into which they are destroyed. By contrast, the flesh (or nose) that is part of snubness is being nasal or enfleshed, not bits of nose or flesh from which particular noses are created or into which they can be divided. Concavity-of-the-nose is not itself a spatially divisible object. It is the way spatially divisible objects are: a material way of being.

In Z.10, so interpreted, the matter in the form (*as a principle of the form*) is not the matter which makes up a particular compound. Aristotle, in effect, distinguishes material objects or quantities of matter from the way those objects or quantities are (material in specific ways: bodily, nasal etc.). This is why, in his terminology, man (the material compound) and being a man are not the same (*Metaphysics* 1043b3). Nor, as Frege once noted, is being a horse itself a horse. Similarly, being bodily is not itself a body nor is being a 12-stone object itself a 12-stone object. If it were, all 12-stone objects would be (at least) 24 stone! Being bodily is a material way of being: the way material bodies are.[36]

Aristotle not only needed this distinction in Z.10: he actually drew it. His discussion in 1035a1ff. focuses on the question: when does the definition of the form include an account of the parts (as it does in the example of snubness and the syllable) and when not (as in the case of the circle)? In the latter, parts of the line may be present in an account of the composite but not in that of its form. When he asks whether flesh and bones are parts of the form or only parts of the composite (1035a19–21), his answer seems clear:

The account does contain the account of such parts in some cases but must not contain them in others, unless it is an account of the composite. (1035a22–3)

---

[36] I shall discuss further in Section 2.6, in considering essentially material capacities, the way in which being nasal or being enfleshed are *material* principles.

In this comment, 'such parts' most naturally includes the cases just given: bones and flesh.[37] If so, his view is that the *account of these parts* will be parts of the relevant, definitional account, of the whole. The account of flesh is part of the definition of man. Not so in the case of the circle where the definition of the form does not contain an account of the relevant parts, even if one must refer to them in giving an account of the composite. Aristotle drew a further consequence:

> For this reason, some things are from those things *as principles* into which they are destroyed and some are not.   (1035a24–5)

In the former cases, the account of the form will contain *as principles* things into which the compounds are destroyed. In the example of the syllable, the account of its form will contain the letters of the alphabet *as principles* because it contains an account of these letters.[38] For similar reasons, flesh, considered *as a principle of form*, will be present in the definition of man: that definition will include reference to flesh or hands *as principles* because it contains an account of them. By contrast, the definition of the circle does not include any reference to segments. The latter are not present *as principles of form* (so understood) because no account of the segments is contained in the definition of the circle.[39]

---

[37] I take *such* parts to refer back to the parts just mentioned: bones, flesh, and letters, not just to the parts of the syllable mentioned in 1035a11 and 14–15 (as Frede and Patzig suggest). Aristotle has just said that flesh and bones are parts of the compound and now adds that the account of such parts will in some cases be part of the account of the whole (as was the case in the earlier example of snubness). The account of the parts just mentioned will be, in these cases, parts of the account of the form: the account of flesh will appear in the account of man. If so, flesh is part of the form of man in the same way as it is part of snubness and letters are parts of the syllable. The account of flesh will appear in the account of man. Aristotle now needs to distinguish the flesh that is part of the form (the account of flesh) from that which is part of the compound. (I am indebted to Sam Meister for detailed discussion of these lines and other issues in Z.10 and Z.11.)

[38] For a highly congenial discussion of the case of the syllable, see Michail Peramatzis (2011: 46ff.). My aim is to show how the 'flow' of argument in this extended context supports the enmattered form interpretation.

[39] I take the separate contrastive (*men... de*) clauses 1035a24–5 to pick up and explicate the contrast drawn in the previous sentence (1035a22–3): between those cases whose account contains an account of such parts (viz: those into which the compound is destroyed) and those whose account does not. (My reading follows the grammatical structure of the two sentences, taking each of the contrasted clauses (marked out by *men* and *de* respectively) in a22–3 and 24–5 to refer to the same cases.) The addition of the phrase 'unless the account is of the composite' in 1035a23, so understood, makes an additional point about the second type of account mentioned in 1035a22–3: it will not refer to an account of the parts unless what is offered is an account of the compound understood as (pure) form combined with the matter in the compound. The first type of account, by contrast, refers to the account of such parts, even when there is no addition which refers to the type of matter in the compound. This is because, as we are now told, the first type of account will contain reference to such parts *as principles*. Aristotle writes 'for this reason' in 1035a24 because the sentence that follows is a consequence of the fact that the first type of account contains an account of parts, while the second does not. Because of this, the first type of account refers to such parts *as principles*, the second does not. This sentence, so understood, does not consider accounts of composites which add to the form reference to matter which is not a principle of this type. The question of how to understand the latter style of account of composites is taken up only in the next sentence, as is marked by its resumptive beginning (*men... oun*: 1035a25ff.), taking up the case of the composites mentioned in 1035a23.

Aristotle's next remark shows that flesh *as a principle of form* is, in his view, different from the bits or quantities of flesh present in the compound. He continues:

> Compounds [things where form and matter are taken together], like the snub or the bronze sphere, are destroyed into these things [their material constituents] and have matter as a part. However, things which are not taken together with matter but are without matter—things whose formula is of the form and nothing else—these are not destroyed at all, or at any rate not in this way. So material constituents are parts and principles of the former [i.e. compounds] but are not parts or principles of the latter. (1035a25–32)

Here he is at pains to distinguish the form (and its principles) from something else which is a part or principle of the compound itself: the material constituents from which it comes to be and into which it is destroyed. While the latter are involved in the process of composition and decomposition, the form—and its parts and principles—are not (as we know from discussions in Z.7 such as 1033b8ff.). The flesh, which is understood as a *part or principle of the form* and referred to in the definition, is different from the flesh which is present in (and a principle of) the compound itself. The former will be a feature, such as being enfleshed (or being nasal), the latter material constituents (such as bits of flesh), referred to in the account of the composite.

Aristotle is, in effect, making two points:

[1] The form of a human (like snubness) contains flesh and bones (as principles) as a part in the way the form of the syllable contains letters (as principles) as parts. (In this they differ from the form of the line (or of the concave line: concavity) which does not contain its segments as principles or parts, and

[2] Flesh as a principle, part of the form of a human, is not the same as flesh understood as the constituent bits of matter involved in the process of composition and decomposition of noses.

[2] distinguishes flesh *as a principle* and part of the form from flesh as the matter of the compound.[40] The former is present in the essence and is explicitly referred to in the definition, the latter is not. Since flesh and bones are referred to as matter (1035a20), the definition will refer to matter *as a principle*. There is no

---

[40] It is important to note that while flesh *as matter* is described as a principle of the compound, flesh *as matter* is not a principle of the form (in the case of a human). The latter role is played by flesh *as a principle* in the way indicated in 1035a24–5: an account of flesh is present in the definition of a human given by specifying our form.

reason to limit the type of matter at issue to matter which plays a given functional role in the organism. Indeed, given Aristotle's focus on the type of matter into which humans are destroyed, there is reason not to see him as restricting matter as a principle to matter defined wholly in terms of its role in living organisms.[41]

Aristotle makes a similar point in the second part of Z.10 when he attempts to re-state his view more clearly. He writes:

> Those parts which are parts of the formula and into which the formula is divided, these are prior [to the formula]...those parts which are *as matter* (i.e. those into which the composites are divided as into matter) are posterior (to formula), but those parts which are parts of the formula (*logos*) and of the substance (*ousia*) as defined by the formula are prior (to the formula)—all or some. (1035b11–14)

This remark recalls his earlier distinction between flesh *as a principle of form* and the bits of flesh in the compound. He distinguishes the substance (*ousia*) as defined by the formula (that is, the essence) of a living creature (such as a human), even if its definition refers essentially to matter *as a principle*, from its parts *as matter*: those into which the human body is spatially divided. That this is his idea is clear in what follows:

> Since the soul (which is the substance of any living thing) is the substance given by the defining account—that is the form and what it is to be for this type of body [*toiōdi*]...the parts of the soul are prior—all or part—to the composite animal, and similarly in the case of the individual, but the body and its parts are posterior to this substance [the form] and it is not this substance but the whole that is divided into them as into matter. (1035b14–22)

The soul, the form of this type of living body (where the body is referred to as *a principle*) is contrasted with matter (spatially divided bits of the body) into which the compound man can be divided *as matter*.[42] The form in question is what it is

---

[41] For the suggestion that the type of matter present in the form is restricted to functional matter: see, for example, Michael Wedin (2000: 38), Daniel Devereux (2010: 183–4), and Riccardo Chiaradonna (2014: 384–8).

[42] It is significant that at this point the relevant matter is understood as what is spatially divisible (1035b12), not as that into which the compound is destroyed (1035a25). While the compound of a living man may be made up of spatially distinct parts (such as hands or feet), these will not survive its destruction. If the matter in question is that into which the composite is spatially divided, some parts of the matter of the compound will be essentially the matter of a living body. But not all need be. Flesh and bones, for example, will not be if they are (as earlier in the chapter) also part of that into which the body is destroyed. Aristotle is not, it seems, concerned to specify precisely what type of matter is, as matter, a principle of the compound (is it a principle of spatial division, destruction, or both etc.?). His attention is, instead, on maintaining a clear distinction between principles of the compound and principles of form, which will—in the case of man—include flesh and bones *as a principle* in the way specified in 1035a24–5.

to be a body of this type. *As a principle*, it is distinct from, and prior to, the body of the composite animal when that is understood simply as made up of spatially divisible quantities of matter.

These remarks provide the basis for Aristotle's suggestion at the end of Z.11 that parts of the flesh and bones are not present *as matter* in the essence or the form of the compound. He is proposing that, as in Z.10, material bits of the compound are not to be referred to in an account of the essence. But he is not excluding matter as *a principle of form*. The essence of a snub nose does not, of course, contain quantities or bits of noses. If matter is present *as a principle* in its essence (nasal-concavity), it will be as a material aspect of what it is to be a snub nose. If nasal concavity is understood as a nasal way of being concave, matter will be present in the essence as a material way of being concave. Material features of this type are not, of course, material constituents (such as bits of matter) or material objects.[43]

Against this background, another of Aristotle's remarks near the end of *Metaphysics* Z.11 falls into place. When he says:

> from the immanent form and matter, the compound substance is described, such as concavity: from it and the nose, snub nose, and snubness comes to be, for nose will be present in these twice...but in the compound, such as snub nose or Kallias, the matter will be present. (1037a29–34)

he is developing a point already made in Z.10. The immanent form is snubness (nasal-concavity) which gives the essence of the compound, where the latter can be understood (but not defined) as a combination of this form and matter (bits of matter). He is not saying, as purists suggest, that (i) the relevant form in the case of the snub nose is a pure form: concavity—not snubness—or that (ii) problems arise in defining the snub nose or snubness when one takes reference to the nose to be part of the definition. Indeed, he must be thinking of the relevant form as nasal-concavity, if nose is to appear twice in talking of the compound snub nose. There is no other way to generate the relevant repetition of nose in talking of concavity and the nose. If so, the immanent form in this case will be nasal-concavity: the specifically nasal type of concavity found in the definition of the snub nose (as in *Metaphysics* Z.10). This inextricably enmattered form, and not the pure form, concavity by itself, is referred to in the definition as the *principle of*

---

[43] There are other proposals to consider. Mary Louise Gill and R.E. Heinaman have suggested that Aristotle is separating the definition of the compound from the definition of the form. However, in the immediate context, Aristotle does not refer to the accounts of compounds as *definitions*. Indeed, while the compound can be described in terms of matter and immanent form (1037a28–30), the definition of the compound appears to be confined to its form and essence and to exclude matter (1037a25–9). In this section, I assume (as my default) that in Z.10–11 (i) the definition of the compound = the account of its essence and (ii) the essence of a compound = its form. One should only withdraw either of these assumptions if one is absolutely required by the texts to do so—which (I argue) one is not.

form. Problems of repetition do not arise in the definition of the form even if they still may in non-definitional accounts of the compound.

Aristotle's remarks at the end of Z.11 can be summed up as follows: in Z.10, he had distinguished between essences and the compounds which result from those essences and matter. Now he is applying and refining that distinction. While the compounds may be particulars (such as the particular snub nose compared with Kallias), they may also be universals (the snub nose as a type of nose, with 'snubness' added to make it clear that one is referring to a type of nose: 1037a31).[44] The accounts of compounds (whether universals or particulars) will refer both to the form (as, for example, nasal-concavity) and to matter *as matter* (such as, for example, the nose understood as a material, spatially divisible object).

However, these latter accounts will not be *definitions* of the compound, which are given (as in Z.10) in terms of the form alone (e.g. nasal-concavity). In these chapters, non-definitional accounts of particular compounds will refer both to the form (nasal-concavity) and to matter understood as particular bits of *matter*. In the case of universal compounds, the matter in question may be particular bits of matter, taken universally, or (perhaps) matter understood as a stuff (such as bronze). (The later parts of Z.10 prepared us for this extension: 1035b27–1036a1.) However, the matter included in this account *as matter* is not matter *as a principle of form*, such as being nasal or being brazen. The crucial difference—between bronze as a spatially divisible material stuff and being brazen (the way the stuff in question is)—remains intact. In the non-definitional account of compounds (whether particular or universal), nose appears twice: once as *a principle of form* (being-nasal) and once *as matter* (whether as particular bits of matter or as stuff).[45]

Aristotle, so interpreted, maintains throughout Z.10–11 the tight connection between definition and form he suggested in *De Anima* A.1, 403b2 and *Physics* B.2, 194b10. Snubness is a clear example of a form (one which makes snub noses what they are) which does not contain flesh (or noses) *as matter* (as material parts) but does contain it *as a principle of its form* (or as a universal).[46] Its definition as enfleshed-or nasal-concavity, as *a material principle of form*, is to be

---

[44] In this understanding of 1137a31–4, I follow a suggestion of Michail Peramatzis' (2011: 51–2, n. 12).

[45] Aristotle does note that he has yet to integrate matter *as matter* in his account: he writes:

> Each thing and what it is to be the thing are in some cases the same, as in the case of the first ousia (such as convexity and to be convex). I call the first substance (*ousia*) that which is not said as one thing of something else—that is, as what underlies it as matter. But in the case of what is said as matter or as things combined with matter, they are not the same as their substance (*ousia*), but nor are they accidentally one as Socrates and the musical are accidentally one. For the latter cases are accidentally the same.

To make progress, he needs to articulate the connection between being nasally concave and the noses which are concave. While he addressed this issue in Z.17 and in H, it remains unresolved in Z.10–11.

[46] These passages show Aristotle's own developed position going beyond what he is explicitly committed to in *Physics* B.

distinguished from accounts of compound objects which refer to flesh, or noses, *as matter*. Aristotle, so understood, maintains in Z.10 and 11 that the relevant forms are inextricably material principles, defined in terms which refer explicitly to bodily conditions or bodily capacities, such as those of hands in Z.11, 1036b31ff. They are not pure forms to which something else is added, such as being instantiated in given types of matter. Bodily conditions and capacities are not themselves spatially divisible bodies, quantities or bits of matter.[47]

The impurist interpreter can offer, or so I have suggested, an integrated and textually well-grounded reading of Z.10–11 as a whole. Purists, in developing their account of these chapters, need to provide an interpretation of the passages which seem to support impurism.[48] Their task is particularly demanding in the case of the mistake Aristotle attributed to Socrates the younger. His error cannot have been, in their view, that of taking the form of man as pure. (After all, that is their own positive thesis!) Instead, some suggest, it arose because he failed to see that the distinctively human form, albeit defined without explicit reference to perceptual matter, requires (or 'hypothetically necessitates') the presence of specific kinds of such matter, which are, nonetheless, not part of the form or referred to explicitly in its definition.[49]

How convincing is this purist reading? In 1036b28–30 Aristotle writes:

The animal is a type of perceptible [*aisthēton*], which cannot be defined without movement; nor, for this reason, without parts in a given condition.

His remark, as already noted, is most naturally taken to say that there is an explicit reference to movement and also to bodily conditions (conditions of the body) in the definition of the animal in question: a human. Purists have sought to avoid this consequence in one of two ways: either by claiming that (a) there is no explicit reference to movement or to the body (such as hands) in the definition of a human;[50] or (b) while there is an explicit reference to movement in this definition,

---

[47] This will be true whether one refers to the manual capacity as a capacity-in-the-hands (compare nasal-concavity) or as hands-when-capable-of (compare noses-when-capable-of). Aristotle does not seem to be concerned in these chapters with which of these ways of describing the enmattered form is to be preferred. (See 1036b23–4.)

[48] See, for example, Michael Frede's attempt to do so, which has been criticized by, amongst others, Jennifer Whiting (1991), Michail Peramatzis (2011), and Riccardo Chiaradonna (2014).

[49] Some suggest that the specific form 'hypothetically necessitates' the presence of specific matter. That is, such a form can only exist if enmattered in some specific way. In this section, I consider explicitly the views of purists who (rightly as I have suggested) take definitions to state only the forms of composites. However, some of my arguments will raise problems for all purist interpreters.

[50] Frede and Patzig in their commentary (1988) suggested, against nearly all other commentators, that the phrase 'cannot be defined without movement' (1036b29) should not be taken to mean that the definition of man must contain explicit reference to movement but only that man cannot be defined without making it clear on the basis of the definition that man is capable of movement. While a proper definition needs, they claim, to have the latter fact as a consequence, it will not itself explicitly refer to it.

there is no explicit reference to a bodily condition (of such parts as hands or feet).[51] On either view, the definitions offered, although pure, isolate features which require the presence of the body. But reference to the latter is not contained explicitly in the definition of the form.

The first purist proposal is difficult to sustain. In Z.10, 1035b15–18, perception was mentioned as a case where the relevant function is present in the definition. If this is a candidate for an acceptable definition, there will be no defining a human without explicit reference to activities such as seeing. Elsewhere, when man is defined as a two-footed animal, reference to walking (and the ability to walk) is part of the definition, since feet are defined in part in terms of their role in walking. The best candidates for an Aristotelian definition of man (and certainly those in this immediate context) explicitly refer to activities. Further, it is particularly difficult to construe the phrase 'cannot be defined without movement' as claiming that man 'cannot be defined without having movement in mind although this is not part of the definition (but entailed by it)'. Had Aristotle wished to say this, he would have needed to add (as elsewhere) a term to designate the relevant type of (non-definitional) thinking at issue, saying, for example, that man 'cannot be defined without thinking (or conceiving) of movement'.[52] He should also have indicated the feature to be included in the definition of man which (i) is other than movement but (ii) nonetheless necessitates its presence. This purist interpretation appears to offer an unparalleled translation of the key phrase and to take it as introducing an unspecified definition of man, of which we are told nothing, but from which we are expected to infer that it does not contain the one feature ('movement') that is explicitly mentioned in the context.

Is the second purist reading more successful? Did Aristotle think that we can define our capacity to move in relevant ways, such as walking or picking up

---

[51] Their view would be this: there are other ways to define human beings in such a way as to avoid creating the impression that they could exist without material parts or without the material parts they have. We can, e.g., define a human being as, among other things, capable of perception, more specifically capable of sight, hearing, taste, smell, and touch. For defining a human being in this way we explicitly only refer to its form, or rather to parts of its form. But we do this in such a way as to make it perfectly clear that a human being cannot exist without material parts (Frede 1990: 120 understands him in this way).

[52] Frede and Patzig point to cases, such as are to be found in Plato's *Phaedo* (such as 99A), where the phrase 'not without T' introduces a necessary condition for T's presence. But what they need (and do not provide) is a case in which 'it is not possible to define A without T' is shorthand for 'it is not possible to define A without thinking of T'. That is: they require a text in which (i) a new (non-synonymous) verb is assumed after 'without' distinct from the one used in the 'it is not possible to…' phrase and (ii) 'T' refers to the object of this new assumed verb. None of the twenty-five relevant cases in the TLG of 'it is not possible to φ without T' exemplify this pattern. (*De Memoria* 450a9 might appear to do so: it says 'why one cannot think of anything without continuity or of things not in time without time: that is a different story'. However, the following sentences make clear that Aristotle is claiming that it is not possible to think of anything without thinking of continuity or to think of things not in time without thinking of time. For he continues: 'it is necessary to grasp (*gnōrizein*) magnitude…and time' (450a10–12). I am indebted to Brad Inwood for discussion of this point.)

objects in the way we do, without explicit reference to feet or the type of hands we have (with thumbs and fingers capable of distinctive movements unlike those of the higher apes)? In the case of walking, our mode of walking cannot, as we have noted, be defined without explicit reference to feet. This is, no doubt, why Aristotle was inclined to define humans as two-footed animals. In any event, it would have been a major undertaking (i) to define walking or gripping without explicit reference to the bodily capacities (the capacities of feet or hands involved) and (ii) to do so in such a way that walking or gripping, so defined, requires hands or feet because of the type of movements they are. Nor is there any sign (here or elsewhere) that Aristotle thought that either project could be achieved or was worth attempting. The second purist reading of these lines, quite apart from its difficulties in construing the grammar of the relevant sentences,[53] attributes to Aristotle a large (and superficially unattractive) philosophical project that there is no indication he was interested in pursuing.

Purist readings of this specific passage will, I suspect, commend themselves only to those already persuaded that there is no satisfactory, impurist, interpretation of the last lines of Z.11. However, if the reading offered above is defensible, there is no need to embark on the strenuous endeavours required to articulate a defensible purist reading of 1036b28–30. They will turn out to be, in one of Aristotle's own phrases in this chapter, 'wasted labour'.

To conclude: Metaphysics Z.10–11, as a whole, support the impurist reading. Natural substances are defined in terms of matter *as a principle of form*, understood in terms of essentially material or bodily features. Any reference to their matter *as matter*, as spatially divisible matter, is confined to non-definitional accounts of such substances. These chapters, so interpreted, parallel the enmattered form reading of anger and fear proposed in Chapter 1. Natural substances resemble these emotions in not being definable by decomposition into a pure form and an additional material component. The forms of natural substances are snub-like, best understood (at least at first approximation) as inextricably material (or bodily) phenomena.

Are these chapters atypical outliers? Do they merely represent one stage in Aristotle's progress, not his final destination? To address this concern, I shall turn to consider his discussion of related issues in *Metaphysics* H.2–4.

---

[53] If one understands 'one cannot define man without movement' to say that reference to movement is part of the definition in 1036b29 and takes (as in the natural and generally accepted reading) 'defined' as the assumed verb in 'nor, for this reason, without parts in a given condition', it is extremely difficult to take the latter phrase to point to something that is a consequence, but not a part, of that definition.

2.5 Metaphysical basis (2): *Metaphysics* H.2–4

In H.2 Aristotle writes:

> For instance: if we had to define threshold, we would say wood or stone lying thus, or in the case of house, bricks, and boards lying thus (and in some cases the goal would be present), or in the case of ice, water frozen or solidified like this, or in that of harmony, this type of mixture of the high and the low, and similarly in all other cases.
>
> It is evident from these considerations that the actuality of one matter is different from that of another and so is the formula: in some cases, this is the composition, in others the mixture, in others some of the other things we have mentioned.
>
> (1043a6–14)[54]

In this passage, reference to the *actuality* (*energeia*) is taken to explicate *form* (1043a20) and is contrasted both with matter (wood and stone) and with the combination of actuality and matter (1043a17ff.) referred to in the account of the composite. Aristotle states that the actuality (or form) of one type of matter is different from that of another. Why did he think this? And why is it evident? For impurists, it is evident *because* the actuality itself is defined as a type of material actuality. Are they correct? And what is the actuality at issue? How is it connected with material capacities or conditions?

Aristotle's examples are revealing: a house is defined *as* bricks and stones lying thus (perhaps with a final cause added), ice as water solidified thus, and harmony as a type of mixture of high and low. Is reference to the matter part of the definition? Can lying thus for the sake of a goal, solidifying thus or this type of mixture be defined, as the purist would suggest, without any reference in the definition to matter thus mixed, solidified, or laid out? Is there, in Aristotle's view, a distinctive type of lying, solidifying, or mixing defined without any explicit reference to matter which is sufficient to define houses, ice, or harmonies respectively? Or is the way of lying or solidifying at issue an inextricably material way of lying or solidifying?

There is, it seems, explicit reference to something distinctively material in the definition of the form (or actuality) in these cases. Three considerations support this conclusion:

(a) In the case of harmony, reference to high and low notes (the relevant matter) is clearly required. There are other types of mixtures (understood as a ratio of numbers: see *Posterior Analytics* 90a20ff.) which are not

---

[54] 1043a13–15 appear to refer in 'on the one hand these (*tōn men*)...on the other hand those...(*tōn de...*)' to the matter in the cases just mentioned...

harmonies. The relevant mixture (or ratio) would not be a harmony unless it was a mixture of notes: an 'en-noted' mixture.

(b) In the case of ice, reference to water is needed to distinguish the relevant type of solidification from that present when, for example, earth is solidified by fire. Aristotle makes no attempt to demarcate the type of solidification in the case of ice except by reference to the relevant matter: water. It is an essentially enwatered type of solidification.[55]

(c) If the definitions of harmony, ice, and houses are essentially material in this way, it will be 'evident', as Aristotle remarks, that difference in matter entails difference in actuality. If this were not so, there would be nothing in the immediate passage to explain why this consequence evidently follows. It is not obvious that distinctive types of mixture or solidification (defined independently of matter) require, or hypothetically necessitate, different types of matter if they are to be realized. Nor is there any suggestion, either here or elsewhere, that there is a type of mixture or solidification, defined without any explicit reference to matter, which has to be realized in one specific type of matter (such as water). Indeed, there could not be since the relevant types of solidification are defined, as in Aristotle's own theory, in terms of the matter with the potential to change in certain ways (as suggested in 1044b8ff.). Nor is it obvious why coverings (defined independently of matter) made to protect belongings need be made of stones and timber. There can, after all, be house-shaped tents, caves, igloos, or even tree awnings, which (as was suggested in Chapter 1) can serve this purpose as effectively. Houses are defined as specific kinds of material (e.g. wooden) coverings.

If this is correct, difference in matter entails difference in actuality (or form) *because* the form (or actuality) is defined in part in terms which refer to it as enmattered in some specific way (such as en-watered or en-bricked). If so, as in *Metaphysics* Z.10–11, the forms in question will be impure.[56]

Aristotle developed this thesis in H.4. He writes:

Things which are by nature but are not substances do not have matter: but what underlies them is the substance. For example: what is the cause of an eclipse,

---

[55] This is clear in his discussion of solidification in *Meteorologica* 388b11ff.: types of solidification are distinguished by their proper subjects: water, earth, fat, etc. Solidification is, in the terms introduced in Section 2.2, the Q-term in an S-structure. It is made determinate in a variety of ways by differing R-terms.

[56] 'Form', I assume, has the same reference in H.2–4 as in Z.17, 1041b8–10 (reading with the MSS), where it is cited in answering the 'why?' question and identified with the essence. Form, so understood, will have the same reference as in Z.10–11, where it is identified with the essence. In *Analytics* terminology they will be specified as the B-term: the basic cause of the other features of the compound. Even if Aristotle in H.2 or Z.17 allows definitions to contain more than their forms, the reference of 'form' remains constant.

what is the matter? There is none. Instead the moon is what undergoes the change. What is the cause which makes the change and destroys the light? The earth. There is perhaps nothing which it is for. The cause as form is the definition which is unclear unless the definition includes the cause. For example: what is an eclipse? Deprivation of light. If one adds: 'due to the earth coming between', this is the account which includes the cause. In the case of sleep, it is unclear what it is that suffers first. Is it the animal?   (1044b8–16)

He is now considering cases where the appropriate 'underlier' is not matter (strictly speaking) but is the proper subject of the change (such as the moon, definable independently of the capacity of the earth to affect it). These examples suggest that some reference to the efficient cause is needed to complete the definition. Although matter (or an analogue of matter: the proper subject) is already in place in the account, reference to a further cause is required for a clear definition. In the case of an eclipse, the definition will be in terms of the moon's deprivation of light caused in a given way (as in *Posterior Analytics* B.8–10). The type of deprivation of light, in the case of an eclipse, is the one caused by the earth coming in between the sun and the moon. In this case, the actuality is a feature (deprivation of light) which is made the type of actuality it is by the presence of the cause: it is the type of deprivation which is caused by the earth coming in between moon and sun. In the case of the house discussed in H.2, the relevant arrangement of the bricks is the one it is by being for the sake of preserving the property of the owner.[57]

This remark supplements the picture introduced in H.2: the form is to be defined in matter-involving terms but also in ones which refer to its relevant efficient cause. In the case of the house, the form, the type of covering cannot be defined without reference to the relevant end: to protect possessions and bodies (1043a16f.). It is a protective covering. Further, this type of covering will be defined as an 'enbricked' material type of covering and, as such, unlike a house-shaped tent or cave. This is why it is said to be obvious that difference in form requires difference in matter: in all such cases the form itself is defined in part in

---

[57] Aristotle adds a further qualification in H.4: he modifies his initial principle (different matter, different actuality) by suggesting that, in cases involving skill, difference in matter by itself need not entail difference in form or actuality. There can be examples in which there is difference in matter but the same form: cases where the efficient cause (such as skill) can produce the same form from different matter. But it remains true that, if one excludes the complexities introduced by the efficient cause, difference in matter entails difference in actuality because (in these cases) the actuality is defined in a matter-involving way. Further, even in cases which involve skill, there are limits imposed from the side of matter. As Aristotle remarks, one cannot make a saw from wool or wood (1044a29). It is not that the relevant matter is simply defined as that on which the efficient cause can operate; it is rather that the efficient cause is one which can operate on certain types of matter. If so, the functional view of matter, even if extensionally correct, will not capture the correct order of exposition. Aristotle, it should be noted, does not hold:

[D]   Different actuality (*energeia*) ENTAILS different matter.

The same matter can be used for many different activities, as bricks can be used in town walls, houses, etc. He holds only that same actuality ENTAILS sameness in matter in the types of cases discussed in H.2.

terms which mark it out as material. The type of lying or mixing in question is a distinctively material way of lying and mixing.[58]

In sum: Aristotle's remarks in *Metaphysics* Z.10–11 on enmattered forms, such as that of man, are not atypical outliers or a first stage in his route to a final different account. His considered view in *Metaphysics* H is also that one cannot define this form, or that of ice, harmony, or lintels without explicit reference to them as inextricably enmattered forms. His remarks in both these books support his suggestion in *Physics* B.2 that the forms of natural substances are to be distinguished in this way from mathematical forms. Aristotle's claims about the forms of anger and fear in *De Anima* A.1 are, as we can now see, of a piece with his theory of the inextricably enmattered forms of natural substances.

In order to secure this interpretation, we need to understand Aristotle's motivation for adopting it. What is the connection in Aristotle's account between the forms of natural substances and movement or change? Why is the type of form required to account for change impure, essentially enmattered? In doing so, we need to specify what Aristotle intends by talking of matter *as a principle of form*. What underwrites his distinction between the (perceptually) enmattered forms of natural objects and those of mathematical objects? What is the precise nature of his distinction between matter *as a principle of form* and matter as *matter*? In addressing these questions, we will achieve a firmer grip on the type of forms he is envisaging.

2.6 Forms and causation

Aristotle's views on causation provide the key. Inextricably enmattered forms are needed to play the causal roles required of them in his account of the natural substances at issue. Or so I shall argue.

Aristotle suggests that forms, as Plato understands them, cannot cause movement or change in material sensible objects (*Metaphysics* 991a11ff.). In his view, they do not come to be from Platonic forms in any of the ways we are accustomed to think. In more polemical vein, he asks: what really does the work if one appeals to Plato's forms to account for cases of coming to be?

---

[58] It is important to distinguish in H.2 those features which are parts of the form and constitute the activity (*energeia*) in question (1043a21), the causes of being (1043a1–4), from matter and its features which themselves are explained by the form. The latter may include reference to matter *as underlying matter* (1043a21) and features of matter such as how in the case of a house bricks and stones are stuck together to form a covering. The latter may include differentiae of the matter but will not be part of the form. In *Analytics* terms, the form (as in Z.17, 1041b8) will be the basic explanatory term (the B-term) and will be contrasted with terms which refer to the matter *as matter* (C-term) and its explained features (the A-term). So understood, proper Aristotelian definition may remain of the form alone (the B-term), even though some would-be definers, such as Archytas, also include the A- and C-terms in their definitions (1043a20ff.). While the cause of being will be found among the differentiae mentioned in this chapter (1043a1–4), not all such differentiae will be causes of being.

One of Aristotle's criticisms is that Plato's forms, as he characterized them, cannot be 'the cause from which the change begins' (*Metaphysics* 992a25). In *Metaphysics* 1033b26ff., he says that talk of the causality of forms understood in the way 'some' (presumably referring, amongst others, to Plato) do is of no use in accounting for coming into being. He concludes, in *De Generatione et Corruptione* 335b18ff., that Plato's forms are not the right type of thing to be efficient causes. Nor can they be teleological causes either. In *Metaphysics* 992a29ff., he writes 'such forms do not have any connection with what we see to be the cause in the case of arts: [that] for whose sake [all minds] in the whole of nature are operative'. In the terminology of *Physics* B.1-2, Platonic forms, so understood, cannot be starting points of change and rest.

What is needed, in Aristotle's view, are forms of a different type. In *Metaphysics* Z.7-9, in constructing his account, he points to a basic connection between forms, as he understands them, and efficient causes. In the case of skill, the form is 'that from which the process in question comes', its starting point: the efficient cause (Z.7, 1032b21-6). In Z.8, he generalizes his claim to all cases of natural coming to be, emphasizing once again that Platonic forms are not useful in accounting for this (1033b29-32). What is required, he suggests, is a type of form which is present in the maker (1033b31ff.) as the cause or starting point of the relevant processes of generation. (Indeed, this claim provided the basis for his synonymy principle: man causes man, because the form of man is the starting point of the process of generation of another man.)

The idea that one and the same thing, the form, is both the formal cause (that in virtue of which the thing is the thing it is) and in the cases of substances that come to be the teleological and efficient cause is a basic assumption in *Metaphysics* Z.[59] The form, the soul in the case of living beings, is both the efficient cause and the formal cause (Z.7, 1032b1-2). He appeals to this idea explicitly in Z.17, 1041a31ff., when he writes:

> the cause is the essence (what it is to be the thing in question, to speak in a general manner), which is in some cases, such as perhaps a house or a bed, the teleological cause, in other cases the efficient cause... The latter type of cause is sought in the case of coming to be and passing away, and the former as well is sought in the case of being.

In natural substances under discussion, teleological and efficient causes are identified with their essence. This is why later in the same chapter the cause in question is identified with the form (1041b8-9).

Our central question is: how do Aristotle's forms have to be to be efficient and teleological causes in the required way? Why do Platonic forms fail to play this

---

[59] For further discussion of this assumption, which reflects Aristotle's basic concerns in the *Analytics*, see my (2000a: 285ff.).

2.6 FORMS AND CAUSATION

role in the relevant cases? In the case of efficient causation, Aristotle holds, I shall suggest, that:

(a) forms, to be efficient causes of the relevant type, have to enmattered (*logoi enhuloi*) in such a way that they are the starting points of processes which are the producing of the relevant effect

and

(b) this causal role could not be played by pure forms which are realized in matter. The latter would not be efficient causes of the required type, even if they have to be realized in matter to exist.

In *Physics* 202a9–12, he remarks:

> That which moves (the agent) will always bear some form, either as such and such a thing or as of a given quality or size, which is the starting point and cause of the process which it (i.e. the agent) produces, as when what is actually a human makes a human from what is potentially a human.

The form is the starting point and cause of the process which the agent produces. In one of his examples, the builder, who grasps the art of building, possesses the form of the house, which is the starting point of the process of housebuilding. The form has to be of a type which can be a starting point of this process. Aristotle identifies the form in question with the builder's art of building (*Metaphysics* 1070b33) as the most basic (or highest) per se cause of the house which is built (*Physics* 195b23–5).[60] A rational capacity, in this case, is the relevant cause of the ensuing material process as its starting point and controller.

We need, before proceeding further, to note some aspects of Aristotle's account of efficient causation. At the outset, he distinguished active causes from potential ones: a per se potential cause is that which is capable of causing the relevant result or effect (*Physics* 195b3–5). In the case of building: the highest per se potential cause is the art of building, a rational capacity, in the soul of the builder (195b21–5). The activity of this capacity is the activity of causing the house to be built: the building of the house. In particular cases, there are particular active causes, as Aristotle notes: 195b19–21.[61] The art of building is not only the first (or

---

[60] For further discussion of Aristotle's views on efficient causation, see Thomas Tuozzo's essay: 2014, 23–47. The builder's art is, it appears, identified with the form in the builder's soul. At very least, they are inter-defined.
[61] I take 'highest' to refer to the first cause (*Physics* 194b20): the efficient cause from which the process of building begins. Since this is a cause within the builder, it is the art—and not the builder— which is the first, or highest, cause. In *Metaphysics* Z.7, 1032b21ff., Aristotle distinguishes the form (as

highest) starting point of the relevant process (that from which it comes); it also causes that process to develop as it does. It is because of their skill that builders act as they do: it is why their acts of building develop in the way they do. Their skill determines the order in which they act, modifies their actions as they encounter problems and difficulties, and determines when they finish building. It is, in this way, the controller of their unfolding actions.[62]

The builder himself (or herself) is also a per se efficient cause, sometimes active, sometimes (as when resting) potential. Aristotle talks of the active cause as the builder when exercising his (or her) art. This is the way in which he or she brings the house into existence. The builder builds in virtue of her (or his) possession of the form (the presence of the form in him or her), which is the basic (or highest) starting point of the process which is her building. Efficient causes can be described as 'the cause...through whose activity the result comes about' (to use Sextus' phrase: *Outlines of Scepticism* 3. 14). This description will be true, albeit in different ways, of the builder and her (or his) skill.

Aristotle's formulations suggest a generalization:

A (the form: e.g. the skill in question) is the highest (or basic) per se cause of B (e.g. the house in question) if and only if A is the starting point and controller of the process (house-building) which is (i) aimed at B and (ii) achieves its goal (e.g. the house).

In the case of building (or weaving), the per se efficient cause is the relevant skill: a rational capacity. When ice forms, the cause would be water's capacity to solidify: a non-rational capacity. These differing capacities are actualized in movements such as building, weaving, walking, and solidifying. It is the weavers' capacity to pull and push the wool and loom, to move their fingers in the way required to produce the desired outcome. Per se causes are required to bring about results (such as the house) and are adequate to the task of doing so through processes of this type. The processes themselves are the bringings about of the relevant result.

grasped by the doctor) as that from which the process starts from the doctor, who is the maker (or doer). While both art and doctor are described as that 'which makes' (*to poioun*: 1032b21, 24) and that 'which moves' (1070b29), they are makers in different ways. The art, which is the starting point and controller of the process (*archē*), is located inside the agent. Suarez described builders as the cause which moves (the cause *quod*—in his terms) and the form (or their skill) as that by or from which they act (the cause *quo*—in his terms).

[62] When Aristotle talks of skill as an '*archē*', he understands it to be both that from which the process begins (1032b21ff.) and as its ruler or controller (1013a14f). Both nature and skill play these roles in accounting for the structured, goal-directed, processes discussed in *Physics* B.8, 199a8–20. I am indebted to Emily Kress for discussion of these issues. Per se causes, so understood, are 'robust' or 'plastic' in their implementation (as Susan Sauvé Meyer noted (1992)), depending on how the causal process (such as weaving) unfolds when guided by the agent's skill.

We can now return to our basic question: how does the form in question have to be if it is to be the highest (or basic) efficient per se cause of results effected through processes of this type? Is the per se cause, whose activity consists in pushing and pulling the wool and loom, an inextricably enmattered capacity? If so, why?[63] (Similar questions, it should be noted, can be raised about capacities of the soul whose activity is causing movements in the *connate pneuma* in the case of bodily actions or in other types of *pneuma* in the case of animal generation.)[64] Are these per se causes of the relevant changes inextricably material capacities?

Three considerations support an affirmative answer to these questions:

(a) Since the activities in question are material changes (such as pushing or pulling, heating or cooling), the capacities in question will be defined as capacities to, for example, pull or push, types of material activity. Similarly, for the capacities to heat or walk, weave or build, considered as capacities for bodily processes. Since capacities, in Aristotle's account (*Metaphysics* Θ.8, 1050a8–12), are defined in terms of, and are present for the sake of, their resultant activities, they will all be defined in terms of the material changes in which they issue. Such capacities will be different in principle from mathematical powers, if the latter cannot be actualized in material processes and are incapable of causing such changes.

(b) Aristotle defines the relevant capacities as ones to—in certain conditions—act in certain ways. There is no defining the capacity independently of the material conditions under which the capacity is exercised. It is the capacity to—in those material conditions—act in a given way. These remarks are in line with his discussion of the identity conditions for capacities in *Metaphysics* 1048a17ff.: the relevant capacities are conditional capacities to, in certain matter involving conditions, act or suffer in given ways. This latter fact is sufficient to make them essentially material capacities. One cannot adequately define the kind of capacity

---

[63] This account applies only to cases in which the relevant starting points are 'physical' (*Physics* 198a36). There may be other cases which are not efficient causes of this type: the prime mover, for example, if that moves by being moved, not by itself doing something. Elsewhere Aristotle talks of what is capable of moving the body as being capable of pulling and pushing, interacting with joints (see *De Motu* 703a19ff. and *De Incessu Animalium* 704b15).

[64] Peck discussed this parallelism in Appendix B of his edition of *De Generatione Animalium* (1942: 576–93). Devin Henry (2019: 182) talks suggestively of 'the entire process [of generation] being regulated and controlled by the formal nature according to conditional necessity... for the sake of the end'. If 'regulating' and 'controlling' are understood as types of (goal-directed) material interaction, the relevant forms will be (in my terminology) inextricably enmattered capacities. Indeed, biological forms, understood as goal-directed capacities, will need to be enmattered in this way if they are to be per se efficient causes of unfolding enmattered processes. For recent contributions to the discussion of biological forms, which support the latter perspective, see the papers by Marwan Rashed (2017: 109–29) and Diana Quarantotto (2019: 333–62).

they are except as a material capacity because it is a capacity—in certain material conditions—to act or suffer.

(c) The type of capacity is one realized in processes such as pulling and pushing, heating and cooling, which exemplify basic material principles of interactions between material bodies (such as dragging and pushing in the case of spatial movement: *Physics* 243a15-17). The relevant capacities have to be material capacities, ones governed by general material principles of this type, to be starting points and controllers of processes of this type. Indeed, this is what makes them material capacities. Such capacities are required for this role as only they are adequate to initiate and control the processes as they develop. Together with connected inextricably material features such as being bulky, being heavy, and being hot, they are relevant aspects of the material nature of the objects that possess them. Their being hot or heavy need not be wholly defined in terms of their capacities to act in certain ways.[65] In this, they differ from mathematical capacities which cannot be causes of change as they cannot initiate or control such processes. This is why Aristotle describes mathematical capacities as derivative cases of capacities 'described as capacities only in virtue of some similarity to capacities which are causes of change' (1046a5-12). They are not instances of, or governed by, general material principles for heating, pulling, and pushing.

If this is correct, forms, in Aristotle's account, are per se efficient causes in the relevant cases because they are inextricably material capacities which initiate and control interactions with material bodies. They must be simultaneously *material and goal-directed* capacities to initiate and control bodily processes such as heating, pushing, and dragging. If they were not material capacities, they would not be adequate to the task of causing the relevant results by means of material processes of this type. If they were not goal-directed, they would not be adequate to the task of causing the relevant results by means of goal-directed processes. The forms of natural objects must be inextricably material goal-directed capacities to be per se efficient causes of material processes of this type. There must be, as Aristotle suggests in *Metaphysics* 1036b29-33, explicit reference in the definition of the form to bodily capacities: the matter of the agent. They are in their nature (*de re*) inextricably material capacities. Only capacities of this kind can be per se

---

[65] Aristotle's comparison between forms and shapes is suggestive. While to be circular is the way a tyre is to be capable of rolling in a given way, their distinctive type of circularity is not wholly defined in terms of this capacity. It is also defined in terms, for example, of the tyres being materially shaped in a given way. But their being materially so shaped, like their being heavy or solid, will not be analysed wholly in terms of their capacities, or dispositions, to roll (or their functional role). Indeed, the capacity to roll may itself be defined in terms of their being materially so shaped. I shall return to this issue in Chapter 7.

causes of the relevant processes. Error will result if one does not take forms to be inextricably enmattered capacities of this kind (*Physics* 193b35).

Contrast these with pure, mathematical, ones:

(a*) Mathematical capacities, such as 2 to the power 3 or the capacity of the side of a triangle to be extended indefinitely, are not capable of producing material changes. They are not the type of capacity which can be a per se efficient cause of, for example, pushing and pulling, or more generally of acting on another object (1046a19–21). In this they differ from those forms (or capacities) which are, in Aristotle's account, per se causes of such movements. Mathematical forms could at best be accidental (or indirect) efficient causes of material changes in virtue of their being realized in bodies with physical capacities realized in pulling and pushing. But this is not the way in which, for example, the capacity to weave is the per se efficient cause of weaving. If it were like a mathematical form, the capacity to weave would not be the starting point and controller of the relevant process. Its causal role cannot be captured simply by its being realized in a material body. Otherwise mathematical form could equally play this role when they are instantiated in material bodies.[66]

(b*) Platonist mathematical forms cannot account for change or movement (*Metaphysics* 997b15ff.). To move non-accidentally forms would have to be essentially enmattered in the way the forms of natural bodies are. Aristotle makes this point in *De Caelo* Γ.8 when he notes, as an absurd consequence, that on certain views 'mathematical entities will heat and burn' (307a20–2), result from objects being burned (307a25–6) or sever other objects (307a17ff.). Indeed, the fact that such entities cannot be efficient causes of changes of this kind is one of his grounds for rejecting the mathematical version of physics advanced by several of his predecessors, including Plato in the *Timaeus*.[67]

Aristotle emphasizes the required distinction clearly in *De Caelo* Γ.1, when he notes that mathematical objects are arrived at by abstraction, natural objects by addition (299a18–19).[68] A mathematical sphere, for example, is arrived at by 'abstraction'. In abstracting, as we saw in Chapter 1, we do not regard the sphere as possessed of perceptual matter or perceptual properties (such as being made of rubber, in the case of the tyre). We, in effect, filter out the essentially enmattered features of the tyre. If, as a further step, we were to define the mathematical

---

[66] Separated mathematical forms can be formal or final causes of phenomena such as order or symmetry (*Metaphysics* 1078b1–2) but not the efficient causes of their generation. What accounts for their coming to be is the geometer's thought of it: the form grasped by his (or her) soul (*Metaphysics* 1032b5), not the mathematical form alone.

[67] For further discussion of this issue, see Brad Berman's essay (2017: 89–106).

[68] I am indebted to Emily Katz who first drew my attention to these passages and to their significance.

sphere, we would present it as a (definitionally) separated entity: as essentially a pure, non-perceptually enmattered, form. Natural objects, by contrast, can be grasped 'by addition', a process which reverses that of abstraction. If the latter filters out perceptual matter and perceptual features, addition removes the filter, allowing us to see natural objects (once again) as endowed with the very features abstraction filters out. The features of natural substances, including their form, recovered when the filter is removed, will be grasped, and properly defined as essentially enmattered. This is why, as noted in Chapter 1, the straight shape of a ruler has causal powers, in virtue of its being an enmattered shape, that mathematical straightness itself lacks. The ontological gap between mathematical and physical straightness (or concavity) is reflected in this difference in their differing causal capacities. The latter type of straightness has to be an inextricably enmattered form to be a cause of the resulting material changes.

Aristotle, it should be noted, distinguished between the objects of optics or harmonics and those studied by geometry. There is, in his view, a difference between a geometrical form like circularity and the kind of circular form studied in optics. The latter does not study circles that are, as a matter of fact, instantiated in sensible objects. If that were the case, the only difference between optics and geometry would be the substratum in which these circles *happen* to be. Instead, optics studies circles *as attributes proper to* visual phenomena (*Metaphysics* M.3, 1078a14–16): its circles are, in Aristotle's terminology, per se features of these phenomena, not the conjunction of a pure mathematical property and a sensible object or light.[69] The objects of optics and harmonics, as proper (per se) attributes of a specific kind of matter, are to be defined as, for example, being circular-in-an-essentially-enmattered- or-enlightened-way (as snubness is defined as being-concave-in-an-essentially-enmattered-way). This is why the study of halos, for example, concerns types of circularity defined as features of light, not geometrical circles which happen to be present in light. They need to be defined in this way to be per se causes of the features they explain.[70]

Snubness, as we have seen, is defined in Aristotle's account as an inextricably nasal way of being concave: being-nasally-concave. Optics studies a distinctive 'enlightened' type of circularity: a distinctive type of circularity that can be a unified cause of other optical phenomena. Had the latter type of circularity

---

[69] Nor are they conjunctions of (what I am calling) abstracted circularity and matter. For since the former is a type of property which can be found in mathematical and physical entities, it too will lack the causal powers of physical properties.

[70] Aristotle accepts that there are proofs in optics and harmonics which use pure mathematical or geometric features (such as: If A is circular, B is circular). But these are not explanations of why sounds travel (in the way they do) or why rainbows have their distinctive effects on light. For the latter we need 'addition', which reverses the process of abstraction, and allows us to see the essentially enmattered properties of sounds, rainbows, and the like. Geometry applies to the latter phenomena only when they are seen in an abstracted way. For further discussion of these examples, see Peter M. Distelzweig's essay (2013: 85–105).

bifurcated into being circular in a way common to mathematical objects and the light of which it is now predicated, there would not have been one unified (per se) cause of the relevant phenomena. Indeed, in Aristotle's view, since pure mathematical properties lack efficient causal powers, all the causal work would have to be done by the light (that is, the matter) involved. And this would have been inadequate since reference to the circularity of the halo is required to account for its distinctive optical effects.[71] Enmattered forms, understood as inextricably material (in this case enlightened) capacities, are required to do the causal work. Forms are enmattered, in the way the impurist suggests, because they are inextricably material capacities. It is because their forms are material capacities of this type that natural substances cannot be defined without reference in their definition to matter (as a principle). They cannot be defined in terms other than those which refer to material capacities of this type.[72]

The same perspective pervades Aristotle's discussion of change elsewhere. Bodies are affected by bodies because their relevant capacities for agency and patiency, the hot in one and the cold in the other, are enmattered forms of heat and coldness (324b20: 'the hot in matter'), not something separable from matter. If the capacity in question had been separable from matter, there would have been no action or passion at all (324b19–21). The capacities have to be essentially enmattered to play the required role. This is why they, as forms, are described as 'capacities in matter' (322a29–30). Features defined independently of matter could not be unified per se causes of the relevant changes, even if such features were always (and necessarily) present in matter. This passage adds a further point: when there is immediate reciprocal activity, such as in heating and being heated, the active and passive objects involved must have the *same* type of matter (322b15ff., 324a32ff.). The relevant capacities (described as 'a type of capacity in matter': 324a6–7) have to be enmattered in the *same type* of matter to be involved in heating and being heated (324b6–8). Aristotle comments:

> Body is by nature such as to be affected by body, flavour by flavour, colour by colour, and in general what is of the same kind by something of the same kind.
> (323b32ff.)

---

[71] While doctors have knowledge about circular wounds (facts concerning their development: they heal more slowly than non-circular wounds), it falls to the geometer to know the explanation of this fact (*Posterior Analytics* 79a14–16). The latter might know, for example, that such wounds have the greatest area relative to their perimeter and so have a bigger area, relative to the perimeter, to be filled. However, the geometer will not know why such wounds heal (or fail to heal) in the specifically material way they do (e.g. by joining up the parts that are healing). For the latter one needs to know something about enfleshed circles which will not be grasped by those who only know about their extension and shape.

[72] This account will be revised in one important respect: talk of capacities will need to be refined. See Chapter 4, Section 2 and Chapter 7, Section 4.

This additional claim, which requires the relevant forms to be defined as enmattered in certain specific types of matter, builds on the same basic idea: the relevant forms (or capacities) have to be inextricably enmattered to be per se causes of the relevant effects. Matter *as a principle* of form is a per se cause because such principles are material capacities of this type.[73]

In *De Caelo* Γ.1 305a28ff., Aristotle criticizes the Platonic suggestion that one can build up the objects of natural science from those of mathematics. The types of shape are, in his view, distinct. His point, as we can now see, is exemplified by his discussion of the case of the saw in *Physics* B.9. There Aristotle writes:

> if one defines the task of sawing as being a certain kind of dividing this will not come about unless the saw has teeth of a certain kind. These will not be present unless the teeth are iron, so there are some parts of the definition which are as its matter. (*Physics* 200b5–7)[74]

In this passage, as we noted above, he appears to refer to teeth of a certain kind as part of the definition as its matter. The saw, like the snub, will be defined as a certain type of shape-in-metal of a given kind. As in the case of snubness, the form of the saw is inextricably enmattered. If one were to define the capacity of the saw as what is realized in dividing, where dividing is defined independently of material change, one would not be able to explain why the saw must have hard teeth, ones able to cut through wood. The kind of division envisaged could be purely mathematical, one which divides the wood in a geometrical manner. What is required is a distinctively material type of division which depends on an enmattered capacity to divide wood in this way. This will be an enmattered capacity of a specific kind. Other instruments, such as axes, are capable of dividing wood but not in the way a saw does: by means of hard, serrated teeth. In *Physics* B.9, Aristotle talks of *iron* as the matter required for the relevant type of cutting (although elsewhere he appears more relaxed).[75] Saws have the capacity to divide wood in this distinctive way.[76] Just as, *pace* Socrates the younger, one cannot define the type of movements

---

[73] For discussion of this further claim, see the discussion of Aristotle's accounts of taste and visual perception in Chapters 4 and 5.
[74] For similar views see also *Metaphysics* Z.11, 1037a15ff.
[75] *De Partibus Animalium* 642a10–14.
[76] Aristotle does not attempt to define the specific type of dividing wood that saws do in the purist style (without explicit reference in the definition to some type of metal, such as iron), and then to show that their form (defined as what is capable of dividing wood in this way) requires or 'hypothetically necessitates' the presence of iron. To do so would have been a major undertaking. He would have needed to show what it is about the capacity (defined in the purist way) that requires the presence of iron rather than bronze. Enmattered capacities, by contrast (such as the material capacity to divide wood with hard metallic teeth), clearly require the presence of iron rather than bronze. Claims of hypothetical necessity are, in the impurist account, grounded in the definition of the type of form at issue. However, purist interpreters cannot simply insist that, for Aristotle, the relevant pure forms 'hypothetically necessitate' the presence of some matter. They need to show how, in his account, pure forms actually require the presence of specific types of matter.

characteristic of man without explicit reference to bodily parts (such as hands) in a given condition, so one cannot define the type of movement characteristic of saws without reference (as part of the definition) to iron (or some such material) in a given condition. The relevant condition, in virtue of which they are capable of moving or cutting in the ways specified, is an inextricably material capacity. If the capacity is identified with the form of the saw, the latter will be inextricably enmattered in a specific type of matter. One needs, to address Aristotle's own question in *Physics* B.2 (194b9–10), to specify in defining the form enough of the matter to account for the saw's capacity to cut wood in the way which saws, but not axes, do. This amount of causally relevant information is required to capture its role as a per se cause of the type of cutting at issue.

In sum: the forms of natural substances (and of many artefacts) must, in the cases considered, be inextricably enmattered to be adequate per se causes of the relevant results. They are essentially material capacities whose exercise is, for example, a specific type of heating or pushing. If they were not defined as a specific type of material capacity, they could not be per se causes. If matter is not present in their definition, as Aristotle remarked in *De Anima* A.1, the latter will be 'empty and vain': not causes in the way required. If a capacity is to be active in certain material conditions and its activity is to consist in material (or bodily) changes (such as heating and cooling, pushing and pulling), it must itself be essentially and inextricably material, not decomposable into definitionally distinct components, one of which is pure. One cannot account for pushing or rolling in terms of a combination of a pure geometrical shape (sphericity) and metal (or rubber). The kind of sphericity which causes a ball to roll has to be an enmattered type of sphericity (as snubness is an enmattered type of concavity) to be the unified per se cause of what results.

Aristotle develops this line of thought further in discussing what he calls 'correlative passive capacities' which (a) are caused to be active in certain material conditions and (b) issue in material change in matter-involving ways (such as involve being heated, pulled, pushed, etc.). If the operation of a passive capacity consists in being heated, pushed, or pulled, it too is an essentially material capacity. More precisely, if its operation is caused by a matter-involving activity, there will be a matter-involving suffering correlative with the activity of the causal capacity.[77] If the agent's activity is essentially material, so too will be the patient's suffering.

Aristotle, I have suggested, regarded the forms of natural objects as inextricably enmattered because of the role they play in efficient and teleological causation. Only essentially material or bodily capacities can be per se causes of the types of activity they generate. This was, we can now see, his underlying motivation in *De Anima* A.1 for understanding the forms of anger and fear as

---

[77] As Aristotle emphasizes in *Metaphysics* Θ.1, 1046a9ff.

inextricably psycho-physical. As per se causes (and effects) of bodily changes, they are, like the forms of natural objects, inextricably enmattered.

In sum: material capacities are not *matter as matter*: spatially extended bits or types of matter or stuff. Aristotle's distinction between matter *as a principle* of form and matter *as matter*, drawn in the case of flesh in *Metaphysics* Z.10 and 11, is underwritten by his view of the relevant forms (and their principles) as essentially material capacities, the per se causes (or effects) of the relevant bodily changes.[78]

2.7 Is the matter of natural substances inseparable in definition from their forms?

How is the matter of natural objects, that which possesses these capacities, to be defined? Is it, as was suggested in *Physics* B.2 (194b8–9) and *De Anima* A.1, defined in relation to form, inseparable in definition from it? Is it posterior to the form in definition? How is it connected with matter *as matter*?

Some of Aristotle's remarks in Z.11 address this question. He writes:

> This is why [man] cannot be without parts in a given condition. For a hand is not part of a man in any condition but only that which can fulfil its function and so be ensouled; if it is not ensouled, it is not part of a man. (1036b28–32)

To be a hand is to be a part capable of fulfilling a given function: moving in given ways. This is the account of hands used as a principle in the definition of man: it is matter as a *principle of form*. Particular hands as material parts of composite bodies are, by contrast, spatially divisible bits of matter defined in terms of their bodily capacities. Hands as parts of the composite are, in Aristotle's account, *posterior* in definition to the form. They cannot be used to define the form in question. Instead, they themselves are defined as the material parts they are in virtue of their being parts with given bodily capacities (as horses are, in Aristotle's account, to be defined in terms of their being a horse). As such they are distinct from 'dead hands': spatially divisible material entities no longer capable of playing this role in the organism. Hands, as material parts of the composite, are not defined simply as matter understood simply as spatially divisible bits of matter. They are defined as the material parts they are in virtue of their causal capacities.

---

[78] Material capacities are parts of the form that can be classified as *material* because they are capacities to change in various ways (*Metaphysics* Λ.2, 1069b14). Such features, unlike matter *as matter* (bits of matter), can be (in the sense explained) both formal and material.

2.7 IS THE MATTER OF NATURAL SUBSTANCES INSEPARABLE

This viewpoint is not confined to *Metaphysics* Z.11. In *Metaphysics* H.5 Aristotle suggests, in similar vein, that the relevant matter is partly defined in terms of form. He writes:

> There is a problem over how the matter of each thing stands to the contraries. For example: if the body is potentially healthy, and illness is the opposite of health, is it then potentially both? And is water potentially wine and vinegar? Or is it the matter of one in respect of a state, I mean the form, and of the other in respect of a deprivation and a destruction that is contrary to nature? (1044a29–34)

The matter, in the case of wine and vinegar, is water, in that of health and sickness, the body which undergoes both conditions. In this example, the body is understood primarily as that which is potentially healthy and only derivatively as what is potentially sick—because sickness is the deprivation of health. However, teleological considerations are decisive (as suggested in some but not all cases in H.4: 1044b1–2, 12). They offer the preferred way of defining the relevant matter as matter for the goal in question, which is to be identified with the essence (or form). This is why the body is defined as potentially healthy: it has the capacity to be healthy. In H.2–4, the identity of form is, as we saw above, taken to be matter-dependent. In H.5, as we now see, the identity of the matter in the composite is form-dependent, defined in terms which refer explicitly to the relevant form or activity with its distinctive goals. It is defined as the matter of (or for) the composite in virtue of its being capable, in certain conditions, of playing the required causal role.[79]

These passages suggest that Aristotle held that:

[B] The matter of natural objects is inseparable in definition from their forms.

However, although the matter of natural objects is defined in a way which refers to their form, it need not be wholly defined simply as what possesses the relevant capacities.[80] Hands, for example, may also be partially defined in terms of their possession of material features, such as being extended, heavy and solid, wet or dry, and being made of flesh and bone, in the way required for them to be capable of playing the causal role required of them. They will not be cases of 'functional matter', if such matter is taken to be defined simply as that which possesses a

---

[79] Both moves are important for Aristotle's attempt to address the dilemmas concerning definition raised in Z.13–16. These issues, together with further detailed analysis of Aristotle's argument in H.6, are discussed in Peramatzis and Charles (forthcoming).

[80] Talk of 'functional matter' is sometimes taken in the latter, stronger, way to signify matter defined wholly in terms of its functional role and distinguished from other types of matter which is not so defined. See, for example, Devereux (2010).

given function (or causal capacity).[81] Indeed, the matter of some natural objects will need to be, for example, extended, solid, or hot if those objects, and their forms, are to be causes of the required kind.[82]

Aristotle developed his own way to implement this proposal. In *Metaphysics* Z.11, matter (that is, matter *as such*) is said to be indeterminate (*aoriston*: 1037a27). He developed this suggestion further in *Metaphysics* Θ.7, where matter is said to be made determinate by the presence of the form. He writes:

> For the universal and that which underlies differ in this way, namely by (the latter) being a this such while (the former) is not a this such. For example: when that which underlies is a human being, both body and soul, and the quality is (being) musical and pale (for when musicality is present, the thing in question is said not to be musicality but musical, and the man is not whiteness but white, nor a walk or a change but walking or changing, as with the 'en-' locution). In all cases like these the last item is a substance; but in those cases which are not like this but a form and a this such is what is said, the last item is matter and mattery substance.

In the latter cases, 'form and this' are predicated of matter or mattery substance (1049a34–6).[83] In these examples, there is not *a this such* nor a thing which underlies (1049a28, 23–4) but a universal. It is like a genus which underlies without being *a this such* (as in 1038a5ff.). In this account:

(a) matter is something which is made determinate in varying ways, and
(b) the form (differentia) is what makes the matter into a 'this such'.

(a) and (b) are both applied in his discussion of a wooden box which he presents as the final point in a sequence:

Fire
[fiery] Earth
[earthen] Wood
[wooden] Box

---

[81] Being extended and being heavy are, of course, the ways various types of matter are. They are not themselves any kind of matter, let alone spatially divisible parts of matter.

[82] [B] introduces a disanalogy with the case of snubness. In that case, the nose (the relevant matter) is, one assumes, defined independently of nasal-concavity. By contrast, hands are defined (at least in part) in terms of their capacities to move objects in given ways (manual capacities).

[83] Earlier in 1038b5ff., Aristotle separated two ways of 'underlying', one which consisted in being a this something, another in being matter. This is compatible with taking the latter case as one in which the *entelecheia* (or form) was constituted by the matter.

In this sequence, fire is matter for earth, earth for wood, wood for box. At each stage, the matter of the next stage is made determinate by the relevant form (as, for example, wood capable, as it now is, of being a box). Fire, for example, if primary, is not a 'this such' (1049a27) as it is not a determinate object. Earth or air, by contrast, will be something determinate constructed from fire and a further relevant determinant. While fire (if a primary) is the final determinable, air would be a modification (*tropos*) of fire. Air is a determinate form of fire, where the relevant determinant (the form: such as being hot) is what makes fire into air.

In this account, matter is, as in Z.12, said to be indeterminate (*aoriston*: 1049b1) because that at each stage below the final level (that of a box in this sequence) matter is a determinable which is made determinate at the next level. This is so even in the case of this piece of wood (1049a24), a particular with its own spatio-temporal position, because it is not yet determined which of its capacities (as wood) will be realized in the final product. *This wood* will not be, in the relevant way, a determinate *this such* until its capacity to be a box (rather than a chair or part of a ship) is realized. Although it is a spatio-temporal particular, it is yet not a *determinate this such* (as Aristotle understands it) because it is not determinate which of its capacities will be realized. *This suches*, so understood, emerge only when there is no further determination to be made. In this structure, one begins with something determinable (matter) which is made into a determinate entity (a *this such*) by the imposition of specific form.[84]

Matter, in this account, is dependent on form to be made determinate as the matter of the composite. When so enformed, it is capable of playing the required causal role.[85] Matter *as such*, at its most general, might be understood as a determinable, made determinate in various ways in various types of object by various types of forms.[86] The matter of a composite is matter of this type enformed in a given way. It can be seen as spatially divisible bits of matter (such as bits of wood, bronze, etc.) enformed so as to be capable of playing the specific causal role that defines it. The form in question is *prior* to the matter in the compound because it makes that matter the type of matter it is. Hands, as material components in a compound, are posterior to the bodily capacities (being capable of reaching out, gripping, and carrying objects) because hands are hands in virtue of their being possessed of these bodily capacities.

---

[84] This overview of parts of *Metaphysics* Θ.7 follows the pattern I discussed in more detail in 2010: 168–97.

[85] In the case of matter, the form (the determinant) is a *differentia* of the relevant genus. As such, it entails the presence of the genus while, by contrast, being nasal does not entail the presence of concavity. There are, after all, aquiline noses! These differentiae are defined as differentiae of the relevant genus, as red is defined as a differentia of colour. If so, the forms at issue will be essentially differentiae of matter: different ways of being material. They can no more be defined independently of matter than redness of colour.

[86] For further discussion of this general approach, see my earlier comments on prime matter (2004: 166).

This model exemplifies the S-structure described in Section 2.2. In the present case, matter takes the place of concavity (in the case of snubness) as the determinable made into the determinate matter of the composite by the presence of the relevant differentia (or form). This is why there is more to being a hand than simply being capable of playing a given causal (or functional) role. To be a hand is to be flesh made determinate by being enformed in the relevant way: so as to be capable of playing the required causal role. Hands are not to be defined solely in terms of their functional role.[87]

Aristotle's model has important implications. One is relevant to his account of efficient causation and material explanation.[88] In the case of anger: there will be a generic (Q) feature, being hot, and a number of determinants picking out various ways of being hot. One of these will be: being-hot-in-the-desiring-revenge way. Other cases which fall under the same generic feature—for instance, the way in which water is hot—will be found in other types of object apart from sentient creatures. In this way, in terms of the S-structures introduced in Section 2.3, a psycho-physical determinant serves to make determinate the type of boiling that is involved. There is no way of defining the specific type of hot material (or heat) that is present in the case of anger except as heat of the desiring-revenge type.[89]

It does not follow, it should further be noted, from the fact that anger is a determinate form of heat, that heat is psychological 'all the way' down: that there are no generalizations covering heat as a material, non-psychological phenomenon. While heat can be determined in this psycho-physical way, it can also be determined in other distinct (non-psychological) ways. If the generic or determinable feature is being hot, there can—in principle—be generalizations governing all hot objects, no matter the ways in which heat is made determinate. All these cases may act in somewhat similar, or analogous, ways in virtue of their all being determinate forms of one such generic feature. There is no inconsistency between adopting this perspective and accepting that there are useful generalizations concerning all type of hot objects. However, there will always be more specific generalizations governing the determinate type of heat present in anger.[90] Generalizations covering all cases of heat can be studied by the physicist in the manner of Aristotle's own investigations in *Meteorologica* Δ.[91] There will be

---

[87] This is to assume that being flesh is not itself wholly in terms of playing a given causal (or functional) role but as being bulky, heavy, composed from something else (not themselves defined wholly functionally). While I return to this issue in Chapter 7, it will be more fully discussed in Peramatzis and Charles (forthcoming).

[88] This important issue is raised by Caston (2008: 46).

[89] This model, it should be noted, allows for 'variable realization' of a limited kind: while this type of desire for revenge requires the presence of heat, the heat itself might be specified in such a way as to include the heat of the heart and of other organs (in different animals) which were also hot. At this level, there could be different sources or types of heat present as long as they were all instances of the type of heat of which the relevant type of desire for revenge was the determinant.

[90] For this reason, Aristotle's view is not—as we shall see in Chapter 7—a version of pan-psychism.

[91] Solidification, for example, is a generic type of drying which is brought about by heat and it occurs in a variety of subjects (384b22–3). This is Aristotle's way of summing up his earlier discussions

features of the type of heat found in cases of angry-blood-boiling not defined simply in terms of its causal role in this organism. Indeed, these would be shared with other determinate forms of this generic or determinable feature.

From this perspective, desire for revenge is a determinant of heat (or blood heat). Without reference to the hot, one will not fully capture the form of anger: that which stands as the basis of an account of the causal consequences and characteristic causes of anger. It is not that the form of anger is simply desire for revenge (which fully specifies a fully determinate entity) which requires supplementation by a further entity (matter) to yield the essence of the compound anger. It is rather that desire for revenge, as it stands, is an incomplete specification of the form of anger, which requires supplementation by reference to the determinable (hot) to yield a full, non-empty, specification of the form. The form in question will be a hot-desire-for-revenge (or the desiring revenge type of heat). Anger cannot simply be defined as a desire for revenge.

The form of anger, so understood, will be identical with its essence, as was suggested in *De Anima* A.1. Both will be defined in terms of a general feature (heat) made determinate by desire for revenge. It is not that the form is simply the determinant (desire for revenge) which is incomplete and needs to be added to the determinable to yield the essence (where the essence is made up of the determinant and the generic feature). Instead, the form itself, when fully specified, is essentially a determinant (desire for revenge) of this determinable. One would not capture the form (or essence) of anger—in the required non-empty way—without taking it to a desiring-for-revenge type of the hot. Being hot, so understood, is the determinable present in anger, made determinate by being the determinant: desiring revenge. The formal aspect of anger is itself essentially matter-involving.

This model has further consequences: if it is correct, there is no necessity that there be, in Aristotle's account, a determinate self-standing purely material process which underlies the relevant psycho-physical one. The relevant processes (those closest to the form) will be, as in the case of anger, psycho-physical through and through. When form and matter are defined in these ways, the form can be the per se cause of bodily changes which are not caused by two definitionally separate components: the form and the matter. There is no risk of over-determination because the matter involved is itself (at least in part) defined as enformed matter. There is no fully determinate, purely material state or capacity defined independently of the form which also causes the bodily changes that result.

Each of the consequences of this model will be explored further in subsequent chapters.

---

in *Meteorologica* Δ.5 and elsewhere. There he introduces different determinate forms of drying corresponding to the different types of material capacities involved.

2.8 Interim conclusions: a problem

There is, I have argued, a more general hylomorphic theory of natural substances which parallels Aristotle's remarks in *De Anima* on passions common to body and soul. In this account, when fully developed:

[A] The forms of natural objects are (in the way specified in Section 2.2) inextricably enmattered, capacities or activities, and
[B] The matter which underlies the form is defined in terms of the form.

It is a consequence of [A] that natural objects are not to be defined in terms of a pure form to which something else is added. Definitions of natural objects in terms of their form are incomplete without explicit reference (in the definition of the form) to material (or bodily) capacities or activities. They are not defined in terms of a pure capacity plus the matter (or body) in which they are present. Had they been defined by composition in this way, their forms could not have been per se causes of bodily movements. Given [B], the matter in question will be defined in terms of an impure form as defined in [A]. There is, in the resulting account, no danger of one and the same bodily result being over-determined by two independent causes, one material and one formal. This is because the relevant causal capacity (the form) is inextricably material and the matter in question (in the composite) is defined as matter possessed of that capacity. There is one and only one per se cause of the resulting bodily result. Further, in committing himself to [A] and [B] in the case of natural substances, Aristotle provided the resources to underwrite the non-accidental unity of the resulting composite. Its matter and form are, in the way specified, definitionally connected. Provided that the form itself is a proper unity (a step yet to be discussed), the composite will be a non-accidental unity.

There remains a problem: Aristotle takes forms to be *prior* to matter. How can this be? If the capacities possessed by hands are examples of inextricably enmattered forms, can they be prior to hands, defined as that which has that capacity? Aren't they simply capacities of hands and, as such, posterior to hands? Equally, aren't bodily (or material) capacities to be defined as capacities of bodies (or matter more generally)? Surely, it will be said, only pure forms can be prior in the required way to hands and bodies?[92]

---

[92] This concern motivated one of Plotinus' objections to Aristotelian forms, which he interpreted as impure. More recently, it has provided a major motivation for the pure form interpretation of Aristotle's own views. On this, see, for example, Marko Malink (2013: 341–62). One cannot escape Plotinus' problem merely by suggesting that impure forms and the matter they enform are simultaneous in definition: a possibility Aristotle, on occasion, considers (for, at least, some such definitions: *Metaphysics* Z.10, 1035b26–7). This is because, even in this account, forms will not be prior in definition (or in being what they are) to the relevant matter.

2.8 INTERIM CONCLUSIONS: A PROBLEM

The relevant manual capacities of, for example, hands are to be defined (or so I have argued) as material capacities for moving or gripping in certain ways, where the ways in question are defined independently of hands. These capacities are referred to in the account of hands: they are principles of the forms of hands. Hands, as spatial objects, are hands because they have certain capacities of this kind, determinate types of more general capacities for pulling and pushing. Material capacities are defined as capacities of this type. While matter is defined in terms of such capacities, these capacities are not, so understood, defined as capacities of matter.

This picture is at work in *Metaphysics* Θ.8 where the forms of natural substances are said to be teleologically prior to the matter which has the capacity: that which comes to be, and is, present in the composite. As he notes:

> the matter is potentially [an F] when it would proceed towards the form; when it [the matter] is actually [an F], it is in the form [enformed]. (1050a15–16)

The form in question is prior in being (and in definition) because it is the teleological cause of the matter being in the state it is. This is what underwrites the priority in being of the form over the relevant matter. In the case of processes and of nature, actuality (*energeia*) is the goal (1050a16–19). He explains this as follows:

> For the result (in the case of action) is a goal and the actuality (*energeia*) is the result. (1050a21–2)[93]

In some cases, the goal is the finished product (1050a25–7, 30–4), in others it is to be active in a given way (1050a23–5, 34–b1).[94] However, in all the goal is prior to matter, understood as that which is capable of achieving and sustaining this actuality. In the case of substances, the form is prior in being to the relevant matter because it is prior in the relevant teleological order. In his account:

[A] The goal for matter is being enformed and
[B] To be enformed is an actuality (*energeia*, in the sense of *entelecheia*).

---

[93] In cases involving matter, the Form (being an F) is the goal both of the process of becoming an F (1050a8–10) and the potentiality to be an F: the Form is the actuality (*energeia*) in question. Further, in this case the actuality (*energeia*) is an *entelecheia*: the completed or perfected result which is to be achieved as the goal in question (1050a21ff.). Aristotle notes that the term '*energeia*' can be used to apply both to actions (such as using knowledge) and to the perfected state (e.g. of a statue): 1050a20. While in both cases the goal is an actuality (*energeia*), in the first it is an activity (in the case of (e.g.) seeing) and in the second the perfected state which results from the process of making a statue (or building a house). '*Energeia*' can refer both to actions and to the results of actions. I discuss the act/result ambiguity of '*energeia*' in 1986: 132–9.

[94] Both could be called 'works': art works (such as statues) and the work of the flute player (e.g. flute playing). For discussion of this ambiguity, see *E.E.* 1219a12–17. Given these considerations, '*ergon*', like '*energeia*', is act/result ambiguous.

From these claims he concludes:

[C] The goal for matter is an actuality (being enformed).

Since

[D] the form is the actuality in question (1050b2)

it follows that

[E] The form is prior to matter in being (1050b3ff.).

The relevant matter, throughout its development, up to and including its final state (as hands), is teleologically explained by the form which is prior in being (and in definition) to the matter.

This picture, however, brings with it some strong commitments: manual capacities (the form) have to be defined independently of the hands they enform. Even if such forms are necessarily the forms of hands, they need to be defined essentially without explicit reference to hands (as matter). In subsequent chapters, I will examine how far Aristotle maintains this precise type of account in his discussion of psychological phenomena.[95]

2.9 Three ways of going (slightly) wrong

Aristotle's general hylomorphic theory (as understood here) can be presented, albeit somewhat schematically, as follows:

1. The forms of natural substances are per se efficient and teleological causes of bodily change

---

[95] Aristotle, on occasion, suggests another type of priority. In *Categories* 12, he says that A may be prior to B even though neither can *be* without the other, provided that the former is the cause of the latter (14b9–14). If the notion of *being* invoked in this passage covers both existence and being what it is (as it does earlier in the chapter), A can be prior in being to B even though both are defined in terms of the other, provided that A is the cause of B. Thus, manual capacities could be prior in being to hands, even though both are defined in terms which refer explicitly to the other. There would be no inconsistency between A and B being inseparable in definition and A's being prior in being (or definition) to B provided that A is causally prior to B. This remark, so understood, would allow for a type of priority beyond those discussed in the Lexicon (*Metaphysics* Δ) where 'some things are called prior and posterior in nature and being…those for which it is possible to be without the other things, but the latter without them' (1019a1–4). While it lies outside this project to investigate this suggestion further, and to test its applicability to, for example, *Metaphysics* Θ.8), it suggests a different (and potentially interesting) way to formulate the material inextricability of form, consistent with the latter's priority (so understood) over matter.

2. To be per se causes of bodily change they have to be inextricably enmattered forms [CAUSE]. They are, in fact, inextricably enmattered in the demanding way in which snubness is inextricably enmattered, as set out in Section 2.2 (and captured above by I.Γ.)
3. The forms of natural substances are essentially inextricably enmattered forms (from 1 and 2)
4. The forms of natural substances are their essences and are prior in being to their matter [PRIORITY]
5. The essences of natural substances are essentially inextricably enmattered forms (from 3 and 4)
6. The matter of natural substances is defined in terms of their inextricably enmattered forms (from 4)
7. Natural substances are non-accidental unities [UNITY] (from 3, 4, and 6).

In this account, forms are inextricably material (or bodily) capacities (or activities) and the relevant specific matter in the compound is defined as the matter for this form, that which is capable there and then of acting in the required ways. Such forms need to be inextricably enmattered to be per se causes of material changes (1). This is why they are impure forms (in the way defined above). Nor is being inextricably enmattered inconsistent with their being, in the way suggested, prior in being (and in definition) to the matter of the composite. In this way, forms of this type satisfy the three conditions, [CAUSE], [UNITY], and [PRIORITY], to which I shall return in Chapter 7.

Several questions concerning the nature of enmattered forms remain unanswered. We have not yet finally determined some basic aspects of their ontological character. In the present chapter, we began by talking of inextricably material *ways of being* (the way material objects are) and then sought to underwrite this description in terms of inextricably material *capacities*. However, since, as we have seen, Aristotle sometimes characterizes forms as 'actualities' (as in the *Metaphysics* H.2 passages discussed in Section 2.5), there is something still to clarify in his account. Nor have we fully considered important aspects of the unity of such forms. How is there a unified form of animal defined by possession of a variety of different capacities (as there would be if humans were defined in terms of separate abilities to reason and to walk)? These issues will be addressed in examining aspects of Aristotle's discussion of the soul in more detail in Chapters 3–6 and in more general terms in Chapter 7.

However, before proceeding, it may be helpful to place the impurist interpretation (as so far developed) on a wider exegetical map by comparing it with other accounts of Aristotle's hylomorphic theory. There are several ways in which, if the impurist account developed here is correct, his theory has been (somewhat) misunderstood. I shall mention three:

(i) Many scholars have emphasized, as the impurist does, that the determinate type of heating present in cases of anger is a desiring-revenge-type-of-blood-boiling (or heating). However, some have pressed a further question: how is this type of heating related to a further fully determinate purely material process of heating, defined without essential reference to desiring revenge, whose presence is, in their view, required?[96]

But their final question rests on a mistake: there need not be, from Aristotle's perspective, a separate determinate purely material process or state present when anger occurs. From his viewpoint, the material processes involved are made the determinate entities they are by being aimed at revenge. Matter, more generally, is a determinable made determinate in this way. The type of matter present when one is angry (the specific type of heat) is not a wholly new type of 'spiritual matter' only found, for example, in angry creatures. It is matter of the same general type (determinable: the hot) as is found elsewhere, now made determinate in the specific way found in cases of anger. It is defined as the matter that is capable of issuing in the relevant bodily processes.[97]

Scholars have searched in vain (or so I shall argue) in Aristotle's writing for the required fully determinate purely material process, defined without reference to anger, which underlies it. Nor should their failure surprise us. If there had been a determinate purely material process of this type, anger itself would have been an accidental unity, made up of two definitionally independent components. If anger is a non-accidental unity, there can be no such definitionally independent purely material process that underlies it. Other interpreters, rightly concerned about issues of unity, have sought to explain how the relevant pre-existing fully determinate matter 'disappears', to be replaced by a new enformed determinate type of matter when we are angry. However, from our present perspective, both lines of investigation can be called off. Matter, in the case of anger, is best understood (as suggested in Section 2.7) as a determinable made determinate by the presence of a psycho-physical determinant.[98]

(ii) Many scholars have regarded the form of natural objects as itself fully determinate without supplementation from anything material. The latter is not, in their view, in any way part of the form of natural objects. In the present chapter, I have challenged this purist interpretation, arguing that an account of the form of such objects is incomplete unless it is defined as a distinctively material principle (or capacity), as it must be if it is the efficient cause of further bodily changes.

---

[96] See, for example, Charles (1988: 1–53), Everson (1997), Caston (2005: 245–320).
[97] For further discussion of this issue, see Chapter 7.
[98] Such matter, when determinate, is not functional matter, understood as matter defined wholly in terms of its function. It is also defined in terms of its heat, mass, volume.

Suarez also objected to the purist view, emphasizing the causal role of the forms of natural objects. He wrote, with great acuity, 'form is a certain type of simple incomplete substance, which as an act of matter constitutes together with matter the essence of a composite substance' (*Metaphysical Disputations* xv.5.1). He was motivated, it seems, by the idea that form is in some way 'incomplete', sometimes talking of it as 'an act of matter' (although his talk of 'act of matter' is elusive). Perhaps he was inclined to think of the form as a determinant of matter.

However, Suarez developed his insight in a distinctive way: the form is 'incomplete' in that it needs to be supplemented by matter to yield the essence of the composite substance. In his view, the essence is, it seems, a (complete) complex made up of a form (a simple but incomplete entity) which requires supplementation from matter to yield the essence. However, Suarez's final step should not be taken lightly: Aristotle, as we have seen, regularly identifies the form with the essence (see, for example, *Metaphysics* Z.17, 1041a29–31, b5–7). The form may be fully specified in terms of the determinant (e.g. desire for revenge) and the generic feature of which it is the determinant (the hot). Indeed, to think of desire for revenge as a differentiating determinant is to think of it as essentially a determinant of this generic feature (as being scarlet is essentially a determinant of being coloured). If so, one will not grasp 'being two-footed' as a differentiating determinant unless one grasps it as a determinant of being footed (Z.12, 1038a5ff.) or perhaps being a walker. In a similar way, 'desire for revenge' will only be a partial and unsatisfactory specification of the form, which will be defined as a *hot* desire for revenge (or the desiring revenge way of being hot). As in *De Anima* A.1 (according to the interpretation of 403b1–2 proposed in Chapter 1, Section 3), the form of anger and its essence (as given in its definition: *logos*) will be identical. Neither can be adequately (or 'non-emptily': 403a2) defined simply in terms of desire for revenge. Both need to be defined in terms which explicitly refer, in the way suggested, to material features (such as heat or heat-involving bodily capacities).

Suarez saw that there is a type of incompleteness in Aristotle's talk of form. But, if I am correct, he misunderstood its nature, taking it as specifying (completely) an incomplete (if simple) entity rather than as incompletely specifying a complete entity: the matter-involving form (and essence) at issue. This entity is completely defined as a distinctively material capacity. Indeed, this is how the form needs to be to do the efficient causal work which Suarez himself emphasized.

(iii) Some recent commentators differ from Suarez in taking the form to be a complete entity while agreeing with him that the essence of the compound involves more than the form in question. To maintain the required connection between form and essence (which I too have emphasized), they distinguish two essences both of which are present in the compound: one identified with the form alone, defined independently of matter, the other with a combination of the form and matter.[99]

---

[99] See, for example, Gill (1989), Heinaman (1997).

Their suggestion brings with it its own difficulties. First, if it is accepted, natural compounds turn out to have two essences. But can man, in Aristotle's view, have two essences? Is there any reason to believe that he departed from his standard practice of attributing one essence to one type of natural object? Further, since he identifies—at the level of reference—the essence with an appropriate cause (such as the teleological and efficient cause: Z.17, 1041a28–30), he does not distinguish—at the level of reference—two separate essences: one logical or metaphysical, the other physical—put forward to account for the required causal role of the form.[100] Second, the present proposal does not give the essence of the compound the unity required. It is now represented as the conjunction of two determinate entities: the form plus the matter which is present with the form. However, Aristotle consistently rejected definition by conjunction or addition: see, for example, *Posterior Analytics* 91b35ff. Such accounts cannot, in his view, ground the non-accidental unity of the resulting compound. If the essence of the compound is to play the role of the middle, explanatory, term in Aristotle's favoured *Analytics*-style account (considered in *Metaphysics* Z.17), it cannot be a combination of two factors (said as one thing of something else). No such combination can be the unified basic cause required in the relevant demonstrations. It would not fulfil the explanatory requirements set out in *De Anima* 402b23ff.: conjunctions of this type themselves need to be explained by a more basic, strongly unified cause. Nor can this explanatory task be discharged by invoking a pure more basic essence unless it can be shown how this pure essence itself requires, or hypothetically necessitates, the presence of the required matter. In Aristotle's view, one has to show what it is about the essence, considered by itself, that requires the presence of this type of matter. The explanation in question has to follow from the nature of the essence itself (the basic feature in the relevant demonstration: *De Anima* A.1, 402b27ff.). This is why in *De Anima* A.4 407b15, he criticizes those who combine matter and form without explaining why, and how, the latter is combined with the former.

There is another way to distinguish two types of essence, more congenial to the approach taken in this chapter. On this view, while some entities, such as various types of sphere have purely mathematical essences (or forms, such as concavity), others—such as man—have physical essences (understood along the line suggested for snubness). However, this suggestion is sometimes combined with a further, more controversial, claim: that the first type of case has a primary type of essence, the second only a derivative, or second-grade, type of essence. Concavity, so understood, might be an example of a primary essence, enmattered-concavity (or snubness) of a second-grade one. Aristotle, it is sometimes suggested, drew

---

[100] There may, of course, be specifically 'logical' or 'metaphysical' ways of describing, for example, the essences of natural substances: in terms which abstract, for example, from their efficient causal role or, indeed, from all their distinguishing features other than those that belong to them qua beings. But they will not have, on this view, distinct logical (or metaphysical) and physical essences (or forms).

this distinction in 1037a30ff. when he entertained the possibility that concavity is a primary type of essence to be distinguished from cases involving matter. The latter cases, it is concluded, cannot be examples of a primary type of essence.[101]

The final step, just sketched, is not required. As suggested above, the type of concavity mentioned in 1037a31 is, it appears, the type of concavity found in snub noses. (This is why 'nose' is said twice, within the framework of Z.4–5, in defining snub noses as concave nose, nose.)[102] Further, the reference to matter in 1037a32–3 is introduced when talking of particulars like Kallias (or particular snub noses). In these cases, snubness is said of the matter in the particular compound (as one thing or something else). The matter as matter in the compound is said not to be defined at all: perhaps particular bits (or quantities) are not defined because they are particulars. Or perhaps they are not defined as determinate particulars because, without addition, it is not specified which of the potentials of this matter are exercised.[103] But, either way, the matter in question is different from the material principle, or capacity, which is part of the form. Nothing follows about the nature of the latter from Aristotle's discussion of particular bits or quantities of matter.

Nor is the additional exegetical step attractive. In *Metaphysics* Z.4, species such as man are introduced as primary objects of definition: ones defined not by something being said of something else (1030a10ff.). It would be strange if the essence of man was now demoted to secondary status in the discussion of definitions *on the basis* that in its account something is said of something else. Even if introducing matter as a determinable in the essence places material substances at a disadvantage in Aristotle's overall ontological hierarchy (see, for instance, *Metaphysics* Z.11, 1037a12ff. or Λ.6–10), it remains true that in their case (if Z.4 is to be believed) there is no predication (in their definition) which is of the 'one thing of something else' type.

2.10 Summary: surviving questions

In the Chapters 3, 4, 5, and 6, I shall suggest that Aristotle's discussion in *De Anima* of desire, perception, and imagination—the passions common to body

---

[101] Alan Code considered this possibility in his 'Comments' (2010b: 197–210).
[102] This type of concavity may be identical with being concave (as Aristotle notes in 1037b2). It is also not said of matter as one thing of something else (1037b3–4). Nor—as a way of being—is it identical with matter or the matter/form compound (1037b4–5). But, as Aristotle also mentions, it is said accidentally of matter. The exact nature of their connection is to be discussed later (for example in Z.17).
[103] As was suggested in the account of *Metaphysics* Θ.7, 1049a25ff., offered above.

and soul—parallels his more general view of hylomorphic natural substances, as understood in this chapter, and is motivated by similar concerns. Consideration of aspects of his specific account of these inextricably psycho-physical activities will enable us to address some of the issues, concerning the precise nature of forms and their unity, which remain unresolved.

3
Desire and Action

3.1 An unnerving silence

In *De Anima* Γ.10, 433b15–18 Aristotle claims that the desiderative faculty (*to orektikon*) is moved by the object desired and moves the animal. His remark is difficult to grasp mainly because he presents the phenomenon at issue as almost wholly unproblematic. He continues in a similar vein:

> The instrument by which desire moves the animal is a bodily one: this is why it must be investigated among the functions common to body and soul.   (433b19–20)

These comments unnerve us. From a post-Cartesian viewpoint, they fail to raise, let alone address, the basic philosophical question: how can desire, understood as a psychological phenomenon, move the animal and its body? Nor is our unease diminished by his next remark:

> for now, to put the matter briefly, that which moves instrumentally is where a beginning and end coincide, as in a ball and socket joint: here the convex (the ball) and the concave (the socket) are respectively the end and beginning of movement; this is why one is at rest and the other is in motion. They are spatially inseparable but differ in account. For all movement consists in pulling and pushing. This is why it is necessary (as in a wheel) that something remains at rest and from it movement is initiated.   (433b21–6)

This observation seems to make matters worse: how can desire interact with 'an instrument' which has weight and magnitude? How can the desiderative faculty be understood as one element in a hinge joint? What sense can be made of talk of it pushing and pulling spatially adjacent parts of the body? However, so far from answering these questions, Aristotle simply concludes that desire (understood as the activity of the desiderative faculty: 433b18) moves the animal in this way. While he notes that the instrument itself is to be investigated 'among the functions common to the body and the soul', he is confident that it is pushed and pulled by desire. From a post-Cartesian perspective, there is a major gap at precisely the point where an account is most needed.

The Undivided Self: Aristotle and the 'Mind–Body Problem'. David Charles, Oxford University Press (2021).
© David Charles. DOI: 10.1093/oso/9780198869566.003.0004

3.2 How to fill the silence?

Aristotle's account of anger and fear in *De Anima* A.1 (as sketched in Chapter 1) suggests a way to address the apparent explanatory gap between desire and bodily movement in *De Anima* Γ.10. In the case of anger, he held (if the account in Chapter 1 is correct) that:

[A] The psychological features essential to being angry (that is, desiring revenge) are inseparable in definition from the processes with physical properties to which they belong: the relevant features are inextricably psycho-physical. (The form of anger is defined as inextricably enmattered.)
[B] The psycho-physical features (specified in [A]) are essential to the identity of the processes to which they belong: the processes to which the psycho-physical features belong are essentially psycho-physical processes.
[C] There is no other process type (other than the one specified in [B]) which is essential to being angry. Individual cases of anger are essentially instances of this type.

Anger and fear, so interpreted, are, as was noted in Chapter 1, 'common to body and soul' in a particularly demanding way. They are not to be defined in terms of two definitionally separable components: a purely psychological component, a pure form, and a further purely physical (or bodily) component. The relevant process is, in the terminology of Chapter 2, the realization of an impure form: an essentially material (or bodily) capacity. Inextricably material capacities of this type are required as unified per se causes of bodily action. Anger and fear, like natural substances, cannot be defined by decomposition into a pure form and the matter in which the form is instantiated. (I use the term 'process' from Chapter 1 for '*kinēsis*': this aspect of the ontology will be discussed further in Chapter 4.)

In *De Anima* A.1, sensual desire (*epithumia*) was described (403a7ff.), like anger and fear, as 'common to body and soul'.[1] Elsewhere, desire generally (*orexis*) is characterized in the same way (*De Sensu* 436a8–9) and placed in the same category as spirit (*thumos*), of which anger is a species. If desire is 'common to body and soul' in the same way as anger, it too will be inseparable in definition into two distinct components. The apparently psychological component of desire (such as aiming at the good or the pleasant) will be defined in an inextricably psycho-physical way as an essentially bodily type of goal-directed activity, the realization of an inextricably psycho-physical capacity. Its form will be impure.

If this is Aristotle's view in *De Anima* Γ.10, 433b15ff.:

---

[1] I take the phenomena in question to be activities and passions although similar remarks will apply to the capacities for such activities or passions.

(1) Desire, like anger, will be defined as an inextricably psycho-physical process (or activity), essentially involving some fairly specific type of bodily change. Its form will be essentially matter-involving,
(2) Desire, as an inextricably psycho-physical process, causes a further process in another part of the body, and
(3) As a result, the limbs move in just the way required for the action desired.

If Aristotle held this view, he will not need to address our post-Cartesian question: how can desire, understood as a purely psychological phenomenon, move the body? This is because desire, in his account, is inextricably psycho-physical, possessed of an inextricably psycho-physical form. The 'instrument' by which it moves the animal is described as among the functions 'common to body and soul' (433b19–20) because the processes located in it, including the activity of desire, are themselves inextricably psycho-physical.[2] While in *De Anima* he speaks of the bodily instruments only in outline (because his focus there is on the actions, passions, and capacities of the soul, not on the mechanisms linking them with bodily movements),[3] when his account is more fully spelled out elsewhere, the mechanisms also will be shown to be inextricably psycho-physical.

If this is Aristotle's view, he would not have been attracted to the options with which we are most familiar. More specifically:

1. His account will not be a dualist one in which a purely psychological phenomenon causes the movements of the body. Desire, in his view, is essentially a psycho-physical, not a purely psychological, process: the activity of a psycho-physical capacity.
2. Nor will his account be a spiritualist or pan-psychist one. The matter at issue is not primitively endowed with the capacity for purely psychological processes. Instead, it has a capacity for inextricably psycho-physical activity.
3. Nor will it be a non-reductionist materialist one. It will contain neither the purely psychological component which specifies what desire is (defined in non-material terms) nor the purely physical component (defined in purely material terms) which realizes the relevant psychological component.[4] Further, since no purely physical process of this type need be present when desire moves our bodies, the account will not be that offered by materialist functionalist interpreters.[5]

---

[2] This instrument itself can be described as 'bodily' not because sensual desire and anger are not themselves bodily processes but rather because it is bulky, not fine grained or light in the way heat-based phenomena are. (For this contrast between bulky elements and fine-grained ones, see *De Anima* 404b31–405a7. It is a distinction between what we would count as bodily elements.)

[3] In a similar style, when discussing anger in *De Anima* A.1, Aristotle offered comparatively little detail about the bodily states involved, preferring to speak, somewhat indefinitely, of 'the blood around the heart or the hot' (403a32f).

[4] For this style of account of non-reductionist materialist interpretation, see my (1984: 217ff.).

[5] For this kind of account, see Putnam and Nussbaum (1995: 39ff.). They talk of Aristotle's 'psychological processes as realised in physiological ones'.

If this is Aristotle's view, we can understand his apparently unnerving silence in *De Anima* Γ.10. He was not seeking to explain how desire moves the body in the grip of the Cartesian assumptions that make the phenomenon appear so puzzling. If desire is, like anger, inextricably psycho-physical in the way suggested, the fact that it moves the body will have seemed relatively unproblematic. Although specific questions remain, about, for example, the way in which it moves the body (e.g. what is the type of mechanism involved?), there is no outstanding general question about the possibility of the phenomenon itself. He was not thinking, as we are inclined to, that:

[1]* There is a purely psychological feature or event involved in desiring (or a purely psychological description), such as desiring (or aiming at) revenge.[6]

[2]* All the relevant features and processes essentially involved in desiring are either purely psychological or purely physical or a combination of the purely psychological and the purely physical.

His silence will be readily intelligible in the light of the model he introduced in his discussion of anger and fear in *De Anima* A.1, which was, in turn, underwritten by his general view of essentially enmattered forms as per se causes of bodily changes (as described in Chapter 2). Desire, the unified per se cause of the resulting bodily movements, is an inextricably enmattered capacity which issues in inextricably enmattered activity.

Did Aristotle, in fact, hold this position? His criticism of the harmony theory (Section 3.3) and his own positive and more detailed account of animal movement in *De Motu* (Sections 3.4–3.5) suggest that he did. His view of desire, and how it is to be defined, follows the pattern of his simple, and intuitive, picture of the emotions. Like these, desire must be defined as inextricably psycho-physical (with a form of this type) to be capable of playing its role as the per se cause of bodily movements. Or so I shall argue.

3.3 The harmony theory: problems for the non-reductionist interpretation

Non-reductionist materialist interpreters understand Aristotle's account of desire in the following way (using their favoured ontology):

[1] Desire is defined as the psychological event type it is without explicit reference to any co-occurring internal physical phenomena (in purely

---

[6] By 'purely psychological' is intended a description which does not explicitly refer to internal physical states of the agent. Certain types of functionalist description, which refer to external physical objects, will be counted as purely psychological.

3.3 THE HARMONY THEORY

psychological terms). (Its form is pure, defined without explicit reference to matter.)
[2] Desire, so defined, is realized in (or supervenes on) a particular event or state of a physical type, and
[3] The relevant type of physical event or state is defined without explicit reference to any psychological phenomena.

In their view, Aristotle posits the presence of purely physical events (or states) which (i) are required to account for the causal role of desire and (ii) are themselves basic per se causes of bodily movement (described in purely physical terms).[7] While desire is made up of purely psychological and purely physical components, the latter do the basic causal work. In their account, desire is made up (in Aristotelian terms) of a pure form, defined independently of matter, and matter, defined independently of form. Even if desire (the compound) is inextricably psycho-physical, its form (the psychological component) is not.

One major difficulty for this interpretation is that in *De Anima* A.4 Aristotle rejected an account of the soul, which, in certain key respects, resembles the very one it proposes. In considering the 'harmony theory', he writes:

> The soul is said to be a type of harmony. Harmony, on this view, is taken to be a blending or combining of opposites which are the components of the body. However, as harmony is either a formula governing the components or their actual combination, the soul cannot be either. A harmony cannot cause movement but all attribute this to the soul virtually above everything else... Again, we apply the term 'harmony' in two ways, first to the combination of things with size which move and have a spatial position when they are 'harmonized' so as not to allow anything of the same kind to be added and second to the formula which governs the things mixed. Neither view offers a plausible account of the soul although the former is most open to criticism.

Aristotle separates two versions of this theory: 'harmony' can be understood either as:

a. the formula which governs the combination of elements (such as the mathematical ratio 4:2:4) or
b. the elements when harmonized by that formula (in such a way as not to allow anything of the same kind to be added).

---

[7] Putnam and Nussbaum (1995: 39ff.).

While he offers several criticisms of both versions, his first objection is the most significant for our purposes. If the soul were a harmony (in either of these two ways) it could not, he says, account for movement. Why not?

If the harmony is understood simply as a mathematical formula (such as 4:2:4), present when one has 4A's, 2B's, and 4C's, it is not the type of thing which can be the per se cause of the relevant movements.[8] As Aristotle notes (408a1–2) such formulae are found in many things which do not cause such movements: e.g. in bone and flesh when they form parts of hands and feet: *anhomoiomerous* parts of the body. They are not specific enough to account for voluntary actions. Further, and more fundamentally, mathematical forms are not, in Aristotle's account, the type of phenomenon that can be efficient causes of movement. In this they differ crucially from physical forms. This is, of course, precisely the criticism he should have made given his general views about physical and mathematical forms (as set out in Chapter 2). It would be a mistake, by his own lights, to think that a pure, mathematical, form can do the required efficient causal work.

He now adds a further criticism. If the relevant harmony were understood as physical elements combined in a given ratio, it still would not be the per se cause of the relevant changes. Aristotle developed this point in two ways:

(a) The elements, even when they instantiate the formula, retain their natural tendencies to behave and interact with each other in their own distinctive ways. He criticizes Empedocles (who he mentions just after this discussion: 408a17ff., as encountering similar difficulties) on just these grounds (*De Anima* 416a5–10). The mere fact that the elements exemplify a given mathematical formula does not alter their causal powers. Indeed, since mathematical forms themselves lack the power to bring about material changes, the elements cannot have different causal powers simply in virtue of instantiating them. By contrast, the soul has a causal role, apart from that of the elements: that of preventing them flying apart. The desiderative faculty, like the other parts of the agent mentioned in *De Motu* 703a29–b2, plays its own per se causal role in maintaining the well-organized whole, a role not derived from the natural tendencies of the elements themselves.

This point can be developed further: the elements would have to be transformed when they instantiate the relevant mathematical formula to generate a new phenomenon capable of playing the causal role the soul plays. If so, what plays the causal role is the new phenomenon, not the elements when governed by the mathematical formula. However, on the present proposal, we are given no understanding of how the elements, when governed by this formula, are capable of generating an entity capable of playing the specific per se causal role played by the soul. As Aristotle

---

[8] The harmony in question could be described as a mathematical capacity: the capacity realized when objects are ordered in the sequence: 4:2:4. For this use of capacity, see, for example, *Metaphysics* Θ.1, 1046a4–7.

remarks, in criticizing another proposal: the theory does not tell us why the bodily elements at issue give rise to the soul (*De Anima* 407b15ff.).

The latter remark is important: it is not enough, by Aristotle's lights, simply to define the relevant bodily states as those which play a given causal role in the organism. One has to explain how they, constituted as they are, came to have that role. What is it about their material nature which gives rise to the causal powers required to account for voluntary action?

(b) The soul (or desire) will only have an 'epiphenomenal' role if this version of the harmony theory is adopted. It (or better the agent) will not be the per se subject (or the controller) of the relevant actions because purely psychological phenomena will, like mathematical ones, lack per se causal powers. What causes the movement will be the elements when they stand in the relation defined by the formula, not the formula itself. When they stand together in this way, the resulting causal powers are, for the harmony theorist, the result solely of the causal powers of the physical parts which make up the whole. However, for Aristotle, the soul of an organism has its own distinctive causal powers, not derived from the causal powers of the individual physical elements that 'underlie' it. This will not be so if all the relevant causal powers belong to the physical elements which are governed by a given ratio.[9]

Nor can this problem be resolved simply by adding to the mathematical form (itself causally inert) the physical elements on which the mathematical form rests. For, in that scenario, the physical elements, not the soul, will do the causal work. In the harmony theory, while the causally inert psychological state may be present for the sake of a given goal, the underlying physical elements are the relevant per se efficient causes of the relevant bodily actions. There is, in this account, no one unified process or state (desire) which is simultaneously and in the same respect both goal-directed and a per se cause of bodily movement.

The harmony theory wishes to understand the relevant causal powers of the soul (or agent) in terms of a combination of a pure form, defined without reference to matter, and a set of physical elements (defined independently of the form) which ground or realize that form. In fact, this seems to be just the view attributed to Aristotle by the non-reductionist interpreter. Hence, in rejecting this theory, Aristotle is, in effect, rejecting precisely the type of account the non-reductionist interpreter attributes to him.

Neither of Aristotle's concerns about the harmony theory can be met by simply suggesting that the physical elements should themselves be defined as those required for the form to be present. Even if the theory were modified in this way,

---

[9] These will act as they are naturally prone to (*De Anima* 415b27ff.): their natural powers, as Aristotle remarks in his criticism of Empedocles, are not changed by the mere fact that they are present in a given ratio. The agent will move, like Democritus' silver sphere, in a robotic, quirky, way (*De Anima* 406b20–5), not through preferential choice and thought.

the purely psychological features of desire (e.g. its goal directedness) would not themselves be per se causes of the resulting voluntary bodily actions. Nor would he have any account of how, or why, the physical elements themselves came to play that specific role. The two central problems which Aristotle isolated will remain.

These problems cannot be addressed by suggesting that the psychological aspects of desire require (or hypothetically necessitate) the presence of the relevant physical elements. Within such an account, the distinctively psychological aspects are not per se causes of the resulting actions. That role is discharged by the underlying purely physical states. Nor are we given any account of how the physical states are modified, or altered, so as to be appropriate per se causes of voluntary actions. Why are the causal powers of these physical states changed by the mere fact that their presence is required if there is to be desire? Of course, if desire itself, the psychological phenomenon, has its own causal powers, one could argue that these require the presence of physical states with 'matching' causal powers. But this would assume that pure psychological phenomena have their own per se causal powers and that physical states can (somehow) come to have matching causal powers. However, it is precisely because he rejected these assumptions that Aristotle criticized the harmony theory.

What is Aristotle's own detailed account of how the soul moves the body? This issue is pressing since, on occasion, he himself uses the very terms employed by the harmony theorist. Thus, later he compares the soul's capacities with the arrangement (*sumphōnia*) and pitch of the strings of a musical instrument (as in *De Anima* B.12, 424a26ff.). Isn't this just a version of the discredited harmony theory?

We are in a position, given the discussion of physical form in Chapter 2, to address this question. If the type of form is, as suggested in Section 3.2, an impure, essentially material capacity, it will be different both from the mathematical form by itself [such as 4:2:4] and from the elements [A, B, C] which instantiate it (and from the combinations of forms and elements just considered). Mathematical forms are defined without explicit reference to change (194a5) or matter (194a13). Even though they need to be instantiated in physical matter (if they are to exist), they are defined independently of it. Enmattered forms, by contrast, are not defined in this way but as essentially material. It is only if desire's form is of this (inextricabilist) type that it can play the unified per se causal role required in the account of action.

To generalize: desire, on this model, will be defined as essentially enmattered capacity, not as a pure capacity, defined independently of matter, which is present in the matter.[10] More generally: the soul, if talk of 'harmony' is still to be employed (as in 424a26ff.), will be defined as a harmony-of-this-material organ, not as a

---

[10] Even if a pure psychological process could (somehow) require the presence of a separate physical state, there would still not be one properly unified cause of the resulting bodily movements. I shall return to this issue in Chapter 7.

type of harmony (defined independently of matter) which is present in this material organ. The form in question will, like snubness, be an inextricably enmattered form.

In Sections 3.4–3.6, I shall suggest that this interpretation is supported by Aristotle's detailed discussion in *De Motu* on how desire causes actions.

3.4 Desire in *De Motu*: Aristotle's four-stage account

In *De Motu*, Aristotle characterizes that which moves the limbs as a bodily part, capable of becoming bigger or smaller and changing its shape under the influence of heat and cold (701b12–16).[11] Its expansions and contractions, changes in its shape and size (703a18–20), move the animal by releasing and slackening its sinews and bones (701b9–10). To act in this way, it must be heavier than fire (703a21–3).

In this account, the *connate pneuma*, that which moves the limbs, is itself moved by heating and cooling, themselves caused by the thought, imagination, or perception of an object. He writes that when we think of or imagine an object which is good or to be pursued or avoided, our thoughts or imaginings are necessarily followed (*akolouthei*) by chilling and heating (701b35ff.), which occur together with (*meta*: 702a4) confidence, fear, or sexual arousal (*aphrodisiasmoi*).[12] As a result, the *connate pneuma* which initiates movement changes in size in such a way as to move our limbs in the required ways.

There are several stages in Aristotle's account of the process (or activity) which begins with perception and culminates in bodily movement. It is important, at the outset, to be clear on these details of his picture of the causes at work in producing bodily movements. The stages are:

Stage [1]   An object of pursuit or avoidance is thought about, perceived or imagined. Such objects might include a cool drink, John (my friend and your enemy).

Stage [2]   Fear or confidence occur and the heat or coldness which occurs with them.

---

[11] I take the necessary connection between the thought or imagination of some object of pursuit and (e.g.) heating to be an efficient causal one (compare that between memory and heating etc. in 702a5ff.). Why then does Aristotle say next that the painful and pleasant are [only] nearly always followed by heating and chilling (701b35ff.)? One might have thought that there are some cases of pleasure which are not followed by heating and chilling (even when grasped by thought or imagination): those that are not objects of pursuit or avoidance (because they are remote in time or place). Such cases might arise if the theoretical intellect thinks of something which is pleasant but there is no desire to obtain it.

[12] Confidence will always occur with, and be suffused by, a type of heating: that type of heating which (if the argument of Chapter 1 is correct) always co-occurs with, and is defined by, confidence.

Stage [3]   The *connate pneuma* expands or contracts.
Stage [4]   The limbs (including bones and sinews) move.

At Stage [1], the subject perceives an object which inspires fear or confidence. Aristotle describes these perceptions as, in their own nature (*euthus*), quality changes (701b17) which give rise to further quality changes in the perceiver. Elsewhere this stage is described as 'perceiving by itself' or 'merely perceiving' (431a8). It consists in seeing the object and is to be sharply distinguished from seeing that object *as* pleasant. When the object perceived is (in fact) pleasant, we may not merely perceive it but as a result (at Stage [2]) also visually respond to its pleasantness (by seeing it as pleasant) and therein desire it (431a8–10).[13] A similar distinction is drawn in the case of thinking of or imagining an object. We begin by merely thinking of or imagining it (Stage [I]). When the object thought of or imagined is, in fact, pleasant or painful, we respond accordingly (Stage [2]). In these cases, Aristotle says 'the form of an object which is pleasant or painful has the same impact [on us] as the object itself' (701b20–1).

At Stage [1], when the object is discriminated perceptually or in imagination or thought, we may be presented as judging, for example, 'This is a drink' (see 701a32). In *De Motu*, when such judgements are attributed to perception, thought, or imagination (in 701a32f.), 'this' refers to the object which is, in fact, pleasant or painful, the one which is, in fact, feared, desired, expected etc. There is nothing to suggest that perceiving by itself, or mere perceiving, involves seeing the object *as* pleasant or good. In the case of fear, you may see, at Stage [1], someone who might harm you, an enemy or someone with a gun, and on seeing them become afraid (Stage [2]). In cases involving imagination or thought, you will initially imagine or think of something which is, in fact, a threat to you, and as a result become afraid.[14]

Aristotle refers to fear and confidence, Stage [2] phenomena, as occurring in the inner regions around the origins of the organic parts (702b21). The heating and cooling, which 'occurs with' them, leads to changes in an adjacent part of the organism (701b15f.), where the *connate pneuma* is situated (Stage [3]: 703a10ff.). It expands and contracts (703a22ff.: see 701b12ff.) in the way required to move the limbs.

Aristotle extends his account to cases in which, at Stage [1], the object in question is remembered or anticipated (702a5–7). Here memory and anticipation, not perception, generate desire which generates further affections (at Stage [3]: 702a12ff.), which result in the animal's walking (Stage [4]: 702a15–16). Aristotle sums up these cases as follows:

---

[13] For further discussion of this account, see my 'Aristotle's Desire' (2006: 19–40).
[14] It may be that in less scientific contexts, such as the *Ethics*, he talks of perception of what is fearful or pleasant which suggests that the latter are part of the content of perception. But even if this is so, it does not undermine the account given in *De Anima* or *De Motu* in his more scientific psychology.

imagination (at Stage [1]) prepares desire (*orexis*), which in turn prepares certain affections, resulting in the 'organic parts' (here, presumably the limbs) moving.
(702a16–20)

The affections at Stage [3] are again caused by heating and cooling, as in the case which begins with perception. Imagining and thinking play the role of perceiving in the earlier account (701b16–18).

In generalizing his account, Aristotle re-describes the second stage of the relevant sequence, presenting the four stages as follows (702a15–18):

[1]* The object of pursuit is imagined (remembered or anticipated or perceived)
[2]* The object is desired (*orexis*)
[3]* Certain affections occur (see reference 'to the account we have given of them', 702a15): the expansion and contraction (mentioned in 701b13ff.)
[4]* The limbs move (the animal walks)

Desire has replaced fear, confidence, and sexual arousal at Stage [2]. This, too, should not come as a surprise: confidence, fear, and sexual arousal were initially introduced as examples of a more general phenomenon: something is perceived as painful or pleasant and cooling or heating follows (702a1–2). The heating which is essential to anger (if understood as a hot type of desire for revenge) will occur whenever what is experienced is painful. But, more generally, heating or cooling will occur in this way in all cases of desire for the pleasant: sensual desires (*epithumia*) (701b33ff.). These too will be inextricably psycho-physical per se causes of the resulting bodily changes.

There is, it must be ceded, considerable unclarity about the range of Aristotle's claims about desire in *De Motu* 702a12ff.[15] It is certainly true that he uses the term 'desire' ('*orexis*') for cases beyond those of sensual desire as when speaking of thought as bringing about states which (in turn) lead to changes in the organ which causes the limbs to move (701b33, 701b16ff., picking up the reference in 701a33). Since the desire that precedes movement (701a35) can be brought about by thought, it will sometimes result from reasoning from general premises (as in 701a15ff.). The final desire can be brought about by reasoning (701a36) and may

---

[15] Nor is this the only unclarity: in 702a19 Aristotle replaces his earlier talk of thought, perception, or imagination (701a16, see 701b34: thought and imagination) by a reference to 'imagination brought on by perception or thought'. However, this may simply be a comment on the example considered in the immediately preceding lines: one involving (e.g.) walking towards some non-present object which is remembered or hoped for (702a7ff.), where the memory or anticipation arises from perception or thought. It need not show that imagination is always present prior to action. (At this point I am indebted to discussion with Jean-Louis Labarrière.) It is also unclear in *De Motu* 701b34 (i) whether the object of pursuit grasped by thought and imagination is an external object (such as a friend or a drink) or an internal one (such as the 'representation' of an external object) and (ii) whether it is grasped simply as (e.g.) a drink or rather as a drink to be obtained (or as pleasant). These issues lie outside the scope of this essay.

be (or be based on) a rational wish (701a37). This is perhaps why he begins his discussion in *De Motu* 8 by talking generally of what is to be pursued or avoided, which presumably includes objects beyond those of sensual desire. So, it may seem that, in his view, heating and cooling occur with all desire (*orexis*), not just sensual desire.[16] However, he is not explicit on this point in *De Motu*. Perhaps he was content to indicate that there are bodily processes involved, while not speculating (beyond his evidence) about their exact nature.

3.5 Desire, confidence, and the *connate pneuma*: their role in action

We need, at this point, to address some basic questions about Stages [2] and [3] in Aristotle's model.[17] Three are central to our investigation:

(1) In what way is fear, confidence, and sexual arousal, at Stage [2] connected with the heating and cooling which occur 'with them' (702a4f.)?
(2) How are the expansions and contractions of the *connate pneuma* at Stage [3] best understood?
(3) How does desire at Stage [2] produce the relevant movements in the *connate pneuma* at Stage [3]?

Aristotle's focus on fear and confidence in these passages recalls his discussion of psycho-physical passions and actions in *De Anima*. We are now told that the heating and cooling which occur 'with' fear and confidence will 'follow' thought or imagination of an object which is pleasant or to be pursued (701b35) because they are caused by those thoughts, imaginings, or perceptions of such objects (701b16f.). Some external objects which are pleasant or painful, when perceived, generate sexual arousal and fear: pleasant or painful bodily affections (702a2–4). If the latter are inextricably psycho-physical phenomena (702b4),[18] heating and cooling will occur 'with them' (702a2–4) because they are to be defined in matter-

---

[16] Perhaps he thought that all such desires involved the object being thought or imagined as pleasant or painful (701b35f.). Or perhaps he thought such desires were cases of being attracted to an appropriate object of desire (e.g. the fine) in ways similar to that in which sensual desire is attracted to the pleasant. Perhaps he thought that all such desires involved the object being thought or imagined as pleasant or painful (701b35f.). Or perhaps he thought such desires were cases of being attracted to an appropriate object of desire (e.g. the fine) in ways similar to that in which sensual desire is attracted to the pleasant. Gabriel Richardson Lear develops this line of thought in (2006: 116–36).

[17] I shall consider Stage [1] and its connection with Stage [2] in Chapter 6, Sections 1–3.

[18] I am inclined to take 'the painful and the pleasant' in 701b36f. as referring to painful and pleasant affections, later referred to as 'bodily pains and pleasures' in 702a3. For what is clear from the passions is something about such bodily states. It is not clear whether in the earlier phrase 'the pleasant is pursued' (7021b36), 'the pleasant' refers to an external object (which is pleasant) or to one seen as pleasant. (My interpretation can accommodate either option.)

involving ways. Heating will occur 'with' anger because the latter is defined as a hot desire for revenge. If so, the way in which anger occurs 'with' heating will be different from that in which it 'accompanies' perception or thought of the object. While the latter indicates the step from Stage [1] to [2], the former suggests that the phenomena at Stage [2], such as desire or fear, will be defined, in the way suggested in *De Anima*, in a way that essentially involves matter. They will be 'common to body and soul' in the same demanding way anger is.[19]

Is this Aristotle's considered view in *De Motu*? To address this question, we need to consider how desire at Stage [2] generates expansion and contraction in the *connate pneuma* (at Stage [3]) in the way required for action. If desire is the unified per se cause of the relevant bodily changes and is so in virtue of its formal nature, its form, the type of capacity it is, will have to be inextricably enmattered.

The contractions and expansions of the *connate pneuma* are caused by heat or coldness. As Aristotle notes: 'The parts expand because of heat and contract because of cold' (701b15f.).

It is the heat that 'co-occurs with' anger (understood as the desire for revenge) that generates this expansion, which—when all goes well—moves the relevant sinews and bones (701b6ff.) in the way required for appropriate bodily action.

How is the effect in the *connate pneuma* to be understood? Aristotle compared its movements with those of pegs and cables set in motion by a puppeteer (701b2–4, 7–8) or of small carts pushed by a child.[20] The activities of the child and of the puppet-master resemble those of the weaver: goal-directed physical movements.[21] In fact, Aristotle's discussion of *pneuma* and its movements develops just this analogy. Thus, in discussing animal reproduction, he compares the relevant processes with the actions of craftworkers (*De Generatione Animalium* 744b32ff.). He writes:

> heat and cold soften and harden the iron, but they do not produce the sword; this is done by the movement of the instruments employed which contains the formula (*logos*) of the art. For the art is the starting point and form of what is produced.

The movements are defined as the ones required for the production of the desired result: they contain 'the formula (*logos*) of the craft'. Sword-making provides a clear example: the spatial movements of the swordsmith contain the formula (*logos*) of the art: one is not able to define the relevant processes without reference

---

[19] For a similar use of 'with', see *N.E./E.E.* 1144b27ff. where full virtue is, it seems, defined in terms of practical wisdom with which it occurs.
[20] The case of the young child may be introduced to exemplify imperfect control of the limbs, leading to actions which are not as planned.
[21] There is, it should be noted, a dispute as to whether the case of the puppeteer is like, or unlike, that of the small child in this respect. We do not need to attempt to resolve that issue here.

to the goals of the craftworkers involved and their skill. Their movements are guided in the appropriate way by their skill when they heat, mould, and hammer the metal in the way required to make the sword they aim to produce. Their actions, like those of the weaver mentioned earlier, are examples of inextricably psycho-physical processes, in contrast to purely physical processes, which soften or harden the iron, but do not produce the sword.[22]

It is important to note that the movements of *pneuma* involved in reproduction will, in a similar way, not be definable without reference to the goals and capacities of the agent. While they will result from the nature of the parent, not art or conscious reasoning (744a33–6, see 740b27–36), their nature and identity will be determined by the relevant capacities and goals of the agent (*De Partibus Animalium* 640b1–3 and *De Generatione Animalium* 734b11–18). Just as swordsmiths move their hands and use certain materials in ways appropriate for their goal, so generating parents operate on certain materials in ways appropriate for their goal.

The expansion and contraction of *pneuma* in cases of action production, if they resemble the movements of the puppeteer, will follow the same pattern: the relevant type of expansion or contraction cannot be defined without reference to the goals and capacities (such as action-producing skills) of the agent. They will be essentially the types of expansion and contraction involved in achieving these goals. The relevant types of increasing or decreasing of the *connate pneuma* will be just the ones required if the agent (like the puppeteer) is to reach his (or her) goal. From Aristotle's viewpoint, nothing more needs to be said about the types of movement involved. He has indicated, by means of his analogies with craft activity, the general category in which these movements fall and pointed to the general bodily features required for expansion and contraction of the required type (703a21–7). In his terminology, they will be, in the sense already explained, 'common to body and soul'. They are not purely physical processes defined independently of matter: they are inextricably psycho-physical, goal-directed, processes.

We are now in a position to address our central question: how does desire have to be if it is to produce hardening or softening and expansion or contraction of the goal-directed type required: bodily changes which, in Aristotle's phrase, 'contain the formula' of what the agent is aiming at? Do the heating and cooling occur 'with it' in the same demanding way as they occur with anger and fear?

It appears that they must do. To produce the changes in the *connate pneuma*, desire, when actualized, has to be a type of bodily process which also contains the formula of what the agent is seeking. Desiring has to heat and expand the *connate*

---

[22] Aristotle gives other examples involving various types of skilled activity, such as weaving and building (*De Anima* 408b10ff.). See, for example, *De Partibus Animalium*. 640b1–3, *Meteorologica* 390b11–14 (craft in general). In these cases, the craft will be defined in terms of its bodily activities.

pneuma (and its surroundings) in the ways required to produce the goal-directed results required. As the situation changes, desire will need to adjust these movements so as to achieve its goal. It is the unified cause of the expansion of the *connate pneuma* in a way which is sensitive to the goal to be achieved. The capacity to desire, as the unified cause, is actualized in this psycho-physical activity: heating the *connate pneuma* in just the way required to produce the agent's goal. (This is how the specific material movements there 'carry the relevant form': *De Generatione Animalium* 734b32ff.).

Desire, when exercised, heats the *connate pneuma* in the ways already indicated. Since there is only one capacity referred to (viz. the capacity to desire), this must be a heat-involving capacity. The type of heating, we already know, is one which has the power to produce just the desired movements in the animal. The activity in question is the distinctive type of heating which is, in its nature, sensitive to the goals to be achieved. (Individual activities are essentially activities of this type.) Desire, in order to move the *connate pneuma* in the ways required, must itself be the exercise of a goal-directed material capacity: a capacity to heat in a way sensitive to the goals to be achieved, exercised in a distinctive type of inextricably goal-sensitive heating. One cannot define the type of heating without explicit reference to its goal-sensitivity. Nor can one define the specific type of goal-sensitivity without reference to heating. If so, desire will be defined (at least in part) as the capacity for this type of inextricably psycho-physical activity. As such, it must be an inextricably enmattered capacity (with an impure form).

It should come as no surprise that Aristotle developed this view of desire and the capacity to desire. That both should be defined as inextricably material phenomena is what was to be expected given his general account of the forms of natural substances (as interpreted in Chapter 2). They need to be of this type to be unified per se causes of the resulting unified bodily movements. In *De Motu* we see his general model being deployed in giving a detailed account of the processes which lead from perception to bodily action.

Desiring, so understood, is a unitary bodily (or material) capacity simultaneously goal-directed and the per se cause of the subsequent bodily changes. There has to be just one capacity at work in initiating and controlling the required goal-directed process in the *connate pneuma*. It is not that desire merely initiates a bodily movement which is intelligible as a goal-directed activity. The activity unfolds in ways which are causally sensitive to the goals, and so the content, of desire. A strongly unified, goal-directed material capacity, is required as the per se cause of the resulting strongly unified, goal-directed, bodily activity. There is no suggestion that the latter activity is the joint product of two independently defined capacities, one purely physical, the other psychological or psycho-physical. Nor is Aristotle concerned to address the issues which naturally arise if one adopts a two-component account: how do the components combine to form a unified effect? Is there over-determination by two independent causes? Is the psychological epiphenomenal? This is because, given his own perspective, they do not arise. (I shall return to these issues in Chapter 7.)

Against this general background, it is not surprising that Aristotle confines himself to remarking that the part of the body in question is one whose movements are naturally well suited to perform its appropriate function (703a35ff.). In expanding and contracting, the *connate pneuma* (i) produces large spatial movements at the periphery of the body as a consequence of (sometimes) relatively small heatings and coolings in the region of the heart (701b24ff.), (ii) brings about the specific spatial movements (such as in the case of weaving) required to achieve the agent's goals, and (iii) is made of the right material to push and pull: 'it is heavy in comparison with the fiery and light by comparison with its opposite' (703a23–5). The *pneuma* is the right type of thing to be impacted by heat in the way required to bring about a complex and desired result.[23] It is the type of material base which possesses the material features required to produce just these movements.[24]

Aristotle, it should be noted, does add one further effect of the heating and cooling which 'occur with' fear or desire: it changes the inner parts next to the organic parts from solid to supple, from soft to hard and vice versa (702a7ff.) as well as generating expansion and contraction of the *connate pneuma*.[25] (It is not clear why this further detail is added.[26] Perhaps hardening of the relevant organ is needed to provide the solid, unmoved container within which the *pneuma* can expand and contract in the ways required to move the limbs of the animal.)[27] In

---

[23] Freudenthal spells out a general theory of this type in his monograph (1995).

[24] Even if several types of material base could play this role, all the varying realizing states would have material features of this general type.

[25] There are several ways to understand his remark:

(a) the bodily organs next to the organic parts (the ones that house the *connate pneuma*: stage 3) change from being hard to soft (and vice versa) as a result of the heating and cooling that occurs with anger and fear;
(b) both the bodily organs next to the organic parts (that 'house' the *connate pneuma*) and those that 'house' desire change as a result of the heating and cooling that occurs with desire.

Aristotle's actual phrase 'the inner parts and those that are around the beginnings of the organic parts' (702a7ff.) might suggest (b), but could equally refer only to (a) (taking the 'and' as epexegetic or clarificatory). However, either way, he is referring to a stage which happens after the heating and cooling which co-occur with 'fear or confidence' but before the movement of the organic limbs. This stage involves, in some way, the *connate pneuma* [Stage [3]].

[26] This issue is discussed further by Klaus Corcilius and Pavel Gregoric (2013: 70–1) and Pavel Gregoric and Martin Kuhar (2014: 99–100). Corcilius and Gregoric conjecture that the alteration within the flesh around the joints is a second effect of the thermic alteration connected with desire (in addition to the pneuma's pushing and pulling), but not mediated by the *connate pneuma*. Gregoric and Kuhar (2014: 99ff.) suggest that the thermic alteration responsible for the solidification and softening of the flesh around the joint is transmitted by blood through the vascular system—as opposed to the pushing and pulling that uses the system of *neura*.

[27] There is talk of platforms also in *De Motu* 2–3. Perhaps this is a place where this material is deployed in the discussion of action. For discussion of platforms, see the papers by Ursula Coope and Benjamin Morison (2020).

any event, this further effect is presented as a second specific type of bodily change for which the relevant heating and cooling are responsible.

3.6 Instruments, joints, etc.

Aristotle's more detailed discussion spells out his general picture. In the course of his lengthy and speculative account of the 'joint-like' nature of the part which moves the organic limbs, he notes that there must be something which moves that part (703a1–3) which is 'distinct from a magnitude of the type of body just mentioned, but in it'. Further he identifies that which moves as the soul (or its desiderative capacity) and contrasts this with the organ which contains the *connate pneuma*. The joint, in some way, connects the desiderative capacity (as the unmoved mover) and the *connate pneuma*. The former, when active, accounts for contraction and solidification in the latter.[28] I shall consider these additional claims for the sake of completeness. It may be reassuring to see Aristotle's general picture at work in the fine details of his account.

Aristotle suggests that 'what first causes movement...must be in a definite starting place' (702a23) and seems to identify the first cause with desire (702a18).[29] This starting point is in a joint [J], one part of which is at rest [A] while the other [B] is moved (702a25–6) [or moves/is in motion]. Since [B] also causes movement: it is a moved mover. In Aristotle's picture, we find:

(i) [J] described as the whole joint that is potentially one but actually two (702a30–1).
(ii) [J] is where the starting place which belongs to the soul is situated (702a31–702b12).
(iii) [J] as a whole is not itself part of any larger joint [J*]: (702b6–8).

Desire, it appears, is located in [A], that part of the joint which is at rest. This is the aspect of the soul referred to in (ii).[30]

---

[28] In 703a1–2, Aristotle points to a type of activity (or way of being) which is not itself a body (magnitude) although it is situated in a body. Compare his remarks on perceiving in *De Anima* 424a25ff. The soul (or its relevant aspect) need not be unmoved (under this interpretation) although the unmoved (spatial) part of the joint is. Indeed, the two should be sharply separated: the soul is not that phenomenon which plays the role of A in the original diagram (*De Motu* 702b26–703a1). At this point, the aspect of the soul which generates movement could be desire (which is itself moved) but is not a spatial magnitude.

[29] Desire may be substituted for desiderative thinking that one should go (702a16f.).

[30] In *De Motu* 9, Aristotle, in considering a more complex case, adds a further relevant detail:

(iv) [J] is in the central part of the body (702b15–21).
(v) [J] is potentially one, but actually more than one (702b26ff.)—a modification of (i) in the light of the more complex case now being considered: 702b25–34.

In the more complex case:

How is desire connected with the magnitude [A] in which it is situated? The very same terminology is employed as in *De Anima* 424a26ff., where perception is said not to be a spatial magnitude but present in one as a capacity of such a magnitude (bodily organ). The soul will be a capacity, not itself a magnitude. If the soul is present in [A], it will be present as a capacity in [A] in the way in which perception (as a form) is a capacity in the perceptual organ. Both will be defined, in the favoured snub-like way, as capacities-in-A, essentially material capacities, not as pure capacities which are present in matter. The forms in question will be inextricably enmattered.

Aristotle had earlier talked of a joint in which one aspect is unmoved and another moved: 'there must be something at rest if one is to be moved and the other to impart movement' (702a28–30). He now adds even more detail:

> So the extended point (*sēmeion*), although potentially one, becomes two in actuality... so that both these starting points [B and C] must both be moved and impart movement. There must be something beyond these [the moved movers] which moves and is not moved. (702a30–5)

Aristotle introduces the complex joint [J] (with physical size) which has two types of parts: one unmoved [A] and another moved (the latter being starting points of the two movements of [B] and [C] respectively, taking 'these' in 701a34 to refer to the moved movers in J, not to J as a whole). On this reading, the unmoved part [A] is distinct in actuality from the moved and moving parts: [B] and [C]: 702b35. [A] is, it seems, the spatial magnitude in which the soul is located, which remains at rest and supports [B] and [C] which push against it.[31]

The soul located in [A], is—to use terminology Aristotle employs elsewhere— the relevant cause. It is the capacity whose exercise is A's moving [B] and [C].

[A] is at rest but there are two (or more) moved movers [B, C, etc.] which produce changes in different limbs:

In this case:
(vi) There is an unmoved mover separate from [B] and [C]: 702b33–703a1.
(vii) [B] and [C] need something at rest which is a mover (702b34–6).
(viii) The mover which moves [B] and [C] is the soul: it is situated in a magnitude of the type described but different from it (taking 'this' in 703a3 to refer to the mover in 703a2 which is presumably unmoved: 702b34–5).

In (viii), it appears that the type of magnitude (*megethos*) in which the soul is situated is [A] while [B] and [C], on the other side of the hinge, are moved by the soul. At this point, the soul is a mover situated in a magnitude which is at rest [A] and which moves [B] and [C]. Further, the soul and [A] are said to be distinct, even though the soul is situated in [A].

---

[31] An alternative would be to take [A] as referring to a spatial part of the joint which is distinct from the soul but affected by it. However, this suggestion seems merely to push the question one stage further back: (i) why is this part of the joint itself unmoved if it is moved by the soul? (ii) how is it affected by the soul if not by a joint? (Perhaps [A] might be regarded as a 'platform' within the joint.)

In this passage, the capacity is taken as the cause of the relevant expansion and contraction in the *connate pneuma*. We also know where this capacity is spatially located: in a joint-like structure at the centre of the body (see 702b25). It has to be there to be a cause, when active, of the expansion and contraction of the *connate pneuma* by heating and cooling (703a8–10). As such, this capacity is essentially spatially located at a given position in the body and is able to cause other parts of the body to move by heating them. That desire is this type of capacity emerges in what follows.

Aristotle continues, relying, it must be ceded, on a less than fully perspicuous analogy:

> The moved mover (the organ for the *connate pneuma*) STANDS TO the psychic origin of movement (the soul/desiderative capacity) AS the moved and moving part in joint STANDS TO the unmoved part of a joint. (703a10–12)

The psychic origin of movement (which we now know to be the desiderative capacity) is located in [A] and its activity causes the organ for the *connate pneuma* to harden, soften, contract, and expand. The instrument (or joint: [J]) has as an unmoved part [A] which houses, in the first instance, the desiderative capacity, while its moved part [B] (or parts if [C] is included) are moved movers—to be identified with the *connate pneuma*, which itself is moved and moves the limbs.[32]

Why talk of 'joints' at all?[33] In Aristotle's account, joints are mechanisms for pulling and pushing: one side has the power to move the other in this way.[34] In the present case, the desiderative faculty, in its operation, has the power (by heating) to move the *connate pneuma* (making it expand and contract) which in turn moves (pushes and pulls) the elbow, hands, stick, etc. Aristotle's talk of 'joints' locates the transition between desiderative faculty and the movements of the *connate pneuma* within the general framework of his general physical theory. He is, in effect, employing that theory, with its distinctive resources of pushing and pulling, to focus on the inextricably psycho-physical desiderative capacity (or desiderative soul) and its activity in moving the *connate pneuma*.[35]

---

[32] For a contrasting view of this passage, see Corilius and Gregoric (2013: 52–97). They see the soul as situated at [A] as the 'unmoved point which turns certain motions in the body into perceptual motions that in turn spawn other motions in the animal's body' (p. 87). In their view, the cognitive activity of the soul, located at this point, makes certain alterations of the heart have an 'intentional dimension' (p. 95) which then serves to account for voluntary action.

[33] I am indebted to Christof Rapp for discussions of this issue.

[34] These issues are helpfully studied by Istvan Bodnár (2004: 137, 156) and Sylvia Berryman (2009: 67–8, 157). For relevant illustrative passages, see *Mech.* 3, 850a 35ff. and *Mech.* 8, 851b 16–21, 154. Most would now agree that these treatises derive from a Peripatetic context. Some are open to the possibility that they were written by Aristotle himself. I do not intend to examine this issue here.

[35] This is why Aristotle emphasizes that the points in question have extension, unlike purely mathematical points: *De Motu* 698a25–b3, 702b21.

Why is the desiderative capacity unmoved? Indeed, how can it be if active desire essentially involves becoming hot under the influence of some external object? Surely desire is, and is recognized to be, a moved mover: 703a5–6?

In Aristotle's picture, the desiderative capacity (and the faculty understood as an organ together with its capacity) is not changed or altered when the person desires to act. Active desire is the realization of a capacity of that faculty, but neither the capacity nor the faculty alters when they are realized in this way. The change in question is, as we shall see in *De Anima* B.5, not a destructive change: one which changes the nature of the thing which changes.[36] The desiderative faculty is, in this respect, like the unmoved side of the joint. Further, as an essentially psycho-physical faculty, the desiderative faculty has spatial position and the power to move other objects. It is, in this respect, an unmoved mover.

That desiring (in activity) is the type of process (or activity) caused by something external (and in the middle) is consistent with the desiderative capacity and faculty themselves remaining unchanged. Desiring is the realization of the relevant capacity brought about in this way by the object desired. However, this realization does not cause the capacity itself to change. The activity of desire brings about changes in the *connate pneuma*, while the faculty (and capacity) of desire remains unmoved.

In sum: when in *De Motu* he talks of the role of joints (698a15ff., 703a12ff.) in spelling out more fully the type of instrument mentioned in *De Anima*, Aristotle is seeking to develop the following ideas:

(a) The desiderative capacity, to be identified with the desiderative soul, the form itself, is unmoved (it is not changed in its operation).
(b) The desiderative capacity is located at a specific spatial position and causes changes in the *connate pneuma* (it is an unmoved mover); it is located near the organ which houses the *connate pneuma*.
(c) The unified activities of the desiderative capacity are types of heating and expanding where the latter generate pushing and pulling (701a17–23, 28–31).

His talk of 'joints' is his way of capturing these ideas about the psycho-physical capacities and organs involved, as well as their distinctive psycho-physical operations. He could have stated his view more simply, if less elegantly, in just these terms. But that said: talk of 'joints' and 'instruments' provides a vivid picture of how bodily movements are caused by desire within the framework of his physical theory. To talk in this way is to emphasize the inextricably psycho-physical nature of the relevant causal capacities and their strongly unified activities. They are essentially material and goal-sensitive bodily capacities.

---

[36] For further discussion of *De Anima* B.5, see Chapter 4.

3.7 Desire and action: an overview of Aristotle's account

We can now better understand the background to Aristotle's initially unnerving remark in *De Anima* 433b13ff.:

> The instrument by which desire moves the animal is a bodily one: this is why it must be investigated among the functions common to body and soul.

Desire, understood as the realization of the capacity to desire, moves the body by generating movements of the *connate pneuma*. These movements are essentially psycho-physical: changes in size and shape of the type required to move the limbs so as to act. In order for this to happen, the *connate pneuma* must itself be heavy (at least compared with fire), capable of expanding and contracting, pushing and pulling (703a22ff.). Talk of 'instruments' and 'joints' locates these processes within Aristotle's general physical theory.

If desire, as a capacity, is to cause the *connate pneuma* to move in these ways, it must itself be an essentially and inextricably enmattered capacity: a capacity for a psycho-physical type of activity.[37] It is because desire is an activity of this type of capacity that it moves the body by means of a psycho-physical instrument. The capacity is actualized in the specific type of heat-involving, goal-directed, activity which generates changes in the *connate pneuma*. Its activity is the basic per se cause of the movements of the *connate pneuma* and of the resulting movements of the body (themselves understood as psycho-physical processes).[38]

If desire, when active, is to impact on the *connate pneuma* in the ways described, it must be a specific type of heating. If sensual desiring is seeing A as pleasant, the relevant type of seeing will be a hot type of seeing ('hot cognition'). The type of desire must itself be defined as an essentially and inextricably material capacity if it is to be the basic per se efficient cause of movements which require heating, pushing, dragging, and expanding.[39] While Aristotle, as we have seen,

---

[37] Since it is of the essence of the relevant process of heating that it is psycho-physical, its nature will be (in principle) distinct from any type of process which is not essentially psycho-physical in this way. One cannot define this type of heating in terms of ordinary heating or cooling since it essentially serves certain goals. It might be labelled 'vital heat', understood as the type of heat which essentially serves certain teleological goals in the organism.

[38] In this respect, the desiderative faculty in activity is like the builder building: the latter, *qua* builder, remains unchanged in the process (*De Anima* 417b9ff.).

[39] Aristotle describes both desire and (by implication) the *connate pneuma* as 'moved movers' (703a4–7), but, as I have argued, this need not commit him to identifying them. He has already marked out the *connate pneuma*, as what is moved and moves (702b33ff.: see 703a13ff.) and may simply be comparing its role with that of desire. Later in *De Motu* 10 Aristotle specifies the nature of the *connate pneuma* as being to expand and contract (703a21) while earlier he had associated fear and sexual arousal with heating and cooling (702a6ff.). If desire plays the same role as fear and anger, it must be connected with heating and cooling, not with the expansion and contraction that follows. So understood, desire should be associated with (e.g.) warm blood moving around the heart (or with what is hot: *De Anima* 403a31ff.) rather than with the different physical properties of the *connate*

attempts to spell out his account in considerable detail, his discussion is motivated through its many (sometimes idiosyncratic) complexities by this overriding, and deeply motivated, perspective.

In sum: in Aristotle's account, one cannot define desire as a capacity simply for a type of heating (without reference to its psychological object or goal) since the relevant type of heating is directed towards this goal. Nor can it be defined in solely psychological terms (as seeing A as pleasant) since the relevant type of seeing cannot be defined without reference to heating and cooling of the type required to produce changes in the *connate pneuma*. Remove that and one will not capture the unified per se causal role of sensual desire in moving the body. Desire, if it is to be a unified phenomenon which is both content-directed and a per se cause in the way described, must be inextricably psycho-physical. It is the unified activity of an essentially embodied, or material, capacity.

Desire, so understood, is not the purely psychological phenomenon post-Cartesian interpreters take it to be. It cannot be defined without reference to the specific physical phenomenon 'with which' it occurs. Active desiring is not a purely psychological activity realized in, or constituted by, a particular process of a specific physical type. Indeed, there are, it seems, no further particular physical processes of this type present which are essential to the person's desiring to act (contrary to the materialist account of these phenomena). Nor is it the case that the relevant matter is 'primitively disposed to desire': specific material features, such as heating and cooling, are also essentially required.

When desire and the movements of the *connate pneuma* are understood as 'common to body and soul' in the way suggested, Aristotle's remarks in *De Anima* and *De Motu* about the causal processes leading to action emerge as a relatively straightforward attempt to indicate the essentially psycho-physical capacities and activities involved in bodily actions. His simple theory of desire follows the pattern set by his simple theory of the emotions. They must be defined as inextricably psycho-physical phenomena (with forms of this type) to be per se causes of actions such as moving one's hand or weaving one's cloak.

3.8 Conclusions

Aristotle's account of desire and action, so understood, is not a version of one of the standard options of post-Cartesian philosophy because it rejects its two basic assumptions, labelled [1]* and [2]* in Section 2 above. In his view, desire (understood as an inextricably psycho-physical process of the type defined above) can

---

pneuma (703a22–5). So understood, it will be distinct from the 'instrument' (*De Anima* 433b19) or joint it uses to move the body, where the latter (as we learn in *De Motu*) essentially involves also the *connate pneuma* 703a12ff.) which, in turn, moves the bodily limbs.

simultaneously be a basic per se cause of action and at the same time a goal-directed way of seeing something as (e.g.) pleasant. Armed with this conception, he had no need to address the distinctively Cartesian puzzle with which we began: how can desire, understood as a purely psychological phenomenon, move the animal? This question simply does not arise.

The silences we are naturally inclined to detect in his account should not unnerve us. They reflect his fundamentally different overview of the phenomena themselves.

The unity of desire, as a capacity, as the per se cause of a developing psycho-physical process is important in this account. The standard non-reductionist materialist account loses this feature, separating the psychological aspect from the physical and attributing the real causal work to the latter. There is not, in this view, one type of feature that is both causally efficacious and endowed with mentality. While the features which are causally efficacious (basic per se causes) are purely physical, those available to consciousness or possessed of intentional content, are not. What is lost in this account is the idea of desires themselves as causally efficacious in virtue of their own content.

Stephen Menn, in an important article, has also rejected what he describes as a 'fashionable' hylomorphic account of the soul,[40] itself a version of the two-component interpretation which I have challenged. Menn takes as his starting point Aristotle's description of the body as 'organic' (designed as an instrument (*organon*) for certain purposes) and his talk of desire as 'moving the body with an instrument' (*De Anima* 433b19f.). In Menn's view, the soul, as the user of the body, is separate from it, standing to it as user to used (as the pilot is to the rudder he uses to steer the ship).[41] Since the soul is separate (in this way) from the body, Menn concludes that it must be non-bodily. Indeed, according to his interpretation, Aristotle only avoided (Cartesian) dualism by understanding the soul as being (somehow) like an art which (somehow) 'uses' the tools of its trade and even the artisan to make its products.

There is, however, a gap in Menn's argument. Even if Aristotle thought of the desiring faculty of the soul as inextricably psycho-physical, he can still distinguish it from those parts of the body (the organ in question, such as the *connate pneuma*) which desire uses as an instrument to move the animal. It does not follow from the fact that desire is different from this instrument that it is not a psycho-physical capacity or that its exercise is other than a psycho-physical process.

An analogy may be helpful. The hand, let us assume, is a purely bodily instrument separate, distinct, from the soul. This assumption is fully consistent with thinking that the soul's moving the hand is an essentially psycho-physical process.

---

[40] Menn (2002: 83–109). [41] See *De Anima* 413a9ff.

It does not follow from the fact that the soul moves the body by means of a purely bodily instrument that its *using* that instrument is not a psycho-physical process, the activity of the hylomorphic faculty for desire. Once we distinguish the bodily instrument itself from the agent's using it, it is clear that the agent's moving it can be a psycho-physical process, initiated by other psycho-physical 'passions' or activities of the soul (such as desiring etc.).

Menn's paper raises a further central issue. Even if desire (or the desiderative soul) moves the animal by an 'instrument' (understood as something designed to play a given role), does it do so by 'using' that instrument in the way helmsmen use rudders to steer the ship? Aristotle's comment may mean no more than that desire impacts on an instrument designed to generate the desired movements. Neither it, nor the goals or skills of the agent, need intentionally 'use' such an instrument as the helmsman uses the rudder.[42] Still less does their skill 'use' the agent (or their desires) to achieve their ends. All that is required, in Aristotle's account, is that desire moves part of the body whose teleological function is to bring about the goals at which the agent aims.

While Menn and I are allies in resisting currently 'fashionable', two-component, interpretations, we do so in different ways. My suggestion is that Aristotle treated the relevant phenomena as inextricably matter-involving, not analysable (as they are for Menn's 'fashionable hylomorphists') into two definitionally separate components, one of which is a purely psychological form. He did not do so, as Menn suggests, by thinking of the skill as literally using the agent's body to achieve their goals. Although the skill is the starting point of the relevant process, it is not itself an agent which does, or uses, anything.[43]

In Chapters 4, 5, and 6, I shall examine Aristotle's account of perception. This too suggests that he was not a hylomorphist of the 'fashionable, two-component, variety'. His account follows the pattern set by his simple theory of the emotions and desire. Or so I shall argue.

---

[42] There are, of course, cases where craftworkers are described as 'using' tools (such as an axe or loom) or phenomena such as heat to achieve their goals, when they use them intentionally. In cooking, for example, the cook modifies the heat provided by an external fire in the way required to produce pleasant food (*De Generatione Animalium* 743a33–5). Here a formal nature (the cook's capacity to cook) intentionally uses something with a distinct material nature (the fire, the fish which is cooked). It differs from the examples discussed above in *De Motu* in that in the latter (i) the desire, unlike the cook, is both the source and the controller of the heat required to move the *connate pneuma* in the way required and (ii) the desirer need not have any intentions at all to use the *connate pneuma* (and, indeed, might even be unaware of its existence).

[43] See Chapter 2, Section 6. In Suarez's terms: skill is the cause *quo* (from which), not the cause *quod* (which). The latter is a substance such as Polykleitos.

4
Taste and Smell
With Some Remarks on Touch

4.1 Introduction

Aristotle's description in *De Anima* and parts of *De Sensu* of how animals, including human animals, perceive by tasting and smelling, is the central focus of this chapter.

Many post-Cartesian theories of perception share, as we have noted, two assumptions:

[A]   There is a purely psychological type of feature essentially involved in perceiving, such as being aware of, or perceptually discriminating, a taste or smell;

[B]   All the types of event essentially involved in perceiving are either purely psychological or purely physical or a combination of the purely psychological and the purely physical.[1]

The first assumption can be developed in a variety of ways. In some accounts, we are, in tasting, presented as aware directly of an internal object, a mind-dependent taste, the content of a sensation, which (in some way) represents the external object. In others, we are aware in addition of an external object on the basis of our direct awareness of an internal, mind-dependent object. In still others, the relevant awareness is directly of an external flavoured object.[2] However, in all these accounts, there is an act of awareness whose definition does not contain reference to an internal physical event or physical property in the perceiver. I shall call awareness, so defined, purely psychological. Such accounts inherit, and need to address, our post-Cartesian problem: how does awareness, so understood, relate to the relevant internal physical events, states with their physical properties?

Spiritualist and non-reductionist interpreters agree that Aristotle, in his account of perceiving in *De Anima* and *De Sensu*, shared assumption [A]. In Chapters 5 and 6, I shall argue, in his account of perception he rejected both of these

---

[1] By 'combination' is intended any relation between two definitionally distinct events or two definitionally sets of features (such as properties). The relevant relations may include necessitation or supervenience and are not confined to mere conjunction (or correlation).

[2] In these views, the psychological extends beyond the body. John McDowell has developed this view in a series of papers: see, for example, his (1998: 431–91).

assumptions. Properly to understand his thinking about perception, we need to recover his fundamentally different conception of the psychological.

4.2 Some reminders

Aristotle, it was suggested in Chapter 1, defined anger as a hot, physically qualified, desire for revenge. The type of desiring is an inextricably psycho-physical process (*kinēsis*) with an impure, inextricably psycho-physical, form. It is, in the terms introduced in Chapter 2, the realization of an inextricably material goal-directed capacity. The relevant processes (and capacities) in Aristotle's account are neither purely psychological nor purely physical. Aristotle offered two sets of considerations in favour of these claims. In the case of anger:

[H.1] If there were no appropriate bodily condition present, there would be no suffering of the relevant type

[H.2] The nature of the bodily condition present causally affects the nature of the suffering [*pathēsis*].

In Aristotle's account, the process (or suffering) in question is defined in terms of its inextricably psycho-physical form: it is a hot (boiling-blood) desire for revenge with certain efficient causal antecedents (403a26–7). He also held that the relevant type of heat or blood boiling cannot be defined without essential reference to revenge: it is a desiring-revenge type of heat. In his view:

[H.3] There is one and only one process essentially involved in being angry: the instantiation of one inextricably psycho-physical process type: boiling of the blood for the sake of revenge. No further purely physical process (type or token) is essentially involved in being angry. (This will be true even if some physical processes are necessary background conditions.)[3]

In Chapter 2 it was suggested that Aristotle's view of these emotions parallels his account of the forms of natural objects, which in turn was motivated by his aim of accommodating the latter's role in efficient and teleological causation. In the present chapter, I shall argue that his discussion of tasting, smelling, and touching follows the pattern set by his discussion of anger, fear, and desire (as set out in Chapter 3). [H.1] and [H.2] considerations suggest that these types of perceiving are essentially enmattered in just the way anger is: they have inextricably psycho-physical, impure, forms. They are not defined by decomposition into separate components, one of which is a pure psychological component, definable without

---

[3] As Burnyeat (2001) suggested they might be.

reference in the definition to matter. His view is motivated, once again, by his view of the relevant psychological phenomena (as captured by the form) as per se causes and effects of bodily (or material) processes. I shall further suggest that his discussion exemplifies the pattern set by [H.3]. This is why there is no threat of over-determination by two independent causal processes, one psychological, the other physical. The processes involved are, as was to be expected, inextricably psycho-physical with unified inextricably enmattered causes and effects. His account follows the pattern set by his theory of the emotions and of desire.

Spiritualist interpreters have argued that Aristotle, despite initial appearances to the contrary in *De Anima* A.1, did not apply the model he developed for anger and fear to perception. Whatever his original intentions may have been, in *De Anima* B.5 he gave reasons not to do so, arguing that perceiving, unlike anger or desire, is not a genuine process at all, and hence (*a fortiori*) not an essentially psycho-physical one. In their account, he defined perceiving as essentially only a change in relation, a 'mere Cambridge change', not as a real process (or activity) in the subject of change itself.

I shall challenge their interpretation. While in *De Anima* B.5 Aristotle refined his ontology, he did not, or so I shall argue, offer an account of perception that differs radically in the way they suggest from that of the emotions in *De Anima* A.1. While he presents perceiving as an activity, it is nonetheless an inextricably psycho-physical activity. In his discussion of perception, he is, in effect, further developing his account of processes, activities, and the relevant capacities: the ontology required for his theory. He is not, it should be noted at the outset, relying on the undifferentiated category of events deployed in most contemporary writing on this topic and exemplified in Assumptions [A] and [B].[4] His account of perception differs in important ways from those with which we are most familiar in part because it rests on his own distinctive ontology. This will become clearer in considering his detailed discussion of ontological issues in *De Anima* B.5.

4.3 Perceiving: ontology refined

In *De Anima* A.1, Aristotle talked of anger as a process (*kinēsis*). In *De Anima* B.5, he distinguishes two types of sufferings (*paschein*: 417b2) or changes (*metabolē*: 417b17), separating:

[Type 1] changes: changes which are 'a type destruction by a contrary' (417b2)

---

[4] We have been accustomed to talk of events because of our familiarity with the work of Davidson, Russell, and McTaggart.

and

[Type 2] changes: changes from potentiality (or capacity) to actuality: *entelecheia* (417b3–5) in which 'there is instead a preservation of what is potentially [in some way] by what is actually [in the same way] where the former is like the latter as potentiality stands to actuality'.

Some or all [Type 2] changes, he says, are either not quality changes at all or else a different type of quality change (417b6–8). Since quality changes are the relevant types of processes (*kinēseis*), these [Type 2] changes are either not processes at all or else a different type of process from [Type 1] changes.[5] He also provides, or so it seems, two examples of [Type 2] changes. While in both the initial capacity is maintained throughout the change, they differ in important respects. In the first case [Type 2A], the subject exercises knowledge already possessed (417b5–12), while in the second [Type 2B], the subject acquires knowledge: as a child does when taught (417b12–15).

Aristotle describes the former case, that of exercising knowledge, as follows:

> The one who has knowledge becomes a theorizer, which change (becoming) is either not a quality change (for it is a change towards itself and the relevant actuality) or a different kind of quality change.[6] This is why it is not a fine thing to say that the thinker, whenever they think, undergoes a quality change or the builder whenever they build. (417b5–9)

The transition to being a theorizer (being an actual, that is an active, knower) consists in the activity of using one's knowledge. In the same way one becomes an actual thinker (or builder) in virtue of thinking or using one's skill as a builder. In the case of knowledge, the change from the state of being a potential to that of being an actual knower consists in the activation of the knowledge at one's disposal. It is not good, Aristotle comments, to describe this activity as a quality change. To do so is either literally false (if it is not a quality change) or, at best, misleading because it conceals the fact that it is a distinctive type of quality

---

[5] These changes are not spatial processes (*phorai*) or changes in quantity either: the other possible candidates. (See for a list of the relevant standard types of process: *Physics* H.1, 243a35ff.)

[6] In this translation I take '*theorizer*' to refer to the state of the one who knows in the authoritative way (*epistamenos kuriōs*: 417a29), 'to itself' to refer to being a knower in this way, and '*entelecheia*' to the state such a knower is in. The transition to this state (*epidosis*) consists in actively using one's knowledge. Hicks, it should be noted, achieves a broadly similar understanding of 417b5–6 although translating it somewhat differently: 'for that which has knowledge becomes an actual knower by *theorizing* which is an advance towards the thing itself'. In the case of knowledge, the transition to being a knower may also be a transition to the nature of the subject in question (if the subject is defined as a knower). But this may be a special feature of the example of knowledge, not a general requirement on all [Type 2] changes.

change, different from standard [Type 1] changes. He does not seem concerned to decide at this point which of these alternative ways of labelling [Type 2A] changes is to be preferred: his goal is only to distinguish them from [Type 1] changes.

Aristotle had discussed both sorts of [Type 2] change in the immediately preceding passage (417a20–b2), distinguishing the person who uses knowledge already possessed (417a29–30) from one who learns (417a31–2) and has, as a result of learning, 'been altered in quality, often changing from a contrary state'. In the latter case, the learner acquires a new state (*hexis*): being possessed of knowledge which they are capable of exercising there and then. Their being in that state, being a knower capable of exercising their knowledge, is the relevant achievement. Their state is not itself a capacity: it is the way they are when they are capable of certain activities. Being capable of speaking French is not itself a capacity.[7] In the former case, by contrast, the final achievement is described as that of being an active speaker of French: the state a person is in when they are exercising the knowledge they possess.[8] Both could be described as changes 'towards' the actuality (*entelecheia*) in question: in one case this would be to the state of being able to speak French, in the other to actually speaking French.

In the passage just cited (417b2–6), Aristotle distinguishes both cases of [Type 2] change from all [Type 1] changes. Later he confirms that [2B] and [2A] cases all differ from [Type 1] changes ('as was remarked', in effect, at the outset).[9] What is the basis for his distinction? One suggestion runs as follows:

---

[7] This point is important for a question raised at the end of Chapter 2: are enmattered forms capacities or actualities? It seems that, in this discussion, forms should be identified not with capacities but with the actual states in which their possessor is capable of acting: their being such as to be capable of acting. This is the way they are: their way of being. (For further discussion: see Chapter 7, Section 6.)

[8] In 417a22–b2, Aristotle focuses on distinguishing different ways of being a knower: being an actual and potential (in various ways) knower. He is separating different states one may be in, not classifying different processes or activities. In 417b2–16, by contrast, he is discussing processes (sufferings) of various types. Since states are not processes, Aristotle is not identifying the state of being a master of French with learning French or the state of being a currently active French speaker with currently speaking French. One will, of course, become a master of French by learning French and a currently active French speaker by (in virtue of) speaking French. But, nonetheless, it is a mistake to identify any of the states mentioned in 417a22–b2 with the various types of processes (sufferings: described after 417b2) which are required for those states to be present. Nor is there any sign that Aristotle, with his customary attention to the relevant ontology, made it. There is no reason to interpret him as identifying one who has mastered a skill (417a25: the knower) with their learning that skill (being led: 417b10ff.). Nor should one identify people coming to be in the state of being an active speaker of French (in virtue of their speaking French) with their transitioning to speaking French (from silence) by beginning to speak (as Burnyeat suggested). They come to be in the state of being an active French speaker by speaking French. At this point, I follow Mary Louise Gill (1989: 179) and Robert Heinaman (2007: 176) in taking using knowledge (or theorizing), not the transition to using knowledge, to be what is said 'not to be a quality change or to be a different type of quality change' (417b5–7).

[9] 'As was said' should, if possible, be retained from the majority of the MSS [CPV]. Its presence implies that the acquisition of knowledge has been said earlier (in effect) not to be a simple case of being affected in 417b3–7. This implication can be accepted if (as I argue) the acquisition of knowledge (learning) is a case of 'the preservation of what something is potentially (a knower)...under the causal influence of what is actually so and so...'. Its omission in some later MSS [S,U] may be explained by their rejection of this view of learning, perhaps influenced by Simplicius' or Philoponus'

[Type 1] changes are those for which it is essential that a contrary is destroyed by a contrary.

In the case of cooling, for example, it is required that when hot water is cooled its heat is destroyed by something cool. The water needs to lose some of its original heat for this change to occur. Cooling, so understood, meets two conditions:

(a) There is a 'type of destruction' of the water's heat in the process of change (417b2–3). Indeed, it is essential that the water's initial heat is destroyed, and the water ceases to be hot. This is because the change in question is defined as one in which one specified contrary state is destroyed.[10]
(b) The change is brought about by a causal agent which is itself cold: possessed of the contrary of the water which was initially hot.[11]

[Type 2] changes do not satisfy the first condition. It is not essential to these changes that the initial condition be destroyed in the change. On the contrary, the subject has to retain that condition throughout, going from being potentially a knower to being one in activity. More precisely: this potentiality (or capacity) is preserved and the change is in the direction of (*epi*) its appropriate end point (or goal): being an active knower. In [Type 2B] cases this transition culminates in the learner's acquiring the ability to speak French (417b16: a state or *hexis*), in [Type 2A] cases in their actually speaking French: being a knower in the fullest sense (417a29). The latter cases, in which the knower develops into being what it is (*epidosis eis auto*: 417b7), can be described as changes in the direction of its nature (*phusis*: 417b16). [Type 2B] transitions, in the case of learning, can also be described as changes in the direction of the nature of the object in question, even though they result in a state of knowledge (*hexis*) not in the activity that defines its nature: the one in which it is truly what it is—a knower. The whole change from its outset in initial learning to its final realization in speaking French is a [Type 2] change (417b16). Its first stage is a [Type 2B] change, its second a [Type 2A] change.

commentaries. I am indebted to Andreas Anagnostopoulos for helpful discussion of this textual issue and many other problems in *De Anima* B.5. For an alternative view of the text, see Lorenz (2007: n. 11).

[10] I take 'negative conditions' (*sterētikas diatheseis*: 417b15) to refer to this case. (Compare the use of similar terminology in discussing the hot and the cold in *Meta*. 1070b11ff.) In these cases, it is essential that the final condition is not the original one: the object is no longer cold. This will be so even if it is not hot. Aristotle's description of a case of the destruction of the cold by the hot is accurate: all that is required for the change described in 417b2–3 is that the object ceases to be cold not that it becomes hot. On this point, I agree with Burnyeat (2002) and Heinaman (2007) and disagree with John Bowin (2012b).
[11] I take the phrase 'by what is contrary' to refer to the causal agent of change: compare the role of the teacher in [Type 2] changes. There is no reason to take all [Type 1] changes as unnatural. On this point, I agree with Bowin (2011: 149).

All [Type 2] changes, so understood, fail to meet condition (a) for being a [Type 1] change. This is because:

[Type 1] changes are ones in which it is essential that the original state (e.g. being hot) is destroyed and replaced by a different, incompatible, condition (not being hot) in the change. These are defined as a transition from one contrary in the direction of another. The initial state, e.g. being hot, is one which has to be lost or negated in the course of the change, if it is to be the very change it is.

[Type 2] changes, by contrast, are ones in which the subject, so far from losing one contrary state to gain another, retains its initial condition (being potentially a knower) and is brought closer to the potentiality's goal: being an active knower) in the course of the change. These are not essentially changes from one contrary, because the initial state is not defined as one which is a contrary, to the final state: being an active knower. Instead, it is defined as the state of a (potential) knower, one who has the capacity to become an active knower at the end of the transition.

Aristotle's distinction, so understood, will classify learning as a [Type 2B] change. However, earlier in 417a30–1, he had written:

The learner has been changed in quality through learning, often changing from the opposite state (*hexis*).

Doesn't this show that learning is, after all, a [Type 1] change: one which always is a change in quality from one state (being ignorant) to its contrary (knowledge), not a [Type 2] change? Have we misunderstood Aristotle's distinction? Or perhaps it was badly drawn.

It is important to note, at the outset, that:

1. Aristotle may best be understood as saying that learning is *often* from the contrary state, not that it *always* is.[12] If so, he is not claiming that it is *required* for learning that one begins from, for example, a state of ignorance. Learning (the type), so understood, will not meet condition (a) for [Type 1] changes. Although he does not develop this remark further, it suggests that one can, in his view, begin learning at a variety of starting points, not simply from the contrary state: ignorance. One might, for instance, begin from

---

[12] As Hicks correctly translates. Aristotle surely did not require, as the alternative translation favoured by Ross suggests, that all cases of learning require *frequent* changes from the contrary state: ignorance. One does not have to go back to square one each time one strives to master French! There are interim starting points in that journey. (Nor is it clear that Aristotle thought that all the intervening stages could be located on a single line between two contraries: ignorance and knowledge. There are, it seems, many ways of failing to know.)

true beliefs. While all learning begins from lack of knowledge (a *deprivation* in Aristotle's term), not all need begin from a contrary state.[13]

2. Even if cases of learning do begin with the learner being in a (contrary) state, what is essential to their being cases of learning is that the subjects of change retain their potential to be a knower throughout. It is in virtue of the presence of this potentiality that they change in the required way and achieve the final state (being a theorizer). Learning does not occur in virtue of the subject's being ignorant. It is their capacity to know that is essential to this change. After all, some subjects are ignorant in ways that preclude them from ever learning (as dogs cannot learn to speak French). Instead, it is because pupils are capable of knowing, not because they are ignorant, that the teacher can teach them. This is why learning is defined as a change in which the original capacity, essential to the change, is preserved throughout.[14]

It is natural to object that in any particular case, the learner must begin in one definite epistemic condition (whether this be that of ignorance or of mistaken or incomplete belief) and end with the acquisition of knowledge. Isn't this enough, it will be said, to make their learning a [Type 1] change, in which one quality is lost and another gained? Isn't their lack of knowledge destroyed and replaced by a new state of knowledge? Doesn't this show that learning cannot be a [Type 2B] change?

This objection too can be met: even if each [Type 2B] change does in fact involve a change from some definite epistemic condition to one of knowledge, what is *essential* to that (very) change is its occurring in virtue of the learner's capacity to know, which is fully realized in their active knowledge. As such, it is essentially a [2B] change which, as it happens, begins at one definite epistemic state. Further, for all that is said, while beginning in that definite epistemic condition may be an accidental description of the particular [Type 2B] change that occurs, it need not be the essential description of a further [Type 1] change. Indeed, there

---

[13] For this distinction, see, for example, *Metaphysics* 1055b14–15 where deprivations (*stereseis*) are contrasted with contraries. Not all deprivations are contraries. What unifies all cases of learning is that they are from some lack of knowledge, not that they are from a contrary state such as ignorance. In fact, in Aristotle's view, there is no separate potential to be ignorant. (For similar restrictions on capacities, see *Metaphysics* 1051a15f.) If so, learning cannot be essentially the destruction of this state (compare 417b2–3). Nor, one might add, is the acquisition of knowledge (strictly speaking) a change to the privative state (417b15) because ignorance is not a positively characterized state and so lacks a privation. (Knowledge, that is, is not to be understood as the privation of the privation!)

[14] This is not simply to say, as Burnyeat suggests (2002: 61–7), that learning is from one point of view a [Type 1], from another a [Type 2] change. My suggestion is that learning, of the type envisaged here, is essentially a [Type 2] change, as too is using knowledge one already has. Both are essentially cases of preservative changes in which the subject comes towards 'themselves and the relevant actuality' (417b7–8): they are both in the direction of one's nature as a knower (417b16–17). Indeed, both cases of [Type 2] changes can, as Heinaman correctly notes (2007: 170ff.), be seen 'from one point of view' as [Type 1] changes: this is because [Type 2A] changes can also be described as changes from the state of not using to that of using knowledge.

need be no such [Type 1] change which is required for, let alone essential to, the activity of learning.[15] Since there is no explicit mention of any additional [Type 1] change 'in the offing' in this passage, all that seems to be required is that there be just one [Type 2B] change which, as it happens, begins with the subject being ignorant.[16]

There is a further difficulty. Some might suggest that any [Type 1] change (such as turning cold) can be re-described as a [Type 2] change. Cooling, that is, might be defined as the realization of the capacity of the object to be cold.[17] This change, so understood, will occur in virtue of that object's ability to be cold. Further, that ability will continue to be present throughout the process as a result of which the object ends up cold. However, if this is the way to understand this change, Aristotle's distinction, as we have characterized it, will collapse. [Type 1] changes will all be, in the final analysis, [Type 2] changes.

This difficulty too can be overcome. In the case of cooling, the original contrary (the heat of the object) has to be destroyed in the course of the change. This is because this type of process is defined as a transition from one contrary state in the direction of the other.[18] In these changes, so defined, the object is deprived of the very condition (being hot) which was essential for the change being a case of cooling. While the water, even when hot at the beginning of the process, may retain its potential to be cold (because it can become cold again in certain conditions: 1048a16ff.),[19] what is essential for this very change is that the potential to be cold does not determine the state of the object at the time when the transition began. Had it done so, the object would have been cool at the outset and cooling could not have occurred. Given the nature of this change, the potential to be cold, the potential that is exercised at the end of the process, cannot determine the state of the object at the outset: that state in virtue of which cooling occurs. The initial condition, essential to this change, has to be determined by its capacity to be hot. It is in virtue of its being hot at the outset that cooling occurs.

In [Type 2] cases, by contrast, the relevant initial state, as in the case of learning, is not defined as one which is a contrary to the final state: being an active knower. Indeed, its initial state is best understood as the state of a (potential) knower, one who has the capacity to become an active knower at the end of the transition.

---

[15] This will be true even if all cases of [Type 2] changes have accidental descriptions of this kind.

[16] In this case, the 'whence and the whither' will not determine the form in question. Contrast what happens in standard cases of processes (*kinēseis*): *N.E.* 1174a31ff. For further discussion of the case of knowledge, see *Physics* H (VII).3, discussed in Section 4.8.

[17] There is a major debate as to whether cooling is, for Aristotle, to be defined as the realization of the capacity to be cool or the capacity to be cooled. However, in the present context, I shall accept (for the sake of argument) the first alternative, although favouring the second for the reasons given in 'Aristotle's Processes' (2015: 186–205).

[18] See, for example, *Physics* 205a6, 224b29, and *De Generatione et Corruptione* 310a25.

[19] At this point, I follow the analysis of conditional capacities (unconditionally ascribed) developed by David Pears (1975) and accepted by Jonathan Beere (2009).

The subject is not deprived of this initial state (being capable of knowing) as the change occurs. Instead, the end state is the realization of the very capacity (to be a knower) whose presence determined the relevant initial state of the subject, the one required for this to be the change it is. It is in virtue of the subject being capable of knowing, and not in virtue of any capacity to be ignorant, that the change in question occurs. Even if there were (contrary to Aristotle's view) a capacity to be ignorant, it would not be in virtue of its presence that the change occurs. Nor would this capacity determine the state of the subject in virtue of which the relevant change occurs. (Remember those who are ignorant in such a way as to be incapable of the relevant knowledge!)

This is why what happens in all [Type 2] cases is to be defined as a transition towards the goal of the relevant capacity: 417b4–5. The end stage in all such cases is the realization of the capacity to know which was present and active (albeit in an incomplete way) at (and even before) the beginning of the change. This first realization of this capacity consists in the learner's achieving the state of being a knower (being a master of French: *hexis* (417b16)), the second in the activity which follows from that state (speaking French) or in the state of being active as a French speaker. When actively speaking French, one will be in the state earlier described as that of being 'a knower in the full sense': 417a28.[20]

What is the importance, from Aristotle's viewpoint, of this distinction? The capacities involved in [Type 2] changes are, in the cases with which Aristotle is principally concerned, ones which are defined by their role in a completed well-functioning organism: such as seeing or actively knowing (*De Anima* Γ.7, 431a5–7), which he describes as 'activities (*energeiai*) without qualification'.[21] This is the goal of the relevant capacity: one which is active and present from the outset up until the acquisition of the settled state (*hexis*) and its exercise. [Type 2] changes are essentially the realizations of goal-directed capacities of see-ers or knowers. They are, as such, defined in terms of their teleological role in the organism in question.

The capacities involved in heating and cooling, by contrast, are defined as the realization of a capacity of an object to be affected by other objects. They

---

[20] If this is correct, there is no need to invoke the distinction, suggested by Heinaman (2007: 175–7), between those uses of knowledge which are and those which are not 'nature-preserving'. Indeed, we should be reluctant to introduce this distinction in a context in which Aristotle focuses only on successful, 'nature preserving', cases: his examples are of use of skills (417a31) and of theorizing (a success term: 417b5). These are not cases where one merely actively thinks one knows. One actively knows.

[21] It does not follow from this that all [Type 2] changes must be directed towards the natural goals of the organism. There can be, for all that is said here, other [Type 2] changes where the capacity realized is, for example, one for vice or vicious activity, not for a natural goal of the organism. Indeed, if all completions are [Type 2] changes, Aristotle will point to just such a case in *Physics* 246b18–20, where he treats both virtues and vices alike as 'completions' of the relevant capacities. There is no reason, *pace* Bowin (2011: 151–2), why [Type 2] changes, as defined in *De Anima* B.5, should exclude the realizations of capacities for vice, illness, or blindness, even if the examples mentioned in *De Anima* are not of this type. It is simply that there he focuses on knowing and perceiving which are directed towards the natural goals of the organism.

are not defined by their role in producing the natural goals of a completed, well-functioning, organism. Even if water has a natural temperature, its being cooled by another cool object will not be defined in terms of coming to be in that natural state: it could, after all, be cooled to temperatures below or above it, depending on the nature of the external cause and circumstances. This is why [Type 1] changes can be described as the activity (*energeia*) of what is incomplete (*De Anima* Γ.7, 431a6–7), best understood as what has the capacity to be cooled or heated.[22] They do not realize the distinctive type of goal-directed capacity, defined by reference to the activity of the completed organism, which is manifested in the [Type 2] changes with which Aristotle is concerned in *De Anima*. In the latter cases, a capacity of this type was, and had to be, present and active (albeit in an incomplete way) at the outset.

Perceiving and knowing are [Type 2] changes, defined by reference to their teleological role in the completed organism. In *De Anima* B.5, Aristotle has, in effect, refined the ontology introduced in *De Anima* A.1 by distinguishing [Type 1] and [Type 2] changes. Once this distinction is drawn, desiring too should be classified as a [Type 2] change: one defined as the realization of a capacity with a role in the completed organism: it is, as Aristotle notes in *De Anima* Γ.7, to be defined as an activity towards what is good or bad for the organism (431a10–11).

Aristotle develops his account in *De Anima* B.5 by suggesting that perception, understood as the exercise of the perceptual capacity, and thinking are both [Type 2A] changes (417b16–19) despite their other differences.[23] While there may be prior [Type 2B] changes, akin to learning, in which the child (or embryo) acquires the capacity to perceive red objects, the capacity exercised in seeing particular red objects is compared with using knowledge one already has. (For a similar claim, see *De Sensu* 441b20ff.)

Why did Aristotle think of perceiving this red object as a [Type 2A] change? Isn't it really a [Type 2B] change, from lack of knowledge to knowledge of the object's colour? Don't we learn its colour in this case?

While Aristotle did not tackle this problem directly in *De Anima* B.5, he provides the resources to do so. We possess at birth, in his account, the capacity to see any red object that is presented to us (with no antecedent learning) because we are born with (e.g.) a capacity to detect all such qualities when encountered. The capacity in virtue of which we see this red object, so understood, is a general

---

[22] I defended this specific view in my 'Aristotle's Processes' (2015: 186–205) and earlier in *Aristotle's Philosophy of Action* (1984: 19ff.). For an alternative interpretation, see Aryeh Kosman's discussion (2013: 50–5), building on his earlier work (1969: 41–62) and Ursula Coope's essay (2009: 277–91). The issue is also discussed by Jonathan Beere (2009: 204ff.) and Andreas Anagnostopoulos (2010: 33–79). There is no need, in interpreting 431a5–7, to attempt to adjudicate further between these suggestions. All can, albeit in somewhat differing ways, make room for the required distinction between those changes which are definitionally connected with a completed goal and those which are not.

[23] They differ in that the objects of perception are external particulars, the objects of thought universals already in some way in the soul (417b19–27).

one: to see red objects. No further capacity (to see *this* red object) is acquired or exercised when I see this red object. The capacity exercised on this occasion is to be individuated in terms of its general role in the organism. Although we learn something new when seeing this particular red object, we do not acquire a new capacity in doing so. It is not the type of learning (acquisition of a new capacity) required for a [Type 2B] change. Perhaps this is why perceiving is classified as a [Type 2A] change.[24]

Aristotle's discussion in *De Anima* B.5 serves to clarify several points about the ontology of perceiving:

(i) Perceiving is not a [Type 1] but a [Type 2] change: it is not a change (like ordinary colouring) in which red is replaced by green (or its relevant opposite);
(ii) It is the exercise of an already acquired goal-directed capacity: it is not a [Type 2B] change (like learning) but a [Type 2A] change
(iii) The sense organ is not itself altered in the way objects affected by [Type 1] changes are affected
(iv) The sense organ is not itself altered in the way objects affected by [Type 2B] changes are affected.

Perceiving, so understood, is neither a [Type 1] nor a [Type 2B] change, one in which the relevant state (*hexis*) is set up. Instead, it is the exercise of a capacity one already has, where the exercise need not involve either the replacement of one contrary by another or the setting up of a positive state (*hexis*). In this type of change, the relevant capacity (of the sense organ) is exercised in perceiving. It is not a case of replacing one contrary by another: a [Type 1] change. The transition from being a potential seer to an actual seer is seeing. This is a case of a [Type 2A] change in which the perceiver is (in some way) made like, or likened to, the object perceived (417a20, 417b5–6). The way in question remains to be spelled out.

Aristotle, in this discussion, draws distinctions not captured by undifferentiated talk of events. He is at pains to distinguish [Type 1] and [Type 2] and to show their differing structures. These ontological issues will be important in our subsequent discussion of other aspects of Aristotle's account of the psychology of complete organisms.

---

[24] An interesting alternative, suggested in discussion by Mary Louise Gill, runs as follows: one comes to possess the capacity to see what is red at that stage when one has acquired (as a maturing child) the capacity to discriminate red objects from those which are like red ones (moving to a determinate grasp on red). In *Physics* 184b2–3, A describes a child who calls any man 'father'. Perhaps there is a stage at which the child calls all non-blue or green objects red. In this understanding, the acquisition of the capacity to see what is red will depend on prior cases of seeing.

4.4 Perceiving: a 'mere Cambridge change'?

There is no commitment in *De Anima* B.5, as understood in Section 4.3, to treating perceiving, or [Type 2] essentially goal-directed changes more generally, as 'mere Cambridge changes', changes in relation alone. There are two ways to see this.

Elsewhere, in *Physics* H (VII). 3, Aristotle discusses phenomena described as 'completions' (*epiteleiōseis*). These changes (such as the house being tiled or roofed: 246a19) are not quality changes (strictly speaking) because they are not defined as changes from one contrary to another.[25] Instead, they are essentially the completions (or perfections) of what something potentially is (and, as such, is described paradigmatically as in line with its nature: 246a15).[26] In the case of roofing, the completion might be the realization of the tiles' capacity to be the roof of a house and will occur as (and when) it does in virtue of their possession of that capacity. While the final stage in house-building, that of putting on the roof, is not a [Type 1] change (as it is not the replacement of one contrary by another), it is nonetheless a matter-involving change: a [Type 2] change essentially involving tiles, bricks, and their material capacities (to bear weight etc.) and, as such (in line with the argument developed in Chapter 2, Section 6), the realization of a goal-directed but inextricably material capacity.[27] Further, since tiling and roofing are not mere Cambridge changes, Aristotle is focusing on phenomena which are neither [Type 1] changes nor mere Cambridge changes.

Aristotle in H.3 claims that neither states of the soul or the body nor their acquisition are quality changes, or at least those which are virtues or vices. Virtues and their acquisition are both described as 'completions' (246a10–11, 13). Virtues are so described because they are the best, or perfect (*teleion*), state of the subject in question (246a14–15), understood as the goal of one of its natural capacities. It

---

[25] In the case of completions, there is no transition from one contrary to another, as there is in ordinary quality changes (including those involving heat: 245b15), because there are no contraries to completions (as *not being complete* is not the contrary of being complete/being in a given relation). Ordinary quality changes, by contrast, are from one contrary to another (*Physics* E. (V), 1, 225b10ff.). In the case of house building, the transition from not having a roof to having a roof is not an alteration (246a20f.) because not having a roof is not the contrary of having a roof. (There are after all many ways of not having a roof!)

[26] At this point, I follow Ursula Coope's interpretation of what is distinctive about completions: they are the manifestations of the nature of the things whose manifestations they are (2012: 69ff.). I follow the MSS (against Ross) in maintaining '*to*' (246a15) and in taking Aristotle to be speaking about the expression 'in accordance with nature'.

[27] It is important to note that while *Physics* H (VII). 3 marks off [Type 2] changes from [Type 1] alterations, it introduces a distinction not to be found in Aristotle's discussion of processes in *Physics* Γ(III) 1–3), where teaching and learning are paradigm cases of alterations: in *Physics* H.3, by contrast, they are not taken as alterations at all (perhaps because they are not, in the required way, between contraries). While *De Anima* B.5 marks off [Type 2] cases in a manner which resembles (in some respects) that employed in *Physics* H.3 to characterize completions as non-alterations, it does not follow *Physics* H.3 in denying them the status of quality change. That question is left open (417b14f.).

may be that, in referring to the state in question, Aristotle intends to extend this description to the exercise of that state in virtuous activity. He certainly envisages such an extension later in the chapter in considering the states of the intellect (247b1–3); there he writes, in similar terms, of their *coming to be used* as a completion, not a quality change (247b10–13). The acquisition of knowledge and its coming to be used are both instances of perfecting the capacity of the subject to know. If so, both [Type 2] changes, the acquisition of knowledge and its subsequent exercise, will be regarded in H.3 as 'completions' because both are perfections of a capacity already possessed (such as the capacity to know or be virtuous). They are, as in *De Anima* B.5, the progressive manifestation of the subject's goal-directed capacity. (I shall return to another aspect of the *Physics* H.3 discussion of knowledge below.)

Aristotle's remarks provide the resources to defuse an important argument in favour of the spiritualist interpretation, advanced by Myles Burnyeat. He presented Aristotle as holding:

1. All alteration is a change with regard to quality [premise]
2. All changes with regard to quality are [Type 1] changes [premise]
3. No [Type 2] change is a [Type 1] change [premise]
4. No [Type 2] change is a change with regard to quality (from 2 and 3)

and so as concluding that:

5. No [Type 2] change is an alteration (from 4 and 1), and that
6. All [Type 2] changes are 'mere Cambridge' changes (from 5).

However, if completions (such as completing the house by putting the roof on) are neither mere Cambridge changes nor [Type 1] changes, Aristotle can, and should, reject premise (2). There are also completions, specifically quality-related matter-involving goal-directed completions, to consider.[28]

In the immediate context of *De Anima* B, Aristotle gives an example of just such a matter-involving completion. In his account of nutrition, he initially distinguishes two stages:

[Stage A]: food (undigested) is taken into the body: as Aristotle describes it 'contrary feeds on contrary' (416b7ff.)

---

[28] Burnyeat is reluctant to countenance use of *Physics* H (VII).3 in discussing *De Anima* B.5 because he regards it as an outlier text, offering a view inconsistent with his own 'mere Cambridge change' interpretation of the relevant *De Anima* passages (2002: 28–90). It is, in my view, a merit of my interpretation of *De Anima* B.5 that it coheres well with Aristotle's discussion, in somewhat similar terms, of apparently similar phenomena in *Physics* H.

[Stage B]: food (digested) is used by the body: like by like (in Aristotle's terminology) (416b7–8).

At [Stage B]:

(a) there is no destruction of the first contrary (as the nutriment at this stage retains its nature and does not change into a contrary: 416b6–7);
(b) the nutriment goes from being a potential energizer of the ensouled body to being its actual energizer: 416b16–20;
(c) As a result of (a) and (b), the nutriment preserves the ensouled body in activity.

At [Stage B], the relevant *capacity* of the nutritive soul converts what is a potential energizer of an ensouled body into an actual energizer of that body. The nutriment itself goes from being a potential to an actual energizer of the ensouled body. This is the way the nutriment preserves the ensouled body in activity. It maintains the qualities of the body. However, this is not a [Type 1] change from one contrary to another because, as in *De Anima* B.5, there are no contraries to completions of what something potentially is (in line with its nature). However, as in the case of tiling or putting the roof on, nutrition (at [Stage B]) is an essentially matter-involving type of change, although not a [Type 1] change. It is a [Type 2] change, because it essentially involves as its object, food, a distinctive type of material composite (*De Sensu* 445a20–1) and its sweetness (*De Sensu* 441b27ff.).[29] This change will be, if the argument developed in Chapter 2 is correct, *the* realization of a goal-directed inextricably material capacity.

Perception and nutrition at [Stage B] are similar in several respects: in both

[1] the object perceived/nutriment does not change into a contrary condition in being perceived/being used as nutriment;

[2] the action of the object perceived/nutriment is to preserve (not to alter) the perceptual faculty/the *ensouled* body.

Given these points of similarity, one should conclude that:

[3] Neither nutrition at [Stage B] nor perception is a [Type 1] change (from contrary to contrary).

Both are better classified as completions (*epiteleiōseis*), if the latter are understood as the perfections of a capacity that is already present. Since nutrition is a

---

[29] For further discussion of these aspects of nutrition, see Thomas Johansen's account (2012: 136–7).

matter-involving completion, the realization of an inextricably material capacity, and not a 'mere Cambridge change', perception may also be a completion of this type. It does not follow from its not being a [Type 1] change that it is a 'mere Cambridge change'.

4.5 Perceiving: the issue

We can now, in the light of the discussion in Sections 4.3 and 4.4, formulate two questions which are central for our present investigation:

(a) Is perception, like nutrition, a type of matter-involving completion (like finishing the house by tiling the roof)? Or is it a 'mere Cambridge change'?
(b) If perceiving itself is a [Type 2A] change, is this the only change essentially involved in perception (as may be the case in coming to know)? Or is there also an additional [Type 1] change in which the sense organ is caused to be a given way and a further [Type 2] change in which the perceiver sees the object or property in question? And, if there are two changes of this type, how exactly are they related?[30]

Spiritualist interpreters deny that perceiving is, for Aristotle, itself defined as a matter-involving completion. They present it simply as a type of awareness, or discrimination, of the object perceived. Some deny that any [Type 1] material change occurs in cases of perceptual awareness. Others, like Burnyeat in his later essays, accepted that some bodily changes (or conditions) are causally necessary for an occurrence of this type of awareness.[31] However, they all deny that such material changes or conditions are referred to as part of the definition of the type of awareness at issue. Even for later spiritualists, no [Type 1] change is an essential feature (or definitional part) of perceptual awareness (which they see as the relevant formal change). Any [Type 1] change that occurs is, in their view, distinct from the purely psychological [Type 2] activity of awareness (or discrimination) which is perceiving.

Non-reductionist materialist interpreters have much in common with the later spiritualists. They too think that there are two changes in Aristotle' account of perception: a [Type 1] change and a second [Type 2] change. They also agree that the initial [Type 1] change is a material change. They differ from spiritualists in

---

[30] This view is adopted, albeit in somewhat different forms, by Victor Caston (2005), Hendrik Lorenz (2007), Mark Johnstone (2012), and Thomas Johansen (2012).
[31] Burnyeat (2001: 136). He writes:
> Moistening is a necessary part of the total process, whether as causal antecedents (sound or smell) or concomitant effects. They are not constitutive of perceiving as such. (2001: 136)

understanding the relevant [Type 1] change as not merely a causally necessary feature, required for the occurrence of the relevant perception. It is, in their view, an essential additional part of perceiving, now understood as a complex phenomenon defined in terms of two definitionally separate component types: an activity of awareness and the material change that underlies it.

There are, it should be noted, several materialist interpretations. In non-reductionist accounts, [Type 2] changes are defined as the type of changes they are independently of the [Type 1] changes that realize them. In this view, perception cannot be reduced to, or defined in terms of, an underlying [Type 1] material change. Instead, it is a combination (of some kind) of a purely psychological phenomenon (awareness of the object) and a purely physical phenomenon. While they (like spiritualists) agree that perceiving contains a purely psychological type of activity defined without reference to any internal, grounding, material change, they differ in taking this physical component to be essential for perception, defined as a combination of a purely physical and a purely psychological activity, where the former (in some way) grounds the latter.[32] Other materialist interpreters take a different view, presenting Aristotle as aiming to reduce the psychological to the physical by advocating a version of type-identity theory.[33] Still others seek to define the psychological properties neutrally in terms of their causal role alone (without essential reference to them as psychological).

These materialist and spiritualist interpretations, however, do not exhaust the range of answers offered to questions (a) and (b) (even if one excludes dualist readings). Others, while accepting that there are two changes and seeing one as purely psychological, take Aristotle to define the material change in terms of the psychological one: as, for example, the one required for the purely psychological activity of perceiving. This latter view, sometimes attributed to Aquinas, combines a pure psychological component with an impure physical component, defined in terms which explicitly refer to the psychological. One might call the physical component, which Aquinas described as 'spiritual matter', quasi-material. Others suggest that Aristotle himself did not commit himself to a view about the relation between the relevant purely psychological [Type 2] change and the material [Type 1] change, preferring to remain neutral between the options just sketched.[34]

All the options just canvassed (excluding the reductionist materialist and neutral functionalist accounts) agree on one central claim: there is a definitionally

---

[32] Caston, Shields, and Johansen take this view, albeit in somewhat different forms. Some of the differences between them are helpfully set out by Caston (2005) and Johansen (2012). Earlier writers who held this type of account include Martha Nussbaum (1978), Richard Sorabji (1979), and my younger self (1984).

[33] As suggested by T.J. Slakey (1961: 470–84).

[34] There are several ways to develop this possibility. Perhaps Aristotle took no view as to whether or not the co-occurring physical process was essential for perception. Or perhaps he thought that it was essential but took (or stated) no view as to whether it realized or grounded the purely psychological activity of awareness. (For the latter view, see Lorenz: 2007: 179–220.)

independent, purely psychological feature or activity, involved in perception. The form of this feature or activity is pure: not defined in terms which explicitly refer to specific internal material states. It is this shared assumption that I wish to challenge.

The relevant psychological activity, such as discrimination or awareness of a red object, is, I shall suggest, defined as an inextricably psycho-physical activity. To discriminate such an object is to be materially affected in such a way that we are perceptually aware of its redness. Perceiving, so understood, is a [Type 2] change: an essentially matter-involving completion, the realization of an inextricably material capacity. There is not a definitionally independent, purely psychological, [Type 2] change (discrimination or awareness) that occurs. The type of perceptual awareness itself, and the relevant capacity for such awareness, is defined as inextricably psycho-physical, not decomposable into two definitionally separate components, one of which is purely psychological.

If Aristotle were to understand perceiving in this way, his account would run as follows: when perceiving red, perceivers, possessed of the general ability to see something red, are causally affected by redness in the world. Before they are affected in this way, their state will be one in which they have the potential to see red—a state which is not the contrary of seeing what is red.[35] Although their perceiving red is not a [Type 1] change from one contrary to another, as Aristotle notes: *De Anima* B.5, 417a8ff., it will not be defined as a purely psychological activity (or a distinct purely psychological part of one). Instead, it will be an inextricably psycho-physical completion, a [Type 2] change. Individual activities of perceiving red will be essentially instances of this type.

The case of nutrition [at Stage B] provides an analogy. Those capable of being fed do not move to a contrary state when fed. There is no contrary essentially destroyed in this transition.[36] What occurs involves nutriment travelling around the body and affecting different parts as it goes. These essentially material movements are defined as integral parts of the [Type 2] change under way at [Stage B] of nutrition. They should not be defined as [Type 1] changes co-occurring with a [Type 2] change of nutrition. Instead, they are stages in a process of nutrition governed by its characteristic goal in a completed organism. As such, they are essentially stages of a [Type 2] change, not a definitionally distinct [Type 1] change which co-occurs with a [Type 2] change.

Is this correct? Are tasting and smelling essentially and inextricably psycho-physical completions, [Type 2] changes? If they are, Aristotle's account will not be captured by either non-reductionist materialist or spiritualist interpretations.

---

[35] We are still at the logical level of analysis prior to introduction of talk of the 'transparent'. There are many states in which one is not seeing what is red (but seeing what is green, blue, or yellow) but has the potential to do so.

[36] Perhaps, one might add (in the style of *Phys.* H.3), in desiring revenge they stand in a relation to a possible future state of affairs (and relations lack contraries).

This is because he is not advocating any of the positions just canvassed because he rejects the two post-Cartesian assumptions [A] and [B] which, as we noted in Section 4.1, encourage philosophers to accept one of these options. I shall further suggest that, in his view, there is no purely physical process which underlies it. All that is essential to tasting is an inextricably psycho-physical discrimination or awareness of the flavour of objects in the world.

4.6 Tasting: an inextricably psycho-physical completion

In *De Anima* A.1, Aristotle, as we noted in Chapter 1, offered two types of consideration to support his suggestion that anger is best defined as the boiling-of-the-blood type of desire for revenge brought on in a given way. His discussion of taste contains the first of these (what I shall call) [H.1]-type considerations:

(1) If the sense organ is destroyed, there is no tasting at all. Some types of perceptual impact are described as being too strong for the sense organ to bear and destroying the relevant 'formula' (*logos*) of the body in the same ways as some heavy blows might break a musical instrument. When this happens, the animal with the damaged sense organ can no longer perceive (424a28–32). It is necessary for perception that a (basically) undamaged sense organ is present (where such an organ is a bodily magnitude: 424a26–7). If there is no such appropriate bodily organ present, there will be no suffering for the relevant objects of sense (424a32ff.).

(2) The sense organ, if tasting is to occur, has not only to be present undamaged; it also has to be in a given bodily condition. In discussing taste, Aristotle suggests that the tongue, if it is to taste flavours, must be neither too wet nor too dry but capable of being moistened by the flavour in question (422b5ff.). It must have the right degree of moisture to be affected by the flavours in question. These remarks show that, in Aristotle's view, there has to be an appropriately moist bodily organ present if it is to taste flavours.

The sense organ, in the light of (1) and (2), responds—if it is an appropriate condition—to the flavour in the way (whatever it is) required to taste it. This response is the actualization of a capacity of the patient to taste. How is this activity to be understood? What is involved in its responding to the flavours that affect it?

[H.1] considerations are consistent with some versions of spiritualism. For later spiritualists, the tongue's being initially dry and being capable of being moistened is a causally necessary condition for tasting to occur. In their view, the physical impact of moistening is a concomitant (or at best a causally necessary) physical occurrence, not constitutive of the sensing itself. It does not make the awareness be the way it is. [H.1] considerations, as they stand, are consistent with both late spiritualist and non-reductionist interpretations.

However, in his discussion of taste, Aristotle introduced further, [H.2]-style, considerations which suggest a different conclusion. Thus, he writes:

> Since the object of taste is moist, it is necessary that its sense organ be neither actually moist nor yet incapable of being made moist. For taste is acted upon by the object of taste as such. The organ of taste which needs to be moistened must have the capacity of absorbing moisture without being dissolved, while at the same time not actually being moist. Evidence for this: the tongue cannot perceive when very dry or very wet.   (422a34–b6)

The organ of taste is, it seems, made moist in the process of tasting the object. This is because the object tasted, *as such*, is itself moist. In becoming like that object, the organ itself is moistened. This is, it appears, an essential part of what it is for the organ to be assimilated to the flavour (*chumos*). Later he develops this point as follows:

(4) Flavours are dependent on the differing dry elements in liquids (such as those of oil or salt: 422b10ff.). Flavours, like juices, are dependent on, for example, the water, oil, and salt they contain. The tongue is affected in virtue of its ability to be affected by them. Oily flavours are sweet, salty ones bitter (*De Sensu* 442a19ff.):[37]

> For taste happens because of the moisture with which one is in immediate contact as when the tongue is very wet, the contact is with the moisture originally on the tongue, as when someone first tries a strong flavour and then tastes some other flavour; or as with the sick to whom all things appear bitter because their tongue is full of bitter moisture.   (422b6–10)

The role of moisture in (3) and (4) is important. It is not simply that a moist object is bound to moisten things in contact with it.[38] The moistening is not accidental to perceiving because the object of taste, as the object of taste, is itself moist. Since what is tasted is the flavour, the flavour is itself in some way moist. This is why the organ, in receiving a flavour, has to be moistened in the very activity of tasting it.

In the light of (3) and (4), tasting is not defined simply as the purely psychological exercise of ability to discriminate, or be aware of, bitterness.[39] It is instead an essentially embodied (moisture-involving) type of discrimination. The bodily organ is defined as that which has the capacity—when impacted by flavours—to

---

[37] As Aristotle's account develops, it emerges that the tongue (or parts of it) is the medium: flavour is carried on (or through) the tongue to the relevant sense organ.
[38] Burnyeat accepts this (2001: 136) while denying that the moistening is an essential part of the tasting itself (*pace* R.Bolton 2005: 227–8n.). Moistening is not, in Burnyeat's view, part of the definition of tasting as 'perceptual awareness, a mode of cognition' (2001: 141)—which is how Burnyeat understands taking on the form without the matter.
[39] For a discussion of this view, see Johansen (2012), who cites several others taking a similar view.

discriminate them in an essentially embodied way. Tasting is an inextricably embodied type of sensory capacity: one whose exercise essentially involves the organ of taste being moistened in a given way. One cannot define what the relevant type of perceptual awareness is without explicitly referring, in the definition, to moisture-involving discrimination.[40] If this is correct, Aristotle's account of tasting will follow the model developed for anger in *De Anima* 403a20ff. It too will be an essentially enmattered capacity defined in terms of a specific inextricably and distinctively psycho-physical type of activity.

Aristotle's detailed account of tasting further develops this pattern: the one at work in his discussion of desire (in Chapter 3) and of natural substances (in Chapter 2) which is motivated by similar concerns.[41] Or so I shall argue.

4.7 Tasting: problems for the spiritualist interpretation

Aristotle's picture, if the model just sketched is correct, is a simple one: the flavour in the medium operates on the sense organ which is moved in such a way that the perceiver discriminates, in a distinctively psycho-physical way, the flavour of the object. Is this his view? Did he fill it out in more detail?

The relevant types of discrimination are defined, in Aristotle's view, by their objects (*De Anima* 415a20ff.). Taste is a discrimination of flavours, smell of odours. We can make progress by understanding his account of the nature of these objects.

Flavours are, it appears, essentially enmattered in water and it is these which we discriminate: we are sensitive to, for example, the bitterness of the water or the sweetness of the apple. By contrast, smells are enmattered in air and water. As Aristotle remarks:

---

[40] That is, the changes involved are defined partly in terms of such material properties as heat and cold, dryness and moisture and, as such, are sensitive to material factors of this kind.

[41] In *De Sensu* 439a6–12, Aristotle writes: 'We have said in general terms before what is colour, noise, smell, taste, and touch but now we need to say what they do and what they are with regard to each sense organ...e.g. what is colour?' This looks like an attempt at definitions of colour and smell which are less general than those in *De Anima* and, in some way, specific to each sense. What is the precise relation between the works? There are, it seems, two, not inconsistent, points of connection:

(i) 436a1–4: focuses more on the actions and processes or activities of the objects sensed while *De Anima* focuses on the soul and its capacities, exposing just enough about their objects as is required for that purpose.

(ii) 439a8ff.: focuses on what each object of sense is and what it does so as to be perceptible: what they do in the medium so as to be perceived by the perceiver.

If this is correct, *De Sensu* offers specific and fuller definitions of each sense object (colour etc.: what they are) in such a way as to show why each is perceptible. However, so understood, it is an attempt to proceed further with the enquiry set out in *De Anima* 415a20ff.: begin with the objects sensed and define senses in terms of their sensitivity to these objects. This project, while it goes beyond what is necessary for basic four-cause style definitions, spells out more fully Aristotle's account, begun in *De Anima*, of what sensed objects are and how they impact on the medium and perceiver.

What the dry produces in the moist, this the flavoured moist does in another area, in air and water in a similar fashion. (*De Sensu* 442b28–9)

Smell in air and water is what flavour is in water. (443b15ff.)

There is a flavour when dry things are placed in water (422a15, 443a8f.). There is a smell when either air or water is affected.[42] Both flavours and odours are essentially matter-involving phenomenon. Flavour is present when water is affected by certain dry objects, odour when a feature found in both air or water is affected by a flavoured object. Aristotle calls the feature common to air and water 'the moist' (443a8) but does not specify its nature. However, whatever it is, it cannot be the same as being water. It is a feature, which like 'transparency', both water and air possess (443a1–2). Some objects, such as grapes, have both a flavour and a smell, their bouquet: the former is a property of water when it permeates dry material (441b18ff.), the latter of the moisture in the air or water, the effect of the dry material which, when permeated by water, gives that water its flavour: a distinctive property (441b18–20). A bitter drink will have, in Aristotle's terms, an enmattered (or, more precisely, an *enwatered*) form. Its water is enformed in a bitter way—which, when we perceive it, we taste as bitter. The form in question is bitterness-in-the-water. A bitter smell has, by contrast, an *enmoistened* form, where the type of moisture is common to both air and water: it is bitterness-in-the-moist. Aristotle needed to refer to the differing ways of being enmattered to define flavour and odour: the former is bitterness-in-water, the latter bitterness-in-the-moist. There is not one thing (bitterness) which both senses access in different ways. Instead, the relevant flavour is bitterness-in-water, the relevant odour bitterness-in-the-moist (as snubness is concavity-in-the-nose). These inextricably enmattered phenomena are prior to tasting and smelling in the way Aristotle required in *De Anima* 415a20ff. Tasting is sensitivity to, or discrimination of, bitterness-in-the-water, smelling to bitterness-in-the-moist. Neither smell nor flavour can be defined without reference to the capacities of the moist or the water involved. They are both inextricably matter-involving features: bitterness-in-the-moist (whether air or water) and bitterness-in-water respectively.[43]

---

[42] Aristotle compares a smell to the dipping or washing of the dry in a fluid: 445a14–15. (I follow the MSS in reading '*plusis*' (washing) rather than '*phusis*' (nature): Cook Wilson's emendation of '*plusis*' for '*phusis*' in 443a8, although tempting, is not required.) A smell is, it seems, regularly presented as a type of process in the medium. In *De Sensu*, he is concerned with the processes in the medium, with what each object of sense is and what it does (439a8ff.). While all such objects are said in *De Anima* to be perceptible and such as to cause perception, *De Sensu* focuses on what makes them perceptible, beginning with an account of what they are, and what they do in the medium. So understood, in *De Sensu*, he is providing specific and fuller definitions of each sense object (colour etc.: what they are) in such a way as to show in what way each is perceptible.

[43] In the case of smell, the relevant medium is found in air and water, both of which are moist, qua possessing the power to be modified by dry substances once they are placed in water (*De Sensu* 443a7ff.; *De Anima* 421b9f.). The effect of dry substances, when placed in water, on the moisture of air and water is similar to what they have when originally placed in water to create flavours (443b7ff.). In

When flavour is received in tasting, its reception is a moisture-involving type of reception. This is not simply because tasting is individuated by its object: a flavour, itself a water-involving form of bitterness. It is also because the reception of an enwatered form must itself involve—as an essential and constitutive part of its reception—the organ itself being moistened. This is, it seems, an essential part of the causal impact of a unified flavour on such an organ: what it is for it to receive, and be sensitive to, an enwatered form.

This conclusion coheres with Aristotle's subsequent remark, when discussing the intellect, that the relevant activities of receiving the relevant forms are enmattered in just the way and to the same extent as their objects are (*De Anima* 429b21–2). If the objects of taste and smell are enmattered, so too must be the activities of tasting and smelling. They will be matter-involving completions. But why did Aristotle hold this view?

One motivation is based in his view of the type of causation at issue. It is, it seems, a special case of his account of the role of forms as causes, discussed in Chapter 2. 'Flavouring' (the activity of flavour on the sense) is said in *De Anima* 426a13–15 to stand to the tasting as action to passion, a relation illustrated elsewhere by teaching and learning in *Physics* 202b16ff. We can spell this out in more detail on the basis of his remarks on active and passive causal capacities and their interaction.

In Aristotle's account, teaching is the providing of the very same form (or informational content) as the learner grasps. If the teacher says more but the learner does not grasp it, this additional information is not something that is taught (in this teaching). Or, conversely, if the brilliant learner (as not infrequently happens!) sees the implications of what the teacher has said but failed to make explicit, the surplus gained would not be what is taught (or learned) but a further implication of what is said. What is taught is precisely the same in content (and form) as what is learned. (For the teaching/learning case: see *Physics* Γ.3, 202b16–22; for the same form being conveyed: see *Physics* 202a9ff.) More specifically: what is transferred is the same form (the learner qua learner grasps what the teacher teaches). In the case of tasting, the form transferred is, for example, bitterness-in-the-water. This is what is tasted.

The flavour, bitterness-in-the water, acts on the sense organ (*poiēsis*), which, when we taste, suffers (*pathesis*) as a consequence of the activity of the flavour. The relevant capacities have to be enmattered in the *same type* of matter to be per se causes and effects in this type of causal interaction.[44] In his view, the agent and the patient must

---

effect, Aristotle compares the creation of smell in the moisture of the air or water with washing or dipping dry substances in moisture and liquid (445a14). They differ in that odours and flavours belong to moisture and water respectively and are caused to exist in different ways.

[44] This is an application of the general principle in *De Generatione et Corruptione* discussed in Chapter 2, Section 6. Aristotle comments 'body is by nature such as to be affected by body, flavour by

be possessed of the same general type of matter to be capable of 'flavouring' (to make up a term missing in 426a15 for the activity of the flavour) and tasting. Indeed, the relevant capacities can only be present in either when both the agent and patient are capable of being moistened in the relevant way. This is why tasting, for example, the bitterness-in-the-water, must itself be a moisture-involving activity. Moisture is required as something common to the agent and patient if they are to undergo this change. The active and passive capacities have themselves to be inextricably material to be per se causes and effects in the required way.[45]

Aristotle's remarks on smell follow a similar pattern. The sense organ of smell, he claims, is potentially dry (422a6ff.) but initially moist and cold (444a31ff.). In the case of taste, the organ was moistened in the process of tasting. In the case of smelling, by contrast, the sense organ is dried in smelling. In the latter case, the object sensed is said to be both dry and hot (in its own way) and to assimilate the sense organ to itself, when the latter smells the object. Something of the dryness and heat of the original dry material must be present in the moisture of the intervening air or water. If the sense organ were simply wet and cold (and not potentially dry or hot) it would not be affected by the dryness of the object: the impact of its dryness would be lost and there be no smelling. The relevant form, the result of the impact of the hot dry object on the moisture in, for example the air, heats and dries the sense organ when it receives (and is sensitive to) this form. There is, it seems, one unified object: bitterness-in-the-moist, which is sensed by the smeller. The discrimination of this object is itself an essentially embodied type of discrimination, the realization of, in our case, an air-based capacity to receive bitterness of this type through the air. The capacity to smell such objects is an essentially enmattered capacity, one enmattered, in air-based smellers, in the same type of 'matter' as the smell itself: air.[46]

These considerations suggest a way to challenge a second spiritualist argument which starts from two assumptions:

(1)   The effect on the organ is of the same general type as the effect in the medium, and that

flavour, colour by colour and in general what is of the same kind by something of the same kind' (323b32ff.).

[45] Whether, as Aristotle notes, actually or potentially in the agent (*De Anima* 422a17ff.).

[46] The type of moisture in the air or water has to retain, if Aristotle's account of odour is to be successful, something of the dryness of the objects which were originally permeated by water to form a flavour. Indeed, this seems to be a constraint on the type of *moisture* which, in his theory, is required in both air and water. However, Aristotle made no attempt to spell out further what *moisture* is in this case. (He, almost certainly, lacked the empirical resources to do so.). *Moisture*, in his account, may be understood as a 'stand in' for the specific way in which odours are enmattered. It should further be noted that while what is smelled is, for example, bitterness-in-the-moist, this is consistent with there being smells in the objects themselves, such as in mature cheese or rotten fish, provided that they too contain *moisture*. However, neither of these issues concerning the nature of *moisture* needs to be addressed for the purposes of the present discussion.

(2) In the case of smell the effect in medium is not identical to a movement in the sense of a body going from place to place

and concludes that:

(3) All that essentially occurs in smelling is the smeller being aware of the odour.

(3) captures, for the spiritualist, the idea that the odour appears to the smeller. However, given what has just been said, Aristotle could accept both (1) and (2) without concluding that what occurs is a 'travelling of (pure) form alone' or that its reception is to be defined simply as a purely psychological awareness of a pure form, defined without essential refence to matter. In fact, these considerations point to a different conclusion: what it is for a flavour or odour to be tasted or smelled by a perceiver is for bitterness-in-water or bitterness-in-the-moist (enmattered forms) to be received by the relevant sense organ. If this is correct, and the effect in the sense organ is of the same general type as the effect in the medium (accepting (1)), the effect in the organ which constitutes smelling will also be a matter-involving type of completion.

(1) is a premise which Aristotle accepts (as we saw in his discussion of causation: Chapter 2, Section 6). In the specific case of taste: the operation of the flavour on the sense organ is a case of agency, of its acting on the sense organ. The organ itself is passive, suffering under the impact of the flavour. When there is acting and suffering of this type, the same form is transferred from agent to patient. In the case of flavour, the relevant type of form is a matter-involving form, such as bitterness-in-the-moist. Indeed, what makes tasting the type of perceiving it is, is that it is the reception of a matter-involving form of this type. Given that types of perceiving are defined in terms of their objects, tasting must be essentially a matter-involving activity (or completion). It is the agent's way of being sensitive to the relevant matter-involving form present in the medium. In cases of this type, the agent and patient must share the same type of matter if they are to possess the type of enmattered capacities which are per se causes and effects of the relevant process in the way suggested.[47]

---

[47] In *Physics* Γ.3 Aristotle describes individual cases of acting and suffering 'as the same but different in being'. Some, amongst them David Ross and Ursula Coope, have suggested that he understood these as cases of numerically one process with different descriptions true of it. Others, including Charles (1984: 14–19) and Anna Marmodoro (2007: 205–32), have taken them to be numerically distinct, but necessarily connected, processes. Others, including Charles (2015: 186–205), have argued that Aristotle did not, and did not need to, decide between these alternatives in *Physics* Γ.3 in order to address the problems at issue there. Indeed, elsewhere he talks of phenomena as being 'one and the same' when discussing cases which are necessarily co-extensive as well as those where there is one (definitional) account: see *Metaphysics* 1003b22–5. The present discussion is intended to be neutral as between these alternatives. When I talk of the 'same individual process (or activity)', it is left open

The spiritualist underestimates what is essential, in Aristotle's account, to the impact of the flavour on perceivers. It is not just that, in successful cases, the flavour of an object is revealed to them (in a pure psychological act): there is an essentially moisture-involving process which, as part of his causal account, results in their being aware, in an essentially embodied way, of an enmoistened flavour. His account of taste, it seems, runs as follows:

(1) The flavour in the moist impacts on the sense organ by moistening it in such a way that it (or the person) senses the flavour (we do not sense its wetness or moisture but its flavour).
(2) Sensing the flavour is the exercise of the matter-involving capacity of such an organ: the capacity to sense the flavour in a moisture-involving way.

The change essentially involved in tasting is, it appears, a [Type 2] change: a matter-involving completion. There is more to tasting than simply purely psychological (or phenomenal) awareness of flavour. What occurs is essentially an embodied awareness of flavour, an inextricably enmoistened activity, essentially the realization of inextricably enmattered, goal-directed, capacity. As such, this activity, like the activity of the angry, has an impure form.[48]

In sum: in the case of taste and smell, one cannot define the relevant type of perceptual awareness without referring, in the definition, to material changes in the sense organ. For these are essential to the occurrence of the relevant types of perceptual awareness and are required to explain the distinctive nature of specific types of perception (why they have the features they do: being of certain tastes rather than others). Further, the material changes involved are partially described in terms of material properties such as moisture and are sensitive to such factors as heat and cold.[49] One cannot define these forms of perceptual awareness without reference, as part of the definition, to material activities in the relevant part of the body. Tasting and smelling, like being angry, are inextricably psychophysical activities, the realizations of distinct inextricably enmattered capacities. This is the core of Aristotle's theory of tasting and smelling, the basis for his definition of the essential inextricably psycho-physical phenomena (the relevant activity type and the capacity from which it flows) in terms of their inextricably enmattered forms.

---

which of these alternatives is to be preferred. The central claims in the inextricabilist interpretation do not rest on taking one or other of these options.

[48] I shall return to this issue in Chapter 6.
[49] Perceptions also produce changes in the size and temperature of other parts of the body (see *De Motu* 701b19ff.). It is difficult to see how they can do this unless they have the physical properties required to induce change in size or temperature.

4.8 Tasting: problems for the non-reductionist materialist interpretation

According to non-reductionist materialist interpreters, Aristotle's account of tasting is not simply constituted by the purely psychological (or phenomenal) awareness of flavour (suggested by the spiritualist). It is this type of awareness *plus* a further [Type 1] physical event which is (i) required for that awareness (ii) defined independently of it and (iii) grounds (in some way) the psychological properties of tasting. These interpreters take the view of the purely psychological recommended by the spiritualist and add to it a further purely physical event to complete the full definition of tasting.[50]

There is, for all materialist interpreters, an ordinary purely physical [Type 1] change, such as moistening, which is systematically correlated with, and in some way underlies the taster's awareness of, the relevant flavour. In some non-reductionist accounts, awareness of flavour supervenes on a moistening of this type; in others, there is a type of moistening, always present when we taste flavours, where the specific type of moisture received 'encodes' information that is essential to a separate act of tasting.[51] But these differences, important though they are, are not relevant to our present concerns. In all such accounts, the initial physical changes, however characterized, will—in some way—underlie a purely psychological activity of perceptual awareness of flavour.

In the non-reductionist account, there is a specific fully determinate type of moistening (and moisture), a purely physical [Type 1] change defined independently of the capacity to taste flavours, which grounds the activity of awareness. However, as spiritualists have noted, Aristotle shows no interest in any such purely physical grounding process in *De Anima* or *De Sensu*. The type of moistening involved is defined as one essential to the realization of a capacity, or an organ, designed to taste flavours (see, for example, *De Anima* 422b15ff.). The activity of the flavour in the sense organ (*poiēsis*) results in the sense organ being moistened in the distinctive way sense organs are. The relevant sufferings (*pathēseis*) are those of distinctive types of perceptual organ. They are not defined independently of organs of this type. Further, what occurs in the sense organ is defined as a bringing of that sense organ into 'actuality'. As such, it is a completion (*epiteleiōsis*),

---

[50] Several recent writers (following Burnyeat) have suggested that there is a further purely physical process required for perception (perhaps as a necessary concomitant) which is not connected to the purely psychological one as 'matter to form'. Even though it is not clear what exactly they intend by the phrase 'not as a matter to form', they wish to contrast the case of perception with that of anger (where talk of matter and form seems required).

[51] For an example of the latter account, see Johnstone (2012: 143–83). Johnstone offers an interpretation, which although non-reductive, suggests a type–type correlation between smelling and the underlying physical process. The latter, in his view, contains a determinate type of dryness which 'encodes' the type of odour of which we are aware in smelling. I am indebted to Mark Johnstone for helpful comments on the issues discussed in this chapter.

not a destructive [Type 1] change—since the capacity in the organ required for the change in question survives the change intact, when all goes well. This completion, which essentially involves the organ being moistened, is the suffering of a sense organ brought about by 'flavouring', where the organ is one designed for tasting. It is not a [Type 1] moistening of the type the non-reductionist requires: an independently defined purely material process essentially involved in, and the material ground for, tasting.

Aristotle, in *Meteorologica* 384b30ff., distinguished types of moisture and heat present in goal-directed bodies in terms of (i) the ways they act on the senses and (ii) their other qualities: such as proneness to solidify, melt, or break other objects. In this context, he makes no attempt to explain their action on the senses in terms of their [Type 1] qualities alone, still less in terms of features of basic elements. That a moist body affects the senses in a given way (in organized bodies) is treated as a way of differentiating the relevant type of moisture. There is no mention of purely material types of moisture in this case, defined in terms of [Type 1] qualities alone. Nor does he seek to use [Type 1] features as a basis for defining the impact of moisture on the senses. Indeed, there is no indication of Aristotle attempting to develop the resources required to give a [Type 1] purely material characterization of the type of moistening which grounds tasting in a complex, goal-directed, body.

Some non-reductionist interpreters have appealed to Aristotle's discussion in *Physics* H (VII).3 to support their suggestion that, in the relevant cases, psychological completions 'supervene' on, or in some other way are grounded by, purely material processes of alteration. In this chapter Aristotle notes that when some completions occur it may be necessary that something is altered. Perhaps, for example, in the case of completing a house, the matter in question needs to be heated or thickened (246a5–8) in such a way as to necessitate its completion. Perhaps here he was aiming to characterize the material features in their own terms in such a way that, for example, psychological states (or form more generally) supervene on them.[52]

What do Aristotle's observations in *Physics* H.3 actually establish? He writes, concerning the virtues and vices of the body:

Neither these states (*hexeis*) nor losing or gaining them are quality changes but perhaps it is necessary that they come to be or pass away when the qualities of certain things are changed.   (246b13–15)

However, even if we disregard the cautionary 'perhaps', this is not a clear statement of the view that the relevant quality changes necessitate (or ground) the acquisition or loss of these states. It could be taken simply as the concession that

---

[52] Michael Wedin (1993: 49–105) and Victor Caston (1993: 107–35). For further discussion of these passages, see Maso, Natali, and Seel (2012).

the acquisition and loss of such states requires (as a necessary condition) some change in quality. It does not require that their acquisition supervenes on, or is determined by, these quality changes.[53] Indeed, this less demanding claim seems to be all that is required in a context in which Aristotle is emphasizing that the acquisition of bodily virtues is a completion, even if some quality changes are necessarily involved. He has no reason to make, out of the blue, the further, upwards determination, claim. It is one thing to suggest that health, beauty, and other bodily virtues require a mixture of material ingredients, quite another to insist that the latter determine health and the rest. Further, there is nothing in this context which suggests that he saw the relevant mixtures as defined in purely material terms. The mixtures (or mixings) could be defined just as those required for health. Indeed, this would mirror his way of talking of the way the ingredients of flesh and bone are mixed (*De Anima* 408a15f.): in just the way required to produce them. There is no reason to think that Aristotle is trying, in these two lines in *Physics* H.3, to introduce an explanatory, materialist, account of conditions sufficient for the acquisition, presence, or loss of health.

There is a further problem: Aristotle's remark in 246b13–15 shows at most that *some* completions require ordinary alterations, not that *all* do. In the case of knowledge acquisition or manifestation, no such alteration is essentially involved (247b7–8). It may be that some [Type 1] changes are needed as a causal background for the [Type 2] changes in epistemic states that occur. A person may need to 'sober up' (in Aristotle's example: 248a4ff.) to be able to become a knower. Their sobering up is what enables them to come to know, not what their coming to know supervenes on. Even if Aristotle had held, contrary to my previous reservations, that ordinary alterations provide the subvening ground for the acquisition of health or other bodily virtues, he did not extend this account to the case of knowledge. Indeed, he seems unconvinced that there are any such alterations in the similar cases of coming to see or touch something (247b8–10).

Aristotle's discussion of the acquisition of virtues of the soul (246b21–247a19) is revealing. He claims that when they (and their opposing vices) are acquired or lost there are bodily pleasures and pains, here described as quality changes of the perceptual part (247a15–17: see 247a5–6). But there is no suggestion that such pleasures and pains (of taste or touch) are to be defined wholly in terms of basic material elements (such as the hot and the cold). Elsewhere these changes are classified as 'common to the body and the soul' (*De Sensu* 436a10f.): essentially psycho-physical phenomena. They are not the type of purely material, grounding, change non-reductionist interpreters require.

---

[53] Similar remarks apply to the equally cautious claim in 246a6–8 and the less cautious claim about the acquisition and loss of virtues of the soul in 247a5–6. In the latter case, the relevant changes in the perceptual part may only be necessary conditions for their occurrence.

How, according to Aristotle's account in *Physics* H.3, are ordinary [Type 1] quality changes involved? Earlier it was suggested that as in the case of knowledge acquisition, a completion, one could describe what happened in any particular case as a transition from one specific state of the soul to another. This would be an accidental description of the relevant completion, which was defined essentially as the manifestation of a goal-directed capacity for knowledge. Its beginning with that specific false belief (rather than another) is an accidental feature of the completion that occurred. A similar account could be offered of a builder's completing the house. Any description of it as a [Type 1] change, such as beginning with five bricks required to finish the job (and not three), would be an accidental description of the completion that occurred. In neither case would there be any further alteration. Indeed, to describe what happened as a quality alteration would not be the best thing to say: this would only be an accidental description of the completion of the house (the one activity that really occurred).

Aristotle's description of the role of pleasures and pains in the acquisition of virtues and vices seems to exemplify just this structure. Although in *Physics* H.3, these are described as quality changes (247a16), elsewhere he notes that some pleasures, those which have a further end, are ones in which 'one is led towards the completion' of one's nature' (*Nicomachean/Eudemian Ethics* 1153a12). He continues:

> And this is why it is not a fine thing to say that a pleasure is a perceived generation (*geneseis*): rather it should be said to be an activity of a natural condition (*hexis*).

These pleasures are best described as 'completions', activities which bring one to one's natural goal. To describe them as [Type 1] quality changes (or comings into being) would not be speaking finely, even if—to make this consistent with his remark in *Physics* H.3, 247a16f.—one is not speaking falsely. To do so is to give an accidental, and incomplete, description of the completion that occurs. To describe it as an alteration, without essential reference to the natural states being completed (or exercised), is to fail to capture the essence of what happened. No separate quality change need occur. In these cases, there are essentially [Type 2] changes described accidentally in [Type 1] ways.

Perhaps this is how Aristotle saw the relevant ontology in these cases. Maybe he generalized this model in his discussion of seeing, touching, and perceiving in general. In these too there will be just one essentially psycho-physical [Type 2] activity which can be described accidentally in [Type 1] ways. All that happens in any case of tasting or smelling is just a [Type 2] completion of this kind.

The evidence of *Physics* H.3 is not conclusive. Aristotle might have thought that, for example, all individual cases of finishing a house were accompanied by some distinct particular ordinary, [Type 1], alteration or other: an instance of the type of lifting, carrying, or heating of bricks required to complete the house. However, even if he did so, the distinct [Type 1] alterations would, so understood, be essentially ones guided by the builder's skill. These intentional actions, like the pleasures or pains mentioned later in H.3, would be essentially psycho-physical alterations: ones common to body and soul. They would not be the type of material ground the non-reductionist materialist interpreter requires. This is because the identity of the [Type 1] alteration, and how it develops, is dependent on the knowledge exercised in completing the house. The type of lifting or heating is a skill-directed lifting or heating, the particular liftings instances of this type. Indeed, which [Type 1] alteration occurs is determined by the way the [Type 2] completion develops: how the builder proceeds to complete the house.

If Aristotle applied this latter model to the case of tasting, the particular moistening that occurs would be an instance of the type of moistening required for tasting. It would be defined in this way, not simply as an instance of a general, purely material, capacity for moistening. This is because to do the latter would be to fail to capture why the [Type 1] alteration develops and ends as it does. Instead, the [Type 1] alteration at issue will, on this model, itself be essentially psycho-physical, whose identity and nature is dependent on the [Type 2] exercise of the enmattered capacity to taste involved. Introducing a further [Type 1] alteration of this type to add to the explanatorily more fundamental [Type 2] completion might have seemed a piece of 'harmless ontologizing'. The further [Type 1] alteration will not, in any event, ground the [Type 2] completion in the way the non-reductionist suggests nor be the realization of a separate purely material capacity.

It is not clear which of these two ontological models best captures Aristotle's intentions. But, either way, his resulting picture will be that of an inextricabilist. The [Type 2] activity of tasting cannot be defined without explicit reference to an enmattered, goal-directed, capacity. Nor can the [Type 1] material alteration be defined without explicit reference, in one of the ways mentioned, to the psychological activity of tasting. Whichever option Aristotle favoured, there will be a unified, definitionally inextricable, response in the taster. Indeed, once his inextricabilist claims had been secured, he might have been happy—given his goals—to use either model to present his central claims. Perhaps he did not need to decide between them.[54]

There is one further aspect of the non-reductionist materialist account of perception that requires scrutiny: the suggestion that the activity of awareness of a taste is purely psychological, defined without essential reference to moistening. If tasting is of flavour and flavour is an enmoistened form, tasting itself must be the reception of an enmoistened form. To taste is to be sensitive to, and receptive of, an essentially moisture-involving form of this type: bitterness-in-the-water.

---

[54] See also note 47 above. For further discussion of this issue, see Chapter 8, Section 6.

There is no receiving of bitterness of this type which is not moisture-involving. To taste is to sense an enmoistened flavour in a moisture-involving way. Absent this, and what occurs will not be a tasting of flavour. (It might be a case of imagining that one was tasting flavour: a way of engaging with the relevant form without doing so then in the specifically moisture-involving way a perceiver does.) Or so I have argued.

The same general type of activity (at least with respect to the form involved) is found, in Aristotle's account, in the agent and patient. It is not that the agent operates without actually possessing the form and the patient (somehow mysteriously) injects it on receiving a lower level prompt received from the agent. Nor does the patient initially lose the form transferred to it from the agent only (again somewhat mysteriously) to regain it later in grasping the form. In the case of tasting, the activity of the agent (the enmattered flavour in the moisture) has to be of the same general type as the activity of the taster. If so, since the former is essentially a moisture-involving activity, so too is the latter. Tasting is to be defined as the moisture-involving activity of receiving the relevant form: bitterness-in-the-moist. This is the type of inextricably psycho-physical activity it is. (These considerations follow the pattern discerned in Chapter 2 and exemplified by the discussion of desire in Chapter 3.)[55]

There is a related issue. Even if one were to concede, for the sake of argument, that Aristotle was (despite appearances to the contrary) assuming that a [Type 1] purely material moistening is present in the perceiver, how does this process, in his view, 'underlie' or 'ground' the perceptual awareness of flavour? How, in his account, does a perceptual awareness of flavour, in his view, arise out of simple moistening? What is it about some types of moistening, wholly defined in purely material terms, that 'grounds' perceptual sensitivity to flavours as flavours? Non-reductionist interpreters cannot allow that, for Aristotle, the relevant moistening is merely a necessary condition for tasting. If it were, their account would be in danger of collapsing into a version of spiritualism.

Aristotle must have thought, if the non-reductionist account is correct, that [Type 1] purely material changes ground the perceiver's awareness of flavour. How do they do so? There is no obvious sign that Aristotle attempted to answer this pressing question. We are confronted, as in Chapter 3 when discussing the relation between desire and bodily action, by an unnerving silence at just the point where, as interpreted by the materialist, a theory is most required. What is it

---

[55] If tasting had been defined, in the purist fashion, simply as the reception (or cognition) of flavour (itself defined without essential reference to the moist), why would tasting (so defined) have required, or hypothetically necessitated, the presence of moistening? That is: if reception of flavour can be defined solely in terms of, for example, awareness of bitterness (or sweetness), without any reference to moisture, why should such awareness, in its nature, require the presence of moisture rather than air? It is not enough to say that tasting, as things are, involves moisture. One needs to explain from the nature of the psychological act of tasting itself why this must be so. For a contrasting account: see Johansen (2012: 168).

about moistening, defined in purely material terms, that generates, in his account, awareness of flavour? Aristotle's silence on this issue is particularly telling. In *De Sensu* 442a30ff., he criticized Democritus' theory of perception precisely because it leaves just such a gap between the physical impact of the atoms on perceivers and their perceiving colours or tastes. Non-reductionist interpreters need to explain why Aristotle thought that his own account, as they understand it, is immune from the type of criticism he levelled against Democritus. It is not an act of charity to present him as (blissfully) unaware of precisely the same type of gap in his own theory!

Sophisticated proponents of the non-reductionist interpretation have addressed this issue, itself a micro-version of our own post-Cartesian general mind–body problem. Some have suggested that the awareness of a bitter flavour instantiates, in Aristotle's account, the same ratio as is found in the [Type 1] change of moistening by a bitter juice. We are aware of a particular *flavour* because the activity of tasting instantiates the same ratio as is present in the relevant type of moistening. On this interpretation, there will be a [Type 1] process of moistening which can ground the activity of tasting bitterness because both instantiate the same ratio. (The activity of tasting is defined psychologically but will be, in their view, necessarily enmattered in something other than moisture: e.g. heat or dryness.)[56]

This last suggestion, in aiming to explain (at least in outline) how the perception of flavour emerges from moistening, marks a significant advance on interpretations which talk freely of 'supervenience', 'upwards determination', and 'grounding', without indicating why Aristotle might have found such claims true or intelligible. However, even this more sophisticated interpretation encounters serious problems, some exegetical, others theoretical.

One might ask, at the outset, the following theoretical question: what—absent moisture—makes the relevant type of perceptual awareness one of tasting a flavour? There are, after all, ratios instantiated in other types of perception. Indeed, as we have seen, the same ratios may be present both in smells and flavours. If we remove Aristotle's suggestion that in the latter case what is perceived is bitterness-in-the-moist and in the former bitterness-in-the-air, what makes one case a tasting, the other a smelling? A major explanatory gap remains. Aristotle, so interpreted, still lacks an explanation of why we taste bitter flavours rather than being aware (somehow) of ratios found in water and air. At the crucial point, there is, once again, an unnerving silence in his account.

While the exegetical evidence in favour of this proposal will be assessed below, the considerable effort expended in constructing these ingenious non-reductionist interpretations on the basis of a few phrases is, from the inextricabilist viewpoint, 'wasted labour'. If tasting is the awareness of bitterness-in-water, a phenomenon

---

[56] See, for example, Caston (2005: 306).

that is essentially enmattered in the moist, tasting must itself be an essentially embodied, moisture-involving, activity. It will not be defined as a combination of an ordinary [Type 1] moistening plus a distinct type of psychological activity, such as ratio detection, where that activity and its object are defined independently of moistening. The specific type of moistening will be defined in inextricably psycho-physical terms as the moistening of a perceptual organ: the activation of its capacity to taste. There is, from this viewpoint, no need to search in his writings, as materialist interpreters do, for specific types of purely physical alterations, still less to devise increasingly subtle and sophisticated accounts of their connection with purely psychological ones. Indeed, we should not be surprised, against the background of his general view of the matter and form of natural substances (as set out in Chapter 2), to find no clear signs of his carrying through this project. The simplest explanation is that he was operating with fundamentally different, non-Cartesian, assumptions about the psychological and the physical. To seek to understand his account on the basis of our post-Cartesian assumptions is to be in danger of losing what is philosophically most significant about it.

Many non-reductionist interpreters reason as follows: there must be, they correctly think, more to tasting than awareness of flavour as defined in the spiritualist account. So, they conclude, there must be a separate independently defined, further purely physical, process (a [Type 1] process) essentially involved in perceiving, which underlies that awareness.

We can now diagnose their misstep. While tasting is, in Aristotle's account, more than simply (pure) awareness of flavour, it is not a type of pure awareness plus a further purely physical underlying process. Instead, tasting is, in his view, an inextricably psycho-physical completion, which is (in its own nature) essentially and inextricably a moisture-involving responding to flavour in the medium. He had no need to supplement his story by hypothesizing the existence of a further purely physical underlying process to ground the purely psychological activity of awareness or to worry about the connection between these two definitionally independent components. The type of moistening at issue could not occur in something other than a sense organ: it is defined as a moistening-of-such-an-organ. The psycho-physical capacities of this organ are the only capacities which are essential to tasting.[57]

---

[57] This formulation is strictly neutral on the issue raised above: is there a numerically psycho-physical distinct process (in the sense organ) which underlies the psycho-physical activity of discrimination? Or is there numerically one activity which can be described in different ways? My immediate aim is to challenge the claim that there is an underlying (grounding) purely physical process, defined independently of discrimination, in these cases.

4.9 Tasting and smelling: a summary

In Aristotle's account of tasting:

[1] The person's discriminating flavour is the same activity as their sense organ's being affected by flavour.
[2] Their sense organ being affected by flavour is the same activity as the flavour affecting the sense organ [acting and suffering: *poiēsis/pathēsis*].[58]
[3] In cases of acting and suffering, the acting and suffering are (i) the same in general type and such that (ii) the patient receives what the agent gives [causal principle].
[4] The flavour which affects the sense organ is essentially a matter-involving phenomenon (such as bitterness-in-water) which (i) affects the sense organ in essentially matter-involving ways (such as moistening it) in such a way that (ii) the patient receives what the agent gives (e.g. bitterness in the water) [from [2] and [3]].
[5] The person's discriminating of flavour is essentially a matter-involving type of activity: its organ being moistened in such a way that the patient receives the bitterness-in-the-water [from [4] and [1]].

Both tasting and smelling are affections 'common to the body and soul' because what is perceived in both cases is an enmattered form (such as bitterness-in-the-water or bitterness-in-the-air) and the perceiving itself is the realization of an enmattered capacity. Tasting is the realization of a capacity of the relevant bodily organ—if affected by the flavour—to be moistened in such a way as to taste that flavour. Smelling, similarly, is the realization of the capacity of a distinct bodily organ—if affected by a smell in the medium—to be dried in such a way as to sense that smell.

Tasting and smelling, if this is correct, are 'common to the body and soul' in the same way as anger, fear, and desire. Tasting and smelling, like the emotions and desire, will both be, in the ways indicated, inextricably psycho-physical, not decomposable into two definitionally independent components in the way post-Cartesian philosophers standardly assume. The relevant type of activity is defined, in Aristotle's simple theory, as inextricably psycho-physical, the realization of an inextricably psycho-physical goal-directed material capacity. Both the form and the matter of tasting and smelling are, in these ways, inextricably psycho-physical.

---

[58] See note 47 above for further clarification of my understanding of Aristotle's talk of 'the same activity'.

4.10 The case of touch

Does touching, in Aristotle's view, follow the same pattern? Some aspects of his discussion suggest [H.1]-style considerations:

(1) Some types of perceptual impact are said to be too strong for the sense organ to bear and to destroy the relevant 'formula' (*logos*) of the body in the same ways as some heavy blows might break a musical instrument. When this happens, the animal with the damaged sense organ can no longer perceive (424a28–32). Clearly, it is necessary for perception that there be a basically undamaged sense organ present (where such an organ is a bodily magnitude: 424a26–7). If there is no such appropriate bodily state present, there will be no suffering for the relevant objects of sense (424a32ff.).

Other remarks suggest [H.2]-style considerations:

(2) In the case of touch, the sense organ is said to be affected by the blow struck as a man is struck through his shield (423b15ff.). Later, Aristotle invokes the analogy with the lyre: here too the way in which the lyre is struck (424b32ff.) determines the sharpness of the note produced.[59] The speed of the blow determines the type of note emitted. In the case of a blow experienced as through a shield, the type of experience will be determined by the speed and heaviness of the blow struck.

(3) The sense organ is, in his view, incapable of sensing objects as warm as it is (423b27ff.) but only ones which are warmer or colder than it. This tells us something more about the way in which the relevant sense organ is struck in these cases. Only warmer or colder objects can produce the type of blow (or change) in the sense organ which is required if it is to register their temperature. Objects of the same temperature cannot do this. In this case, the effectiveness of the blow to the sense organ depends on its heat and that of the striker.

Why is (3) the case? If all that occurs is a purely psychological act of touch-perception, why should the perceptual faculty not be able to sense an object of the same temperature as its sense organ? Why couldn't it simply register the external object's temperature as being the same as its own? Something more must be involved: a type of suffering which is dependent on the initial heat of the organ

---

[59] Aristotle makes a similar correlation between the quickness of the movement of air in the relevant sense organ and the sharpness of the sound heard. In the case of hearing, animals only hear because the air inside their ears is moved (420a2ff.). Aristotle speaks of the part to be moved as containing air and being ensouled (420a7).

and which is not possible if that is the same as that of the external object. It is hard to see how a suffering of this type, one determined by these factors, is not either a physical or psycho-physical change in the sense organ, which requires it to be of such a temperature that it can be affected in some way by the impact made by the heat of the external object (via the medium). For if the change essentially involved in touching is not physical (or psycho-physical), why should its occurrence (and non-occurrence) be dependent on the initial heat of the sense organ?

Aristotle does not (in B.11) attempt to specify the type of physical (or psycho-physical) change involved in the case of touch. There is, however, no need to assume that the organ of touch is itself heated in the way water is in being touched. That which is of mean temperature could register the heat of an external object by being affected by it in some other way. Consider a possible analogy: red objects fail to absorb red light *not* because they cannot be made even more red by the source of the light but because they have limited abilities for absorption: they cannot respond in this way to the colour in question. By contrast, the 'transparent' will respond when red light is played on to it. In a similar way, the organ of touch might fail to register objects of the same heat because it lacks a similar quasi-reflective ability. By contrast, when it responds to objects of greater or lesser heat, it is enough that it responds to them in this (quasi-reflective) way. It need not be literally made hotter by them. (Analogy: a thermometer might be designed to register on its scale only temperatures greater or less than its own.)

Consider Aristotle's case of the lyre. Here, the speed of the blow determines the sharpness of the note produced. The quickness of the movement is, as we noted, registered perceptually in the sharpness, not in the speed, of the sound heard. It is enough that the impact of the blow is registered in some way or other. It need not be registered by the sense organ (or string) affected itself being literally speeded up.

In the case of touch, one cannot, given [H.2] considerations, define the relevant type of perceiving without reference to some material movements in the sense organ. For these are essential to the occurrence of tactile perception and are invoked to explain why it sometimes fails and why specific perceptions have the features they do. Further, these changes are described in part in terms of their physical properties (force and speed) and are sensitive to such factors as heat and cold.[60] As in the case of anger, one cannot define this form of perception without essential and explicit reference to physical movements of the relevant part of the body. Sensing heat is the inextricably material realization of an inextricably material capacity.

---

[60] Perceptions also produce changes in the size and temperature of other parts of the body (see *De Motu* 701b19ff.). It is difficult to see how they can do this unless they have the physical properties required to induce change in size or temperature.

In the case of touch, when the sense organ is affected, that which is in the mean state is moved in a given way. The mean is what discriminates hot and cold (424a5–7) by being affected by them. It appears that the very same process is the mean's being moved in a given way and its discriminating a given temperature. There is no suggestion that there are two separate changes: the mean's being moved and its discriminating heat. The mean is, it seems, the ensouled part which is affected by the relevant movement (see 420a7), the one which discriminates heat or coldness.

4.11 Taking on the form without the matter

Does Aristotle's account of tasting, smelling, and touching, as interpreted in the previous sections, provide the basis for understanding the summary of his views on sense perception in *De Anima* B.12? In this section, I shall seek to show that it does.

Aristotle speaks elsewhere of perceptual discrimination as *the* activity of sense in the sense organ (426b7ff.). He is, it seems, committed to the following claim:

[I]   that which is in the mean state being active in way A is the same activity as the sense's discriminating B.

He does not, as we have seen, seek to account for the mean's being moved in a given manner solely in terms of the sense's discriminating its object in the pure, non-matter-involving, way the spiritualist interpreter suggests. The relevant type of discrimination essentially involves some bodily processes in the sense organ. Nor is the movement in the sense organ to be defined independently of the sense's discriminating its object. If so, the bodily process and the relevant discrimination will be inter-defined: in Aristotle's terminology, the same activity.

Is this Aristotle's consistent view in *De Anima* B.12? More specifically: is (i) the relevant bodily process, as understood in this chapter, defined by reference to the end it serves and the psychological capacity with which it engages: one directed to the discrimination of the relevant sense objects? and (ii) the relevant discrimination itself defined as an embodied reception of an enmattered form, the essentially embodied exercise of an inextricably embodied capacity? Is there just one essentially psycho-physical activity (type) in each of these cases?

I shall sketch an affirmative answer to both questions. Aristotle begins this chapter as follows:

The sense (in each case) is that which receives perceptible qualities without receiving the matter [of those things which have the perceptible qualities] just as the wax receives the sign on the ring without receiving the lead or gold. It receives the golden or bronze sign but not in so far as it is golden or bronze. (424a17–21)

At this stage in his discussion he does not distinguish between the sense and the sense organ but speaks freely of the former being affected by sensible qualities. (This issue is clarified later.) His point is that in cases of sense perception the relevant sense is affected by the relevant sensible qualities of objects, without being affected by the matter of the objects to which those sense qualities belong.[61] He seeks to make this idea more precise on the basis of an analogy with marks made in wax, noting two things:

(1) the wax receives the sign on the ring but does not receive the lead or gold of the ring;
(2) the wax receives the golden or bronze sign but not in so far as it is gold or bronze.

What do these claims say about the change involved? According to (1), the wax is affected by the sign on the ring but not by the lead or gold of the ring. In one way this is true: the wax receives the sign but does not receive gold or lead from the ring. That is, the material nature of the wax is not changed so as to become more like gold or lead. It certainly does not take in gold or lead matter from the ring but remains wax throughout. However, it is not true (at least without qualification) that: if the ring is golden, the wax is not affected (in some way) by the gold in the ring. The gold presses down on the wax to leave the mark. So, Aristotle adds a further qualification to (2): whether the sign belongs to a golden or bronze ring makes no difference to what is received by the wax. That is, there is nothing about the mark imprinted in the wax that shows that it is made by a bronze rather than a golden ring. The wax registers some features of the ring (its sign/shape) but not others (its material composition).
Aristotle, so interpreted, is making just two points:

(a) the material nature of the wax (as wax) is not changed by what happens (in contrast with cases where the wax is heated and melts); and

---

[61] I understand the phrase 'receiving the form without the matter' adverbially as shorthand for receiving the Form without receiving the matter. This reading does not require Aristotle to talk of a new entity: *the Form without the matter*, which is received when we perceive. This distinction is important as the adverbial reading allows Aristotle to maintain that it is the very same form that is in the object and received by the perceiver. The second reading, by contrast, commits him to there being two objects involved in perceiving: the enmattered Form in the object and a matter-free Form which is received by the perceiver. The latter account is the basis for talk of a separate 'intentional' object which is perceived; the first has no such commitments. I am indebted at this point to discussion with Paolo Crivelli.

(b) the wax is unaffected by certain features of the gold ring (its being golden) and only affected by others (such as having a certain shape). It is, we might say, selectively affected by certain aspects of the ring.[62]

Both ideas are at work in his immediately preceding discussion of touch. The sense organ, when all goes well, is unaffected by the object in question: its material nature is not changed to be made more golden or even hotter by the impact on it of the hot golden object. Second, it is responsive (in the way it is) only to certain features, such as the heat of the object. Whether the heat belongs to a bronze or golden object makes no difference to the perceiver's experience. There is nothing about the experience that shows that it is made by a golden rather than a bronze object. The change in the sense organ (1) does not change its material nature and (2) is based only on certain relevant features of the object. The tactile mean, introduced in *De Anima* B.11, allows Aristotle to describe in outline how this can happen: the tactile sense organ can register heat without its relevant material nature being changed (or itself necessarily being heated). It is enough that it responds in some way to the heat of the object (424a5ff.). This discriminatory response is to a specific type of enmattered form: the heat of the object involved in this case. It does not discriminate the iron in the poker which is hot.

Similar features are present in the case of taste. The sense organ is responsive to certain features of the drink tasted. We taste, as we have seen, the bitterness-in-the-water not the water itself. The sense organ is sensitive to this type of enmattered (or enmoistened) form not to the matter itself. This is why in tasting we receive the form without receiving the matter: we taste bitterness-in-the-moist not the moist, the matter in which the form is presented to the sense organ. While tasting essentially involves that sense organ's being moistened, what is tasted is the enmattered form: bitterness or sweetness in the moist. Similarly, smelling is sensitivity to bitterness-in-the-air or the-moist, a different enmattered form. One does not smell the air or the moisture but the bitterness therein. In this way, both tasting and smelling receive the form without receiving the matter.

Aristotle develops these points in what follows:

> In a similar way the sense for each object is affected by that which has colour or flavour or sound, not in so far as each of those things is said to be [what it is:

---

[62] I understand the phase 'without the matter' as indicating just these two claims. It does not mean that there is no physical (or material) change in the organ (or wax). After all, the latter is physically moulded by the mark on the ring. (Indeed, in *De Anima* 412b6–8 the wax and the shape there are mentioned as a paradigm case of a unified phenomenon.) Instead, the phrase indicates that (i) the wax does not take in matter from the gold, (ii) the wax does not change so as to become more like gold (it is not in either way assimilated to gold), and (iii) the golden nature of the ring does not (in the appropriate way) affect the nature of the impact made. ((iii) would be true even if this very type of impact could only be made by a gold ring. The fact that the imprint had been made by a gold ring would not be clear on the basis of the impact alone. One would need a lot of additional background information to work this out.)

such as a house] but in so far as it is of this type [coloured, flavoured . . .] and in accordance with the formula (*logos*). (424a22–4)

What does the last phrase mean? If it is understood as 'in accordance with the formula of it as a sense', it matches the earlier phrase ('in accordance with the account of each as the thing they are') and explains the transition to the following sentence: 'the sense organ is the first thing in which this kind of capacity is present' (424a24–5). It is because the capacity is the one required for tasting that the sense organ can be correctly described as the first thing in which this kind of capacity is present.[63] This is, it seems, why Aristotle continues:

The sense organ is the same as that in which this kind of capacity is underivatively present [viz. the sense], but they are different in being. For that which perceives [viz. the sense organ] is a kind of magnitude but neither that which is capable of perception nor the sense itself is a magnitude; they are rather a kind of formula or capacity of the sense organ. (424a26–8)

The sense organ is essentially extended. It is the place in which the perceptual capacity is located. But the capacity to taste is not itself essentially extended. Neither is the sense (that which is, in the first place, capable of perceiving). Rather the sense and the capacity to perceive are the formula or capacity of the sense organ. They are, in the terminology of Chapter 2, inextricably enmattered capacities, not extended bits of matter.

Aristotle, at this point, clarifies his earlier talk of the sense being affected *in accordance with the account* (424a23ff.). The sense organ is affected by the object in the world in accordance with the formula which makes it that sense. It is affected, that is, in the way required for the object in question to be perceived as, for example, hot or cold. Since perception essentially involves discrimination, his idea can be summarized as follows: the sense organ is affected in the way required

---

[63] Victor Caston (2005: 306) has suggested an alternative reading of this passage. It runs as follows:

Perception of each special sensible suffers from each of what has colour, flavour or noise, not in so far as each of those things is said to be coloured, flavoured but in so far as each is a given type of thing, one understood as in line with the relevant proportion (*hē toiondi kai kata ton logon*).

This reading has several disadvantages: (i) it introduces talk of 'proportion' apparently out of the blue, with no immediate contextual support; (ii) it breaks the parallelism between each of these things (what has colour and flavour) and gold or bronze in the previous line (424a21): one would expect 'each of these things is said to be' to specify the object/matter that has the colour etc. not the fact of its colour which appears to be captured by 'as such'; (iii) it understands the phrase 'and in line with the relevant proportion' as explicative of the type of thing just introduced *(toiondi)*: being such that is in line with a given proportion. However, since I have not been able to find a parallel use of the Greek expression '*toiondi kai*' introducing a new kind explicated by '*kai*' (understood as 'that is'), it seems preferable to take 'such *(toiondi)*' to refer back to being coloured or flavoured and to understand the expression '*kai*' to mean 'and' and to introduce a further claim.

for the perceiver to discriminate the object in question. The determinate type of affection is defined as the affection of a sense organ with this capacity. It is the essentially embodied activity of a similarly inextricably embodied capacity.

If this is correct, the way that which is in the mean state (viz. the sense organ) is active will be precisely that required for the sense (or better the perceiver) to perceptually discriminate the object in question. Indeed, definition of how the former is moved (way A) must involve reference, in the definition, to the way required to discriminate the objects at issue. There are movements in the relevant organ when we perceive but these are defined in terms of the goal of perceptual discrimination. In any particular case, there will be one physical process in the sense organ (analogous to wax being imprinted) which is also a discrimination of the sense object. One cannot adequately specify the relevant changes in the sense organ except as the ones required for discrimination of the relevant objects. If there were a type of physical change which resembled this one in some (perhaps many) physical respects but did not serve the same goal or engage with the same perceptual capacities, it would be a different type of change. As in the case of anger, one and the same process is essentially and inextricably a psycho-physical change.

The remainder of *De Anima* B.12, when seen from this perspective, tells a coherent story. Aristotle first draws an immediate consequence from his suggestion that the sense is a capacity of the sense organ:

> It is clear from this why excessive sense objects destroy sense organs (for if the process is too strong for the sense organ, the formula—that is the sense/capacity—is destroyed, just as the harmony and attunement [of the strings] is destroyed when the strings are hit too strongly).

If the sense is the defining capacity of the sense organ, the sense organ will be destroyed if the capacity is destroyed. For the sense organ will cease to exist if it loses its capacity to perceive. In this passage, Aristotle calls attention to the fact that there is one process (*the* process: 424a30) which is both too strong for the sense organ and destructive of the sense as there is one process which is a too heavy hitting of the strings and is destructive of their harmony (their ability to mix high and low notes) and attunement (their ability to hit the correct note). In the former case, there is one process which is both a physical (a strong hitting) and a psychological change (destroying the capacity to perceive/discriminate). This is precisely what we would have expected if (as has been argued) in the normal (non-destructive) case there is one process which is inextricably both a physical change (the mean being moved in a given way) and a case of perceptual discrimination.

Aristotle suggests that excessive (too strong) blows destroy the sense organ because they destroy its capacity to perceive (as excessive blows destroy the strings because they destroy their capacity to play notes). But what counts as an excessive blow? In the present context, it is one which destroys its capacity to see (play the notes). The relevant characterization of the physical blow (as too strong for the sense organ) will depend essentially on the psychological effect it has (as when destroying the capacity to perceive). Here, as in the case of normal perception, the physical description of the impact of the blow on the sense organ is inextricably connected, in definition, with its psychological impact.

Aristotle draws out a second consequence of his view as follows:

[It is also clear] why plants do not perceive, although they have some soul-like function and are affected by the objects of touch (for they are heated and cooled). The reason is that they lack a mean, the type of governing feature which can receive the objects of sense. Rather they suffer along with the matter.   (424a32–b3)

Plants cannot perceive because they lack a mean. Their lack of a mean does not consist simply in their lack of an ability to perceive (for, if so, there would be no explanation). Rather they lack the type of sense organ that can (e.g.) register heat without its relevant material nature being changed. That is, they lack the type of organ which, while remaining materially the same, can respond to the heat of the object. As a result, they cannot perceive heat (even when they are heated). However, while the type of organ has these physical aspects, it is defined as 'that material organ which can receive the objects of sense', using terms which refer to its psychological role. Nor should this surprise us if Aristotle holds (as suggested above) that the mean's moving in these ways just is, in the inextricably psychophysical way suggested, our discriminating the relevant sense objects. In the present case, the organ is moved materially in just the ways required for us to perceive heat and cold. Plants, by contrast, when they get hot or cold, 'suffer with the matter'. Since they lack a mean of the relevant type, the impact a hot object has on them is simply to change their material nature (as that of wax would be changed if heat melted it). They become in some material respect more like the object that heats them (e.g. in heat).[64]

These remarks suggest a convincing interpretation of Aristotle's closing remarks in B.12:

---

[64] This understanding of this passage does not commit Aristotle to either of the following claims:

[1] plants actually take in warm material from the sun when they suffer with the matter; for they could suffer in this way if the sun induced a material change in them, one that altered their matter (as in an ordinary *alloiōsis*);

[2] we, in perceiving, receive the Form without receiving any material bearer (from the medium); for while the Form may not change our material nature, it may call into play its capacity to see (a special kind of change marked out in *De Anima* B.5, 417b15–17).

For an alternative view of this passage, see Burnyeat (1992: 19–24). His interpretation of this and other aspects of *De Anima* B.12 is convincingly criticized by Stephen Everson (1997).

> Tangible objects and flavours affect lifeless objects and change them...and indeed even smell and noise affect some lifeless objects too...but not all: smell affects air for example. What is smelling beyond being affected in some way? Or is it that smelling is perceiving, while the air is affected quickly and becomes perceptible? (424b12–21)

The crucial difference, to which he draws attention, between smelling and the way the air is affected is that the latter (like other lifeless things) lacks a mean: a physical organ of the type required for perception. Air lacks a definite nature (424b15) and is easily moved. By contrast, the sense organ (in the case of smell) is enclosed and, as such, can retain the air in place long enough for it to be smelled (422a2–3). These features, the presence of the mean and the relative persistence of the smell in the enclosed air there, are essential for this type of perception. Our smelling an object is for our relevant mean to be materially affected by something retained in the air in the nostrils. Smelling, so far from being a purely psychological activity of perceiving, is defined in terms of the inextricably enmattered capacity of the relevant sense organ (with its mean) to be affected in such a way as to discriminate the smell in question. There is, as in the case of tactile perception, an essentially psycho-physical activity to which defining physical and psychological elements inextricably belong.

Throughout this discussion, Aristotle treats receiving the form of the object without its matter as the same activity as the sense organ being affected materially by the form of the object. Tasting is a unified inextricably psycho-physical type of activity: it is the activity of one psycho-physical capacity of the relevant sense organ. Smelling is another. Touching another. This activity in the sense organ is the same activity as its being likened (or made similar to) the relevant property of the object sensed.[65] It is an example of the distinctive type of [Type 2] suffering which perceiving turns out to be. There is no need to, and reason not to, postulate an underlying [Type 1] purely material change in the sense organ to do justice to Aristotle's account of tasting, smelling, and touching. No such definitionally distinct kinds of change occur.[66]

---

[65] I rely at this point on my discussion of the 'likening' involved in perception (2000: 112–18). It should be noted, however, that in that discussion there are suggestions of my earlier two-component account which I now reject (as when writing of a change in the eye-jelly as 'a physiological change' occurring 'as well as awareness of an object' (p. 117). For a helpful, and congenial, discussion of the relation between receiving the form without the matter and being made like the object, see Hendrik Lorenz (2007: 179–220).

[66] This is why there is no need to answer the further question raised, but not addressed, by Lorenz in the final section of his paper: how are two such kinds of affection related to one another (2007: Section 3)? This is, if I am correct, a pseudo-question which Lorenz wisely did not attempt to answer.

4.12 Interim conclusions

Aristotle, I have argued, developed an account of tasting, smelling and touching as inextricably psycho-physical phenomena, which provides a way to interpret his summarizing discussion in *De Anima* B.12. He did not accept either of the post-Cartesian assumptions, [A] and [B], set out in Section 4.1. In fact, he rejected both, understanding the relevant psychological and physical features as, in the ways explained, inextricably psycho-physical. In his simple theory of these phenomena, they have to be defined as inextricably psycho-physical (and possessed of forms of this type) to be causally produced in the way they are by flavours, smells, and the impact of hot, heavy objects.

Did he apply the same style of account to hearing and to seeing? While we should expect a positive answer to this question on the basis of his generalizing remarks on perception in *De Anima* B.12, I shall seek to confirm this impression by considering the details of his discussion in Chapter 5.

5
Hearing, Seeing, and Hylomorphism

5.1 Hearing: the issue

In Aristotle's discussion of taste, smell, and touch, two types of consideration played an important role:

[H.1] If there were no appropriate bodily process present, there would be no suffering (*pathēsis*) of the relevant type (such as tasting or smelling).

[H.2] The nature of the bodily features present affects the nature of the suffering itself.

These considerations, taken in conjunction with some of his ideas about efficient causation, led Aristotle to view these types of perceiving as inextricably psycho-physical phenomena possessed of impure, inextricably enmattered, forms. Or so it was argued in Chapter 4. Are similar considerations at work in his account of hearing and of seeing? Are these also inextricably psycho-physical completions (*epiteleiōseis*) with similarly enmattered forms: the exercises of inextricably enmattered capacities? Does he extend to these phenomena the type of simple theory he developed in defining tasting, smelling, desiring, and the emotions (with their inextricably enmattered forms)?

Aristotle's account of hearing appears, at first sight, to follow the pattern of his discussion of taste, smell, and touch. Some of his comments introduce [H.1]-style considerations:

(1) As in the case of touch and taste, if the relevant sense organ is destroyed, there is no suffering of the relevant type. Aristotle says that some types of perceptual impact are too strong for the sense organ to bear and destroy its 'formula' (*logos*) in the same ways as heavy blows can break a musical instrument. When this occurs, the animal with the damaged sense organ can no longer perceive (424a28–32). If there is no such bodily state present, there will be no perceiving (424a32ff.). In the specific case of hearing, if water enters the ear and drives out the air within, the capacity to hear will be destroyed (420a15ff.), as it is also by excessively high or excessively low notes (426b3–4).

(2) In the case of hearing, air has to be present, lodged inside the ear, if the animal is to perceive accurately (420a8–10: cf. 420a3–7). This air moves in its

The Undivided Self: Aristotle and the 'Mind–Body Problem'. David Charles, Oxford University Press (2021).
© David Charles. DOI: 10.1093/oso/9780198869566.003.0006

own distinctive way (420a16–18). Further, the walls of the ear must be smooth so that the air inside can vibrate and rebound as one mass (420a25–6).

Other remarks indicate [H.2]-type considerations:

(3) Aristotle claims that rapid movements of air make the resulting sound high while slow movements make the resulting note low (420b1–3: see also [Ar]. *Prob.* XI. 6, 17).[1] (Indeed, this seems to have been a standard view in Greek musicology: see Archytas fragment 1.) The note is high because of the rapidity of the movement of the air up to and including that in the ear. Which type of sound is heard is the effect of the type of vibrating air that impacts on the sense organ (425b32ff.). For instance, the sense organ is such that, if affected by rapidly vibrating air, it hears a high note.

(4) In the case of touch, as we noted, the sense organ is said to be affected by the blow struck as a man is affected when struck through his shield (423b15ff.). Aristotle compares perception (of sound, colour, and flavour) with the hand's impact on the lyre, where the way in which the string of the lyre is struck determines the nature of the note produced (424a32ff.). In this case, the speed of the blow determines the pitch of the note emitted. If the sense organ for hearing functions in the same way, the speed of the movement in the air will determine the pitch of the sound heard.[2]

These considerations suggest that, if tasting, smelling, and touching are inextricably psycho-physical completions, so too is hearing. However, to confirm this result, we should look at the details of his account of the relevant medium and auditory sense organ. In doing so, we need to address the following specific, exegetical, issues:

(a) Is sound in the medium itself an inextricably matter-involving phenomenon, with an inextricably matter-involving form?
(b) Is hearing, as a form of perceptual sensitivity to sounds of this type, itself inextricably psycho-physical with an inextricably psycho-physical form? Is it the exercise of an essentially embodied capacity of this type?

There are, I shall argue, grounds for an affirmative answer to both questions.

---

[1] The discussions in the *Problems* merit further analysis. In this chapter I shall refer to them only when they support claims made in *De Anima* or *De Sensu*.
[2] Aristotle is thinking only of the lyre (a stringed instrument) at this point. In these cases, the more rapid the movement of the string ([*Prob.*] XIX.35a), the higher the note. (Of course, once the pitch has been set by the tension and length of the strings, the string of a lyre, if tuned on A, would sound like A no matter if I strike it violently or softly.) In extreme cases, if one strikes the string too hard, the tuning (i.e. the tension) of the string is altered.

5.2 Hearing: what is the sound in the medium?

It is instructive to begin by considering an influential spiritualist interpretation of hearing. It can be presented, albeit somewhat schematically, as follows:

1. The effect on the organ is the same in general type as the effect in the medium [premise]
2. In the case of hearing the effect in the medium is not the movement of a body going from place to place [premise]
3. There is no genuine movement in the medium (from 2)
4. What occurs in the medium is the travelling of audible form alone: a quasi-movement or 'mere Cambridge change' (from 3)
5. What occurs in the medium is 'a re-shaping' without any change in the matter (air) (from 4)
6. What occurs in the organ is the reception of audible form alone (without any change in its matter) (from 1 and 5): it is a purely spiritual phenomenon.

Premise 1 seems correct (at least in the form discussed in Chapter 2, Section 6 and Chapter 4). It is, of course, true, as premise 2 states, that the air in the medium stays put (419b21): there is no wind when noises are heard at a distance! But why accept (3) or (4)? Why think that the changes in 'shape' in the air (or water) are 'changes in form alone', independent of all material changes? Spiritualists need to show that there is no relevant material change at all in the medium if they are to secure their radical conclusion that the reception of audible form is a purely spiritual phenomenon.[3]

Aristotle's account of what goes on in the medium is complex. He thought of the relevant air as a unified mass of air: 'not scattered' (419b21-2). In the case of echoes, successive bits of air are moved and 'reshaped', one after the other (419b25ff.: see also [Ar] *Prob.* XI.6: 899a34-b7, 14-15). Each bit (or parcel) of the air induces a change in the next bit (or parcel: 899a34-5, b10: 'air is pushed by air'). It is because of this successive impact of one parcel of air on the next that echoes bounce off walls or shiny surfaces. Echoes do not involve (in his picture) bodies travelling through space (like missiles: [Ar] *Prob.* XI.6, 899b1ff.: see also *De Anima* 419b23ff.).[4] But, even so, there is a process under way in the medium: (i) each successive parcel of the air interacts with the next parcel, inducing the

---

[3] In this section, I shall focus on cases where the relevant medium is the air not water. Aristotle does not attempt to specify what feature common to air and water allows them to play this role.

[4] Philoponus rightly emphasized this point (discussing *De Anima* 419b25-7) in his commentary on *Analytica Posteriora* (Philoponus 1909: 340, 32ff. and 360, 19ff.). In (2000a: 133) I developed this point in assessing the spiritualist account of sound and hearing. For further discussion of this aspect of Aristotle's view, see Mark Johnstone (2013: 631-48).

movement in that parcel required to cause the reception of the auditory form (*De Sensu* 446b30ff.) and (ii) the parcels of air, re-shaped in this way, can interact with walls or shiny surfaces by, for example, bouncing off them. In this way, air is progressively 'reshaped' and sound (in a somewhat surprising way) 'travels'.

At each stage of the process, Aristotle suggests, there is shaped parcel of non-scattered air which moves internally (or vibrates). Each parcel, if it is to interact with other parcels and with solid surfaces (as in the case of echoes), must have extension and size (*megethos*).[5] What happens is not a travelling of form alone: at each step, air as matter is reshaped. The form is present in one vibrating parcel of air and then the next. As such, it is an essentially airborne, 'en-aired,' form present in the relevant vibrations of the air.[6] Although what occurs in the medium is not the movement of a body, it is a matter-(or better air)-involving process involving a matter (or air)-involving form. Matter-involving transitions of this type are essential to Aristotle's account of the processes that occur.[7]

Against this background, if, as the first premise in the spiritualist argument states:

1. The effect on the organ is the same in general type as the effect in the medium,

the effect on the organ will be a matter-involving change: the sense organ, in receiving the enclosed air in the ear, will also undergo a matter-involving change (or completion). Indeed, this would explain why the ear, like the external medium, contains air and is resonant (420a25ff., 11ff.). There needs to be the same type of matter (in this case air) in both for one to act and the other to suffer. This is, as was argued in Chapter 2, a requirement of Aristotle's account of the correlative powers of acting and suffering.

However, to secure this conclusion, we need to consider, as far the evidence permits, Aristotle's more detailed account of the medium. Some aspects, it must be ceded, remain elusive. Sound is sometimes described in the Aristotelian tradition as a process (*kinesis*) or a kind of movement in the air (see Philoponus on *De Anima* vol. 15, 366.25–7). But what kind of process is this? What is going on at each stage in the process, when the form of one parcel of air is induced on the next? What type of form is present?

Some have talked of sound as 'shaped air' ([Ar] *Prob.* XI.23 and 51) but this view was rejected by others ([Ar] *De Audib.* 800a1ff.). While Aristotle, on occasion, compares pitch with shape (*De Anima* 420a26–b4), it is not clear that he himself

---

[5] The sound in the medium will contain intervals [*diesies*], divisions within the parcel of air. Perhaps some parts of the parcel vibrate more quickly than others.

[6] There is a further issue here: is the enmattered form to be found in the parcels of air or in the whole medium? One might think of the whole pattern of vibration (in a *melos*) as being enmattered in the whole mass of unscattered air that is in between the sounding object and the hearing organ, as opposed to being enmattered in particular parcels of air.

[7] Air is, along with fire, earth, and water, a basic material element.

developed this analogy in this way. What is needed is a better understanding of what is meant by his talk of the form (or 'shape') of the relevant movement.

High notes, as we have seen, are associated with rapid movements of air, low notes with slower ones. In *Problems* (XIX.35, 37) it is suggested that the more violent the movements, the higher the sound. Elsewhere, the air is described as rough (violent) or calm (VII.5). When the air is heavier (with moisture), the note is deeper (XIX.37, XI.17) because the movements of air are slower. When many voices sing, the force of their voice pushes the air in unison so that the noise travels further (XIX.2, XI.6). However, the air has to carry not just individual notes but also intervals and sequences of notes in order. (*Melos*, in Greek musicology, is the term for the pattern of the movements in the music heard.) In each individual parcel, there will be differing speeds of movement, or vibration, in the air. If the melody is ascending, the movement of the first vibrating parcel leaving the string will be slower than the next one leaving the string (and so on). There will also be intervals between these parcels. One might think of each parcel as vibrating in a given way (some parts of the parcel quickly, some slowly, all members of a defined sequence with set intervals). In some cases, there is a type of unity (a *sumphonia*) when a parcel (with differing speeds of movement) affects the ear. In these there is a unity of high and low notes (like a voice: 426a28ff.). Each parcel may contain portions of vibrating (moving) air, moving internally at differing speeds in a given unified dynamic sequence (or pattern). If the parcels account for individual notes, the sequence of such notes (together with the intervals) will account for the pattern of the music as a whole: its melody.

How to interpret these remarks? In Aristotle's account, we distinguish notes and intervals (*dieseis*) by ear (the relevant type of perception: *Metaphysics* 1087b33–88a2). The smallest interval is the smallest an ear can detect. One note and one interval are what is heard as one (*De Sensu* 448a10ff.). This is one reason why, for Aristotle, harmonics is an empirical (or perceptual) discipline, not a mathematical one. The basic units are not arithmetical but perceptual units (see *Posterior Analytics* 78b34ff.). (The other reason is that harmonics is concerned with the *melos* (the dynamic movement through the harmony not the *harmonia*, the static formal structure itself.) The movements in the medium which concern Aristotle are the ones we discriminate. The relevant parcels of air are those whose vibrations and intervals impact on the perceiver. They are those parcels of vibrating air which have the power to interact with the hearer as a discriminator of notes, intervals, and melodies.

Did Aristotle define the movements in the medium in part in terms of their impact on the hearer? Or as sounds in the medium? Or in terms of the speed and shapes in the air defined independently of both the sounds they exemplify and their impact on the perceiver? Similar questions arise for the movements in the medium in the cases of musical and spoken sounds used to convey meaning. Are the latter to be defined in terms of (i) their impact on the hearer, (ii) their speed and shape in the medium, or (iii) as meaningful sounds, uttered by a speaker aiming at conveying meaning?

Aristotle shows no interest in the project of defining sounds solely in terms of the types of movements in the medium without any reference to their musical or semantic features: the ones that have a potential impact as sounds on perceivers. Further, if sound (as opposed to sounding: the actual impacting of sound on us)[8] is to be prior in definition to its impacting on us (as suggested by *De Anima* 415a18–22), notes, melodies, and spoken sounds cannot be defined in terms of their effect on the hearer. The movements in the air are to be defined in terms of the sounds, whether musical or semantical, present in the air. Further, if voice and hearing are correlative, as Aristotle suggests in 426a27, these sounds will be defined in part in terms of their source in the speaker (or musical instrument). So understood, the relevant patterns of shaped air will be individuated in terms of the sounds created by speakers or musicians using their instruments or vocal cords.

Sounds will be distinctive air-involving forms (or patterns) of air, individuated (in part) by their source. We are, in effect, perceptually sensitive to such forms (or patterns) of vibrating air. One cannot define the relevant form (or pattern) independently of the air that vibrates. As flavours are inextricably 'enwatered' forms, sounds are inextricably enaired forms, patterns-of-the-air. In this respect, their forms will be snub-like: they cannot be defined without reference in the definition to the air they enform.

More occurs in the medium than the travelling of (pure) form alone, suggested by the spiritualist interpreter. In their view, all that is present in the medium is a bare, ungrounded, pure capacity for something to be heard by a perceiver. But this claim seems inconsistent with Aristotle's insistence that movements of shaped air in the medium are required if high and low notes are to be heard. If these movements are enformed by sounds (whether musical or spoken), sounds will be present in the medium waiting to be heard.

5.3 Sounds, sounding, and hearing: the message

What is involved in the hearer's discriminating sounds? The original spiritualist argument took as its first premise:

---

[8] Sounding occurs only in the hearer (426a12–13) as does sound, understood as a type of sounding (426a16–17). But this is consistent with there being another type of sound which is present in the medium and would be present even if no one heard it (426a19ff.). The latter type of sound is potentially an object of hearing, the former is actually one. The cause of the sound in the medium is what creates it: things which are capable of making sound in the medium (419b6–8, 420a20–2): the bronze when struck by the gong or the vocal cords of the singer. But what we hear is not the bronze or the vocal cords but the sounds (the note or voice) created by them, when they are 'struck'. Indeed, so understood, we hear the instrument being struck only derivatively: in virtue of the sound it creates in the medium when struck.

1. The effect on the organ is the same in general type as the effect in the medium premise.

Sounding stands to hearing as acting (teaching) to suffering (learning). The acting, which occurs in the patient (in Aristotle's view), is the imposing of the form on the sufferer, while the suffering is the form being imposed on the patient. Aristotle describes the acting and the suffering as 'the same but different in being' (*Physics* 3.3, 202b12ff.).[9]

Given that the acting in question is the impacting of patterned (enformed) vibrating air on the sense organ, the suffering will be the reception of such patterns by the sense organ. If the acting is defined as an air-involving activity, so must be the suffering. Hearing is not simply the grasping of high and low notes but the receiving of enmattered phenomena, enaired forms, present in the medium. As such, hearing is essentially a matter-involving sensitivity: an embodied type of response to the patterns of vibrating air present in the medium. Hearing is the realization of an air-based capacity to be acted on by enaired forms of this type. This is the one and only type of strongly unified activity essential to hearing. Aristotle's account, once again, rests on his general views about causation, as discussed in Chapter 2.

The hearer, in receiving patterns of vibrating air from the medium, hears sounds, intervals and melodies. How are the latter connected with the vibrating parcels of air in the medium? After all: we discriminate notes *as notes*, not as parcels of air. Equally, what we hear (auditorily discriminate and enjoy) are melodies or voices (446a28ff.: 421a31–3) not varying speeds of air movement (420a28). Aristotle notes that a body, without a mean, is simply affected by vibrating air (in the same way as the sound emitted by thunder smashes fragile objects: 424b10–12). A mean is what enables the hearer to discriminate notes, melodies, and intervals as such when the sense organ is affected by patterned parcels of vibrating air. It is in virtue of having a sense organ (with its mean) that we discriminate the musical properties of sounds and not differential speeds of vibrating air.[10]

---

[9] While this remark conceals hidden depths, and has been the subject of much scholarly controversy, I shall leave those aside in the present discussion. See Chapter 4, n. 47.

[10] Auditory discrimination involves our being able to tell one note or interval apart from others. The role of the mean, so understood, is to discriminate actual sounds present in the medium. It renders heard the sounds which are, when present in the medium, only hearable. It does not make them actual sounds as they were there as actual sounds in the patterns of vibrating air in the medium. (Compare: learning does not consist in making actual the information that the teacher passes on. That was actual enough before the learner grasped it! Of course, the learner's grasping it makes that information active in him (or her). But the information, on this view, was there in the speaker's words all along waiting to be grasped before the learner finally did so.) This claim is consistent with the sounds in the medium being only potentially audible before they are heard (a possibility Aristotle notes in *De Anima* 426a22ff.). Actual sounds are potentially audible before they are heard.

What is involved in the sense organ achieving this result? The causal model, exemplified by teaching and learning, once again proves helpful. In the case of hearing, the notes, melodies and intervals are present in the medium in the relevant patterns of vibrating air. They are themselves essentially en-mattered (or better en-aired) forms. It is these en-aired forms which are heard. It is not that hearing involves vibrating air impacting on the sense organ which generates a further purely psychological act of hearing. The sound that is heard is itself essentially an en-aired form created by its source. Hearing is a receiving of a form of this type, sounding is the impacting of notes, intervals, and melodies, thus created, on the hearer (equipped with a mean). The hearer discriminates as notes or sounds the notes and sounds in the medium. Since these notes are en-aired forms, our receiving them is essentially a matter- (or air-)involving phenomenon. The relevant form of discrimination cannot be defined without reference to the en-aired objects it discriminates. Hearing is, it seems, an essentially matter- (or air-)involving form of discrimination. The form received (the sound) and the mode of its reception are both essentially impure, matter-involving.

Some may hesitate: couldn't one, they may ask, accept that hearing is essentially a receiving of a matter-involving sound but deny that it is itself an essentially matter-involving completion? Perhaps hearing is, for Aristotle, simply the awareness (defined in a pure, non-inextricably enmattered way) of a matter- (or air-) involving object (sound). Why should it follow from that fact that the sound heard is essentially matter-involving that hearing itself is essentially matter-involving?

Aristotle does not seem to have demurred at this point. He held both that:

(i) the type of psychological activity is individuated by its object (415a20 objects as prior to activities and capacities of the perceiver), and that

(ii) activities are matter-involving in the way their objects are (429b21–2).

If so, the activity of hearing will itself be as essentially matter-involving as its object, sound, is. But why did he take these steps? Even if discrimination is typed by what it discriminates, why did Aristotle regard the activity itself as essentially matter-involving?

If sounding is the cause and hearing the effect, the former will be the impacting of patterned parcels of vibrating air of a given kind on the sense organ, the latter the sense organ being impacted by such parcels. Hearing is, in effect, the receiving of patterns of vibrating air impacting on the sense organ. As in other cases of acting and suffering (*poiēsis/pathēsis*), the per se active causes and per se effects are the giving and receiving of the same form (the sound) and are present only in agents and patients with the same type of matter.[11] If so, sounding and hearing

---

[11] This is an application of the general causal principle discussed in Chapter 2.

will be defined with essential reference to a shared form (the sound) and will both be the realizations of correlative material capacities essentially enmattered in the same type of matter: air.[12] The capacity to hear, so understood, is an inextricably enmattered capacity whose goal is the discrimination of sounds which reach it through the medium.

This account of hearing differs from that suggested by non-reductionist materialist interpreters. In their view, sounding is a purely material process (defined in exclusively material terms) while the hearing is a further psychological phenomenon, defined, for example, as attending to sounds, high and low notes, melodies, etc. However, if that were the case, sounding and hearing would not stand to each other in the way premise (1) requires: as teaching to learning. For, the teacher imparts a given piece of information they possess to the learner. If sounding is understood simply as vibrating air in an enclosed space while hearing is grasping notes and melodies, the medium will contain far less information than the perceiver grasps, who (in some unknown way) injects auditory content (such as notes) onto movements of vibrating air. It is not just that the latter is a mysterious process (how does the perceptual capacity do it?). It also violates the Aristotelian requirement that the teacher pass on (in teaching) just the information which the learner grasps (in being taught). There has to be, if he stands by this requirement, the same form (or object) present in, and passed on by, the sounding and received in the hearing.[13]

5.4 Hearing: interim conclusions

Aristotle, if the argument so far is correct, held that in the case of hearing:

(A) The sound in the medium is essentially matter-involving: it essentially involves patterns of moving air

(B) If sound in the medium is matter-involving, then sounding also is matter-involving

(C) If sounding is a matter-involving activity, hearing must also be (Causal Principle: correlative activities of acting and suffering)

---

[12] It does not follow that throughout its operation the sense organ itself contains vibrating patterns of air. The latter may be present in parts of the ear but their impact on the rest of the sense organ need not be, for all that has been said so far, airborne. It is not clear that the whole process of hearing is confined to the ear (see for instance *De Anima* Γ.7). (Indeed, receiving the form without the matter may in this case amount to receiving the pattern present in the vibrating air without receiving the air, even if the form, at a later stage of the process, is the form of some other type of material bearer.)

[13] Further, since the form is what is heard, and what is heard are sounds, the form itself cannot be simply a mathematical ratio, defined without reference to matter. If sounds are ratios of any kind, they will be ratios of high and low notes (as suggested in *Metaphysics* 1043a10–11), enaired-ratios (as snubness is nasal-concavity).

(D) Hearing = the hearer's sense organ's being affected by sounds

and

(E) Hearing = the hearer's discriminating sounds

and concluded that:

(F) Hearing is essentially a matter-involving activity (a completion).

Aristotle, it seems, regarded hearing, like tasting and smelling, as an essentially and inextricably psycho-physical type of suffering. All of these types of perception will exemplify the pattern of the simple theory outlined for those 'passions of the soul', of which emotions were paradigm cases in *De Anima* A.1. They are inextricably psycho-physical because they are caused by the relevant matter-involving activities in the medium. What it is for a sound to appear to a perceiver is for the sound-in-the-air to be received by the organ of hearing in a matter-involving way. If this is correct, and the effect in the sense organ is of the same general type as the cause in the medium (as the spiritualist maintains in accepting premise 1 above), the effect in the organ which constitutes perception will be, like its cause, a matter-involving completion.

5.5 A spiritualist argument concerning seeing

Did Aristotle's account of seeing follow a similar pattern? Are there relevant differences between them?

It may be helpful to consider a further argument in favour of the spiritualist interpretation. It can be presented as follows:

1. Colour, in its nature, is such as to move the transparent when actual (i.e. light) [premise (418a31, 419a10f.)]

2. When the light (the transparent when actual) is moved, it is coloured in a derivative way (418b4–6) [premise]

3. The light's being coloured in this derivative way is the same activity as the colour of the object appearing through it [premise]

4. The light being moved is not a real alteration in medium but a mere Cambridge change [from 2 and 3].

In this account, the sole role of the medium is to separate object and perceiver (and the matter and form of the object seen). If one asks: 'what happens in the medium?', the spiritualist answer is, surprisingly, 'nothing'. While the colour appears to the perceiver through the medium, there is no genuine change in the medium itself (or, at least, no change that is essential to the colour's appearing to the perceiver). The spiritualist interpretation continues as follows:

5. The effect in the eye is of the same general type as the effect in the medium [premise]

6. The effect in the eye is colour appearing through the eye to the subject [from 5 + 3].

All that essentially happens in seeing (as understood by Aristotle) is that the colour of the object appears through the medium to the subject. No genuine change is essential to visual perception. Although the medium and the perceiver stand in a relation to the perceived object (when perception occurs), this relation is not essentially dependent on (or constituted by) any real (non-merely Cambridge) change in the medium or the perceiver.[14] There are, in this account, no essentially material changes essentially involved in perception (as such changes would be—according to the spiritualist—'real', not mere Cambridge changes).

This spiritualist interpretation rests on three claims:

[A] The light's being coloured is the same activity as the colour of the object appearing through it

[B] The light being moved is not a real alteration in medium but a mere Cambridge change

[C] The change in the medium and that in the eye are of the same general type.[15]

From [A] and [C] it follows that all that (essentially) happens in the eye is that the colour of the object appears to the perceiver. This is what seeing is. It follows, given [B], that no genuine changes or alterations are essentially involved in either the medium or in the eye in visual perception. For the spiritualist, Aristotle emerges as a direct realist: we are, in his view, directly aware of the colours of objects. There is no intermediate object present between us and that of which we can be aware.

For the spiritualist, Aristotle's account has this distinctive, and for many attractive, feature. If seeing is simply the colour of the object appearing to the perceiver, perceivers directly see the colour of the object. Colour perception

---

[14] There are two ways to formulate the spiritualist claim: (a) no genuine change occurs at all in the medium or the eye and (b) no genuine change occurs in the medium or the eye which is essential to perception. I shall consider, and reject, the weaker claim (b). Rejecting (b) entails rejecting (a).

[15] While spiritualists usually take this as an identity claim, they could take it to mean only that the two are inseparable in definition, provided that nothing more is added to either definition.

occurs without there being an intermediate object, such as a sense datum, which is directly perceived and represents (in some way) the colour of the external object. Since there are no intermediaries of this kind in the spiritualist interpretation, Aristotle's talk of visual perception as the perception of the colour of external objects in the world is vindicated.

According to the spiritualist, if there were matter-involving states in the eye in cases of visual perception caused by matter-involving states in the medium, perceivers would not directly see the colour of the object (the distal object). At best, they would see something which represents the colour of the object, the visual aspect of the material state produced in the sense organ by material (proximal) states in the medium. This is why, in their view, many non-reductionist materialist interpreters present Aristotle as taking the immediate objects of visual perception to be internal representations of external objects, not the objects themselves. But to do so is, from a spiritualist perspective, a major interpretative error: Aristotle talks consistently of external objects and their colours as what is visually presented, not the internal mental representations of such objects. He can do so, they conclude, only because nothing at all happens in the medium between the perceiver and the colour perceived.

5.6 What happens in the medium?

In assessing the spiritualist account, I shall focus first on assumptions [A] and [B] and, only after examining them, turn (in Section 5.10) to consider [C].

Several considerations have been offered in support of the spiritualist view that nothing occurs in the medium. Three have been particularly influential.

(i) In *De Anima* 418b4–6 Aristotle writes: 'the transparent is that which is seen (or see-able) but is not seen (see-able) in itself but in virtue of the colour of something else (*allotrios*).'

Spiritualists interpret his remark as saying that there is nothing at all see-able in the transparent. In so doing, they reject an alternative, apparently plausible, suggestion that the transparent is visible because it is permeated (in some way) by the colour of the object seen. In their account, the medium is seen (or see-able) only when we note the contrast between it (as something without colour) and the colour of the object seen (as one might see a hole in a wall by contrasting an empty space with the wall that surrounds it). Nothing is seen (or see-able) in the transparent because, like the hole in the wall, there is nothing there to be seen. The role of the transparent (when active) is, in their view, merely to provide an appropriate (motionless) space through which the colour of the object can appear to the perceiver.

But why interpret 418b4–6 in this way? Some spiritualists think that if the medium were permeated by the colour of the object seen, the medium itself would have to be coloured *in the same way* as the object is. If this were the case, they conclude, we would see the green in the medium in the same way as we see the green of a leaf. In their view, we would see the green in the medium, not the green of the leaf. The latter, although the initial cause, would be occluded from us by the green produced in the medium. However, as spiritualists point out, this is not Aristotle's view. Since only the green of the leaf is seen (or see-able) 'in its own right' (418a29–30), the medium, they conclude, cannot itself turn green or be permeated by greenness.

A second consideration might be offered to support the spiritualist interpretation. If some parts of the medium become green when I see a leaf (in the same way as the leaf itself is), no one (it will be said) could see anything red through them. Nothing, it seems, can be red and green all over. However, since intersecting perceptions of this type occur, charity prevents us from attributing such a view to Aristotle. The medium cannot literally be turned green or permeated by greenness.

Neither consideration is decisive. The colour of the leaf, in Aristotle's account, is what is seen in itself because 'it contains within itself the cause of its being seen' (418a31). This remark distinguishes the way in which it and the borrowed colour in the medium are visible: the latter is visible only because of the causal operation of the colour of the leaf. The leaf has its own colour (*oikeion*: 419a2), the medium takes over the colour of something else (*allotrion*: 418b6). If the direct object of vision is what is seen in itself, only the leaf will be directly seen.[16] How does this happen?

There is certainly no reason to require that the medium (light) and the leaf are green *in the same way*. The medium's being permeated by colour may simply consist in the light being affected in some unspecified way (whatever it is) by the greenness of the object perceived. While there is a light-based continuous activity in the medium beginning with the colour of the leaf and ending in the perceiver, this need not be one in which the light itself becomes green in the same way the leaf is. All that is required is that the greenness of the leaf is conveyed (in some way) through the medium to the perceiver. This is what it is for the colour of the object to permeate the medium. While the light (the relevant activity of the transparent) between the object and the perceiver must be modified in some way by the greenness of the leaf for this to happen, it does not follow that the modification itself consists in the light becoming green in the same way the leaf is or itself becoming an object of visual perception.

---

[16] Aristotle was clearly interested in the (excellent) question: why is the sky coloured blue?

One should note that, for similar reasons, the light (when permeated by the greenness of the leaf) need not become green in the same way as when water or a white wall become green when they reflect green light (as when green light is played upon them).[17] There is no requirement that the light between the green object and the perceiver is affected in precisely the same way as water or solid reflective objects. If it were, we would see the greenness of the object in the same way as when we see water (or white walls) as green when green light is directed on them. But this does not seem to be the case. We see these cases as being quite different. There may be quite distinct types of activity at work in these differing cases. Indeed, it seems that there are.

The way in which light is modified need not prevent two people seeing different colours through the same patch of medium. Indeed, since we can do this, the relevant way must allow for its possibility. Reflections can clearly intersect with other reflections in some way without disrupting each other (as when one bit of a mirror looks red at one angle, blue at another). The same model may apply in other cases. One piece of mirror can be red and green all over when reflecting colours from different objects and seen from different angles.

While these two spiritualist arguments show that Aristotle's medium (or the eye) does not become green in the same way as a leaf or a wall reflecting the colours of a stained-glass window do, they do not exclude the possibility that there is a genuine process (or activity) in the medium or in the eye. Aristotle cautiously remarks: there is some way in which that which sees is coloured (425b23). Whatever way this is, it need not be the same as that in which, for example, a leaf is coloured.[18]

---

[17] Ross suggested that 418b5-7 is best taken as referring only to cases where air, water, and solid bodies are visible because of reflection (involving rainbows, white walls appearing green when reflecting green stained-glass windows, the sea appearing green when the sky is grey) and not to cases where the light between the observer and the object is affected by the object's colour. However, Aristotle may use the phrase, 'of this kind' (*toiouton*) to indicate a more general type of phenomenon which is exemplified in cases of reflection (solid objects and rainbows) and in those where the transparent receives the colour of the object (418b26f.). If the transparent receives colour, it is appropriate to describe it as taking on colour and, as such, derivatively visible. One could not visually detect the transparent if there were no colours there to be seen. One can visually detect its operation when one sees a colour. (This may be a case where we are aware of something by sight but do not—in some strict sense—see it. See 425b20ff.)

[18] What of intersecting colours in the medium? Aristotle has several moves available to him, given his remarks in *De Sensu* about colours more generally: perhaps some colours in the medium are unaffected by other colours (*De Sensu* 440a24f.). Perhaps the two colours can be mixed at one point but recover their identity when they emerge from the mixture (as in cases of mixture elsewhere); perhaps there are differing manifestations of the transparent in different, if overlapping, parts of the medium. So, for example, while one part of the medium [T] may manifest redness by itself, when part of a larger whole [T + R + W], the whole of which it is a part may manifest greenness.

While these moves are, no doubt, problematic (in distinctive ways), they suggest some of the resources which Aristotle could deploy to address the problem. He could go beyond simply saying: the difficulty must be soluble since when A and B face one another and look at one another's pullovers, A sees B's blue pullover and B sees A's green pullover.

(ii) In *De Sensu* 440a16ff., Aristotle rejects the idea held by Empedocles that colours are 'emanations' from objects and visible as such. He also rejects the atomist account in which the medium is set in motion by the perceived object by contact (*haphē*: 440a19ff.: see also *De Anima* 418b15f.). Since there is no process of this type in the medium, the spiritualist concludes, nothing at all is going on there. All that occurs, the change of which Aristotle speaks (*De Sensu* 438b4–5), is that the colour of the object becomes visible to the perceiver. (Light is simply that through which the object becomes visible to the perceiver.)

The spiritualist interpretation rests on a simple dichotomy: everything that occurs in the medium is either a process of the type favoured by Empedocles or the atomists (with one material phenomenon travelling between the object seen and the perceiver) or else a mere Cambridge change. Since it is not the former, they conclude, it must be the latter. All that happens there is that the object perceived comes to stand in a relation to the perceiver. Nothing more is required.

But why think that Aristotle succumbed to this, slightly simple-minded, either-or way of thinking? He would not have done so had he accepted that there are genuine activities in the medium which are not movements of particles or emanations from the object to the perceiver. There could then be continuous activities through his medium carrying the colour (or visual form) of the object to the perceiver which are neither movements of particles nor mere Cambridge changes. When so understood, his account of visual perception would provide a further example of an essentially matter-involving completion (in line with the interpretation advanced in Chapter 4 about tasting and smelling).

There is, however, a complication: in the case of light and colour, Aristotle thought that the effect on the perceiver was strictly simultaneous with the cause and that, as a result, there was no process in the medium (*De Sensu* 447a3–4, 7–11). What happens is not sequential: all parts of the medium, near and far, are affected at the same time. However, this does not require that nothing at all relevant to perception happens in the medium. Instead, in this case—unlike that of the other media involved in perception—everything 'suffers' at the same time (as Aristotle remarks in *De Sensu* 447a9). Although there is, it seems, a distinctive type of non-sequential activity in the visual medium, it is still a type of (fire-based) material suffering.[19] There is no suggestion that this case differs more fundamentally from all the others in that it alone is a mere Cambridge change. It is simply that the relevant media have other, somewhat different, features in these two cases.

(iii) Light, as the positive condition of the transparent, is a state (*hexis*: 417b27). As a state, it must be constant, unaffected by the colours that we see. However, if

---

[19] In, at least, the extended sense of 'suffering' and 'quality change' canvassed respectively in *De Anima* 417b2 and 417b7.

light borrows colours from the objects seen, it would have to be affected by them. The most it can do, while remaining unaffected, is—the spiritualist concludes— enable us to see the colour of the objects themselves.

This consideration is not, as it stands, decisive. Light itself must remain unaffected *as light* through the varying changes that occur in it. In a similar way, health, virtue, skill, or knowledge will remain unaffected even though the skilled or virtuous person reacts to situations in virtue of their skill or courage. Indeed, it is, for example, their unchanging skill that enables them to do so. In the same way, the light, while remaining light, can be affected by the colours which impact on it. They simply do not change it from being light.

In order to to make genuine progress, we need to understand some further details of Aristotle's discussion of light and the impact on it of the colours of objects. In the cases of smell, flavour, and sound, there was more going on in the medium than merely the sound, flavour, or smell appearing to the perceiver. Did Aristotle take a similar view in the case of colour? He certainly draws attention to features which these cases share. Here are three examples:

(a) The impact of colour in the medium is likened to that of flavour in its medium (*De Sensu* 442a16ff.). Both are compared with people mixing dyes in water, suggesting that the way in which the medium is coloured involves more than merely that the colour of the object appears through it. There is, after all, more to dying (and the skill of dying) than allowing the colour purple to appear to the perceiver! In dying, the water takes on, or borrows, the colour of the injected material. If so, while light may not be visible in itself, it will be when it is permeated by colour of the objects it illuminates. It will borrow their colour.

(b) Aristotle compares reflections with echoes (*De Anima* 419b28ff., *Posterior Analytics* B.15, 98a25ff.) where there is (as we have seen) more going on in the air than merely the object being heard by the auditor. He was clearly impressed by the improving grasp on reflections since the days of Democritus (*De Sensu* 438a9–10) and their role in producing certain visual phenomena (such as flashing lights in water: *Meteorologica* 370a16ff.). Here, too, there is more happening in the medium (in the case of echoes) than the sound's being related to the hearer (as in a mere Cambridge change). Further, his detailed discussion of rainbows and other kinds of visual effects in the *Meteorologica* (described as 'chasms', 'trenches', and blood red colours seen in the sky: 342b1ff.) suggests that, in these cases, more is going on in air or water than merely the colour of some existing object being visible to a perceiver. Their study falls within the field of optics, which Aristotle compares with harmonics (*Physics* B.2, 194a9).[20] Since harmonics, as we have seen, is

---

[20] Aristotle's discussion of optics and harmonics applies, in my view, mathematical models to enmattered forms. Further investigation of this topic lies outside the scope of the present project.

concerned with sounds in the medium, optics should focus on colours in light. There is certainly more to the study of optics and of reflection than noting that reflections enable the colour of the object to be seen by the perceiver.

(c) Aristotle presents the impact of colour on the medium and the observer (*De Anima* 419b6–10) as being similar to that found in the case of sound ('sound' and 'sounding') and the other senses. If the account just given of sound is correct, there will be more going on in the case of colour also (apart from the colour of the object appearing to the perceiver). What happens in the medium will also be distinguished from the effect of what is in the medium on the sense organ (where the latter is the unnamed analogue of sounding: 426a14f.).

These passages suggest that more occurs in the medium in cases of visual perception than is allowed for in the spiritualist interpretation. How far did Aristotle seek to spell out the details of what happens in the medium and in the eye when we see colours? How did he understand the way in which the colour of the object 'permeates' the medium?

5.7 The medium (1)

The 'transparent' (to use a standard translation), which plays a central role in Aristotle's account, cannot be understood simply as that which allows colour to be seen (as in the spiritualist interpretation). He held that:

[1] In unbounded areas (such as air and water) the activity of the 'transparent', under the influence of fire, is light (*De Anima* 418a29–31: air/water), and
[2] On the surfaces of determinate bodies, its activity, under the influence of fire, is something which receives, shares in, colour (*De Sensu* 439b11–12: cf. 439b8–10).

Since the 'transparent' is present in both bounded and unbounded phenomena, it cannot be simply that whose activity allows colour to be seen. In bounded phenomena, its activity is to be receptive of, or to share in, colours. For similar reasons it cannot be defined simply as what is visible through the presence of the colour of another object.[21] Since in bounded phenomena the activity of the 'transparent' is to be receptive of colour on the surface, it must have a role there beyond that of merely allowing colour to be seen.

Aristotle suggests that the 'transparent' is active both in unbounded phenomena such as air and water and, to a greater or lesser degree (439a21–5), in bounded

---

[21] Compare Mark Eli Kalderon (2015). 418b4–6 is not, in my view, a definition of the transparent.

ones.[22] In the former, its activity is light, in some of the latter whiteness (439b16–18). So, we must ask, what is the capacity which is exercised in these differing ways? Did Aristotle have good grounds for believing that there is one capacity exercised in these two ways?

It is important to exercise due caution in interpreting Aristotle's terminology: 'transparency', the most favoured recent translation of '*diaphanes*', does not capture what occurs in the case of bounded surfaces. This is because it fails to account for the role the transparent plays as the *receiver* of light inside the eye (438b12f.). The pupil, in addition, also lights other things (like a lamp: 438b16f.). In response, some have suggested that 'translucent' is a better translation.[23] However, even if this is a good translation of the term when applied to light, it is less successful in the case of bounded surfaces. Light does not pass through dense or black surfaces. Its activity on the surface consists in the boundary of the object being coloured (439a27f., b17–18). Perhaps 'illuminable' is a better translation. A boundary could not be coloured unless it was illuminable. The inside of the eye is illuminable and when illuminated lights other things. It is capable of illuminating other things in virtue of its being illuminated.[24] Indeed, while for these reasons, I favour 'illuminable' as a translation of '*diaphanes*', my major task is to understand its complex role in Aristotle's theory of colour and colour perception not to identify one English word with the same meaning. (For this reason, in what follows I shall, on occasion, transliterate the Greek term '*diaphanes*'.)

Aristotle suggests that the same capacity whose exercise produces light in the unbounded illuminable produces whiteness on bounded surfaces (*De Sensu* 439b8–10, 15–17). The whiteness of a bounded surface is a distinctive state of the same capacity whose exercise in some unbounded phenomena is light.[25] This does not require that the colour of the surface is itself a manifestation of actual light—an idea that could be developed by taking the colour of objects as (for example) a reflectance property of light. Instead, it may be expressing the simpler (and less committal) idea that there is one capacity exercised in these two differing ways. Further, when Aristotle describes light as 'like (*hoion*) the colour of the illuminable' (418b11), this remark does not require that light itself is coloured in the way a surface is. It may simply be the exercise of a capacity whose exercise in bounded surfaces is whiteness, a type of colour.[26]

---

[22] What does 'unbounded' mean? The sea is not unbounded in any ordinary sense. Nor are puddles of water. Or pieces of glass or ice.
[23] This was suggested in earlier discussions by J.L. Beare 1906. I am indebted to Justin Broackes for many insightful remarks on this issue.
[24] As noted by Justin Broackes.
[25] I take the reference to the '*diaphanes*' in 439a15 to be to what is an illuminable body (something capable of the relevant type of activity), not to the activity of the illuminable in that body. This matches the use in 439b17 referring to water etc., which are taken as examples of bodies.
[26] In *De Sensu* 439a19ff., light is said to be—in an accidental way—the colour of the illuminable. Aristotle spells out his idea in what follows: illuminability is a common nature or capacity found in

Aristotle, once again, is cautious, perhaps even non-committal, in his discussion of the capacity in question. He does, however, make one bold claim: that there is *one* capacity which is exercised in two differing ways in bounded and unbounded phenomena. Why go this far? It is, of course, true (as he remarks) that colours are not present without light. It is also the case, as he himself remarks in *De Sensu*,[27] that the sun can appear to be coloured (at dawn or dusk or near campfires). However, these observations do not establish his claim that there is one capacity exercised in two ways in the two differing phenomena. Perhaps his further step is simply an ingenious way of giving an apparently unified account of a wide range of phenomena: they all manifest one capacity albeit in differing ways—depending on the degree of the illuminable present, on whether they are bounded or unbounded.

Aristotle's strategy seems to be: take light and the colour of objects as his basic notions (as activities are, in general, prior to their relevant capacities) and then hypothesize that there is just one capacity manifested in both. If so, the basis of his theory is his ideas about light and the impact the colour of objects has on it. But, even so, his introduction of the illuminable (*diaphanes*) represents a further, ambitious, theoretical postulate: both light and colour are manifestations of the same capacity under different conditions. Was this one hypothesis too many?

Aristotle's thought, at this point, may, once again, have been motivated by his ideas about efficient causation discussed in Chapter 2. If the surface colour of bounded objects is to cause changes in the light, both need to belong, in his account, to the same genus, something shared by both cause and effect (*GC* 324b1ff.). It is because they are the same in genus that light can be affected by colour. Even if Aristotle was not clear about what the genus is, he could talk of one capacity manifested in these two different ways. If colour and light are to interact causally, they must (in his account) share the same type of capacity, grounded in the relevant matter, which allows this to happen (even if he himself could not spell out further what this capacity was). The 'illuminable' is the shared matter in this case.[28]

In any event, Aristotle thinks of the colours of bounded surfaces as dependent on (a) the amount of the illuminable present there and (b) the way in which it is

---

both bounded and unbounded phenomena (439a24ff.). Air and water are said to be coloured (439b1): but this seems to be because their brightness is the same kind of phenomenon as colour. That is: their brightness is the manifestation of the same capacity as yields colour in bounded objects.

[27] *De Sensu* 440a13ff.

[28] His idea could be developed in several ways. One might think (as already noted) of the colours of bounded surfaces as the reflectance properties of the light present there. On this view, colour at the surface and in light will both be types of reflectance, although of differing sorts. Alternatively, one might think of colour in light and on bounded surfaces as manifestations of colouring, albeit in differing types of illuminable features. But, there is, as far as I can see, no evidence that Aristotle himself developed either of these lines. He seems to have been content with the less committal claim: there is one type of capacity, that of illuminability, which is manifested in two different ways.

actualized. He is required to do so given that the effect of colours in objects on the medium is (in his view) an effect on the illuminable. This must be so, given his views on efficient causation, if there is something of the appropriate type present both in the cause (the bounded surface) and the effect (the medium). While Aristotle did not spell out further the nature of the capacity common to bounded and unbounded objects, he did go far enough for his purposes, providing an account of light and colour which, although incomplete, defined them as manifestations of a capacity, not itself defined in terms of our capacity to see. When we see the colours of objects, we are sensitive to objects and to properties defined independently of us. In this he follows his own advice: in arriving at the relevant definitions one should define the objects of perception prior to the activity of perception itself (415a18ff.). Neither colour nor light is to be defined, in his account, simply as what brings about perceptions of colour in us.

In *De Sensu*, Aristotle uses the idea of the illuminable (*diaphanes*) in discussing the colour of objects (in the case of bounded surfaces), suggesting that the extent to which it is found in them determines the extent to which they share in colour (439b9–10). Further, he takes white and black as the basic colours, thinking of these (it seems) as the two extreme cases of activity of the illuminable in bounded surfaces (439b15ff.). In the case of white, there is an activity of the illuminable as such (analogous to that of light in unbounded surfaces). Black can be seen as the absence of this activity or as the activity in which the illuminable is exercised to the least possible extent. All other colours arise out of mixtures of these basic colours, depending on the ratio of each which is present (440b15–25). It seems that the intermediate colours of objects correspond to differing types of activity of the illuminable in bounded surfaces, intermediate between the type of activity found there in the cases of whiteness and blackness.[29]

5.8 The medium (2): the 'illuminable', fire, and the colours in the 'illuminable' (*diaphanes*)

Fire is one of the things that cause the illuminable (*diaphanes*) to be active (418b12). When it is active, there is light. This is why light, Aristotle says, can be

---

[29] Aristotle does not attempt to give a reductive definition of differing colours (in bounded surfaces) in terms solely of the amount of the illuminable or the distinctive type of actualizations found when there is a given mixture of black and white. For all that he says the relevant type of mixture may be defined only as the one present when there are red, purple, or green surfaces (in a non-reductive fashion). Indeed, it is not even clear that he is offering a reductive definition of whiteness and blackness. For while these are, I have suggested, the two extreme cases of activity of the illuminable in bounded surfaces, he does not specify what the relevant extremes are. It may be that one cannot define what the relevant extremes are without reference to whiteness and blackness. Aristotle may be keeping his options open, waiting for future work to determine whether the reductive or non-reductive option is to be preferred.

thought of as 'the presence of fire or something of this type' in the unbounded illuminable (418b16). The phrase 'presence in the illuminable' suggests not only that fire is the cause of the activity of the illuminable by its immediate proximity but also that when it is active, fire (or something fire-like: *De Sensu* 439a20f.: see 439b15f.) is immanent (*eneinai*) in that activity. Its being immanent in this way does not, of course, require fire or any kind of body to be literally present as fire (or that type of body) in the light. One might think of its presence as consisting merely in the illuminable (*diaphanes*) being illuminated (as when a room is illuminated by a torch). Its absence is darkness (*De Sensu* 439b15ff.).

One might even attempt to define light as this type of presence of fire (or something like it) in the unbounded illuminable. But this would be to take a further step. Light (as an actuality) should be prior in definition to the potentiality involved. Nor is it clear that one can define the unbounded illuminable or the way in which fire is present in it without reference to light. Nor are we told which things like fire produce this state.[30] Aristotle is, no doubt, committed to the claim: when there is light, fire (or something like it) is present in the unbounded illuminable in some way. But there is no indication that he attempted to define what that way is or what other things are like fire in the relevant respects. Indeed, it seems that he takes light as a more basic idea than that of the illuminable being acted on by fire.

Aristotle's more cautious view can be presented, in outline, as follows: the basic actuality (in the unbounded cases) of the illuminable is light. The relevant capacity is one whose exercise in such cases is light. Its activity, in the language of *De Anima* B.5, is not a destructive process but rather a change of a different type, one which realizes the nature of the illuminable. When this completion occurs under the causal activity of fire, the illuminable is illuminated. There is, as we have seen, more to his account of light than its being something which enables colours to be seen. It has to be modified by colour in some way if the latter is to be seen. Colour is what modifies light. How is the latter idea to be understood? How does colour permeate the illuminable?[31]

---

[30] Lindsay Judson suggests that the *aithēr* of the shining heavenly bodies is causally responsible (2015: 173–9).

[31] The activity of the colour of the object is, in the first instance, its impacting on the medium. Guided by this thought Aristotle can say: to be a colour is to have the ability to colour the medium. The medium has the ability to be impacted by colour in this way. This will be a matter-(light-) involving completion of the medium. Thus, things can have a colour without being seen (426a20ff.: colour without sight). Indeed, there could be a coloured world without perceivers. This is one reason why Aristotle distinguishes being coloured and being visible (*Metaphysics* 1065b32). The activity of colour in the medium will be individuated in terms of (a) the colour of bounded surface which produces it and (b) the way in which light in the medium is affected (intrinsically). There is, it should be noted, no requirement that the medium itself will have colour in the same way as the bounded surface does. It will become coloured in that way (whatever it is) in which the unbounded illuminable becomes coloured. In cases of perception, the activity of the colour of the object extends further and includes, as a further stage, its impacting, through the medium, on the sense organ (that is, its 'colouring' the organ), in such a way that the perceiver discriminates the colour of the object. There are, in this case,

Colour, we are told, is such as to move the illuminable (417a31–b2), when the latter is actual. Since light is the actuality of a given type of nature (418b7–8), colour must make a certain impact on the light. Aristotle does not attempt to say what impact this is. Colour, in some way, modifies the light but does not alter its capacities. Being modified in this way is the actuality of a potential of the light. One might compare it to a second actuality of the illuminable. Light is capable of being modified in a variety of ways.

One might suggest, taking a further step, that colours modify the light by modifying the degree of (active) illuminability there.[32] Aristotle does indeed say that sea water which is easy to see through (*eudipoton*) appears light blue (*glaukon*) while water which is less easy to see through appears pallid and water where one cannot measure the depth looks dark or dark blue (*De Generatione Animalium* 779b31ff.). However, these differences depend on the volume of water involved not the degree of illuminability. Aristotle also suggests that the smaller the amount of water present (as in blue eyes) the greater the movement set up by visible objects in the illuminable (780a3–5). But it does not follow from this remark that the variation between changes in the illuminable (*diaphanes*) brought about by objects of differing colours (in the same type of eyes) depends on the degree of illuminability present. Aristotle talks of some changes as being 'more' and 'less', others as 'stronger and weaker' (780a4–7, 11–14) but, unfortunately, does not specify what the strength or weakness of such movements consists in. While there are differing types of movement associated with differing types of visible object, there is no attempt to characterize these more fully. (This may have been a wise move on Aristotle's behalf, lacking—as he did—the resources to define more precisely what is involved in differing types of movement in the illuminable.) While he is happy to talk of the movement from the visible object as being destroyed or dissipated (781a5ff.), he does not offer a positive characterization of its nature. Indeed, he did not have resources to do so.

Aristotle, as already noted, rejected the idea, favoured by the atomists and Empedocles, of 'emanations' travelling from the visible object to the perceiver. However, as we have seen in the case of hearing, this is consistent with his thinking in terms of successive parcels of the illuminable, each inducing a given pattern of movement on the next. There might be cases of processes continuing across distances which are made up of a series of intermediate structure-preserving movements, without one object travelling through space from beginning to the end of the process. However, this is not Aristotle's view of light

---

two stages in the activity of the colour of the object: the first in the medium, the second in the perceiver. We see the colour of the object in virtue of its ability to impact on our sense organs through the medium.

[32] As has been suggested by Justin Broackes.

which he thinks of as instantaneously, in a non-sequential fashion, illuminating vast areas of space (*De Sensu* 447a5ff.).

Aristotle, it is important to note, does not define what it is for colour to be present in the medium without reference to light: colours are essentially 'enlightened' phenomena, features present in the light, itself the realization of the illuminable in the unbounded. He needs to refer to the unbounded to distinguish it from the colour of bounded surfaces. If colour in the medium is defined in this way, it is light and fire dependent: it will, like flavours or smells, have an essentially enmattered form. The activity of the colour of the object is its instantaneously affecting the light in the medium in this way. The medium has the ability to be affected by colour in this way. What occurs there is an essentially light-involving activity, even though it is not a temporally sequential process.

Aristotle, as we noted, distinguishes being coloured and being visible (*Metaphysics* 1065b32). The activity of colour will be individuated in terms of (a) the colour of the bounded surface which produces it and (b) the way in which light in the medium is affected. The medium itself will not have colour in the same way as the bounded surface does: it will be coloured in that way (whatever it is) in which the unbounded illuminable (*diaphanes*), when active, is permeated by the colour of the object.

5.9 The sense organ: seeing

Aristotle's discussion of seeing contains elements which parallel those found in his accounts of tasting, smelling, and hearing. There Aristotle relied, as in his treatment of anger, on two types of consideration:

[H.1]   If there is no appropriate bodily state present, there will be no suffering of the relevant type (*pathēsis*), and
[H.2]   The nature of the bodily state that is present affects the nature of the suffering.

Consonant with [H.1], he suggests that in the case of seeing:

(1)   The eye contains water (*De Sensu* 438b20ff.: 438b8ff.) and the illuminable (438a16ff.: *De Generatione Animalium* 779b26ff.). Eyes are affected in so far as they are both moist and illuminable (780a3ff.).

(2)   If the illuminable aspect of the eye, the pupil, is cut off, people cannot see: darkness falls (*De Sensu* 438b15ff.).

In line with [H.2], he notes that:

(3) The skin on the pupil must itself be thin and illuminable (780a27ff.), so that the incoming movement may not be adversely affected. If the skin becomes wrinkled and thicker (as in old age), the incoming movement is affected by the presence of the dark (non-transparent) shadow cast. Cataract arises when there is too much dryness in the eye (780a16ff.). At this point, sight resembles taste which (as noted above) is adversely affected by excessive moisture and strong tastes (*De Anima* 422b7ff.). Too much moisture in the eye leads to night blindness (780a20ff.).

(4) If the water in the eye is set in motion too much in respect of its illuminability, we do not see well (780a8–10).

He writes that:

> This is why people who have been looking at strong colours or those who go from sunlight into the dark do not see. This is because the strong movement that is already present in the eye drives out the weaker one which comes from without. When the movement of the liquid in the eye is excessive—as when one looks at bright objects—one cannot see them. (780a10–16)

(5) 'The movement in the eye that occurs in virtue of its being illuminable, not in virtue of its being wet, is seeing' (780a5–6).

In the case of tasting, smelling, and hearing, [H.1] and [H.2] considerations were taken to suggest that the definition of the relevant type of perceptual discrimination will refer to what is present in, and received from, the medium: an enmattered form. Given that the types of discrimination in question are defined in terms of their objects and that the types of objects are matter-involving in the way suggested, it follows that the type of discrimination itself must be matter-involving. If so, seeing—in line with the view of causation captured by the *poiēsis-pathēsis* requirement—will be, like perceiving smells or flavours, an inextricably psychophysical process. Both the form received and receiving of that form will be essentially matter-involving (in this case light-involving)

The spiritualist argument, noted above, rested on three claims:

[A] The light's being coloured is the same activity as the colour of the object appearing through it.
[B] The light's being coloured is not a real alteration but a mere Cambridge change.
[C] The change in the medium is of the same general type as that in the eye.[33]

---

[33] While spiritualists usually take this as an identity claim, it need mean no more than that the two are inseparable in definition, provided that nothing more is added in either definition. See discussion of this issue in Chapter 4: especially note 48.

In Sections 5.7–5.8, I have argued that, *pace* [B], there is considerably more going on in the medium than the spiritualist allowed. We should now assess [C].

The basic line of thought is as follows: there is an impact of the colour in the medium on the organ which is, in some way, the same activity as the organ's discriminating the colour of the object. There is, it seems, no definition of the type of discrimination without explicit reference to the light-involving medium which impacts on the sense organ. Given these considerations, seeing, like colouring, will be defined as an essentially matter-involving completion, the one relevant activity of an embodied capacity.

This line of thought can be developed further: colouring is the impacting of colour of the object via the medium on the sense organ in such a way that the latter discriminates the colour of the object. The perceiver sees the colour of the object in virtue of the sense organ being affected by the colour of the object through the medium. The sense organ is such that when impacted by the colour of the object through the medium it discriminates the colour of the object. What we see is the colour of the object (as we hear the voice of the singer) not the colour in the medium. We see this in virtue of the colour's ability to permeate the medium in such a way that, when our sense organ is affected, we see the colour of the surface of the object.

The colour of the object impacting on the sense organ through the medium will be, if the account follows that of smelling, tasting, and hearing, 'the same but different in being' as our seeing it. Aristotle describes the colour of the object impacting on the sense organ as the same activity as that of the sense's discriminating the colour of the object (426a16ff.). The former is the causing of an effect in the sense organ, the latter the correlative suffering of the sense organ. They are both essentially modifications of the illuminable (diaphanes). This is required if seeing is understood as sensitivity to an enlightened-form. Both form and the mode of receiving it, the relevant type of sensitivity, must be light- (that is, matter-)dependent (in line with the general account of causation, as discussed in Chapter 2).

Aristotle speaks of the sense organ as that which has the capacity to discriminate coloured objects on the basis of the impact of colour through the medium. There is one capacity which takes colour delivered via the medium as its input and delivers visual discrimination of coloured surfaces as its output. On this view, the sense organ's being affected by the colour of a surface through the medium is the same activity as discriminating that colour. One and the same inextricably psycho-physical activity occurs. The type of discrimination is defined as the operation of light-based discriminatory capacity. The type of colouring there is defined in terms of its impact on this capacity. Neither visual discrimination nor the material change in the sense organ can be defined without reference in their definition to the other.[34]

---

[34] For discussion of the phrase 'the same activity', see Chapter 4, n. 47.

What is distinctive about this aspect of Aristotle's view, so understood, emerges when it is contrasted with that offered by non-reductionist materialist interpreters. In their view, there are two distinct types of activity which are essential in his account of seeing: the activity of colour in the medium inside the sense organ and the distinct (purely psychological) discrimination of that colour. While both are activities within the sense organ, they should be distinguished. One is defined independently of discrimination (e.g. the impact of colour on the eye) and the other is the discrimination itself, our perception of colour. For these interpreters, when Aristotle talks of one capacity, his remarks are to be understood in the standard two-component way: there is, it is supposed, a purely physical type of change, defined independently of the psychological, and a purely psychological type of change (discrimination), defined independently of the former purely physical change.

It is important to note, in assessing this interpretation, that the activity in the sense organ appears to be defined, in Aristotle's account, in terms of its role in the organism as a whole: to discriminate colours. He does not appear to split the effect in the sense organ into two components: a purely physical change brought about by the medium and a further purely psychological change (such as discriminating colours). Indeed, the suffering in the organ appears to be just the sense organ's discriminating colour. There is one unified capacity at work. There is no attempt to define the impact on the sense organ without explicit reference to seeing the colour of the object or to define seeing the colour of the object without explicit reference to the impact on the sense organ. Further, if the type of impact on the organ essentially involves the illuminable (*diaphanes*), one cannot define visual discrimination without essential reference to the way this type of perception is embodied in a sense organ or to the types of impact made by colour on that organ (which require reference to the illuminable (*diaphanes*) therein). Seeing is, in this way, an essentially embodied type of cognition of the colours of objects.

5.10 Seeing: a more general perspective

Aristotle's account of seeing, so understood, follows the pattern of his discussion of the other senses. He held, that is, that:

(A) Colour in the medium is essentially matter-involving: involving light and the illuminable, which are modified by fire

(B) If colour in the medium is essentially matter-involving, then colouring (the impact of colour on the sense organ) also is essentially matter-involving

(C) If colouring is essentially matter-involving, seeing must also be (the correlative activities of acting and suffering)

(D) Seeing is the perceiver's sense organ's being affected by colours and:

(E) Seeing is the perceiver's discriminating colours

and so concluded that:

(F) Seeing is essentially a matter-involving activity (completion).

Seeing colours, so defined, is an inextricably psycho-physical activity: the exercise of a similarly inextricable capacity. The activity cannot be defined without reference to the impact of the colour of the object on light in the medium and the sense organ. It does not essentially involve the purely psychological act of awareness spiritualists and non-reductionist materialists alike assume.

Aristotle's position can be presented as follows:

(1) Colour, in its nature, is such as to move the illuminable when actual (i.e. light) [premise]

(2) When the light (the illuminable when actual) is moved, it is coloured in an essentially light/fire-involving process [premise]

(3) The change in the eye is of the same general type as that in the medium (i.e. the illuminable) [premise]

(4) The change in the eye is an essentially light-involving change (from 2 and 3).

Given that:

(5) The change in the eye is the observer's seeing the colour,

it follows that:

(6) Seeing is an essentially light-involving change, the realization of an inextricably psycho-physical capacity to discriminate colours.

His account of visual perception, so understood, is similar to those of hearing, tasting, smelling, and touching. All these perceptual activities are, in the ways indicated, inextricably psycho-physical, not definable in terms of a purely psychological component and a separate purely physical (or purely material) one. The relevant capacities are defined as essentially goal-directed enmattered capacities. If this is correct, none of these accounts exemplify either of the two post-Cartesian assumptions mentioned at the beginning of Chapter 4:

> [A] There is a purely psychological type of event essentially involved in perceiving, such as being aware of, or perceptually discriminating, a taste or smell; and

[B] All the types of event essentially involved in perceiving are either purely psychological or purely physical or a combination of the purely psychological and the purely physical.[35]

By contrast, Aristotle develops in his discussion of these cases of perception the inextricabilist account he introduced in considering the emotions in *De Anima* A.1 and deployed elsewhere in analysing desire. From a wider perspective: his simple theory of these psychological phenomena follows the pattern set by his account of the forms and matter of natural substances (as interpreted in Chapter 2).

There is one further feature of Aristotle's account of visual perception which requires comment. Although he did not accept that to see the redness of an object is just for its redness to appear to you (in the way the spiritualist interpretation suggested), he did think that seeing is direct awareness of its redness. In this respect, he differs from those non-reductionist materialists for whom there is an internal psychological act of perception, realized in an internal material state, which in some way 'represents' the redness of the external object (whether by being itself literally red or by 'encoding' in some way the redness of the object). On the latter account, the immediate object of perception is an internal object (of some kind) which represents the qualities of external objects in virtue of possessing certain sensible or structural qualities. Non-reductionist materialists are drawn to this picture by the thought that there must be an internal psychological act of perception of this type which is realized by, or grounded in, an internal purely physical state.

It is natural to suppose that any theorist must choose one of two alternatives: either (i) all that is essential to seeing is an awareness of the colour of an object or (ii) seeing is essentially grounded in material internal events or states which represent the colours of external objects. The first alternative combines direct realism about perception with spiritualism, the second non-reductionist materialism with representationalism.[36] In the latter combination, in all cases of colour perception there is a sequence of events beginning with one on the surface of the object and culminating in one which constitutes perception. Each of these events 'encodes' or 'borrows' the redness of the object (the distal object). What I am directly aware of, in this account, are the properties of the final event in this sequence (or, in some versions, the penultimate, proximal, one). If so, I can only be aware of the redness of the object indirectly in virtue of its causing an event

---

[35] By 'combination' is intended any relation between two definitionally distinct events or two definitionally distinct sets of features (such as properties). The relevant relations may include necessitation or supervenience and are not confined to mere conjunction (or correlation).

[36] If one takes redness to be a pure form of which one is directly aware without anything occurring in the medium, the spiritualist account of perception will follow, given the assumption that the object of perception and the activity of perceiving are enmattered in the same way (*De Anima* Γ.4, 429b22–3). For the spiritualist, neither is enmattered.

which, in some way, represents or 'encodes' it. There is some psychological feature of our experience which represents the redness of the object. This representation of the colour of the distal object is realized in the final physical event in the sequence, located in the brain of the perceiver.

This picture has its attractions: if one thinks of perception as the last event in a sequence of events, each individuated in terms of their physical features, perceiving is naturally taken to be of an object caused to be present by the antecedent events which in some way 'stand for' the colour of the original object. Since the final event is a seeing of a colour, it is best understood as seeing something internal to the subject, perhaps an image or sense-datum, with features which represent the colour of the object and are determined solely by the physical features of the final physical event. This line of thought leads materialist interpreters of Aristotle to present him as a 'representationalist': what we are directly aware of are features of the final physical event which, in some way, stand in for features of the original distal object. (Indeed, it has encouraged many broadly materialist philosophers to be representationalists.)

Aristotle offers, I have suggested, an alternative, non-spiritualist, form of direct realism. In his view, there is no need to postulate a further internal, representational, entity seen by the perceiver but distinct from the (external) object.[37] This is because, in his account, seeing the colour of an object—or its colour appearing to a perceiver—just is that colour impacting on the perceiver through the medium. For us to see the colour of the object is for our perceptual faculty to be assimilated to it. Our seeing its colour is the same activity as its impacting on us through specific light-based movements in the medium. Indeed, the relevant impact of the colour of the object on us (*tupos*) just is our seeing its colour. This is why, when all goes well, we see the colour of the object, not an internal object caused by that colour. In this way, Aristotle proposes a non-spiritualist version of direct realism. In effect, he is seeking to show how to be a direct realist, in a non-ad hoc way, without being a spiritualist.

There are several aspects to Aristotle's suggestion. He focuses on the activity of the colour of the object impacting on the perceiver via the medium (by permeating the medium) and takes the final stage of this activity to be the perceiver's seeing the colour in question. Seeing, so understood, is not identified with the last event in a sequence of events, an event which (i) is caused by an antecedent event in a chain of events which begins with an event on the surface of the object and (ii) is individuated in terms of the internal physical event which realizes it. Instead, seeing the colour is the final, completing, stage of the activity of the colour of the object 'reaching out' to the perceiver. This activity ends, when successful, with our perceptual organ being assimilated to that colour. What

---

[37] Deborah Modrak (2001: 239) correctly describes this style of representationalist interpretation as 'unnecessary and not true to Aristotle's description of perceptual processes'.

occurs in the medium, in this case, is to be understood not as a series of separate events, each caused by antecedent events, but as the activity of the colour of the object instantaneously spreading through the light-based medium to the observer. When this occurs, the colour of the object impacting on the observer is the same activity as the latter's visually discriminating that colour.

If what occurs in the perceiver is the last stage in a causal activity, individuated in terms of its originating colour, Aristotle has no need to seek for an intrinsic feature of the final event which stands for, or represents, the original colour of the object. Indeed, from his viewpoint, this search would, once again, be 'wasted effort'.[38] All that happens in perceivers is a light-based visual discrimination of the colour of the external object, the exercise of our enmattered capacity to see such colours. From this perspective, he had no need to address the problems which arise for representationalist accounts: (i) does the final event instantiate the same type of redness as is possessed by the external object or does it 'encode' (in some way) information present in it? (ii) how does a purely material event, if one is present, come to have mental properties of this kind? Still less need interpreters search for texts which might, with considerable ingenuity, be construed as addressing some of these questions in ways consistent with representationalism. This is because, in his account, perception is not to be analysed in terms of a final event, internal to the perceiver, caused by a sequence of antecedent events in the medium, each of which, in some way, borrows or encodes the colour of the object. Instead, the activity in the transparent, whatever it is, conveys, in some way, the redness of the original object to the perceiver. Their perceiving that redness just is their being impacted by it through the relevant light-based medium. There is one matter-involving activity whose endpoint can be described in one of two inextricably psycho-physical ways: as a light-based perceptual sensitivity to the colour of the object or as a light-based affecting by the colour of the object of that perceptual sensitivity.

This said, Aristotle's accounts of seeing and hearing differ in one significant respect. In the former, what is seen is the colour of the object, a property of its surface. By contrast, what is heard is a sound which results from, for example, the vocal cords (or a drum) being struck. One hears the sound caused in the air by this striking not the striking itself. If one were to describe oneself as hearing, for example, the bus approaching, this would be elliptical, in Aristotle's view, for hearing its sound of the bus approaching. This is because the sound heard is not a property located on the bus (or its periphery) even though the bus has the capacity to cause such a sound. By contrast, the colour of the bus is located on its surface and it is this which is presented to the visual perceiver via the medium.

---

[38] Had Aristotle thought in terms of events, the final event in the perceiver would have been defined as the final stage of the process (perhaps best seen as an abstraction from that process).

It is important to note, in addition, that, for all Aristotle says, the activity in the medium could convey the redness of the object to the perceiver in ways comparable with that in which, in the case of a craft, the form of the craft is present in the movements of the craft-worker (see *De Generatione Animalium* 735a2ff., cited in Chapter 2). In the latter example, it is not the case that each separate stage in the sculpting 'encodes' or 'borrows' the original form of the statue present in the mind of the sculptor. While sculptors' movements are guided by, and manifest, their skill and goals, they do not contain at each stage some likeness of the form to be produced, a specific feature which 'encodes' or represents the form of the statue she envisages. The final product, the result of a complex process, need not be 'pre-figured' in this way at each previous separate stage in its creation. So understood, the activity by which the colour in the object impacts on the observer through the medium need not be analysed as a specific, isolable, chain of events (distinct from the rest of the background conditions) each of which carries, or encodes, a likeness of the one before, going back to the colour of the object. The activity involved may be more complex, and more context sensitive, than this. How precisely it unfolds and generates the relevant perception of colour is, of course, a matter of further, detailed, scientific activity.[39]

While Aristotle's account of seeing is a version of direct realism, it differs from the one suggested by the spiritualist interpreter. This is because it presents seeing as the final stage of an essentially matter-involving activity beginning with the colour of the object and ending in the perceiver's seeing it. Aristotle is, it seems, offering a way to avoid representationalism without defining visual perception, as spiritualists do, simply as the perceptual organ's pure (or matter-free) awareness of the colour of the object. His aim is, in effect, to combine direct realism about the special sensibles with an inextricably psycho-physical account of visual perception as the final stage in a light-involving activity which begins with the colour of the object and ends in the relevant perceptual system. This is how the colour of the object presents itself to the perceiver. (Whether he succeeds is a further question which I shall not seek to address here.)

---

[39] For discussion of an analogous issue in Aristotle's account of animal generation, see Diana Quarantotto's essay 'Aristotle on the Order of Embryonic Development and the Homonymy Principle' (forthcoming). The similarities between Aristotle's discussion of biological and psychological phenomena, as they relate to issues of hylomorphism, require further investigation.

6
Perception, Desire, and Action
Inextricably Embodied Subjects

6.1 Introduction: further extensions?

Aristotle understood emotions, desire, and the perception of tastes, sounds, and colours (the so-called 'special sensibles') as essentially and inextricably embodied activities (or completions), not definable in terms of two definitionally distinct components, one purely psychological, one purely physical. Or so I have argued in Chapters 1, 3, 4, and 5.

His simple theory of these phenomena enabled him to present the emotions, desire, and perception as per se causes and per se effects of material movements. Had they been defined in terms of two definitionally distinct components, one purely psychological, the other purely physical, they could not have played this role. To be per se efficient causes or effects, their forms needed to be inextricably enmattered capacities. This view is a special case of his hylomorphic account of the forms of natural bodies as, at first approximation, inextricably matter-involving capacities. They had to be such, as was argued in Chapter 2, if they were to be unified per se causes of material changes.

Aristotle applied the same style of account to the perception of size, movement, and number (the so-called 'common sensibles') and to imagination and practical thought. His discussion of these topics, so far from being inconsistent with his account of the emotions, desire, and perception, is, or so I shall suggest, an attempt to develop an integrated picture of how perception in general, common as well as special, leads to bodily action in unified, essentially and inextricably psycho-physical human subjects.

The first task is to consider Aristotle's discussion of the perception of objects and their 'common' properties. I shall then examine how, in his account, perception generates pleasures, pains, desires, and actions in essentially psycho-physical subjects with bodily, nutritive, needs. Chapter 3 focused on the causal consequences of desire, Chapters 4 and 5 on the causal antecedents of perception. The present chapter considers the connections between perception and desire: the causal consequences of the former, the causal antecedents of the latter. After doing so, I shall examine some aspects of his treatment of imagination and of thought, which was initially presented as different from activities and passions 'common to body and soul' (403a8–10). This task is important since perception of objects, imagination, and human thought have been interpreted, mistakenly in my view, to be purely psychological capacities.

The aim of this chapter, it should be emphasized, is limited. There are many central aspects of Aristotle's discussions of imagination and thought which lie beyond its scope. My present aim is only to assess the extent to which his account of these phenomena is consistent with the inextricabilist interpretation developed in previous chapters.

6.2 The perception of moving objects: 'common sensibles'

While Aristotle's account of the perception of flavours, smells, sounds, and colours has been centre-stage in Chapters 4 and 5, we have not considered his remarks on the perception of the objects which are coloured or flavoured, or of those properties which are accessible to more than one sense. Is our perception of these, as some have suggested, purely psychological, not essentially psycho-physical? Or is perception 'as a whole' (403a7) common to body and soul in the way perception of taste and colour are?

Many interpretations of Aristotle's account of the perception of objects and of 'common sensibles' such as size, movement, and number, are guided by the assumption that seeing is confined to colours, hearing to sounds, and tasting to flavours. Interpreters take each sense, by itself, to discriminate only what might be called 'modal-specific properties'. They then need to explain how, in Aristotle's view, we can perceive moving objects with a given shape, which are accessible to different senses. (I shall call such objects and properties 'cross-modal'.)

The standard interpretation rests on three claims: it sees Aristotle as holding that:

(A) Special senses, such as vision and hearing, perceive colour and sound (modal-specific properties) and nothing else;
(B) The common sense perceives:
   (i) one cross-modal object as, for example, bitter and yellow, and
   (ii) two different cross-modal objects as different.
(C) The common sense goes beyond the special senses but, in some way, arises out of them.

Anna Marmodoro has recently developed a sophisticated version of this interpretation. She writes:

> Common sense empowers and enriches its constituents with functionalities their union could not alone secure. Its operation results in the generation of new content (awareness of common sensibles) over and above unifying the existing content from the special senses (for example, discerning white from sweet). The

generation of new perceptual content and the unification of existing perceptual content into further contents, is the nature and role of the common sense.[1]

Her remarks prompt the key question: how does common sense do this? Is something fundamentally different added: the exercise of a new capacity or power? Is the additional capacity essentially psycho-physical? Or is it 'pure', defined without essential reference to material sense organs or the type of material change found there?[2]

We need, in assessing this interpretation, first to examine whether Aristotle, in fact, accepted (A): are the special senses, in his view, confined to modal-specific properties, such as seeing colours? Or do we, in his account, also see objects and their movement? And if we do, are the objects or properties seen or tasted modal-specific or cross-modal, accessible to different senses?

In *De Anima* 418a22–4 Aristotle writes:

> Of the two types of sensibles (*sensibilia*) which are perceived in their own right, it is the objects special to different senses that are in the paradigmatic way perceptible and it is these to which the essential character of each sense is naturally directed.[3]

According to the orthodox interpretation, this remark establishes that even though the colours, sounds, and flavours are the colours, sounds, and flavours of objects, sight only perceives colours, hearing only sounds, and taste only flavours.[4] The object itself, and its movement, is not something that can be perceptually discriminated by any special sense operating alone.

Aristotle, I shall suggest, took a different view. In his account, what is seen is a coloured moving (or stationary) object, what is heard a noisy moving object and what is tasted a sweet moving object. Even if colour is what is seen in a paradigmatic way, this does not mean that seeing (the special sense) is confined to seeing colours.[5] Further, since the objects are cross-modal, we see (and visually

---

[1] Anna Marmodoro (2014: 75).
[2] For discussion of Anna Marmodoro's interpretation, see B. Berman (2017: 89–106).
[3] I translate '*kath' hauta aisthēta*' as 'perceived in their own right' to capture the thought that they are *per causes* of perception. I understand '*kuriōs*' as 'paradigmatically' or 'principally' in line with the use in *Categories* 2a11–13, where it is conjoined with 'firstly' and 'most of all' (*malista*). See also *Nicomachean Ethics* 1098b14, where it is conjoined with 'most of all' (*malista*) and *N.E.* 1157a31, where is used together with 'firstly'.
[4] Those inclined to this view interpret Aristotle as saying that colours and sounds (etc.) are not just *principally* but *strictly speaking* perceptibles: the only objects of the special senses.
[5] Those who take this view understand Aristotle to say that the special sensibles are the principal or basic type of perceptibles: those to which the nature of each sense is specifically directed (perhaps taking the 'and' in 418a25 as epexegetic). So understood, a person can (non-accidentally) see the common sensibles, even though vision is not specifically targeted at them. They are accessible to other senses as well.

discriminate) large moving coloured objects. No further step is required to arrive at the perception of cross-modal objects and their cross-modal properties. We see on the basis of vision alone objects and properties of this type.

Aristotle writes, in *De Anima* B.6, that movement is perceived both by vision and by touch (418a18–19). It, together with size, shape, and number, is a cross-modal feature: a common sensible. If it, as a common sensible, can be perceived individually both by vision and by touch, what each sense perceives will be a cross-modal object, one which other senses can also sense. We will, on occasion, see a small red object moving towards us, even though its oneness and movement are not accessible only to vision.

The preceding passage supports this interpretation of Aristotle's remark:

(i) In 418a10 he writes that a specific *(idion)* type of object of perception cannot be perceived by any other sense. By contrast, common objects can be perceived by more than one sense (perhaps by all). If such objects are common to, for example, vision and touch, both these senses must have access to them. If so, we will see and touch the same cross-modal objects and features (such as shape and movement), not different modal-specific objects or features (such as visual-movement). These senses will perceive the same moving object, even though one sense perceives it visually, the other tactually (418a19–20).

(ii) In 418a16 Aristotle notes that each sense (such as vision) cannot be deceived with regard to whether it sees, for example, a colour or hears a sound, but can be deceived as to which object is coloured and as to where it is. If this is so, visual perception must be able to discriminate (and can be deceived about) a determinate object at a specific location. While this remark, taken in isolation, might be about modal-specific objects, his further claim—about movement, size, and number—suggests that the objects discriminated by sight and touch are cross-modal, accessible to both senses. There is no suggestion that we see modal-specific visual-objects with modal-specific properties such visual-size and visual-movement.

Aristotle's remark in 418b24–5, cited above, should be interpreted in the light of these two comments. When Aristotle says that the essential character of vision is uniquely directed to colour, he is noting that it alone perceives colour. However, this is consistent with our seeing, on the basis of vision alone, both colour and cross-modal objects (which are coloured). Perhaps the essence of vision is to see the colour of objects, that of hearing is to hear the sounds of such objects. However, even though seeing alone detects the colour of objects, other senses can detect other features of the same objects. Or perhaps seeing has a complex essence: one aspect is unique to it, another shared with other senses. Or perhaps seeing cross-modal objects is a necessary feature of visual experience, even though its essential character is limited to what is unique to it (seeing colours). In any of these ways, we can see (non-accidentally) moving objects as well as their colours. It is not clear that in his concluding remark in *De Anima* B.5, Aristotle decides between these alternatives.[6]

The suggestion that what is seen is not restricted to colour is supported by Aristotle's next comment at the beginning of *De Anima* B.7. He writes:

> The object of sight is the visible. What is visible is colour and that which can be described but has no name...and colour is that which is on that which is in itself visible...because it has in itself the cause of being visible. (418a28–30)

If what is 'in itself visible' and what 'has in itself the cause of being visible' refer to the 'transparent' surface of objects, they, as well as colour, will be seen (and so visually discriminated). This seems to have been his view throughout this chapter. He notes, at 419a2ff., that certain types of object (such as the fungus) are not seen in the light in contrast with coloured objects, which are. This suggests that the per se objects of sight include coloured objects. As Aristotle later states explicitly: what is seen can be either colour or that which has the colour (425b19).

Nor are remarks of this type confined to vision. The object of taste is described as a tangible object and as a body (*De Anima* 422a7ff.). Since bodies are cross-modal objects, the object of taste will be an object with a given taste (or the taste of that object). Objects of taste include what Aristotle calls the 'drinkable' and the 'undrinkable' (422a33ff.), cross-modal objects such as juices and water.[7]

Nor is this style of account found only in *De Anima* B. In *De Anima* Γ.1 Aristotle writes:

> If sight had been our only sense and what is white its only object, the common sensibles would have been more likely to escape our notice and all sensibles to have seemed the same because colour and magnitude always co-occur. (425b7ff.)

This observation suggests that the common sensibles, the objects of the common sense, would be present to visual perception, even if we had only one sense and so would be more likely not to notice them.[8] These objects would be cross-modal, even though their cross-modal status might more easily escape us if we had only one sense. In that (unhappy) situation, we would, in fact, be discriminating cross-modal objects, even though we were not always aware that we were doing so.

---

[6] I shall not attempt to adjudicate between these alternatives.

[7] There is, it should be noted, a persistent ambiguity in Aristotle's use of phrases such as 'the white' or 'the bitter'. They can refer either to the whiteness of the object or the white object and need to be disambiguated in context.

[8] This remark suggests that the perception of cross-modal objects does not require us to have, and is not grounded in, an integrated perceptual system involving many senses. For an opposing view, see Pavel Gregoric's account (2007: 28–39, 52–61).

In sum: there is reason to believe that for Aristotle, vision and touch (along with the other special senses) individually and by themselves perceive cross-modal objects. They are not confined to modal-specific properties (as in the standard view) or to such properties and modal-specific objects.[9]

How, then, does an Aristotelian perceiver perceive one cross-modal object? Does this require the presence of a new capacity different from the essentially psycho-physical capacities involved in colour or flavour perception? Is the additional capacity pure, defined without essential reference to matter or material changes?

Aristotle's most extended discussion of the perception of common sensibles is in *De Anima* Γ.1. It begins as follows:

There is no special sense organ for the common sensibles with which we perceive with each [special] sense accidentally: such as movement, being at rest, shape, size, being one or number. All these we perceive by movement—as we perceive size by movement (and shape—a type of size), being at rest by not being moved and number by the discreteness of the object—and by the individual sense organs (for each sense perceives one thing).

The first sentence is best taken as sketching the view that Aristotle himself rejects: that there is a special sense organ directed at the common sensibles, which we perceive accidentally by every special sense.[10] He is committed to rejecting this if,

---

[9] In the main text, I have proceeded as if the standard view is, as it stands, clear and properly formulated. However, it is not clear how exactly its proponents understand the object of vision. Some speak, somewhat uncritically, of redness, a universal, as what is discriminated by perception. However, Aristotle notes that, in his view, it is particulars and not universals that are perceived (as in, for example, *Posterior Analytics* 87b37ff., *De Anima* 417b22, 428a16ff.). Others may suggest that the object of vision is a patch in one's visual field or some quantity of redness, perhaps redness here and now (as in some empiricist accounts). But, one must ask, what for Aristotle determines the relevant 'here and now'? Surely this must be, in his account, an object, since he describes colours as a type of quality (*poion ti*: *Topics* 103b32, 120b35), and—as such—a quality of an object. In *De Anima* B.6, as already noted, Aristotle talks of the coloured object as a determinate and spatially locatable particular.

Another suggestion might be that the object of vision is modal-specific: a coloured object, not a cross-modal object. However, this too is problematic as Aristotle notes that movement is accessible both to sight and to touch. What is seen and touched must be a cross-modal object (418a19–20).

A final suggestion would run as follows: Aristotle held that what makes a colour one colour is its being the colour of one cross-modal object but denied that the cross-modal object itself is seen. However, this too is problematic: he talks elsewhere, as already noted, of the object itself being seen at a given place and of vision being deceived as to which object is seen and where it is. These phrases suggest that it is cross-modal objects that are seen and visually discriminated. Deception is a way of going wrong about where the object is and which object it is. If so, seeing (when all goes well) will involve, in the case of common sensibles, the successful discrimination of the object and its location. Both will be part of what is seen.

[10] This use of 'accidentally' in 425a15 has caused problems. Torstrik (1862) suggested adding a 'not' to read 'not accidentally' to make this passage consistent with Aristotle's remarks in *De Anima* B.6. But his radical move is unnecessary. One could interpret this term as indicating only (as Christopher Shields notes in his 2016: 261) the view of Aristotle's opponent, not Aristotle's own. The opponent

as in *De Anima* B.6, the common sensibles are perceived non-accidentally by the special senses. Even if the essence of seeing were confined to the discrimination of colour alone (as in the most restricted reading of 418a23–4), seeing itself can also non-accidentally discriminate moving (or stationary) cross-modal objects.

The final sentence suggests that he retained this earlier view. He writes: 'we perceive the common sensibles by each of the special sense organs' (*tois idiois*: 425a19) and explicates this by noting that 'each sense perceives one thing'.[11] This remark, in its immediate context, suggests that each sense perceives one and the same common object (referring back to number as a common sensible in 425a16). It is needed to support his contention that the special senses perceive genuinely common sensibles (such as movement and shape). Without it, it might well be the case that one sense perceived visual-size another tactile-size on the basis of different movements specific to each sense. To block this possibility. Aristotle adds that all the senses perceive one and the same object with its cross-modal shape.[12] (I shall consider below his telegrammatic remark: 'by movement'.)

Aristotle seeks to argue for his conclusion: common sensibles are not grasped by a further sense over and above vision, taste, hearing, touch, and smell. Had this

would suggest that (on his—the opponent's—hypothesis) we detect common sensibles accidentally with each of the special sensibles. This interpretation is of ancient vintage, dating back to Themistius, Philoponus, and Simplicius (see Joseph Owens' essay (1982: 215–36)). Alternatively, if one were to take Aristotle himself as endorsing the claim in 425a15, he need only be saying (as Hicks (1907) suggests) that the seeing of common sensibles is not part of the essence of vision—even though it is still a necessary part of the operation of seeing (as he suggested—on one reading—in *De Anima* B.6, 418a24–5). In scholastic terms: seeing an object's cross-modal features would be a necessary accident of seeing. (See, for the latter notion, *Metaphysics* 1025a31.) While Shields' proposal is the more elegant, it is not necessary for our present purposes to adjudicate between them.

[11] 'Sense organ' is the nearest relevant noun (425a14) where it is qualified, as here, by 'specific'. On this reading, the next phrase 'for each sense senses one thing' is taken to refer to the cross-modal object they sense and so to explain how individual senses grasp one common object and its properties. Some commentators have supplied the term 'objects of sense' (*aisthēta*) to qualify 'specific', even though there is no noun in the immediate context to underpin this reading. They support their suggestion by understanding the phrase 'each sense senses one thing' to mean that each sense senses one type of sense object (vision coloured objects of sense etc.). However, this clause, so understood, seems irrelevant to Aristotle's claim (which is required in these lines) that the special senses discriminate movement, size and shape.

[12] 425a16–20 point to two features shared by all cases of perception of common objects: such objects are always perceived both by movement and by the special sense organs. Aristotle adds the phrase 'for each sense organ perceives one thing' to emphasize the central importance of perceiving one object for perception of size, shape, movement etc. It is only if a sense organ perceives one object that it can see its size etc. (I am indebted to Juan Piñeros for his advice on this issue.) This sentence (425a16–20) shows that there is not a special sense organ for perceiving common sensibles and so supports the claim in the preceding sentence (425a14–15). The further, stronger, claim that it is *impossible* that there be such a common organ (made in the next sentence: 425a20–1) is supported, in my understanding, by the considerations that follow. These aim to show that if there were such an organ, there would be no genuine cases of perception of common sensibles (425a21–30). The stronger impossibility claim (introduced by 'as a consequence': '*hōste*') is not grounded solely on the fact that there is no such organ. It requires the further considerations introduced by the next sentences (as is suggested by 'for': 425a21–2). These explain why such an organ could not account for common perception.

been the case, he continues, one of two undesirable consequences would have followed. He writes:

> It is clear that there cannot be a special sense for these common sensibles, such as movement; for then the situation will be as it is when we now perceive what is sweet by sight. This happens because we have perception of both and grasp on this basis when they co-occur. If this was not so (that is, if there were a special sense for common sensibles and we perceived objects moving not in the way just mentioned), we would never perceive the common sensibles except accidentally in the way in which we see Kleon's son not because he is Kleon's son, but because he is pale and what is pale happens to be Kleon's son.[13] But we have, in fact, a common or shared perception of the common sensibles non-accidentally. Thus, they are not specific to one sense; if they were, we would not perceive them otherwise than in the way in which it has been said we see Kleon's son. (425a20–30)

If the perception of common sensibles had been the work of a further sense, dedicated to perceiving just them, we would have had to perceive a moving red object in one of two ways indicated: either that in which we see what is sweet or that in which we see Kleon's son. But neither of these is, in fact, how we do it. In the former scenario, we would have seen a yellow object and in addition perceived by the common sense that it is moving. When these two perceptions co-occur, we would have grasped that they do so. It would be as when we taste something sweet, see something red, and grasp that these perceptions co-occur. But, as Aristotle plausibly remarks, this is not what actually happens: we immediately see one moving object. We do not begin with two distinct acts of perceiving and note that they co-occur. No further step is required to identify the yellow with the moving object. What happens is best explained by our non-inferentially seeing one yellow moving object. This is also different from what happens when we see Kleon's son. The movement, shape, and colour of an object, unlike its being Kleon's son, are immediately given to us in visual perception. These are per se causes of our seeing what we see.[14] Our visual system is able by itself to register these cross-modal features.

Aristotle concludes by reiterating his positive claim: we have, non-accidentally, a shared (or common) perception of common sensibles (425a27–8). Each sense, it seems, has access to the same common sensibles. They are not the unique preserve of a new sense dedicated only to perceiving one moving object. As in

---

[13] In 425a26, I follow those MSS who read '*toutōi*' (referring to the pale to which it belongs to be Kleon's son) rather than those which read '*touto*' (where the presence of '*einai*' in 425a27 looks cumbersome).

[14] Movement could be a per se cause of visual perception even seeing it were a necessary accident of visual perception.

6.2 THE PERCEPTION OF MOVING OBJECTS: 'COMMON SENSIBLES'

De Anima B.6, one such object is visually perceived, touched, smelled, or tasted. The object seen or touched must be cross-modal, open to these different senses.

Aristotle attempts to develop his account further. He writes:

> But the different senses do perceive accidentally each other's specific objects, not as the senses they are, but as one sense when there is a simultaneous perception of the same object, as when, with respect to bile, they perceive that it is yellow and bitter; for it is not the task of another sense to say that one thing is both (yellow and bitter). (425a30–b2)[15]

This condensed observation raises several questions. What exactly is meant by Aristotle's talk of 'as one sense when there is simultaneous perception of the same object'? Is it enough that vision and taste perceptually discriminate the same object? Or is it required that, acting as one, they perceptually discriminate it as one and the same object? Is it perception that says that one object is both yellow and bitter? Or, is this further step the task of thought?

Whichever way these questions are answered, it is important to note that even if vision perceives accidentally the bitterness of the object (e.g. the bile), it does not follow that it perceives the cross-modal object itself (the bile) accidentally. Each of the senses may perceive another's special objects accidentally even though they all discriminate the same object. We may, that is, visually discriminate its bitterness only accidentally because this is not a property directly accessible to vision or its per se cause. However, by contrast, its being one moving object may be a per se cause of, and directly accessible to, vision. Common sensibles, in virtue of being what they are, are perceived by each of the senses. We see and touch one and the same cross-modal object at one spatial position (418a16f.).

So far, so good. But how, in Aristotle's view, do our special senses perceive cross-modal objects and their location? How does vision see one moving object? When Aristotle speaks of sight, he talks of the medium as being affected by colour (424a121ff.). How can cross-modal features of objects impact on the relevant medium (the illuminable) or on the visual perceiver? Can we locate them in space on this basis alone?

In the case of sight, there must, it seems, be a distinctive impact on our visual system made by large triangular moving objects as opposed to small stationary circular ones. In Aristotle's terminology, we will receive different forms in these cases. Further, we will see objects as moving through space, occupying differing spatial positions at different times. How, if at all, does he account for this?

---

[15] At 425b1, I read with the manuscripts E and L, '*cholēn hoti*'. Ross' '*cholēs hoti*' (1961) has no MSS support. One could take '*cholēn*' grammatically either as the direct object of perceive (with Hicks (1907)) or as an accusative of respect.

Aristotle comments telegrammatically in *De Anima* Γ.1: 'we perceive all the common sensibles by movement' (*kinēsei*: 425a17). The Greek commentators understood him to refer to movements set up in us by cross-modal objects and their cross-modal properties.[16] Their idea was that we perceive an object's size because it moves us continuously (as one unit), we perceive it at rest because it does not move us at all and we perceive number (e.g. of two different objects) because there is some discontinuity in the movements set up in us. In support of their view, one might cite Aristotle's discussion of contrary movements set up in us by sameness and difference (see 426b30) and his talk of movements in what discriminates as 'proportionate' to what is big and far away (*De Memoria* 452b9–11). There are, it seems, types of movement caused in perceivers by cross-modal objects and their cross-modal properties.[17]

There is, however, another interpretation: Aristotle may be suggesting that we perceive all the common sensibles because of movement, whether theirs or ours. If so, we will in fact perceive them by *perceiving* such movement. Perhaps we perceive an object's size by perceiving it moving continuously (with all its parts) and its being at rest by perceiving it as not moving. Or perhaps we perceive these factors by perceiving our movement in relation to them. We may perceive an object's size as we move towards it or as it moves towards us.

The second interpretation enjoys two advantages. It takes 'movement' to refer to the movement of (or in relation to) external objects throughout the whole passage (425a15–21). By contrast, the former understands the first and last occurrence of 'movement' to refer to the movements of objects while the intervening three occurrences refer (without any marker of the transition) to internal movements in the sense organ. Further, according to this interpretation, this passage adds a new and important point: our perception of common sensibles is constituted by our perception of objects, including perhaps our own bodies, moving in relation to each other. On this basis we can see objects as far away or as near us—a phenomenon Aristotle mentions in *De Memoria* 452b10. To do so is to locate them in relation to us and our bodies. We certainly need, in his account, to be able to visually discriminate where they are (*De Anima* 418a16) in order to act successfully. (Where is the cricket ball? Can I catch it?) By contrast, since in Aristotle's view, all per se sensibles set up movements in the sense organ, why add this comment now specifically about the common sensibles? Even if true (as it seems to be), it does not add anything immediately relevant to the present discussion.

---

[16] Hicks summarizes their views in his note on 425a17 (1907: 428).

[17] Hicks, commenting on this passage, rejects this view, thinking (I believe, mistakenly) that it blurs the distinction between special and common sensibles. But this need not be the case: the former can have effects specific to one sense even though that sense is affected by other different movements as well (to which other senses also are subject).

Aristotle, in any event, seems committed by his remarks elsewhere to two claims:

(i) We see size, shape, movement, and location on the basis of what reaches our sense organs through the illuminable *(diaphanes)*. What reaches us will vary as objects of different size move. We are affected by movements which are, in some way, analogous to those of the objects seen (as Aristotle comments in *De Memoria* 452b7ff.). He probably lacked the resources to specify in detail the relevant movements in the medium or to show exactly how we are impacted by them—something that might be achieved, for example, through an empirical study of depth perception. But there is reason to believe that, in his view, we are (somehow) visually sensitive, on the basis of what we receive through the medium of light, to a red circular ball moving quickly towards us. The relevant media will convey to each sense separately information about the location and movement of such an object.[18] In his account, we (unproblematically) see movement which requires us to visually discriminate the same objects over a period of time.

(ii) Part of what we see, in seeing an object's location, is its position relative to us (*De Memoria* 452b10). To do so requires us to be, and to see ourselves as, embodied subjects, objects capable of interacting with other objects. In seeing objects coming nearer to us, what we see will be partially constituted by our being embodied subjects. This form of perception is particularly important in guiding our actions. If all goes well, I'll adjust to the flight of the cricket ball and catch it! We typically interact with particular objects which we see as close to us, within our reach, as the embodied agents we are.

Given (i), perception of common as well as of special sensibles will be, for Aristotle, 'common to body and soul' (*De Anima* 403a7). The relevant media will convey forms of moving, spatially located objects to the perceiver, who will be visually (or tactually) affected by their movement, location, and number. Our capacity to see is itself an ability to discriminate objects of a given size at a spatial position on the basis of their impact on us via a light-based medium. Each sense will have an ability to detect features of cross-modal objects. There is no need for a step beyond the essentially psycho-physical special senses, such as vision and touch, to a further

---

[18] Of course, had he thought that we or the medium were confined to registering momentaneous snapshots ('*Blicks*') of static colours, his account would have been different. But why think that he was attracted to this, frame-by-photographic-frame, way of thinking? More generally: it should not be assumed that the medium, in Aristotle's account, yields only two-dimensional information on which we as perceivers project a three-dimensional array. If we see size (*megethos*), we will see three-dimensional objects extended in, and moving through, space. Indeed, he appears to argue against the possibility of unextended perceptibles in *De Sensu* 7, 449a21–2.

purely psychological capacity for perceiving cross-modal objects. One and the same psycho-physical capacity to see coloured objects will do both.

Given (ii), what we see, when we see objects coming near us, is dependent on our being enmattered subjects, capable of interacting with cross-modal objects. The content of what we see, as well as our way of seeing it, will rest on vision being the capacity of an essentially embodied agent to move towards or away from enmattered cross-modal objects.[19]

In these two respects, seeing cross-modal objects is, like seeing their colours, inextricably psycho-physical. In the next sections, I shall consider the way in which, in Aristotle's account, our perception of such objects and their properties generates a desire to interact with them. The relevant types of perception have to be inextricably psycho-physical to play this role, not decomposable into a purely psychological and a purely physical component. So, too, we have to be inextricably psycho-physical to be agents who act on the basis of perception of this type. Or so I shall argue.

6.3 Perception, pain, pleasure, and desire: the basic model

Perceptions produce, in Aristotle's view, changes in the size and temperature in other parts of the body. In this section, I shall examine the connections he proposed between perception and desire in his account.

In *De Motu* 701a3–5, Aristotle writes:

> The animal is moved, that is walks, from desire or preferential choice, when some alteration has occurred on the basis of perception or imagination.

Subsequently he adds:

> Imagining, perceiving, and thinking cause alterations: for perceptions are in themselves some type of alteration,[20] while imagining and thinking have the same power as the objects they grasp. In a way the form of the hot or the cold, the pleasant or the frightening,[21] when thought about, is like each of the objects themselves: this is why we shudder and feel fear just having thought about them. For all these are things suffered—that is alterations—and when alteration takes place in the body, some parts become larger, others smaller. (*De Motu* 701b17–22)

---

[19] Aristotle's suggestion has important epistemological consequences. I discuss some of these in 'Aristotle on the Perception of Objects' (2020).

[20] I translate so as to remain neutral on whether Aristotle is speaking of a specific kind of quality change or something which is kind of a quality change (employing the '*alienans*' use of *tis*).

[21] Retaining the text as its stands: in this I follow *De Motu Animalium*: Primavesi and Corcilius (2018).

Perception is the per se cause of the next stages in a process that culminates in bodily interaction with them. It is because tasting, smelling, and hearing certain objects are pleasant or painful that they heat or cool other parts of the body in the way described. Perceiving is inextricably psycho-physical not only because it is defined as an embodied capacity which receives enmattered forms (as suggested in Chapters 4 and 5) but also because it is the cause of essentially embodied effects, such as shuddering, in virtue of the embodied forms it receives. Its form—being the receiver of enmattered forms—has to be psycho-physical to be the per se cause of bodily effects of this type. (This is a further application of Aristotle's account of per se causation, as discussed in Chapter 2.)

Aristotle's picture of the bodily impact of perception has intuitive appeal. We describe tastes and smells in ways which suggest that they are inextricably psycho-physical when we say that they are disgusting, nauseating, noxious, mouth-watering, delicious, fragrant, relaxing, alluring, and stimulating. The ways in which flavours and smells are attractive or repugnant, pleasant or painful, also often refer essentially to bodily phenomena.[22]

That Aristotle himself saw the matter in this way is suggested by his detailed account of smelling. He distinguishes, at the outset, two kinds of smells: one pleasant in itself, the other only accidentally so. The latter are described as follows:

> One kind is classified in line with flavours, as we have said, and is accidentally pleasant or unpleasant. But because flavours are attributes of what is nutritive, smells are pleasant to animals which experience appetite, but not pleasant when they are full and not in need of anything. Nor are they pleasant to those who do not find the food which produces the smell pleasant. These smells, as we have said, involve pleasure and pain coincidentally and hence are common to all animals. (*De Sensu* 443b17ff.)

The first kind of smell is different: it is

> peculiar to humans and involves a state of the region around the brain; for the brain is cold by nature and the blood in the vessels around it is thin, pure, and easily cooled, which is also why exhalation arising from nourishment is cooled by this region and produces sickly discharges. This class of smells has been generated for humans to support their health. Indeed, it has no other function. It obviously performs this function for food that is pleasurable, both dry and moist, is often noxious while the fragrance of a smell that is pleasurable in itself is almost always beneficial to those who receive it in whatever condition they are. (*De Sensu* 444a8–19)

---

[22] For discussion of these cases, see Antonio Damasio (2000).

This type of smell has a distinctive impact on human physiology: it cools the blood vessels around the brain in a specific way. It, together with the correlative type of smelling, is distinguished in terms of its distinctive physiological nature and location which account for the changes it produces. It too has to be psycho-physical to cause results of this type.

Aristotle develops his view further:

> This kind of smell is peculiar to humans because they possess the largest and moistest brains relative to their size. For this reason, humans are almost the only animal to perceive and enjoy the smell of flowers and similar objects. For the heat, that is the movement which is smell, is commensurate with the excess of moistness and coldness in this region of the body. (*De Sensu* 444a29ff.)

Smelling, in the final sentence, is explicitly identified with a kind of heating appropriate to the relevant part of the body. One cannot mark out what this type of smelling is without referring to it as a type of heat-involving bodily movement. Smelling, as we saw in Chapter 4, is defined as inextricably psycho-physical, the receiving of a distinctive enmattered form: the odour which itself is essentially enmattered. Its distinctive causal impact on the body arises from its being psycho-physical in this way.

Aristotle develops his argument by referring to what we might now call 'killer' smells.[23] He writes:

> No non-human animal is troubled by the smell of objects that are malodorous in themselves unless they happen to be destructive. But they are killed by these things in the same way as humans get headaches and are often killed by vapour from charcoal. Non-human animals are killed by potent fumes and brimstone and avoid them because of their effect. But they do not heed or smell it as bad in itself, though many plants have malodorous smells, unless it contributes somehow to its taste or edibility. (*De Sensu* 444b28ff.)

These smells have a direct physical impact on the perceiver. To smell them is to be affected in ways which are physically destructive. Since smelling is defined as the reception of smells, it must be an essentially psycho-physical sensitivity to be the per se cause of these disastrous bodily effects. Indeed, the forms themselves need to be enmattered to be such that, when received, they have these effects.

This type of smell is contrasted with another, shared by all animals, which is relevant to nutrition. Aristotle writes:

> The fact that flavours are not affections or privations of anything dry, but instead of the dry which is nutritious must be inferred from the fact that neither the dry

---

[23] For this terminology, see C.B. Martin (1994: 1-8).

without the moist, nor the moist without the dry are flavour and nourishment. It is not one of these alone, but only the mixture of them that is nourishing to animals. Of the nourishment received by animals, the perceptual qualities which are tangible produce growth and decline. But it is in so far as the food is taste-able that what they receive is nourishing. Everything is nourished by what is sweet— either by itself or when mixed with other flavours.   (*De Sensu* 441b24–442a2)

His focus is here on tastes targeted on what is dry and nutritious. Aristotle takes sweetness to have several functions: it nourishes the body but also is something which we taste as pleasant. It has an impact on growth and nutrition and on our perceptual system, as we find it pleasant to taste. If what is sweet, when tasted, has these two effects, one purely material, sweetness itself must be enmattered. There is one activity, tasting what is sweet, which is the per se cause of the two effects mentioned.

There is, it seems, a further reason to define tasting as an inextricably psychophysical activity: it is the per se cause (in virtue of the sweetness it receives) of bodily effects connected directly with nutrition.[24] Aristotle, in fact, seeks to develop his account further: when what is tasted is sweet, we naturally respond, when hungry, by taking pleasure in it and desiring to have it. By contrast, we are inclined to avoid bitter smells. Pleasures and pains mediate the connection between tasting and desire. We respond to something bitter by finding it disgusting or nauseating (or, more generally, painful in a bodily way) and seeking to avoid it. We respond to something sweet by finding it delicious, 'tasty' or 'mouth-watering' (or, more generally, pleasant in a bodily way) and seeking to eat it, or, if already eating, to continue to do so. Tasting sweet objects, which is the per se cause of our bodily pleasures, is identified as a type of heating and cooling, generated by the objects tasted (the enmattered forms received). This identification is required if tasting is to be the per se cause of the relevant bodily effects.

Tasting and smelling are not the only cases of perceiving which have bodily effects. Aristotle comments elsewhere on the pleasures of hearing music (*Politics* 1340a15–17, 23–8), noting the differing effects of differing types of melody (1340b10, 1340a7–14, 33–5): some produce hate, others love. Differing melodies have a differential impact on us (*Politics* 1340a26ff., a40–b10: see also *Prob.* XIX.27). This is how music makes us angry or calm. Musical sequences have an impact on us, as we saw in Chapter 5, in virtue of the speed and vibration in the parcels of air present in the medium and the sense organs. We understand the impact of the varying melodies on the basis of the enmattered patterns of sound in the medium (the relevant forms) received by the sense organ. On receiving these we become angry, mild, or even courageous. Hearing, like smelling and

---

[24] I shall return to the question of nutrition below.

tasting, must be an essentially matter-involving activity if it is to be a per se cause of these body-involving emotional responses.

We can now spell out an additional aspect of the early stages of the process that leads from perception to action (initially sketched in Chapter 3). The first two stages were:

[1] The object of pursuit is perceived
[2] The object is desired (*orexis*)

These stages can now be more fully described:

[Stage 1]:   The cross-modal object is presented perceptually to the perceiver: they perceive the object, and

[Stage 2]:   The perceiver sees that object as pleasant, takes pleasure in it, and desires to have it,[25] where [Stage 1] precedes and causally generates [Stage 2].

In the case of tasting, as we now know, it is because tasting sweet objects is pleasant (at [Stage 1]) that we are attracted to them. In being attracted to them, we undergo some psycho-physical changes which lead, in certain conditions, to action. In *De Anima* Aristotle develops this point as follows:

> Perceiving is like merely saying or thinking, but when it (either perceiving or the object perceived) is pleasant or painful, the soul, as if making an assertion or denial, pursues or avoids the object. To enjoy and to be pained is to be active with regard to the perceptual mean in respect of what is good or bad as such. This is what avoidance and pursuit are when actualized. Nor is the capacity for desire and for avoidance different, neither from each other nor from the capacity for perception, although they differ in what they are.   (431a8–14)[26]

These changes—'being active with regard to the perceptual mean'—are the effects of tasting an object which is, in fact, sweet. Tasting such objects (at [Stage 1]) must itself be essentially psycho-physical (a form of heating or cooling) to account for the effects it has on us: our being attracted to the object in this way.

Take the case of pain. Aristotle describes it as a disturbance of the soul which drives it from its natural state (*Rhetoric* 1370b35ff.). In extreme cases it destroys the nature of one who suffers it (*Ethics* 1119a23f.). It is said to be a bodily affection (*Ethics* 1173b7ff.), sometimes, in the human case, identified with a type of cooling

---

[25] If Aristotle also describes [2] as a kind of perceiving, there will be two kinds of perceiving: seeing (or tasting) the object (at [Stage 1]) and seeing it (or tasting) it to be pleasant (at [Stage 2]). The latter is identified with enjoying or being pained by the object in question.

[26] I discuss these comments in my 'Aristotle's Desire' (2006: 19–40).

of the area around the chest (see [*Prob.*] XI, 900a27f.). Aristotle focuses on the essentially psycho-physical nature of pain: it is a unified type of affection which cannot be defined without explicit reference to bodily changes. This is, no doubt, why the pleasures and pains associated with taste and touch are described as 'bodily' in the *Ethics* (see, for example, 1150a24). This is why they are described elsewhere as 'common to body and soul' (*De Sensu* 436a10).

In sum: Aristotle defined perception 'in general as common to body and soul' (*De Anima* 403a7) not only because of the nature of the objects that cause it and the way they do so (as was argued in Chapter 4 and 5) but also because it is the per se cause of further material and psycho-physical changes in the body which lead to action. Perception has a central role in the essentially psycho-physical process that begins with perceiving an object and ends in our interacting with it. In addition to being defined as the per se effect of material phenomena, it is, in virtue of its form, the per se cause of subsequent bodily changes.

6.4 Imagination and desire: the basic model extended

In *De Motu*, Aristotle writes: imagining, perceiving, and thinking cause alterations (701b17f.) and talks of the desire for specific objects as coming about through perception or imagination or thought (701a35–6). Since imagination and thought, as well as perception, play an important role in accounting for action, we need to consider whether they too are inextricably psycho-physical.

Did Aristotle distinguish, in the case of imagining, the stage at which the object of pursuit is imagined from a subsequent stage when the imaginer desires it? Is the object presented to the subject's imagination at [Stage 1] and then subsequently at [Stage 2] taken to be pleasant, when the subject is attracted to it and desires it? If this is what occurs, imagining an object will, as Aristotle suggest, be similar to perceiving it in that both will generate a desire to have it (*De Anima* 428b10–12, 429a4–9). If the cases are strongly parallel, imagining the object at [Stage 1] will, like perception, be an inextricably psycho-physical activity.

Did Aristotle see these cases as parallel? He certainly held that, in certain cases, thought and imagination have the same impact as perception. He wrote, as already noted:

> Sense perceptions are in their own nature a type of alteration, while imagination and thought have the same power as the actual objects. For the form thought about, when it is hot, cold, pleasant, or frightening, is just like the thing itself.
> (*De Motu* 701b17ff.)

Imagining or thinking of an object can lead us to shudder and feel fear, to desire or avoid it, in the same way as perception does. If perceiving is a psycho-physical per se cause of these bodily changes, so too is imagining. Both cause bodily changes, such as heating and cooling, in virtue of their being receivers of forms of objects in this way. They must be inextricably psycho-physical to initiate and control these bodily changes on this basis.

Aristotle develops this account further by considering cases where desire follows anticipation and memory. If a frightening object is anticipated, our response is to avoid it. Memory and anticipation of pleasurable objects at [Stage 1] cause a desire for them [Stage 2] in the same way as perception does.[27] This is the way in which imagination 'prepares' desire (*De Motu* 702a18ff.). Our memory and anticipation will, if they resemble perception, be inextricably psycho-physical causes of desire, a type of heating (or cooling) essentially directed at the objects imagined (as suggested in Chapter 3). Imagining, like perceiving and desiring, must be defined as an activity of this type if it is to be a per se cause of the resulting bodily changes.

Aristotle's account of memory in *De Memoria* supports this suggestion.[28] In 450a25ff. he sets up a problem of how we remember what is not present. In doing so, he describes memory (the relevant affection) as, in some way, present even though the object remembered is absent. He writes:

> We should...think that what comes about (viz. memory) as a result of perception in the soul and in the part of the body having it, is like a sort of painting. (450a27–30)

What comes about is an affection, described as an impression (*tupos*), caused by perception. Its creation is compared with making seals (presumably in wax) with signet rings. If Aristotle intends his comparison strictly, there should be something bodily in the case of memory which takes the role of the wax. That he intends his comparison in this way is confirmed by the clarifying phrase 'in that part of the body which has the soul' used to describe the affection which occurs in the soul. It is the bodily faculty which possesses the relevant capacity (or activity) of remembering—and not the capacity or activity itself (the soul)—which receives impressions. This point is developed in what follows: no memory impression is made in certain cases because of the movement in, or hardness of, the receptor. In one case, that of people strongly moved by passion, what happens is compared with the failed attempt to make a mark on running water. In another, it is the hardness of the receptor that accounts for the problems the aged face in

---

[27] There is need, in a fuller account, to understand Aristotle's distinction between perceptual and deliberative imagination. One might, at first approximation, take the former as imagination of an object based on perception, the latter as imagination based on deliberation. Indeed, perhaps this is why deliberative imagination is described as 'the capacity to make one imagined object out of many' (*De Anima* 434a9–10).

[28] In this section I shall focus on the role of memory, leaving anticipation to Section 6.7.

retaining memories. Similar differences are used to explain differences in memory between the very young and the very old and the very quick and the very slow. Aristotle concludes:

> Members of one group are too fluid, of the other too hard. So, in the former case, the impact on the imagination (viz. the impression: *tupos*) does not remain in the soul, or in the latter it does not attach at all.   (450b9–11)

That differences in memory result from differences in type of bodily receptor is evidence for the claim that remembering is itself the receiving of an impression made by perception on a bodily organ. The bodily organ has material features (such as hardness and fluidity) which account for the differences noted.

Aristotle's point needs careful statement. It is not simply that the very old and the very young have distinctive bodily features which make memory difficult. Nor is it that the rest of us possess bodily features which make memory easier. Remembering is in its very nature the receiving in a material bodily organ of a perceptual impression. So characterized it is an essentially enmattered type of cognition. Further, what is received (the impression: *tupos*) is itself essentially enmattered: a bodily (or in-this-matter) impression of a given object previously seen. Receiving (and retaining or 'having') an impression of this type must be an inextricably psycho-physical activity: it is an essentially bodily receiving (and retaining) of an essentially enmattered impression.

Imagining, like perceiving, is, and needs to be, inextricably psycho-physical to be the per se cause of bodily movements such as heating and cooling. In the specific case of memory, Aristotle developed his account further by presenting the relevant type of imagining as the receiving of an essentially bodily type of impression. Remembering, so understood, cannot be defined without explicit reference to the bodily reception of a bodily impression. It is because it is essentially an activity of this kind that memory is, on occasion, the per se cause of the heating and cooling essentially involved in desiring.[29] This type of imagining plays a similar role to perceiving in Aristotle's account of the essentially psycho-physical activity which results in bodily actions.

Aristotle regards recollection, which he distinguishes from remembering, understood simply as the receiving of a perceptual impression, in a similar fashion. After describing it as a type of search and reasoning (453a13–14) which is limited to humans, he adds that 'recollection is a bodily affection: the search for an impression (*phantasma*)', and adduces as evidence the fact that some people

---

[29] The relevant bodily part is itself defined in terms of the soul (450a29): it is, presumably, the part defined as that capable of imagining or remembering. Further the type of bodily imprint made there is introduced in terms of the affection of memory (450a25–7). There is no attempt to define it solely in material terms.

get flustered when they cannot recollect even when concentrating and that others without concentrating recollect no less than when concentrating.

Aristotle's suggestion is that—in both cases—people are moved by impressions (*phantasmata*), understood as a bodily affection (*pathos*), when they try to recollect. This bodily phenomenon accounts for both phenomena. People become flustered when attempting to recollect because, in so doing, they set up phantasms which make them flustered. Indeed, they become even more flustered when there is moisture around in the perceptual area (*topos*). These cases are said to suggest that recollection and the phantasms involved are bodily. Since the impressions have a bodily impact and the impact they have is sensitive to bodily conditions, they themselves must be bodily. So too is recollection, which essentially involves impressions of this type. The impressions in question have content: indeed, we become flustered because of their content. They must be both content-bearing and enmattered to play the required causal role. In other cases, the movements set up will not easily stop until the subject reaches what is sought, even though how the movement develops is sensitive to physical conditions. This is further evidence that recollection is subject in its operation to bodily conditions. However, the activity involved is a goal-directed bodily movement which unfolds under certain physical conditions, although not under our control. It too is essentially and inextricably psycho-physical activity, the realization of an inextricably material capacity.

6.5 The human subject: the unity of our soul

Aristotle talks of the human soul 'as the activity of a body possessed of life' (*De Anima* 412a20–1). His discussion of taste and smell illuminates one aspect of this suggestion. The type of soul characteristic of, for example, humans is that of creatures with certain nutritional, bodily, needs. Aristotle suggests that tasting is present for the sake of living well (*De Anima* 435b22ff.: see also 422b5ff., 414b13, and 413b23ff.). It is, it seems, defined as the selective discrimination of flavours with the goal of benefitting the organism in question. More specifically, as we saw in Section 6.3, it is the activity of an embodied organism with needs for certain types of food. To play this role tasting itself must be defined as a type of discrimination of objects which are beneficial or destructive to organisms with such nutritional, and hence bodily, needs. This gives a further reason for viewing tasting as an essentially embodied, inextricably psycho-physical, form of cognition. It is, in Aristotle's terms, 'common to body and soul' not only because it is defined as a form of sensitivity to moist flavour which is the per se cause of bodily changes but also because it is required in organisms with given bodily, nutritional, needs.

As 'the form of a natural body potentially having life' (*De Anima* 412a20–1), the soul will be a specific kind of form: one which is the form of a natural body with, for example, given nutritional needs. We misunderstand Aristotle's account of the soul if we think of it as separable into two definitionally independent components, a pure form (understood as an activity or way of being defined independently of bodily capacities) which is realized in a body of this type. Instead, the form is an inextricably psycho-physical, bodily, phenomenon: one defined by the goal-directed bodily capacities required for the type of life in question (as snubness is defined as nasal-concavity). This is why it is, in his view, the task of physicists to examine the soul to the extent that it is enmattered (*Metaphysics* E.1, 1026a5–6) as they might study snubness (*Physics* 194a13). They will study desire or perception as the embodied capacities of an animal with a way of life defined in part in terms of its bodily, nutritional needs.[30]

Aristotle has, as we have seen, deployed several considerations in favour of this conclusion. The human soul itself, in whole or in part, is a per se cause of bodily movements in that its specific capacities (such as the capacity to desire, perceive, and imagine) are the starting points of these movements. If these capacities are, as I have argued, essentially and inextricably psycho-physical, so too must be the human soul (either in whole or in part). This is because the human soul is that in virtue of which these capacities are present. It must be inextricably and essentially enmattered to be that in virtue of which we have capacities such as that for moving one's arm. The soul, it should be noted, is not itself affected when this capacity is realized: it remains as that which is capable of the relevant activities. Indeed, if the soul is, for example, a state or activity in virtue of which its possessor is capable of desiring and perceiving—it would not be the type of thing to be moved.

If the soul is that in virtue of which its possessor is capable of eating, desiring, perceiving, imagining, and acting in the way described, what accounts for its unity? It is not enough that there be a separate capacity for each of these. They must be unified in such a way as to ground the integrated four stage sequence which begins with perception and ends in action.

Aristotle develops an account of the unity of the soul in *De Anima* B.3, 414b28ff., when he describes the nutritive as 'present potentially' in the perceptual soul. He writes:

> The types of soul resemble the series of figures. For in a similar way in figures and in animate things the earlier form exists potentially in the later: the triangle potentially in the quadrilateral, the nutritive in the perceptive.

---

[30] In this formulation, the form in question is not defined as the form-of-a-natural-body (with explicit reference to the body in the account of the form). It is defined as the type of essentially enmattered form which is present in a natural body of this type. This formulation expresses the type of priority of form over matter suggested in Chapter 2, Section 8. If reference to the body is an essential part of the definition, the priority at issue will be understood differently (perhaps in the way, for example, noted in Chapter 2: n. 95).

In animals capable of perception (and nothing more), there is a perceptual soul which contains (in some way) the nutritive soul. Their distinctive type of nutritive capacity is best understood as a feature (or 'part') of their perceptual capacity. Such animals possess a distinctive type of nutritive capacity which is made what it is by their being perceptual creatures. In this, they differ from plants whose nutritive soul is not shaped in this way. Perhaps, if animals lost their perceptual capacities, their nutritive soul would be reduced to that of a plant (they would be in a purely vegetative state). However, this should not mislead us into thinking that the souls of such animals, when all is going well, are perceptual souls plus nutritive ones. There is no separate actual nutritive soul in their case. These animals are best defined as nutritive-perceptual creatures.

What applies to the perceptual applies also to the locomotive soul. The perceptual (or, better, the nutritive-perceptual) soul is—in these creatures—something shaped by the presence of the capacity for locomotion. The type of perception present in animals capable of locomotion will differ from that in stationary animals. There is not one type of perceptual soul present on the two cases. The soul of animals capable of locomotion (but endowed with no higher capacity) will be a nutritive-perceptual-locomotive soul. In a similar fashion, animals capable of reasoning and calculation will have a different desiderative and locomotive soul from that found in animals without that capacity. Their soul is a nutritive-perceptual-locomotive-rational soul. It is governed, and shaped, by reason in ways in which the soul of the other animals is not.

The capacities in question are not simply combined by addition. The human soul, in Aristotle's view, is, so understood, not a bundle of separately defined capacities. Although it is not a simple unstructured entity,[31] it exemplifies the distinctive type of unity possessed by a nutritive-perceptual-locomotive-rational soul. It is in virtue of being rational in this way that we move, perceive, eat, and reproduce in the way we do. Souls of different types are unified when their lower capacities (such as that for nutrition) are shaped in this way by their higher-order ones.

There is a further complication: the soul, understood as that in virtue of which its bearer is capable of perceiving, eating, desiring, and acting, is not itself a capacity. It is described as 'an activity'. However, if it is an activity, it must be distinct from the activities of perceiving, eating, and the rest. For these are activities we engage in in virtue of capacities we possess in virtue of being ensouled. Aristotle's account in *De Anima* B.5, considered in Chapter 4, helps to clarify this view: the 'activity' of knowers (the first actuality of their capacity to speak French) is their being capable of speaking French here and now. 'Activity' refers to the state or condition in which they are capable of speaking French when the opportunity arises, not

---

[31] As Suarez suggested: see Chapter 2, Section 10.

6.5 THE HUMAN SUBJECT: THE UNITY OF OUR SOUL

their capacity to do so. Analogously, the activity characteristic of the human soul will be that of being capable of engaging (here and now) in the activities of perceiving, eating, desiring, and acting. It is not itself the capacity to do so. Nor is it the resulting activities themselves. Our soul is not to be identified with our doing these activities (second actuality) but with our being capable, as we now are, of doing them: the first actuality of the relevant capacity of a natural organized body. Our human soul is our way of being alive (our *zōē*: *De Anima* 415b27, *Metaphysics* 1050b1–2): that way of being alive in virtue of which we are capable, as we now are, of perceiving, desiring, and acting in the integrated way Aristotle describes.

In Aristotle's account, if this is correct, our essence is to be capable of a range of activities. In a similar fashion, the essence of an eye is to be capable of seeing, that of an axe to be capable of cutting wood in a given way. To be an eye or an axe is, in his view, to be capable of seeing or cutting. Their respective forms do not consist in seeing or cutting, activities that flow from their being capable of so acting. They remain eyes or axes even when not actually doing any seeing or cutting. When Aristotle describes the essence of an eye as seeing (412b19), he is referring (as the context makes clear: 412a21–4) to the first actuality of the relevant capacity of the body: its being capable of seeing. This is, in the terminology used in Chapter 2, the way of being which defines the eye.

Aristotle describes being capable of living, so understood, as the 'activity' or, perhaps better, the 'realization' (*energeia*) and the success condition (*entelecheia*) of the relevant capacity of the organic body. The success in question is being alive, being capable (here and now) of engaging in perceiving, desiring, and the rest. It is not something we do, an action like running, weaving, or seeing. While the latter are the final realizations of our capacities to act (second actualities), to be alive is to be capable of acting in these ways.

In the human case, our distinctive essence, our soul, is our being alive in the distinctive nutritive-perceptual-locomotive-rational way described above. Our soul is a unified nutritive-perceptual-locomotive-rational soul, in which the type of nutritive or perceptual soul is that required for locomotion and ultimately for reason and the type of reason, in question, is one which governs locomotion, perception, and nutrition in this way. This is why our type of nutritive soul (being capable of eating) differs from those of plants or other animals which are not, in Aristotle's account, governed by reason.[32]

Humans, defined as the possessors of souls of this kind, are essentially and inextricably psycho-physical subjects. We are unified subjects (and agents) in virtue of possessing an integrated, nutritive-perceptual-locomotive-rational soul. Both we and our souls are inextricably psycho-physical.[33]

---

[32] For further discussion of closely related issues, see Thomas Johansen (2012: 67–72).
[33] For further discussion of these and other directly related issues, see Mariska Leunissen (2017). She traces in considerable detail the processes, states, and activities involved in human ethical character

6.6 Practical thought: an essentially enmattered type of thought?

Aristotle, as we noted, commented in *De Motu*:

> imagination and thought have the same power as the actual objects. For the form thought about, when it is hot, cold, pleasant, or frightening, is just like the thing itself. (701b17ff.)

If thought is to generate desire or bodily action in agents like us, it will need, if the arguments in Sections 6.3–6.5 are correct, to be definitionally enmattered. Even if thinking *as such* is not definitionally enmattered, this species of thinking will be.

In considering the intellectual soul in *De Anima* Aristotle writes (431a14–16):

> In the case of the intellect, images take the place of percepts, and when the soul asserts or denies that the thing is good or bad, it pursues or avoids.

If he is to maintain his analogy with the perceptually based desire for pleasure, his two descriptions:

(1) 'The soul asserting that it is good' and
(2) 'The soul pursuing it'

should refer to the same type of activity, one in which the agent is drawn towards the object [Stage 2]. To have an intellectual desire for A will not merely be to register the fact that A has a good-making feature: it is also to be active towards A. To assert in this way that A is good will be to be attracted towards it. There will not be two definitionally separate occurrences: asserting that A is good and being attracted to it (or pursuing it). The relevant type of assertion cannot be defined without explicit reference to being attracted to the object. Nor can the type of pursuit be defined without similar reference to assertion.[34]

Aristotle adds a further feature: 'for the thinking soul, impressions (*phantasmata*) take the place of *percepts (aisthēmata)*' (431a15). The *percepts* in question are the effects of perceptually presented objects on the subject's perceptual system: those that occur at [Stage 1] when one sees this sweet object. What takes their place, impressions, will be the effects of non-perceptually presented objects such as the enemy (if approaching but not yet here: 431b6) or a drink (around the next

---

formation. Leunissen's discussion strongly supports, and develops further, the type of inextricabilist account defended in this chapter.

[34] Does thinking of the object as good involve the agent being drawn to the object pursued on the basis of their finding the prospect of possessing it enjoyable?

corner on a hot day) on the subject's imagination. As the former are the effects of objects on our perceptual system, the latter should be the effects of objects on our imaginative systems.[35] When their imagination is affected in this way [Stage 1], agents at [Stage 2] will form a complex judgement such as, 'It will be good to pursue (or flee) A.'

Aristotle develops his picture as the chapter proceeds (431b2–10). He writes:

> That which is capable of thought grasps the forms of objects in impressions (*phantasmata*). It is affected [*kineitai*: moved in desire], when not perceiving but affected by images, depending on how what is to be pursued is determined for him in the forms [taking *ekeinois* to refer to the forms]. For example: when you see with respect of a beacon that it is a fire, and see with your common sense that it is moving, you realize that it is the enemy. At other times, you may calculate and plan, as if seeing, from the future to the present. And when you assert that there will be something pleasant or painful in the future, here and now you flee or pursue it. And so generally in the case of action. (431b2–12)

He is concerned with how the thinking soul grasps what is to be pursued and is affected by it (431b5, see b9). In his examples, the object to be pursued is not present to the senses. Instead, we realize what is to be pursued in grasping the forms of the objects involved. Aristotle offers two examples. In one of these, subjects work from their present perception to grasp that the enemy is approaching. They then grasp that the enemy is to be avoided (or pursued) and are moved to action (that is, desire) accordingly. In the other example, subjects anticipate, for example, a cold drink on a hot day (which is not presented to them perceptually) and work out what to do to obtain it. When attracted towards a cold drink they will have in the future, here and now they desire it.[36]

Aristotle generalizes from these cases, which involve pleasure and pain, to any which concern what is good or bad for the subject. The resulting actions may be based, for example, on one's understanding that the enemy is to be resisted (or avoided or appeased) or that objects of such and such a type are worth going for. If one thinks that a given object is good or will be pleasant, one is moved accordingly. If the analogy with perception of a present object is maintained, in

---

[35] The imprint they make (*tupos*), on this understanding, will not be defined as an internal psychological object of which they are directly aware. It might be defined, in a world-involving fashion, as the imprint of the relevant external object on us (its mark on us). Alternatively, it might be, as Verity Harte suggested in conversation, the vehicle for our awareness of that object: what enables us to discriminate it.

[36] Recollection, which is compared with searching and deliberating in *De Memoria* 453a13–14, is said to move something bodily. It is, nonetheless, a type of thinking and for this reason is not, like memory, a feature of the perceptual soul (453b11: compare 449b4ff.). In fact, it is restricted to animals capable of knowledge, perhaps to humans (453a9). This type of thinking, like anticipation, will be essentially enmattered because it is a way of engaging with *phantasms* (453a14–15).

judging (now) that the object is good or will be pleasant, one is therein attracted to it (and desires it).

Aristotle's subsequent discussion in *De Anima* 434a14ff. confirms this account. He begins by examining the suggestion that desire and practical intellect can both separately move us to act (433a14–16). According to this suggestion, while desire and practical intellect both begin with a desired object, in some cases desire causes action, in others practical intellect (or imagination): 433a18–22. In this account, explanations of action in terms of intellect and desire will share a common form. Both begin with the object desired and the action would result from either desire or intellect grasping that object and triggering action. Aristotle, however, emphatically rejects this proposal in 433a22–5:

> As things are, intellect does not move without desire (for wish is a form of desire and when one moves in accordance with intellect one moves in accordance with rational desire).

Why is it that 'when one moves in accordance with intellect, one moves in accordance with rational desire' (433a23–5)? Intellect and rational desire, it now appears, play the same role in the account of action. Both begin with a grasp on the goal, work out how to implement it, and lead to the relevant action. The intellect is guided in its reasoning, judgements, and subsequent action by the desirability of the goal in the same way as rational desire is. We can see why this is so. In the light of the analogy between the perceptual and intellectual soul, the intellect grasps that something is good and is therein attracted to it. There is one activity which can be described both as the operation of practical intellect and of rational desire. Desire will not be an independent component present before practical intellect begins to do its work. It will be present whenever the practical intellect is actively sensitive to the desirability of the object.[37]

Practical intellect, it seems, begins by grasping the object of desire as good (or desirable), finds ways to achieve it, and leads to action. Rational desire is present throughout this process because the practical intellect is sensitive to the desirability of the object and (derivatively) of the ways to achieve it. To be sensitive in this way is to be attracted to the object desired and to the means required to achieve it. This is why practical intellect and rational desire can both play precisely the same role in the explanation of action. The expressions 'practical intellect' and

---

[37] Nor is rational desire present only when the agent thinks rationally and takes the further rational step of desiring in line with rational thought. For that would not explain the presence of rational desire from the beginning to the end of the process. Nor would it explain why when one is apt to move in accordance with rational thought one is apt to move in accordance with rational desire (*De Anima* 433a23–5). For it would not rule out the possibility of rational thought pushing in one direction without any support from rational desire.

'rational desire' describe the same phenomenon.[38] This is why the final stage in deliberation, that of preferential choice (*prohairesis*), can be described equally either as a deliberative desire or desiderative intellect (*nous*: N.E. 1139a31ff.). There must be, in his account, more to the practical operation of reason than the purely cognitive judgement that something is good.[39] Practical thought, connected in this way with desire, will be inextricably psycho-physical as is required if it is to be a per se cause of bodily action. It must be essentially enmattered if it is to be (in line with the central argument of Chapters 2 and 3) a per se efficient cause of actions of this type. Whatever is true of other species of human thought, human practical thought, like perception, imagination, and desire, is definitionally enmattered.

6.7 Thought and subjects of thought

Thinking remains a problematic case. While Aristotle notes that although it cannot occur without a body if it involves imagination (403a8ff.) or memory (408b18ff.), it does not, he suggests, involve a body in the way perception or desire does (432a5ff.). Thinking is not, if my hypothesis is correct, inextricably psycho-physical in the way they are: it is not the realization of an essentially embodied capacity. However, practical thought appears, as we have just seen, to be inextricably enmattered. Further, our thought is, I have suggested, the thinking of inextricably psycho-physical subjects, endowed with unified nutrio-perceptual-rational souls. Are these claims consistent? Or do we need to revise our earlier conclusions?

Aristotle's discussion of thought is complex, often highly telegrammatic, and has been the subject of much controversy. In this section, I shall leave aside nearly all of its complexities and focus only on the issues just raised. My aim is to offer only an outline of an answer to these questions and to do so only to the extent required by the major themes of our present investigation. Many other important questions will be laid aside.

---

[38] In *De Motu* 701a31–2 Aristotle remarks 'the activity of desire takes the place of questioning (in dialectical reasoning) or knowledge (in demonstrative reasoning)'. The desire that takes the place of knowledge (in theoretical matters) accepts 'Let me drink this!' and generates action. One could equally describe what happens here in terms of the activity of the practical intellect moving from premises to conclusion and action. There is, it seems, one activity which can be described either as that of desire or of thought.

[39] The rational desire to do A here too will involve more than merely the cognitive judgement that A has a good feature. One also has to be attracted to it. (See, for a graphic description of this, *Metaphysics* 1072b3: the good is loved (*eromenon*) and thus leads to action.) In *De Anima* 433b5–12, Aristotle emphasizes the similarities between sensual and rational desire. His aim is to maintain the unity in form of the capacity for desire in these two cases. He would have failed in this project had he sought to combine a dual component (or purely cognitive) view of intellectual desire with his quite different account of sensual pleasure in *De Anima* Γ.7 (as analysed above).

Aristotle offers several arguments in favour of his distinctive view of thinking: he suggests that:

(a) thought is not mixed with the body; it is not impacted adversely by any of its objects (429b1ff.);
(b) there is no organ of thought (429a23ff.);
(c) Anaxagoras' god can think of anything without being a body. The same, no doubt, is true of Aristotle's divine, pure thinkers.

(a) and (b) are often taken to suggest that human thinking itself is not an inextricably psycho-physical activity, even if it is dependent on the existence of human bodies. (c) points to a type of thinking, available to some favoured beings who lack bodies, that does not require the existence of any body.

This way of understanding (a) and (b) supports the claim that perception, desire, and action are definitionally psycho-physical. Thought may be existentially but not definitionally dependent on bodily states, while perception, desire, and human thought are definitionally inseparable from the body. On the two-component accounts, by contrast, this difference between them disappears. All will be definitionally distinct phenomena which cannot exist without material bodies. However, if—for Aristotle—human thought is different from perception and desire, this should be because, unlike them, it is separable in definition from the body. While our thought may be existentially dependent on our being embodied if it depends on perception an imagination, it will not be definitionally dependent on the presence of bodies. If this is correct, there are two types of hylomorphic activities: some, like perception or desire, are definitionally inextricable, others—like thinking—are inextricable in existence but separable in definition.

We must proceed with caution. Certain aspects of human thinking seem not to be definitionally enmattered: we are capable, for example, of thinking of mathematical objects which are not defined in terms which refer to matter. Perhaps we can also think of still higher entities, the province of first philosophy (403b15ff.), whose existence does not depend at all on the existence of matter. These types of human thinking resemble divine thinking. If so, even if human thought is necessarily embodied, it is not—as such—essentially (or definitionally) psycho-physical.

That said: other types of human thinking seem to be essentially enmattered. Aristotle comments that thinking of essentially enmattered objects is enmattered in just the same way as the objects themselves (429b21–3). Thinking of flesh, like thinking of the snub nose, will be enmattered in the same way as flesh or the snub is. Practical thinking, I have argued, if it is to per se cause action in agents like us, will also be definitionally enmattered. Even if human thinking *as such* is not definitionally enmattered, many of its species will be. Further, these types of thinking will be definitionally enmattered even if there is no specific organ of thought and thought itself is not 'mixed' with the body or affected adversely by its objects. These types of thinking will, as such, be definitionally enmattered in different ways from perceiving or desiring, but definitionally enmattered nonetheless. (Imagination, after all, is, it appears, definitionally embodied although it lacks its own organ and is not mixed with the body.) Thus understood, (a) and (b) distinguish different types of essential embodiment. Since there are types of thinking which are not definitionally enmattered, thinking itself is not definitionally an embodied type of cognition. However, specific types of thinking, such as our practical thinking or our thinking of enmattered phenomena, may be.

There remains an issue about human thinking: is our thinking of mathematical objects, for example, a definitionally embodied type of thinking? Is it only the gods' thinking that is not definitionally embodied? It is not clear that, in Aristotle's view, we are ever capable, even at our best, of thinking in precisely the way gods do. Sometimes he may suggest that we do so a short time (as on one reading of *Metaphysics* 1075a6ff.). Or is all our thinking inferior to the type they enjoy because while ours is based on (and arises out of) memory and perception through abstraction etc., the gods' is not. Is the best we can achieve something which is like, but not of the same type as, their thinking (as may be suggested in *N.E.* 1178b28)?[40] It is not clear that Aristotle takes a view on this question. In any event, his remark at the end of *De Anima* Γ.7, 'we will investigate later the issue of whether an intellect which is not separable from magnitude can think of things which are separated' (431b17–19), suggests that he wishes to leave this further question open in his discussions of the soul. For present purposes, I am happy to follow his example.[41]

It should be noted, however, whichever of these views Aristotle took (if, indeed, he arrived at a settled view), the human soul will—for the reasons already given—be essentially psycho-physical: it is defined as the activity of a natural body in virtue of which we are capable of nutrition, perception, locomotion, desire, and thought. As such, our soul will be inextricably psycho-physical in virtue of the

---

[40] Some might think that this must be the case if all human thinking is defined as the thinking of nutritive-perceptual animals. In their view, if there were beings (such as angels) which could perceive but were incapable of nutrition, their type of perception would be different from our own. On this view, our nutritional needs play some role in determining the type of perception and thinking we enjoy.

[41] Whichever way his highly telegrammatic remarks on the active intellect in *De Anima* Γ.5 are best interpreted, they are not inconsistent with this basic insight. Elsewhere, I have suggested (2000a: 130–43) that the active intellect is best identified with the intelligible world which exists outside of us (as light does). On this understanding, we will—in Aristotle's account—be able, like Newton, to grasp the mind of god in the order of the intelligible world. Since the active intellect is deathless and eternal while our capacity for thought comes into being and dies with us, we will not have access via recollection from our existence before birth to the eternal activity of the divine mind (as Plato may have supposed). Thus, the reason that 'we do not recollect' what is eternal and deathless is simply that we were not there to experience it and as such have no memory of it. It is not that we have Platonic powers of recollection and fail to exercise them. In Aristotle's view, it requires memory, and past experience on the part of one who recollects (*De Memoria* 451b4–5). No one today can remember (or in this sense recollect) the fall of Troy assuming that none of us was there to see it!

first four capacities, the per se causes of material changes. Even if our types of perception and desire were defined (in part) by our being capable of thought of a matter-free kind, they would still be essentially enmattered, modifications of our nutrition-based way of being. So, too, will our entire soul, our way of being alive, if partially defined in terms of them. Since we are essentially nutritive-perceptive-thinking animals, our essence will differ *au fond* from that of the gods if (as is generally supposed) they can think without perceiving, desiring, or eating. While they may be essentially pure, disembodied, beings, whose way of life can be defined without reference to any type of body, we are not them. Human thinking is essentially the thinking of inextricably psycho-physical subjects.

Aristotle could, of course, have concluded that the human soul is not essentially psycho-physical if he had identified it exclusively with that feature in virtue of which we are capable of thinking in the same way as the gods do. Perhaps some of his predecessors had taken this step, identifying us with our capacity to think. However, Aristotle's insistence, in *De Anima*, that the human soul is the form of a natural body with certain biological and material needs, shows that this was not his settled view. Our rational soul is one feature, or part, of our way of being alive, the latter being defined in terms of our capacity for unified nutritive-perceptual-locomotive-rational activity. As possessors of souls of this type, we are essentially and inextricably psycho-physical subjects.

6.8 Summary

Aristotle, I have suggested, extended his theory of the emotions, desire, and the perception of colours and tastes to the perception of common sensibles, imagination, and practical thought. In doing so, he offered an integrated picture of how these differing ways of grasping objects and their properties are per se causes of bodily actions. There is an essentially psycho-physical activity which begins with perception and continues (sometimes via imagination) to desire and bodily action. As humans, we engage in this activity when we act on the basis of what we perceive.

The stages in this activity, such as perceiving or imagining, cannot, in this picture, be analysed into purely psychological and purely physical components. This is because, so far from being causes only indirectly in virtue of the purely physical states or events which realize them, they are per se causes of bodily processes in virtue of their distinctive content (or the forms they receive). To initiate and control processes such as heating and cooling in the required way the relevant capacities need to be inextricably bodily capacities. Neither they, nor the pleasure and pain that are essential to this sequence, can be defined in terms of definitionally separate, purely physical and purely psychological components.

We are, in Aristotle's account, unified essentially psycho-physical subjects, capable of perceiving, imagining, desiring, and acting in these essentially body-involving ways. In this account, we are to be defined in terms of our distinctive soul: that in virtue of which we are capable of percciving and acting in these ways. His integrated picture of how human perception leads to action rests on a view of us as, in the way explained, inextricably psycho-physical subjects. Further, as we have seen in this chapter, our type of soul (our form) cannot be defined without explicit reference to our bodily needs for nutrition. We possess nutritive-perceptive-reasoning souls, which, as such, are essentially and inextricably embodied. We are defined as inextricably embodied subjects with unified, essentially enmattered, souls of this type.

7
Aristotle's Viewpoint

7.1 Common to body and soul

Aristotle presented the emotions, desires, perception, and imagination, as inextricably psycho-physical, not definable by decomposition into two definitionally distinct components, one purely psychological and the other purely physical. These activities are all realizations of inextricably psycho-physical capacities. He defended and developed, or so I have suggested, two inextricability theses:

[A] Psychological activities, such as are involved in the emotions, desire, and perception, are defined as inextricably psycho-physical, not analysable by decomposition into two separate types of activity or feature, one purely psychological, the other purely physical.[1] Their form is inextricably psycho-physical.

[B] The relevant specific types of physical activity are defined as inextricably psycho-physical, not definable without explicit reference to some psycho-physical activity.

Both of his claims demand detailed scrutiny. Aristotle, in holding [A], in effect, rejected the idea of the purely psychological used to set up our post-Cartesian mind–body problem. Nor did he think that we can define the relevant psychological features in a neutral way, consistent with their being pure, and then ask how they are connected with the physical. This is because, in his view, these features cannot be adequately defined without essential reference in their definition to some specific internal physical or physiological features. Several of his arguments are designed to show that the emotions, desire, perception, and practical thought are inextricably psycho-physical.

It may be helpful to provide a summary overview of the three types of consideration that I have suggested led Aristotle to adopt this view:

[1] It provided an intuitively attractive way of defining phenomena such as fear, anger, sensual desire, pleasure, and perception. To be angry, for example, is not merely to desire revenge, but to do so in a specific matter-involving

---

[1] I use the term 'mental' to indicate (in general terms to the modern reader) the type of process at issue. For Aristotle, nutrition is also to be analysed in the same way (as inextricably psycho-physical).

way, which essentially involves heat in the definition of the relevant type of desire (or, we might say, physical tension or adrenalin rush). This is the type of desire which defines anger. Aristotle extended this account to pleasure and pain, to desire more generally, and to sensory perception, presenting the latter as an essentially embodied form of discrimination, only to be defined in terms which explicitly refer to specific bodily capacities of the perceiver (for instance, in the case of seeing, their eyes understood as light-based receivers etc.). This is the type of essentially embodied discrimination sensory perception is. Its nature is, in itself, inextricably psycho-physical. There is no definitionally separate purely psychological feature involved in its definition. It has an essentially enmattered form.

[2] His account presents the per se causes of bodily actions, such as desire or skill, as inextricably psycho-physical. The relevant capacities must be defined as similarly psycho-physical to cause such actions to occur and unfold in the way they do. These capacities are, in Aristotle's terminology, the forms which initiate and control the resulting bodily actions. Purely psychological capacities could not cause such actions in this way; nor could purely physical capacities defined without reference to the goals and skills of the agent. Nor, Aristotle argued, could a combination of the two, understood as definitionally independent phenomena. Instead, the relevant capacities and their causal properties must be inextricably psycho-physical to be the starting points and controllers of the resulting bodily actions (such as weaving). They need to be defined as, in themselves, embodied in specific types of matter to be the per se causes of these actions.[2]

Desires causally interact with non-psychological phenomena, causing changes (which we would describe as 'physical' changes)[3] in parts of the body and in the world beyond it. Perceiving is caused by external objects and their properties. Our causal interactions with these objects are inextricably psycho-physical, not analysable in terms of two definitionally separate phenomena, one psychological, one physical.

To make this point vivid, consider, once again, the case of Penelope's weaving: her activity is, so understood, essentially her manually operating a loom on a woollen thread in such a way as to achieve her desired goal (such as making a cloak). Her individual acts of weaving can develop in different ways as she encounters and seeks to address difficulties in making the cloak in the way she originally planned. Equally, they could be interrupted or, when all goes well, succeed in arriving at her goal. In these two respects, her actions have (what I call) 'modal depth': the same particular act can vary in duration and in manner as

---

[2] They have this causal role in virtue of being essentially embodied capacities. They are not defined as embodied capacities simply because they interact with physical bodies. They have to be embodied capacities to interact with such bodies in the way they do.
[3] Using 'physical' in the post-Cartesian sense specified in the Introduction.

it unfolds.[4] Penelope's skill, the capacities exercised in her weaving, are, together with her desire to weave, the per se causes (in Aristotle's terminology) of her acting as she does. It is because of them that she weaves when and in the manner she does. They are not only required for, but also adequate, to cause her skilled bodily actions to unfold as they do.[5]

Aristotle's claim is that Penelope's skill and desire must be inextricably psycho-physical to be per se causes of these actions. Only embodied goal-directed capacities, indeed ones embodied in specific types of matter, can be causes of the required type. There is not a purely physical cause of some features of her weaving and a purely psychological cause of others. The very same features of her skill cause her to weave in the way she does. There is, in Aristotle's terms, one strongly unified per se cause, an inextricably embodied goal-directed capacity, which results in her skilled actions developing in the way they do. If her skill had been composed of two different, definitionally separable, components, there would not have been one unified per se cause of the resulting actions. Further, the causally relevant properties are, in Aristotle's account, real features of her skill and desire, not merely artefacts of our preferred way of describing them.

[3] His view presents perception, pleasure, desire, and action together as the activity of a unified, inextricably psycho-physical subject. Some of our capacities, such as perception, are activated by physical causes; others, like desire and pleasure, are the per se causes of physical effects. However, there is a continuous inextricably psycho-physical activity beginning with perception and unfolding through desire into action. This is possible because perceiving, desiring, and acting are all activities of the psycho-physical causal capacities of one unified, essentially psycho-physical subject. Being capable of such activities (the form of the subject) is an inextricably psycho-physical way of being.

These considerations constitute a challenge to what I have called 'the philosophical idea of the purely psychological': the idea that being angry, desiring, or perceiving are to be defined as purely psychological phenomena without explicit reference to specific internal bodily states. In Aristotle's account, by contrast, while the capacities and activities involved are essentially psychological, they cannot be defined without explicit reference to specific physical states of this kind. There is no neutral way to define them. The psychological, in what I have called his 'simple theory' of these phenomena, is defined as the psycho-physical.

Aristotle advanced a second thesis, listed as [B] above: he suggested that, in the case of anger, there are no further purely physical features which are present. In this case, as in that of perception and desire, there are, in his view, no essential

---

[4] For further development of this account, see my 'Aristotle's Processes' (2015: 186–205).
[5] For further discussion of Aristotle's view of per se causation, see Chapter 2.

underlying physical (or physiological) features or processes defined without reference to the psychological. The relevant physical capacities, properties, and processes of the agent are themselves inextricably psycho-physical: defined in terms of their role in the life and capacities of the agent. In Aristotle's terminology, the relevant matter is the very matter it is in virtue of the presence of the form. There are, in his account, no brute unexplained correlations between physical and psychological properties. Nor is there any danger of over-determination by separate physical and psychological phenomena. This is because he takes both types of phenomenon as, in the way explained, inextricably psycho-physical.

In Aristotle's view, Penelope's skill and desire (and their relevant mental properties) are not causally inert epiphenomena, dependent (in some way) on a set of underlying purely physical causes which do all the causal work in generating her actions. Nor can her skill, desire, or action be defined wholly in terms of those underlying physical causes, themselves defined without essential reference to her goals or know-how. There can be no successful reduction of psychological to purely physical.

There is a further distinctive feature of Aristotle's account: while Penelope's actions are caused per se by her desire and her skill, there is no additional physical per se cause of those actions. He did not need to address the question which immediately arises if one thinks that there are two distinct sets of causes, one physical, one psychological, both of which determine her actions: how to explain their regular and reliable co-occurrence in the organisms in question?[6] This is because the per se causal connections, exemplified in Penelope's actions, are, in his view, ones between inextricably psycho-physical desires and skills and her essentially embodied actions. Neither her skill or desire, nor their causally relevant psychological properties, can be defined without explicit reference in their definition to some specific material aspects of the agent. Further, the latter aspects cannot be defined without explicit reference in their definition to the psychological. There is no place in his model for two definitionally independent causes which could over-determine the resulting bodily actions.

Aristotle's account of perception follows a similar pattern. Our perceptual experiences are, in his view, psycho-physical discriminations of physical objects and their features which causally interact with us through the medium of, for example, light. These experiences need to be inextricably embodied in this way to be unified per se effects of these physical features of our environment. Like our desires and skills, they cannot be defined without explicit reference to some specific physical aspects of the perceiver. Nor can the latter be defined without explicit reference to the psychological. As in the case of action, Aristotle can in this way represent our perceptions as caused per se by the external physical world

---

[6] This degree of co-occurrence, I assume, cannot plausibly be taken as a 'miraculous co-incidence'.

without embracing either epiphenomenalism or reductionism. Nor are our perceptions, in his account, over-determined by two separate sets of causes, one purely physical, the other psychological.

7.2 A first comparison: non-reductionist materialism

It may be helpful to compare Aristotle's account with one of the subtlest of recent attempts to account for the causal role of the psychological, when that is defined (in a non-Aristotelian fashion) as distinct from purely physical phenomena.

Donald Davidson sought to retain the causal efficacy of the psychological while regarding the latter as autonomous with respect of the underlying physical domain. In his account, the psychological alone is governed by rationality. However, particular psychological events, such as Penelope's desiring at a given time to weave, are causes of particular bodily movements because both causes and effects are identical with particular physical events. In his picture, the causal laws governing these events are purely physical, stated in the language of physics alone. While the psychological aspects (or properties) of these events (such as their content) supervene on physical properties, they are not, what Aristotle would call, per se causes of the resulting acts. These psychological aspects (or properties) do not cause the event to happen when and in the way it does. While they may render the action intelligible, the type of explanation involved, in Davidson's account, is non-causal. It consists in locating the relevant psychological features (or properties) in a rational pattern designed to make optimal sense of agents, their goals, and their actions. Since they are not themselves per se causes of the resulting bodily movements, there is no threat of causal over-determination by definitionally distinct features (or properties).[7]

Contrast Aristotle's view: desire or skill and their relevant properties, when defined as inextricably psycho-physical, are per se causes of the resultant bodily actions. Had Penelope's desires been different, her actions would have been correspondingly different. Her skill might have caused her to develop the same action somewhat differently—had she encountered difficulties in carrying out her original plan. It is because she has certain goals, sees the situation in certain ways and knows how to respond to it that her actions occur in the way they do.[8] Her skill is, in virtue of just these features, essentially goal-directed, content-sensitive, and the basic per se cause of her actions.

---

[7] Donald Davidson developed this view in a series of important essays: 'Mental Events', 'Psychology as Philosophy', 'The Material Mind' (1980). Davidson's account itself has been subject to various interpretations, several of which are ably discussed by T.W. Child (1994).

[8] For a fuller version of these concerns, see my essay 'Supervenience, Composition and Physicalism' (1992: 277–9).

There is a problem: has Davidson's account succeeded in capturing the basic causal role of the relevant psychological states? Token identity and property supervenience do not, it seems, sustain conditionals and counterfactuals such as:

[1] If Penelope had seen the situation differently, she would have woven in a different way.
[2] In roughly similar circumstances, if Penelope were to judge it best to weave in a given way, she would do so.

If this is correct, Penelope's skill and desire (and their causally relevant properties) are not causes of her resulting actions in the way we standardly assume they are. Kim, commenting on a similar difficulty, once wrote:

> the...outcome [promised by non-reductive materialism]...is not to be had. The next best outcome, in fact our only hope at this point if mental causation is to be saved, is physical reductionism. Physical reduction would save causal efficacy for mentality, at the cost of its autonomy. Reductionism allows only one domain, the physical domain, but the mental may find a home in that domain.[9]

Davidson fails, Kim notes, to capture (what I am calling) the basic per se causal role of the psychological properties of Penelope's skill and desire. This causal role could have been captured by reductionist materialist theories. However, the latter—even if they were to be successful in this regard—would, Kim suggests, lose the *distinctively mental* contribution of mental powers, the efficacy of the mental *as such*.

The causal contribution of mental properties and powers is particularly important when one considers actions, as Aristotle did, as activities or processes rather than as events. This is because the content of the desire (what is aimed at) and the nature of the agent's know-how cause these activities to develop in the way they do: they make a difference to how they unfold. Aristotle focuses not only on the occurrence of particular actions but also on the way in which they develop and are, on occasion, modified to adjust to circumstances. And for this, the 'mental' properties of the agent's desire and skill are relevant causes.

While Kim pointed to a genuine problem in Davidson's account, he did not consider all of the available ways to address it. If desire and skill are, together with their relevant properties, inextricably psycho-physical phenomena, they can be both 'mental' and the basic per se causes of the resultant bodily movements. They will be, in virtue of the very same properties, unified, essentially goal-directed, per se causes of action. However, there is no space for Aristotle's suggestion on

---

[9] 'The Myth of Non-reductive Materialism' (1989: 31–47).

Kim's conceptual map. This is because, from his perspective, all the relevant causes must, it seems, be either purely psychological or purely physical.

That said, it should be noted that, in Aristotle's account, desires and skills are, in Kim's apt phrase, 'autonomous' with regard to the physical, understood as what is definable in purely physical terms. While they are inextricably psycho-physical—and this feature accounts for their causal efficacy—the latter does not rest on anything purely physical (or something reducible to the purely physical). The relevant capacities and properties are, for Aristotle, essentially and inextricably psycho-physical and, in virtue of being such, per se causes of the resulting inextricably psycho-physical activities. It is in virtue of these activities that there are causal connections of the relevant type between capacities, their properties, and their physical effects (such as the woollen cloak parts which Penelope wove).

There is a further difference between Davidson's and Aristotle's account. In the former, psychological features 'supervene' on physical features. There are necessitation conditionals linking the physical and the psychological: indistinguishable physical properties necessitate the presence of indistinguishable psychological properties. However, there remains an issue: how to explain why these conditionals are true: how does matter, understood as purely physical, give rise to psychological properties?[10] Confronted with this problem and finding no adequate solution, non-reductionist materialists sometimes suggest that these conditionals simply express a brute, and basic, metaphysical reality which we lack the conceptual resources to understand. Psychological properties, so understood, simply emerge from the physical in the way required to sustain these conditionals. There is, it seems, a mystery at the centre of their account.

For Aristotle, by contrast, the relevant material states are defined as the ones they are in virtue of their psychological forms. The matter, so far from brutely necessitating the presence of various psychological properties, is defined as the type of matter it is in virtue of certain psycho-physical states of a psycho-physical organism. There is no need to explain how purely physical properties, powers, or processes in the subject give rise to purely psychological ones because both are defined as inextricably psycho-physical: in terms of their role in the life of the agent, defined as a psycho-physical organism.[11] There is no further problem to address.

---

[10] Galen Strawson (2006).

[11] In Aristotle's account, the psycho-physical types (such as desiring revenge in the heat-involving way) and the underlying physico-psychic types (such as revenge-directed heat) are definitionally interconnected. One might regard them as type identical. Or alternatively, they could be defined as distinct but inter-defined types of activity. Given that they are inter-defined, necessarily co-occurring realizations of the same capacity with the same goal, the first view may appear preferable. However, for all that has been said, they could be separate activities with differing definitions: in one, desire might be the genus while in the other, heating. Aristotle himself seems, on occasion, to have thought that, provided the two accounts were inter-defined in the way he suggested, he did not need to rule on the issue of identity (vs. definitionally required co-occurrence). For him, it may have been a side issue.

Since Aristotle had no need to explain how psychological features 'supervene' on purely physical ones, he is not correctly described (in Bernard Williams' vivid phrase) as an early advocate of 'a polite form of materialism' (which I have called, more prosaically, non-reductionist materialism).[12] This is because 'polite materialism', together with its impolite cousin (reductionism), requires the presence of a determinate purely material or physical basis, defined independently of the psychological, which underlies the psychological and grounds its causal powers. Aristotle rejects these options because he does not accept their shared assumption: there is, in his view, no determinate purely physical basis, defined independently of the physical, which underlies and grounds the psychological (in the way they suggest). Nor does he present the psychological as causally inert, lacking an essential role in the causal explanation of action.[13]

Aristotle's approach, so interpreted, is distinctive. If Penelope's psychological capacities and properties are essentially and inextricably psycho-physical, they can be unified per se causes of her resulting inextricably psycho-physical action of weaving. But, that said, was Kim nonetheless right not to consider it as an option? Are the costs of accepting it too high? Is it, as some suspect, frankly incredible? Can we really give up the hard-won conceptions of the purely psychological, inspired by Descartes, or of the purely physical, rescued by the scientists of the seventeenth century and their successors from the wreckage of the Aristotelian project?

I shall return to these questions in Chapter 8 in assessing some of the arguments which motivate our post-Cartesian understanding of the psychological and the physical. However, it may be helpful, before doing so, to locate Aristotle's own position on a broader conceptual map.

7.3 Partial overview

One consideration in favour of Aristotle's two theses was based, I have argued, on his understanding of efficient causation. In the case of the emotions, desire, and action, his line of thought can be summarized as follows:

1. Some psychological features involved in the emotions and desire are the forms of the composite organs or activities they enform.
2. Such forms are per se causes of or per se effects of bodily changes: they are required for and adequate to account for the changes that unfold. [CAUSE 1]

---

[12] Bernard Williams, 'Hylomorphism' (1986: 189–99).
[13] Howard Robinson raises this concern (2014: 203–14).

3. The psychological features, the forms of the emotions and desire, are per se causes or per se effects of bodily changes (from 1 + 2).
4. Per se causes and per se effects of bodily changes must themselves be defined as bodily features.
5. The psychological features, the forms of the emotions and desire, must be defined as bodily features (from 3 and 4).

If these psychological features are capacities, they will be defined as essentially bodily (or enmattered) capacities. If they are actualities, they will be defined as bodily actualities. This is the type of capacity or actuality they are. They will differ, in this respect, from purely mathematical capacities, which—even if the latter must be instantiated in material bodies to exist—are not defined as essentially bodily capacities. The relevant per se efficient causes or effects of bodily changes are, in the way explained in Section 7.2, inextricably psycho-physical. This is how they have to be if they are to be unified per se causes of the resulting, unfolding, bodily changes.

Additional steps are required to underwrite Aristotle's second thesis:

1. The bodily processes or activities that result are not over-determined by two sets of independently defined causal capacities. This is because, in his account, there are no definitionally independent physical causes. [CAUSE 2]
2. The bodily causes are to be defined as psycho-physical: they too are inextricably and essentially psycho-physical.

These additional steps rest on two further assumptions which Aristotle endorsed:

[PRIORITY]   Forms are what make the underlying matter (identified as the physical cause) be the way it is. The form is prior in being to the matter in question.[14]

[UNITY]   Forms are what make the resulting composite phenomena non-accidental unities. They do so by making the matter in the composite be the way it is.

Aristotle's view differs from that suggested by non-reductionist materialists, such as Davidson, in several respects. In Aristotle's view, psychological states and their properties are per se causes of bodily changes. They are not efficient causes only in so far as they are instantiated in bodily states with their own causal powers. It is in virtue of their own features that they initiate and control the processes they do. Further, there is, as I have emphasized, no threat of over-determination by two

---

[14] As was argued in Chapter 2.

independent causes, one physical and one psychological. This is because they are, in the ways specified, inextricably psycho-physical phenomena. If the form of anger is PURE (like mathematical forms), it cannot be a per se efficient cause of bodily change. Such forms, like mathematical harmonies, are causally ineffective.

There is a further point of difference: in some non-reductionist accounts, while psychological properties supervene on physical properties, no explanation is offered of why (or indeed how) such supervenience claims are true. The resulting composite does not satisfy Aristotle's [UNITY] condition. Since the matter is not the way it is in virtue of the form, the resulting composite is an accidental unity. It just happens that the psychological supervenes on the physical. We have, in effect, an accidental unity, not the type of genuine unity that Aristotle took to be characteristic of natural substances.

Non-reductionist accounts also differ in respect of [PRIORITY]. They present the relevant psychological features (the form) as metaphysically dependent on purely material (or physical) states. The form, so understood, is a property of, or relation between, some more fundamental material elements: the matter in question. But this conclusion runs strongly contrary to Aristotle's insistence that the Form is prior in being to matter *as matter*, not ontologically dependent on it.[15]

7.4 Aristotle and functionalism

Aristotle's account differs from that proposed by functionalist philosophers and interpreters of his work inspired by functionalism.[16] While there are several varieties of functionalism, I shall contrast his approach with (what might be called) materialist functionalism: the view that the relevant states, defined wholly in terms of their function, have to be realized in material states. Other versions of functionalism, including Putnam's early formulations which allowed psychological states to be realized by Cartesian soul stuff, are further removed from Aristotle's own position.

If Aristotle had been a precursor of 'materialist functionalism', he would have been committed to a proto-version of one or both of the following theses about, for example, anger:

[1] To be angry is to be in a material state which plays a given efficient causal role in a total system of other states.

In his view, the form of anger would be wholly given by its efficient causal role: being such as to be caused by given states and to cause others in a system of other

---

[15] I understand ontological priority as priority in being, not as priority in existence. Explanatory priority is not by itself enough. Priority in definition tracks priority in being.

[16] For this style of reading: see Christopher Shields' suggestion (1990: 19–33).

such states, including other internal states. He would have developed a version of what is now called 'role-functionalism'. He might also have held:

[2] Anger [in an organism] is the state [in that organism] which plays a given efficient causal role in a total system of other states.

Had he accepted [2], he would have identified anger in humans with a specific realizing state in a given organism (the realizing state type), such as the boiling of the blood or T-fibre stimulation (depending on what turns out to be that state in the best empirical theory of the organism in question). In other organisms, the realizing state might be a different physical one (D-fibre stimulation). What makes the realizing state a state of anger is that it realizes the causal role of anger in the total theory of the organism. This latter view is sometimes called 'realizing state functionalism'.

Aristotle was not a role-functionalist. Aristotle's forms, as we saw in previous chapters, are not wholly defined by their efficient causal roles: teleological and specific material causes are also essential to their definition.[17] They are per se causes in virtue of being the specific goal-directed material capacities (or actualities) they essentially are. They must be capacities of this type (as in the case of anger a hot, pain-driven, desire for revenge) to play the efficient causal role required of them. It is because desire for revenge is (i) directed towards revenge and (ii) pain-driven and (iii) a hot desire (one defined by its being enmattered in heat) that it causes the changes it does.

Each of these points is important. It is because Achilles' desire is directed towards the goal of revenge that his actions develop as they do. His pursuit of this goal causes him to leave his tent, drive ferociously into battle, kill Hector in the way he does, and mutilate his body. It is only when his goal has been achieved, and he has revenged the death of Patroclus, that his pain at the death of Patroclus begins to abate. It is because he has this goal that his actions begin, unfold, and conclude as they do. Their controlling cause is an inextricably goal-directed desire. In the case of skilled actions (such as weaving), the skill, as the controlling cause of the unfolding goal-directed process, is similarly goal-directed. This is why the weaver's actions develop as they do. Further, in the case of Achilles, his desire is driven by the painfulness of the loss of his friend. Aristotle makes no attempt to define painfulness in terms of its causal consequences. It is because of the painfulness of his loss that he believes that he is pained and also desires

---

[17] See Chapter 1, Section 3. He had reason to reject the attempt to define all the essential features of the psychological in terms of its efficient causal input and output, where the latter are understood in terms of purely physical changes. In his view, one needs to introduce teleological considerations to capture the goal-directedness of the weaver's reasoning and the characteristic features of her ongoing skill-guided action. I discussed the first of these features, in resisting functionalist interpretations of Aristotle's account: see my (1984: 238–40).

vengeance. There is no sign of his being attracted to the suggestion, characteristic of role-functionalism, that all essential psychological features of pain can be analysed solely in terms of their causal input and output and, as such, be defined wholly in terms which can be unproblematically realized by purely physical states.

The resulting actions are themselves inextricably psycho-physical. They are unfolding goal-directed processes or activities, not specific types of purely physical events (such as spatial movement of parts of a body) which can be defined independently of the desired goal. Desires, as causes, initiate and govern goal-directed bodily processes of this type. To be causes of such processes they must be enmattered in certain quite specific ways: the ones required to account for the specific bodily actions that unfold. Functionalist accounts do not satisfy Aristotle's conditions on per se efficient causality because they fail to state what it is about the relevant phenomena, taken one by one, in virtue of which they are causes of the resultant specific bodily actions or processes. From Aristotle's viewpoint, the relevant desires must be enmattered in the specific material ways if they are to produce and control the required bodily movements. They are, as such, defined as enmattered in just those specific types of matter that are required for and adequate to account for the relevant outcome. The desires have to be inextricably material capacities to cause the unfolding inextricably psycho-physical bodily actions that ensue.

Forms are defined, according to the functionalist interpreter, wholly in terms of their efficient causal role, itself defined independently of the specific material states that realize them. This is why, in this account, psychological states can be variably realized. There is nothing about them, considered by themselves, which requires them to be realized in any specific kind of matter. In Aristotelian terms, they do not—in themselves—'hypothetically necessitate' the presence of specific types of matter. However, this cannot be Aristotle's viewpoint. He criticizes those who:

> join together and place the soul in the body without adding to their defining account why this is so and how the body in question is in a given condition.
> (*De Anima* 407b15–16)

adding:

> they attempt to say what type of thing the soul is but do not add to their defining account anything about the body that receives it as if it were possible—as in the Pythagorean stories—for any type of soul to be tied into any type of body. It seems that each of these has its own distinctive form and shape but they speak almost as if one were to say that one could tie the art of building into pipes. For the art must use instruments, the soul, the body.   (407b20–6)

In Aristotle's account, the relevant forms are essentially material in a quite specific way: they are material in a way that requires the presence of the relevant specific type of matter. In his discussion of the saw, the form in question is defined in terms which include explicit reference to specific types of matter. If the form in question is a capacity, it is an essentially material capacity: the capacity-of-hard-metal-to-cut-with-hard-serrated-teeth. It must be such to cause the wood to be cut in the specific way it is. This is why Aristotle compares such forms with being snub: the inextricably nasal type of concavity which defines snub noses (*Phys.* B.2, 194a13ff.).

This said: Aristotle need not reject the idea of 'variable realization', suitably understood. Perhaps saws can be made from various types of metal. But, nonetheless, all these metals must meet certain specific material conditions. Saws need to be endowed with the capacities-of-hard-metal, whether that metal be iron or steel. They could not be made from bronze, let alone blue cheese. Similarly, while animals without hearts may be angry, they must be endowed with some shared material features (which Aristotle describes as the 'hot') to be per se causes of their relevant effects. While 'heat' may have a causal role, it may also be described as possessed of the lightest parts, and the least bulky of the elements.[18] Indeed, it has its causal role (at least in part) in virtue of possessing these material features.

Some may suggest that Aristotle is better understood as proposing a proto-version of realizing state functionalism. If so, he will have held that:

[2] Anger [in an organism] is the material state [in that organism] which plays a given efficient causal role in a total system of other states.

The total system, thus introduced, may have some teleological goals which require the presence of anger with its distinctive efficient causal role. Further, given the demands of the total system and the distinctive causal profile of anger, boiling of the blood will be required as the realizing state. Aristotle, it must be ceded, did not himself make much progress in spelling out the details of this type of account. He did not, for example, consider whether anger is the same state when there are differences in other parts of the total system. Nor did he explain why the goals of the organism require a state with precisely the causal role anger has. (Why wouldn't a desire to get one's own back without heat have been equally good? Why is just this type of material basis required (or best)?) But, it might be said,

---

[18] *De Anima* 405a7ff. Nor is there any reason to believe that being possessed of lightness of parts or bulkiness is to be defined solely in terms of their causal role. Similar considerations apply to talk of shape. In Aristotle's picture, it is because it is circular (in a material way) that a bronze ball rolls. For further discussion of this point, see Chapter 2.

his is nonetheless a proto-type for the fuller, more worked out, realizer-functionalist accounts we now have.

There are, however, several reasons to doubt that Aristotle held a view of this type. He held throughout that desires and skills were the per se causes of the resulting processes and activities. It is not the case, in his picture, that the real causal work is done at the physical level by the realizing states under their physical descriptions (such as boiling of blood). Desires and skills are not, in his view, causally redundant. Nor are they epiphenomenal features, present when (and only when) the genuine physical causes are in operation. Nor do they explain only in virtue of being invoked in a distinctive a priori pattern of explanation present at the psychological level. The resulting processes and activities are caused to occur and unfold as they do because of their per se causes: skill and desire. This is because the per se causes, in his view, do not bifurcate into two separate types of entity: a purely material realizer state and a purely psychological state or set of properties that it realizes. There is one inextricably psycho-physical cause of the resulting bodily actions.

There is a further difference: in Aristotle's picture, psychological forms are not realized in material states in the way the functionalist suggests: by material states defined independently of such forms. Instead, in his view, it is an essential feature of the relevant type of material state (whether T-fibre stimulation or boiling of the blood) that it be a state of anger. It could not have been that very material state and realized different psychological properties (or none at all). It is essential to its being that material state that it is the exercise of the essentially psycho-physical capacity for anger. Indeed, its being the exercise of this type of capacity is what makes it the material state it is.

This difference is significant. Had Aristotle been a realizer functionalist, he would—given his insistence on the genuine per se causal role of desire and skill—have been committed to the presence of two definitionally independent causes of the same resulting bodily movements. The latter would have been over-determined by two causes of this type. However, Aristotle avoids this undesirable consequence by defining both the relevant material and psychological states in essentially psycho-physical terms. He meets his own [UNITY] requirement by defining the psychological form as essentially enmattered and the matter as essentially enformed by this form. The result is an essentially unified state. The resulting psycho-physical state is not an accidental unity made up of two definitionally independent phenomena.

There is a second, related difference: realizer-functionalism treats psychological phenomena as functions of material states. Forms are, once again, defined as dependent entities: properties of or relations between material states which are metaphysically prior to their properties and relations, structures and functions. Even if the latter are irreducible properties of matter, they are properties of matter nonetheless. Matter itself is metaphysically primary. But this is not Aristotle's view. In his account, forms are definitionally prior to the matter that instantiates them. His definitional, and metaphysical, order is quite different: matter and the relevant material states are the way they are because of the presence of the form. This is why his account satisfies his [PRIORITY] condition: form is metaphysically primary.[19]

To conclude: Aristotle's account, however it is best to be understood, is not a version of either role or realizer functionalism.

7.5 Ackrill's problem: different perspectives

The distinctive aspects of Aristotle's inextricability theses, and their connection with his more general views about hylomorphism, come into sharper focus if we consider a problem, once raised by John Ackrill (1972–3), for a sophisticated contemporary version of hylomorphism. Ackrill noted that, at least if understood as an interpretation of Aristotle, David Wiggins' account of hylomorphism generates an unacceptable consequence. As Wiggins notes, when a sculptor makes a statue from clay, the clay which goes to make the statue might not have been used to do so. It could have been used for other purposes. Wiggins suggests in a series of studies culminating in his 2001 book:

[1] The matter [this clay] is only contingently enformed by the form of a statue.

However, as Ackrill noted, Aristotle was clearly committed to the claim that:

[2] The body of a composite is necessarily enformed by its form (*Meta.* 1035b20–5, *De Anima* 412b10–17).

Hence, if he also held that:

[3] The matter which is present in the composite [this lump of clay] = the body of composite

it will follow that, in his view:

[4] The body of the composite is contingently and necessarily enformed.[20]

---

[19] The relevant psychological forms could not exist, in Aristotle's view, if there were no matter of an appropriate type and no material objects. But, equally, in his view, there would be no matter of an appropriate type and no material objects if there were no such forms. Mutual existential dependence of this kind is consistent with forms being definitionally prior to such objects and their matter. Existential symmetry is, for Aristotle, consistent with asymmetry in definition or being. (Consider definitional asymmetries between necessary entities: two is prior to seven.)

[20] There is also, it should be noted, an alternative, even more threatening, formulation of Ackrill's problem:
 [1] The matter present in the composite is not essentially/definitionally enformed...

But [4] is, as it stands, incoherent. Aristotle cannot, on pain of inconsistency, have accepted [1]–[3] as stated.

One attempt to solve Ackrill's problem, considered as an exegetical puzzle, has been to suggest that while Aristotle accepted [1], [2], and [3], he distinguished two distinct entities with different determinate causal powers. According to this proposal, [2] and [3] are true of the body defined as the body of the composite ('proximate matter' as it is usually described). By contrast, [1] is true of non-proximate matter, which is not identical with but underlies (or realizes) proximate matter. Non-proximate matter, sometimes referred to as BODY, continues to exist and is present in a living organism. It is contingently enformed. By contrast, the body of the composite, which is also present in the composite, is necessarily enformed. BODY, exemplified by this lump of clay, is a persisting determinate entity (with its own nature) which retains its distinctive causal powers in the enformed body, which also has its own new causal powers. In some versions of this account, the latter supervene on (or emerge from) the determinate causal powers of BODY which persists in the composite.[21]

This solution to Ackrill's puzzle faces its own problems. Nor is it easily reconciled with Aristotle's own account. There are several reasons why this is so.

First, if the BODY and the body are definitionally separate entities, each with its own causal powers, the resulting bodily action will be over-determined by two independent sets of per se efficient causes.[22] Desire (as a bodily capacity) is, as we have seen, a per se cause of the relevant bodily movements and is so in virtue of its form.[23] It is not a cause in virtue of being realized in a BODILY state (or process) which is the per se cause of these movements.[24] However, as we have already noted:

[CAUSE] Aristotle's forms are per se efficient causes. They are per se efficient causes in virtue of the same features in virtue of which they are formal causes.

However, if BODY retains its own causal powers and generates the same movements, there will be two independent determinate causes of the same result. At best, there will be an unexplained coincidence of the type Aristotle criticized

[2] The body is essentially/definitionally enformed
[3] The matter present in the composite = the body.
So: the body is essentially enformed and is not essentially enformed.

[21] This approach is developed by Jennifer Whiting (1995: 75–92). For further discussion, see Christopher Shields (2016: xxviiff.).
[22] William Jaworski suggests that, to avoid the problem of causal over-determination, one is well advised to postulate two different types of explanation, one causal and the other 'rationalizing': see Jaworski (2016: 280ff.).
[23] There is no sign of two distinct effects: one a bodily movement, the other a BODILY movement.
[24] As was argued in Chapter 2.

elsewhere.[25] But the situation is potentially worse: if the same (token) BODILY movement could have occurred without the presence of the body, the latter would not be its per se cause. This is because, in his view, something can only be a per se cause if it is necessary for its effect.[26]

There is a second problem: how do the body and BODY together compose anything other than an accidental unity? Even if this suggestion upholds the non-accidental unity of the form with the body, it does so by postulating an accidental unity between the enformed body of the composite and BODY: a move which undermines the unity of the composite object. Some recent writers, aware of this difficulty, have written of the powers of BODY being 'directed by', 'harnessed by', or 'dictated by' the wholes to which they belong.[27] However, their formulation, suggesting the presence of two distinct components, the director and the directed, undermines the required unity of the composite substance. One has, it seems, a team of causally interconnected players. Further it is hard to see how this formulation can offer a solution to the mind/BODY problem (as is sometimes claimed). The relations it invokes, such as directing or harnessing, are just the ones that such a solution needs to elucidate. (Descartes could, after all, talk happily enough of the soul 'directing' the body.) In any event, their proposal does not, as it stands, satisfy Aristotle's UNITY requirement.

Some have sought to mitigate the latter difficulty by treating BODY as the underlying subject and taking being as an enformed body as one of its properties. While BODY might have lacked this further property, the property itself, being an enformed body, is defined as an enformed type of property. When BODY instantiates this property, it is described, *qua* instantiator of this property, as necessarily embodied. That is: BODY is itself contingently enformed but—when described as instantiating this property—is necessarily enformed. It is only so decribed that BODY is necessarily enformed.

BODY, according to this latter suggestion, is a genuine unity which happens to be, at certain times, an enformed body and, at those times, to possess a form. Thus understood, the form is a property of BODY. However, this proposal is not one which Aristotle could accept without surrendering his commitment to the definitional priority of the form:

[PRIORITY] Forms are not defined as properties of, or relations between, metaphysically more basic entities: rather they make those entities the ones they are.

---

[25] See, for example, his discussion of Empedocles' account of animal generation in *Physics* 198b26–199a8. For further discussion of this passage, see my essay (2012: 239ff.).
[26] See *Post. An.* 98a35–b4. For further discussion, see my (2000a: 204ff.).
[27] As Jaworski suggests: see his (2016: 123).

In fact, the present suggestion reverses Aristotle's favoured order of explanation, making matter, understood as BODY, prior to form. In common with the other versions of modern hylomorphism, it does not capture his idea that matter, in this case BODY, is the way it is because of the presence of the form.

Other writers, impressed by these difficulties, have proposed a different approach, suggesting that BODY, identified with the underlying matter, ceases to exist when the body of a living organism is formed.[28] All that is present, in their account, in the composite substance is body defined in terms of its function (which has the same nature as its form). Features of BODY are not essential to body; when present in body they are contingent features of the body of the composite.

This suggestion has its merits: it sidesteps the problems concerning over-determination and the unity of the resulting composite substance which beset the first proposal. It also succeeds in maintaining the priority of the form. However, it does so at a high cost since, in this account, the underlying matter, this lump of clay, is 'annihilated' or 'altered' in the new composite by the presence of the form. That is, BODY is destroyed and replaced by another entity, the body. The form, so far from 'harnessing' or 'directing' BODY, or underlying matter, now alters it in such a way as to deprive it of its pre-existing nature.[29]

This consequence is problematic. In Aristotle's hylomorphic accounts of change, the matter survives in the new composite as the clay survives in the statue.[30] This piece of wood or lump of clay should retain its causal powers as wood or clay in the finished product. However, in that eventuality, both it and the proximate matter of the composite will be present in the resulting composite—and once again Aristotle will be confronted with problems of over-determination. Conversely, if the original matter (BODY) does not persist into the new composite, its properties must, it seems, 'jump' from one determinate entity to another. But how can this happen? If the original object (e.g. this wood) is destroyed, how is its essential property (being wooden) retained in the final product? Further, how does it cease to be an essential feature of the resulting composite, when it was an essential feature of the pre-existing matter, BODY?[31] Most contemporary hylomorphists, finding these questions unanswerable, reject this style of account.[32]

Wiggins discerned two distinct particular objects in the case of the statue. In addition to the statue itself, there is a particular lump of clay which is not identical with the statue (defined in terms of the shape or structure of this matter). There are two numerically distinct determinate but presently co-occurring particulars with different life histories. The particular lump of clay matter was present before

---

[28] See, for example, Anna Marmodoro (2013: 5–22).
[29] How does the form 'annihilate' or 'alter' the matter at all, if it is not itself material?
[30] Aristotle, *Physics* A.7. For further discussion see my (2018: 178–205).
[31] One might also ask: how does the form 'annihilate' or 'alter' the matter if it is not itself material?
[32] See Jeremy Skrzypek's discussion of these issues in (2017: 360–408).

the statue was created, is present while the statue exists, and may persist after its destruction. It retains the causal powers it had before the statue was formed: it is, in its own right, an efficient cause. But the statue, with its own shorter life history, also has its own causal powers. However, if both these claims are true, the lump of clay and the statue will be distinct efficient causes. Thus, when Penelope bumps into a statue of Odysseus and injures her foot, both the statue and the lump of clay will be causes of the resulting damage. Penelope's injury is, in fact, over-determined by two distinct causes. Indeed, there will, it seems, be over-determination of this type in any case when a hylomorphic compound, so understood, interacts with other objects. The threat of over-determination, which we first encountered in reflecting on the causal role of the psychological, has generalized to apply to all hylomorphic compounds.[33]

None of the suggested solutions to Ackrill's puzzle satisfy Aristotle's three relevant conditions: [CAUSE], [UNITY], and [PRIORITY]. Nor should this be surprising. They share a common assumption: either BODY is present in the composite as one persisting determinate object with its own causal powers (the ones it had before being made into the composite) or it is not present at all. But, as we saw in Chapter 2, Aristotle rejects this assumption: BODY is made determinate in a given way in the composite by its form. When so determined, it is the body of the composite. BODY is not a persisting determinate entity, present before the composite is formed and persisting in the composite. His suggestion, in effect, rejects [3] in Ackrill's original argument, as set out above:

[3]   The matter present in the composite [viz. this lump of clay] = the body of composite.

The body of the composite is, instead, this lump of clay made determinate as the body it is only when in the composite.[34]

In Aristotle's account, so understood, the original matter continues to exist in the resulting composite but not as precisely the same entity as was present before the composite came to be. Nor does the matter retain its original causal powers in their pre-existing form. The general material causal powers of matter are made determinate in the resulting composite. For example, the determinable powers of matter (BODY) to heat and cool are made determinate as the power to heat in a given way (for example: the way which is caused by an insult and aims at revenge).

---

[33] For helpful discussion of this issue, see Skrzypek (2017: 360–408).

[34] For discussion of these issues, and of the conceptual machinery of determinables and determinants, and its usefulness in interpreting Aristotle's view of matter, see Chapter 2, Section 7 and my earlier essay (2010: 168–97). Michail Peramatzis, in (2018: 12–32) and his subsequent review of Kathrin Koslicki's *Form, Matter and Substance* (2019: 235–45), showed the role of this machinery in arriving at a proper understanding of the Aristotelian response to Ackrill's problem. I am particularly indebted to Peramatzis' contribution at this point. For further discussion of this issue, see Chapter 8, Section 5.

This is the determinate form of heating found in angry people. It is not that the power to heat is mysteriously 'whisked away' and replaced with a wholly new power. Nor is this determinate power precisely the same as was there before it was made determinate in this way in the composite. When BODY is made into this body, the causal power that results is the determinate power of this body (the one required for the maintenance and flourishing of the body in question).

The determinable power of BODY, it should be noted, could have been made determinate in other ways. The power to heat could, for example, have been made determinate in the power to heat or cool in some other determinate way (in, for example, other types of bodies, including non-animate ones). This is how the intuition behind [1] in Ackrill's original argument is retained. However, once the relevant causal power of the original matter has been made determinate in the specific way characteristic of anger in the resulting body, the power to heat or cool in other ways is no longer present. As long as that body remains, the only relevant causal power of BODY is the determinate causal power of the composite body. (This is an application of the S-structure discussed in Chapter 2.)

An example may help clarify Aristotle's position: in making a statue, a sculptor takes a particular lump of clay with generic causal powers (e.g. to cohere) and moulds it into a persisting unified object with its own determinate causal powers (to cohere, for example, in the way required to represent a human). For the latter to exist, the determinable causal powers of its matter have to be made determinate by the presence of a given form (being a statue). Further, neither the form nor the new object can have causal powers defined independently of the matter, thus enformed. If either of them did, there would be over-determination by two independent causes. Since there are not two determinate entities present in the resulting composite, each with their own causal powers, there is no threat of over-determination by two independent causes.[35] Nor is there a threat to the unity of the resulting composite. It is a non-accidental unity in that its determinate causal powers are grounded in its specific form.

In Aristotle's account, BODY (this lump of clay) is not, as we noted in Chapter 2, Section 7, what he calls a '*this such*' at the beginning of this process but becomes (turns into) one when, and for as long as, it possesses determinate causal powers of the type just specified (*Physics* 191a12–14). Why is this the case? Why does this lump of clay fail to be a 'this such'? Is this merely a matter of grammatical stipulation on Aristotle's part? But what, if anything, motivates it?

We can, I suggest, best understand his claim from a causal perspective. Since the statue needs a certain amount of clay to retain its determinate causal power, it will have non-arbitrary persistence conditions: it will be destroyed just when it

---

[35] It was noted in Chapter 2 that this proposal offers a rejoinder to pan-psychism along the lines suggested in *Metaphysics* Θ.7, 1049a20ff. The form is the determiner or differentia of matter (see also Z.12, 1043a12–14 and 1044a15–25).

loses the amount of clay required to possess this determinate causal power (e.g. to represent Odysseus). Its persistence conditions are based on what is needed for it to possess this causal power. Once that is lost, and the statue is destroyed, it is arbitrary (or a matter of stipulation) how much clay can be lost consistent with the lump of clay that remains persisting as the same lump through time. Absent the relevant determinate causal power, there is no longer a *this such*, understood as a determinate entity with non-arbitrary persistence conditions. One can, of course, refer to a given lump of clay as 'this lump of clay' at any moment one encounters it during its evolving history. However, what is referred to will not be, in Aristotle's terms, a *this such* (so understood) because its persistence conditions are radically indeterminate or a matter of stipulation. By contrast, the statue will be a *this such*, something with non-arbitrary persistence conditions, in virtue of its possessing the relevant determinate causal powers required of statues. There must, in our example, be enough clay left to represent Odysseus.[36]

In Aristotle's account, there is no threat to the unity of the resulting composite statue. It is not an accidental unity made up of two distinct entities. The matter in the composite is defined in terms of the form of the statue. Its specific causal powers are determined by the presence of the form. Further, the non-accidental unity of the statue is based, in part, on the definitional dependence of the matter on the form. In addition, the form itself (and its relevant capacities) will be defined in an inextricably matter-involving manner (as material forms) if they are to be per se causes of the relevant effects (such as injuring Socrates when he bumps into it). Using these resources, Aristotle can underwrite the essential unity of the resulting composite while avoiding the danger of over-determination by two definitionally independent causes. In this way, he seeks to account for the existence of strongly unified hylomorphic composites, possessed of determinate causal powers. Further, he does so without being forced to accept any of the apparently unattractive solutions: 'annihilation' of the relevant matter, denying a per se causal role to form, or reducing the statue to its matter. (Further work is, of course, required to see whether this strategy is successful.)

Consideration of Ackrill's problem, and of the subsequent attempts to address it, highlights one feature shared by Aristotle's treatment of psychological phenomena 'common to body and soul' and his general account of hylomorphism. Both are motivated by a desire to accommodate the per se causal role of form while, at the same time, avoiding the threat of causal over-determination by definitionally

---

[36] Peramatzis suggests in his essay (2018: 26) that 'ostensive or demonstrative resources will not yield material terms with a sustained definite reference' when applied to this piece of wood here and now and concludes that 'they would not, therefore, secure rigorously the metaphysical subjecthood of matter'. In my view, this failure arises because this piece of wood or clay (demonstratively introduced) lacks determinate (non-arbitrary) persistence conditions. The latter are supplied, as was noted in Chapter 2, Section 7, by the imposition of a form of, for example, a cricket bat or a statue, with the distinctive causal (and goal-directed) powers required of the objects in question.

distinct formal and material causes. His two inextricability theses represent a sustained attempt to achieve this goal, maintaining the essential unity of the enformed composite (whether they be objects or activities) without reducing form to matter.

7.6 Aristotle and neo-Aristotelian hylomorphism

Aristotle's account of psychological phenomena 'common to body and soul' points to more general differences between his version of hylomorphism and some contemporary, neo-Aristotelian, versions. These differences, which parallel those already noted in the discussion of the psychological, relate to Aristotle's three major conditions: [CAUSE], [UNITY], and [PRIORITY]. My aim in this section, it should be noted, is limited to marking some points of contrast, not to assessing which viewpoint is preferable.

One salient difference between Aristotle's hylomorphism and some neo-Aristotelian accounts is, I have suggested, based on his view of forms as efficient causes:

[CAUSE]   Aristotle's forms are per se efficient causes. They are per se efficient causes in virtue of those features in virtue of which they are formal causes.

Since Aristotle held [CAUSE], he cannot have understood forms as 'operations' (not an item in the ontology) or as abstract objects. Nor can his forms be mathematical structures. None of these is capable of being the per se efficient cause, the starting point and controller, of material processes such as pulling and pushing (as Aristotle understood it). If talk of 'structure' is appropriate, it must refer to an essentially enmattered structure, one defined as enmattered in certain specific types of matter, to be capable of being an efficient per se cause: the starting point and controller of the bodily processes that result. Aristotle's distinctive understanding of efficient causation is a thread running through many of his discussions of specific issues.[37]

A second difference concerns the priority of forms: for Aristotle, as I have emphasized:

[PRIORITY]   Forms are not features of metaphysically more basic entities: rather they make those entities the ones they are.

---

[37] See, for example, the references to heat in the discussion of anger. It is not enough to suggest, as materialist functionalists might, that there has to be some type or other of matter present.

If he held this view, his forms cannot be defined as relations between or properties of more basic entities, defined independently of forms. Nor can they be defined as 'structures', if these are understood as relations or properties of this type, nor as supervening on more basic entities. Even if the relations or properties are understood as making the items whose properties they are 'whole', they are nonetheless not prior to those items. They are dependent on them even if their presence brings with it (in some way) the further property of making them whole.[38]

Aristotle, I have suggested, sought to address this problem on the basis of his understanding of what it is to be a *material principle*. If the interpretation developed in Chapters 2 and 4 is correct, in his view:

[1] Material principles are defined in terms of capacities for distinctive interactions, such as pushing/pulling/heating. They are the ways substances are when capable of such interactions. Examples of such material principles might be the way hands are when capable of moving, the state or condition of hands in which they are capable of causing such movements.

[2] Matter is defined as the bearer (or subject) of principles of this type: hands would be one example, bodies another. Matter, so understood, is not prior in definition to the relevant principles. Although one could not have material principles unless they were enmattered, these principles are not defined as properties of matter. Indeed, it would be a mistake to do so, reversing the correct order of being (and definition).

Aristotle took a further step: in his account, forms, understood as states (or ways of being) in which we are capable of certain activities, are teleologically prior to the matter arranged so as to be capable of such activities. If the relevant matter is understood as the body which is capable of being a starting point for material interaction, it will be definitionally dependent on matter *as a principle*, defined as that which is capable of the relevant interactions. In this account, enmattered form is prior in being to the matter it enforms. Forms, so understood, are not features of metaphysically more basic entities: instead, they make those entities the ones they are. In this way, impure forms are prior in being to matter. The latter is defined as what realizes forms of this type: ones capable of causing such changes as heating and cooling, pulling and pushing. To be an enmattered form is to be a causal, teleological, principle for changes of this type.[39]

---

[38] See, for example, Mark Johnston (2006: 652–98). Johnston's development of this idea, together with the proposals of Kit Fine (1999) and Kathrin Koslicki (2008), are helpfully discussed by Jeremy Skrzypek in his (2016: 360–408).

[39] For support for this view, see Aristotle's discussion in *Metaphysics* Λ.2, where matter is defined as what is capable of various specified types of change (1069b15ff.). The type of matter which belongs to perishable substances is genetic matter, defined in terms of its capacity to come to be the substance in question. Similarly, topical matter is defined in terms of the relevant capacity for spatial movement. What makes these varying kinds of matter matter is their capacity for given types of change. So

7.6 ARISTOTLE AND NEO-ARISTOTELIAN HYLOMORPHISM

Aristotle in *Metaphysics* Z.10–11 separated matter as a *principle* of form from matter understood *as matter*. However, matter can (like hands) be defined as that which is capable of moving in certain ways. It is matter of this type because it is what can play the relevant roles.[40] Matter by itself *as a principle* is not a type of material object at all: it is to be capable of certain activities, that way of being the possession of which makes matter (*to dunamei on*) what it is.[41] One can also look at hands simply *as matter*: as spatially divisible bits of matter or types of stuff, not defined in terms of these capacities. As a *principle*, matter is distinct both from what possesses the relevant capacity (*to dunamei on*) and from material stuff, defined without reference to these capacities (quantities of material stuff), present in the composite. Matter as a principle is prior to both.

Thinking of matter as what has the potentiality to be a substance allows Aristotle to maintain the essential unity of the composite substance: what results when the potentiality in question is actualized. Indeed, it seems essential to this matter being the matter it is that it is what is actualized in this way in certain conditions. The matter cannot be properly defined except in terms of potentiality to be so enformed. This prevents the new composite from being a merely accidental unity in which matter (specified independently of its connection with the form) happens at a time to play a given role.[42] Part of what it is to be this matter is to have the potential to be enformed in the relevant way: to be potentially something of this kind (*to dunamei on*). The matter in question is intelligibly connected with the enformed composite in question (in virtue of the latter's connections with its form). The composite is not an accidental unity since matter and form (once conceptualized in this way) are essentially connected.

This understanding of matter makes the unity of the composite intelligible in the ways captured in [C] and [D]. From this perspective, the nature and unity of the composite becomes fully perspicuous. One can see why its matter is as it is and why, given that its matter is understood in this way, the compound of matter

---

understood, material principles, defined as principles for change, are more basic than matter. Indeed, they make matter what it is. For further discussion, see my earlier essays (2000b: 81–110) and (2004: 151–69).

[40] This defines what it is to be matter as a modern physicalist might define matter as (e.g.) 'what is studied by physics' or as 'what is essentially spatio-temporal'.

[41] It is a mistake to think of matter, *the principle*, as an actual body or type of stuff. Anaximander (one of the subtlest of Aristotle's predecessors) erred because he took the Unbounded (best conceived as a principle) as a body, albeit one without any actual bodily attribute. His mistake (in Aristotle's view) was to understand a principle as an actual body or element. If Anaximander had not reified the relevant principle (a capacity to become a variety of things) as a body or element, he would not have been forced to accept the (apparently absurd) conclusion that the Unbounded is an actual existent, but one which lacks all the relevant characteristics of actual things. He was driven to this paradoxical consequence by mistakenly construing matter as a principle, understood as a type of capacity or potentiality, with a body or type of stuff.

[42] For a contrasting view, see the functionalist account of the realization of a mental description by a physical state.

and form is non-accidental (and captured in a properly unified definition). The nature of the matter and the composite become clear once we follow Aristotle's advice and see them as teleologically explained and defined by the presence of the relevant goal-laden actuality. In its light we can see why matter and composite are as they are (when all goes well).

The type of intelligibility which Aristotle seeks is distinctive. It cannot be secured simply by setting out an efficient causal story of what happens (in this case), still less by specifying the materials required for the composite in teleology-free terms. For both these routes would fail to explain why the organism has to be made up or brought about in the way it is. To meet this latter requirement Aristotle introduces the idea of a goal which simultaneously defines the nature of the organism and explains why it is the way it is. As in *Posterior Analytics* B.2 (90a14–15), there is one feature which answers both the definitional (what is it?) and the explanatory (why is it the way it is?) question. If one grasps this, the nature of the matter and the composite will be properly intelligible.

By contrast, it is not possible to state the intelligible and general principles of construction required to obtain the composite without reference to the form in question: they will be the ones required for this form to be present. These claims follow from the demand that it be intelligible why the relevant matter is present and why it is changed or altered in the way it is for its potential to be realized. One cannot state in a sufficiently general or perspicuous way why this matter is required or why it is acted on in the way it is without reference to the form in question. And, for these reasons, one cannot state in sufficiently general or perspicuous terms what the matter in question is.[43]

On this understanding, there need be no conflict between the form-involving 'top-down' approach to matter, which makes it fully perspicuous why the matter is as it is (in the ways indicated in the first part of the section) and a 'bottom-up' account which begins with matter, characterized in non-teleological terms, and works in the direction of the form. For even if the latter account could be completed, it would not yield the fully perspicuous understanding we seek of the matter of the composite. It could not tell us what blood was, why it needs the constituents it has, or why they have to be organized as they are. The 'bottom-up' account would fail to specify essential features of the matter of blood: what is required for the relevant goal. It could only describe in non-essential terms what the matter in question is like: hot, wet, etc. It could not offer the type of intelligibility provided by the top-down, form-first, approach.

---

[43] There is, nonetheless, more to the specification of the matter in question than the bare idea of its potentiality to be enformed. For Aristotle introduces the idea of matter as that in which no further changes or additions are required if the capacity is to be present (and the strictly correlative idea of there being changes or additions which will undermine that capacity and destroy the matter in question: 1049b10–11).

There is a further difference between Aristotle's hylomorphism and versions proposed by many neo-Aristotelians today. It concerns the ontological nature of forms. For Aristotle:

[ACTUALITY] Forms are actualities (*energeiai*), not merely capacities. The soul, an efficient cause, is defined as the first actuality of a body capable of living.

On his view, to be a human is to be capable of acting in the way which is characteristic of humans. The form (being a human) is identified with being capable of acting in given ways. But to be capable of acting is not itself a capacity: it is to be such as to be capable of so acting. The form itself is to be compared with being capable of speaking French, the state a person is in when they have learned French and are capable, here and now, of speaking French. The latter is not itself a capacity to speak French here and now which those people have. It is the way people are when they are capable of speaking French: they are such as to be capable of doing so. The human form is the way we are when we are capable of engaging in the activities which are characteristic of humans: nutrition, perception, desire, thought, and the rest. Forms, so understood, are the ways things are when capable of their characteristic activities.[44]

If Aristotle subscribed to [ACTUALITY], the human form cannot be properly understood as:

(i) a power or set of powers (or capacities),
(ii) a power or set of powers which are essentially manifested, or
(iii) a power to unite powers which depend on cooperative manifestation of other powers.[45]

His forms are not, when fully analysed, capacities but actualities: being such as to be capable of living (in Aristotle's terminology, the first actuality of a natural body capable of life). In the case of a human, the actuality in question will be

---

[44] For further discussion: see Chapter 4, Section 3. In this account, the 'actualities' *energeiai* of natural substances are analogous to the *energeiai* of capacities for change. The latter are activities (such as seeing) or processes, the former the way things are (their way of being) when capable of certain activities. In *Metaphysics* Θ, Aristotle, so understood, introduced capacities for processes and activities to provide the basis for introducing a different, but analogous, feature of substances: the way they are when they exist. To refer to their 'way of being' is to refer to the way they are in virtue of which they are capable, here and now, of certain activities or processes. For further defence of this reading of central aspects of *Metaphysics* Θ, see Peramatzis and Charles (forthcoming).

[45] William Jaworski develops the second suggestion (2016: 97–8), Michael Rea the third in his essay (2011: 241–58). Kathrin Koslicki (2018: 354–5) discusses a variety of ontological options: relations, properties, activities, powers, without committing herself to any one of them. However, clarity on this point may finally be required to spell out her description of forms as 'structural components' (2008: 252) or 'robust individuals' (2018: 354f.). Robert Koons raises a number of important questions about the unity of forms in his essay (2014: 151–78).

being such as to be capable, as presently constituted, of living in the distinctively human way. Being capable of doing something is not itself a capacity. It is to have the capacity in question.[46]

(i)–(iii) fail to capture Aristotle's thought in a different way. The relevant form (in this case the soul) needs itself to be a unified entity, not a collection of other entities. The capacities in question (to eat, perceive, move, and desire) need to be integrated in a nutritive-perceptive-reasoning soul. To be a human is to be capable of integrated nutritive-perceptive-reasoning activities of this kind. This is not to be understood in terms of a further power which (somehow) unites other independently defined powers so that they co-operate in some favoured way. Instead, in the human case, the relevant powers for nutrition and perception are modified, or determined, by belonging to a nutritive-perceptive-reasoning soul. Our type of nutritive soul is determined by its being the nutritive soul of a perceptual and reasoning being. (i)–(iii) fail to satisfy Aristotle's [UNITY] condition or to do justice to the distinctive conceptual resources he deployed (as we saw in Chapter 6) in satisfying it.

This point needs careful statement. While being such as to be capable of acting in the ways specified may require us to be structured or organized in given ways, the form, being such as to be capable of so acting, is what explains why we are structured in a given way. It would be better to describe the form, being capable of so acting, as the 'structurizer': that which requires the relevant structure to be present. It is because of the form's presence that our bodies are structured as they are. The human form, so understood, is not itself a bodily structure. Being capable of acting in the way humans do is definitionally prior to the structure which being capable in this way requires.[47] Being capable of the relevant activities will itself be being inextricably enmattered in the way the relevant capacities are. Indeed, to be capable in this way is essentially to be a given way materially: to be heavy or bulky and of a given material shape, the way required to be capable of acting on and interacting with other objects. Forms of this type, we can now see, will be

---

[46] At this point, I address the question raised, but not settled, in Chapter 2, Section 9: are forms best understood in terms of capacities or actualities, such as the way things are when capable of activities?

[47] Aristotle drew a similar distinction in discussing the harmony theory: 'harmony' may refer to the harmonizer (a formula that induces harmony) or to what is harmonized (such as the notes which instantiate that formula): see *De Anima* A.4, 407b30–3. Kathrin Koslicki captures the idea of the 'harmonizer' when she writes: 'we may thus think of an object's formal components as a sort of recipe for how to build wholes of that particular kind (2008: 172). Her account faces, as she acknowledges (2008: 252, n. 19), a serious challenge in accounting for the unity of the resulting compound. If it is composed of form and matter as *quantitative parts* (as defined by principles of quantitative composition), and the form is a *proper part* of the whole in which they are present, what unifies the form and the matter? (This is a version of Aristotle's own regress argument in *Meta.* Z.17, 1041b19ff.) For a critical discussion of Koslicki's subsequent attempts to address this problem, see: Peramatzis (2019: 235–45).

inextricably enmattered: they are to be identified with being capable in these specific material ways of certain inextricably enmattered activities.[48]

If Aristotle's forms are defined in this manner, they will not be defined, at least without serious qualification, as activities, such as the activity of living.

This is because talk of 'activity', taken literally, prompts further questions: what is the activity which is being a stone or a mountain, let alone a house or an axe? What is gained by describing the way of being characteristic of a stone or a house in terms of 'activity' (*actus*) as Thomas Aquinas once suggested? Indeed, why is being a human or being an axe an *activity* (or an *act*) at all? Isn't something's being an axe, or a mountain or a stone, simply its being capable, as things stand, of certain activities?[49]

Aryeh Kosman has recently developed Aquinas' suggestion, writing:

The activity of a thing being what it is...is its substance being, its ousia.
(2013: 182)

In his view, being a human or being an axe is being active, engaging in an activity analogous to end-inclusive activities such as seeing. In spelling out his idea, Kosman talks of objects 'busy being' what they are and, more generally, of their 'self-determining', 'self-expressive' activity, and 'self-manifesting' activity. It remains natural, however, to ask: what is involved in 'being busy' being an axe, mountain, or stone? Surely stones simply exist as stones. What is the explanatory value of the further, elusive, addition of the activity of being?

The case of being an animal may initially seem more congenial to Aquinas' suggestion. Kosman correctly notes that a dog's being active ('being busy') as a dog is not to be identified with its actually engaging in those activities which are characteristic of a dog: breathing, digesting, or seeing. Something can be a dog and not be actively engaged in any of these (at least for a short time!). Nor is 'busy being' a dog to be identified with its *capacity* to engage in breathing, digesting, or seeing. As Kosman accurately notes, to be a dog is to be capable of these and

---

[48] The way in which cricket balls or car tyres are circular may be defined partly, but not wholly, in terms of their capacity to roll. Their so-called 'categorical' features (such as being of a certain weight or density) also need to be added to define their distinctive way of being circular. There is no reason to define their way of being circular solely in terms of their being capable of roll (or as that plus a definitionally independent, pure, mathematical idea of circularity). Their relevant dispositional and 'categorical' features are, it seems, inextricably connected in definition. For some initial discussion of this problem, see my essay on topical matter (2000b: 89–110). Its full resolution requires a further study.

[49] Without a clearer articulation of Aquinas' idea, one may suspect that he was misled by Albertus Magnus' (apparently somewhat broad-brush) translation of both '*entelecheia*' and '*energeia*' by the same Latin term '*actus*'. Indeed, some might think that his (mis)translation led directly to later talk of the 'unbearable lightness of being', matching the evanescent lightness of the type of activity presupposed!

other activities. The relevant way of living is not itself a capacity: it is being alive in such a way as to be capable of acting in these ways.

So far, so good: but what, if anything, is added by Aquinas' talk of a distinctive activity (or act): the activity of living? What is this beyond the fact that dogs, when they are alive, are capable of engaging in certain activities? Why add a further activity, the activity of living, to account for their continued existence? Is this an activity too many?

Being alive as a dog (or indeed being a dog) need not, it seems, itself be an activity (understood as an act). While it may be described as an '*energeia*', this does not make it an act of any type. Being a human, I have suggested, consists in being such as to be capable (in the integrated way sketched in Chapter 6) of certain activities. This is neither an activity (like seeing or walking) nor the capacity to engage in those activities, although it is analogous to activities of this type.[50] It is the way we are when we are capable of those activities. If the form in question is, as I have argued, essentially enmattered, being human must be an essentially material way of being alive if it is to be a per se cause of our bodily actions and movements. Nothing is added by describing this as 'an activity'.

7.7 No longer credible?

Aristotle, I have suggested, is not an advocate of non-reductionist materialism, functionalism, or any of the forms of neo-Aristotelian hylomorphism discussed. However, even if these 'modernizing' approaches misrepresent Aristotle's actual position, it may be that they are the most that today can be salvaged from its wreckage. Maybe he is to be seen, in the most charitable light, as offering some remarks which point forward to one of these later, more sophisticated, theories. Perhaps the other distinctive aspects, which I have emphasized in this chapter, are simply no longer credible.

In Chapter 8 I shall seek to address these concerns and some aspects of the distinctive post-Cartesian mindset that motivates them.

---

[50] Aristotle indicates that he is pursuing this as an analogy in *Metaphysics* Θ.6, 1048b7–10. For discussion of the analogical approach, see Stephen Menn (1994: 73–114), Charlotte Witt (2003), and my (2018: 860–71).

8
Aristotle's Undivided Self

8.1 Two inextricability theses

Aristotle's philosophy of mind, I have suggested, is non-Cartesian. The activities and capacities characteristic of anger, desire, and perception cannot be defined, in his account, in terms of two definitionally separate psychological and physical components. The relevant phenomena, ones 'common to body and soul', are essentially and inextricably psycho-physical.

Aristotle's viewpoint is, in fact, radically non-Cartesian. It is not that he adopts a standard non-Cartesian option (whether some version of materialism, either reductive, eliminative, or non-reductive, functionalism or neutral monism). He challenges the way that Descartes formulated our mind–body problem. This is because, in his account:

[A] there are no purely psychological features essential to being angry, perceiving or desiring defined without explicit reference to some specific internal physical features or capacities;

[B] there are no purely physical features or capacities essential to being angry, perceiving or desiring defined without explicit reference to some relevant psychological features.

From this viewpoint, the Cartesian mind–body problem is badly set up. It is not, as many believe, a properly formulated problem to be solved by a good theory, were one ever to become available. Nor is it a genuine problem so difficult that no human mind can resolve it.[1] Still less does it require the introduction of a mysterious, non-scientific, pan-psychic, view of matter,[2] or a special type of neutral stuff which is neither physical nor psychological but from which both (somehow) follow.[3] These conventional responses address what they take to be a well-set-up problem, framed in terms of the two-component view of the relevant phenomena. Aristotle, I have argued, rejects this two-component mindset. There are not, in his view, two definitionally separate components, one purely psychological, one purely physical, about which we can ask: how are they to be connected? Since the basic phenomena are themselves inextricably psycho-physical, this

---

[1] Colin McGinn (1990).   [2] As Galen Strawson conjectured (2006).
[3] Bertrand Russell (1921) and David Chalmers (1996).

The Undivided Self: Aristotle and the 'Mind–Body Problem'. David Charles, Oxford University Press (2021).
© David Charles. DOI: 10.1093/oso/9780198869566.003.0009

question simply does not arise. From his perspective, the reason why there are no good answers to our mind–body problem is that it is not, in the form we have received it from Descartes, a genuine question. It may be best regarded as a 'pseudo-problem'.

Aristotle's first thesis challenges the suggestion that being angry, desiring, and perceiving are purely psychological phenomena, essential aspects of which are to be defined without explicit reference to any specific type of internal bodily capacities. According to [A], while the capacities and activities involved are essentially psychological, they cannot be defined without explicit reference to specific types of physical features of the body. There is no neutral way to define them. Phenomena, which we ordinarily regard as psychological, are in the way explained inextricably psycho-physical. Their forms, to use Aristotle's terminology, are essentially enmattered.

To see the impact of Aristotle's ideas, consider the following admirably clear formulation of our post-Cartesian mind–body problem:[4]

(1) The mind is a non-physical phenomenon.
(2) The body is a physical phenomenon.
(3) The mind and body interact.
(4) Physical and non-physical phenomena cannot interact.

From Aristotle's perspective, since the relevant 'passions and actions common to body and soul' are inextricably psycho-physical, there is no difficulty in accounting for their interaction. He rejects (1). In his view, the capacities and activities that define the mind are inextricably psycho-physical, although, unlike bodies, they are not composed of material, spatially divisible, parts. But nor are the bodily capacities to run and to fall or the running and falling which result. Further, although the body in question is made up of spatially divisible parts (and, as such, a physical phenomenon), it is to be defined, in Aristotle's account, in terms of the same inextricably psycho-physical capacities and activities which define the mind. Aristotle, characteristically, might regard (2) as 'in one way true' (a human body is spatially divisible into material bits) but 'as in another way false' (since that body is defined in terms of its psycho-physical capacities and activities).

Aristotle's second thesis strikes us as problematic. Wouldn't he have been better advised to maintain [A] but reject [B], taking perceiving and desiring, for example, as inextricably psycho-physical activities which rest (in some way) on underlying purely physical ones? Doesn't he, in defining the latter as essentially psycho-physical, pay too high a price to avoid the threat of the resulting bodily actions being over-determined by independent causes? Some may suspect that

---

[4] Jonathan Westphal (2016: 1). This formulation is a modified version of one initially proposed by Keith Campbell (1984).

my earlier talk, in the case of anger, of 'physical tension' or 'adrenalin rushes' introduces precisely the type of purely physical feature at issue. Isn't Aristotle's second thesis, as presented here, undermined by the very considerations adduced here in its support?

To understand Aristotle's viewpoint, it may be helpful to consider, once again, the case of weaving: in his account, this activity is an instance of pulling and pushing, both types of physical interaction with the world. However, what makes an action (type) one of weaving is that it is a specific type of pulling and pushing: one that realizes the skill, or capacity, of the weaver. One cannot define the types of pulling essential to weaving without reference to the skill and goals of the weaver. (If someone were to move in the way the weaver does—perhaps as some form of St Vitus' dance—unguided by the relevant skill and goals, they would not be weaving.) While weaving is a determinate type of pulling, there need be, in his view, no underlying specific type of determinate purely physical process (or activity), defined independently of the relevant skill, on which it rests. Furthermore, no particular (or token) purely physical process of this type is required to play an essential grounding role in his account of the particular act of weaving. The physical processes (whether type or token) that occur are essentially psycho-physical, the realization of a psycho-physical capacity to weave. Were a process to occur which appeared physically the same but had a cause other than this skill (whether as part of a nervous attack, a cosmic fluke, or as the result of the intervention of a brain surgeon manipulating the weaver's arms or brain while she slept), it would not be a process of the same type. Further, since the particular processes at issue are individuated in terms of the capacities from which they spring, the particular (or token) processes would have been different had they not been the realization of the goal-directed capacity, or skill, of the weaver.

In a similar way: in the case of anger, the type of adrenalin rush will, if we apply the same model, be defined as the type of phenomenon it is by explicit reference to the psycho-physical capacity, to be angry, from which it issues. If an apparently similar type of adrenalin rush were to have occurred that had been initiated and controlled by a different capacity (such as a capacity for fear or to be thrilled by opportunity), it would not have been an adrenalin rush of the same specific type. While these varying types of adrenalin rushes may share many similarities, they differ in that they are manifestations of distinct psycho-physical capacities. The relevant psycho-physical capacities, essential to the identity of the processes, have different goals and are prompted by different types of perceptions. The capacity for anger, for example, is 'triggered' by perceived insult and its resulting activity is directed towards achieving revenge. This capacity cannot be adequately defined, in Aristotle's account, in terms simply of the purely physical features involved.[5] It

---

[5] In Aristotle's account, the psycho-physical types (such as desiring-revenge-in-the-heat-involving-way) and the underlying 'physico-psychic' types (such as revenge-directed heat) are definitionally

is an essentially goal-directed capacity. Further, the particular activities that result from it are essentially realizations of the psycho-physical capacity for anger. They spring from and are guided by the goals of that capacity and are successful when (and only when) they achieve them.

Nevertheless, Aristotle's position is not seen as a live option in most current discussions. Have [A] and [B] been refuted? Is his simple theory of the relevant phenomena, the basis for his definition in terms of their forms, simply preposterous, frankly incredible? In addressing these questions, I shall examine some arguments that, if convincing, would justify the wholesale rejection of his ideas.

My approach in this chapter is not primarily historical. I shall not examine the specific arguments that led Aristotle's successors, whether Stoic, Epicurean, neo-Platonist, or Cartesian, to reject his account (in the precise form they presented them). Nor shall I investigate the ways that Aristotelian commentators, some influenced by neo-Platonism, modified his views to accommodate ideas drawn from some of Aristotle's critics. A historical study of this type is of major philosophical interest, showing how Descartes and others actually came to formulate our own 'mind–body' problem in terms of two definitionally separate phenomena: mind and body.[6] However, my present aim is to consider some arguments that can be used to challenge Aristotle's distinctive viewpoint (as I have interpreted it), even if they are not precisely in the form deployed by his successors. My goal, it should be noted, is only to show *in outline* how a defender of Aristotle's viewpoint might respond to them, using (as far as possible) the resources he developed in his discussion of the topics considered in Chapters 2–6. It is not to spell out, let alone defend, a fully articulated neo-Aristotelian account of the relevant phenomena.

It may be helpful, at the outset, to note that Aristotle's account, as interpreted here, is similar in some respects to three more recent proposals. Peter Strawson in *Individuals* described (human) persons as individuals of a certain unique type: one to which must be ascribed both consciousness and corporeal characteristics (1959: 104). While he focused mainly on what is required to *attribute* states of consciousness to a person, not on the metaphysical issue of what it is (e.g.) for a

---

interconnected. One might regard them as type identical. Or alternatively, they could be defined as distinct but inter-defined types of activity. Given that they are inter-defined, necessarily co-occurring realizations of the same capacity with the same goal, the first view may appear preferable. However, for all that has been said, they could be separate activities with differing definitions. One might regard them as type identical. Or alternatively they could be defined as distinct but inter-defined types of activity. It is not clear that Aristotle finally made up his mind on this issue. See p. 231, n. 11. A similar question appears to be left open in his account of process identity in *Physics* Γ.3, which I discuss in (2015: 186–205). Indeed, it may have been, in his view, a side issue.

[6] This type of investigation will be conducted by a number of authors in a collection of essays, *The History of Hylomorphism*, Oxford University Press, forthcoming.

person to perceive or be angry, some of his most direct positive arguments depend on understanding actions such as coiling a rope, playing ball, taking a catch, and going for a walk (like weaving) as essentially and inextricably psycho-physical.[7] In this he, like Aristotle, points to activities that appear to resist decomposition into distinct psychological and physical processes. However, Strawson did not apply his account to the range of activities (such as perceiving or desiring) that Aristotle considered or seek to define them or their subjects as inextricably psycho-physical (in the manner of the snub-like).[8] This is perhaps why Strawson was willing, at certain points, to entertain seriously the possibility of disembodied existence.[9] Further, in his later writings, Strawson came to advocate a dual-aspect account in which definitionally distinct psychological and physical properties are attributed to persons as he conceives them.[10]

Another approach that, in certain respects, resembles Aristotle's was initially proposed by Susan Hurley and Andrew Clark, and has subsequently been developed by those who emphasize the importance of 'embodied cognition'.[11] They see many features of cognition and cognitive processing as dependent upon characteristics of the physical body of an agent. This viewpoint is, at a general level, similar to Aristotle's. However, in his account, the body is not simply a causally necessary condition for anger or perception. Instead, the latter capacities and activities are inextricably psycho-physical: one cannot define the type of desire or perceptual discrimination involved without explicit reference in their definition to the body. This is how he accounts for their distinctive causal power. The body, so understood, is not simply a *constraint* on cognition or a *regulator* of cognitive activity, which ensures that cognition and action are tightly coordinated. In Aristotle's view, the type of cognition characteristic of perception or desire at issue cannot be defined other than as inextricably psycho-physical. Nor, it should be noted, can the relevant bodily states be defined without explicit reference to these psycho-physical phenomena. Aristotle is, at the very least, proposing, and developing, a radical version of the embodied cognition thesis, and doing so on the basis of a distinctive set of causal and metaphysical considerations.[12]

Aristotle's position is also, it should be noted, similar to some formulations of neutral monism.[13] Indeed, if the latter is understood as the purely negative thesis

---

[7] Strawson (1959).   [8] As discussed in Chapter 2.   [9] In Strawson (1959: 115–16).

[10] Strawson did not engage in detail with issues concerning the causal role of the two aspects thus isolated. Brian O'Shaughnessy argued (in a somewhat similar vein) that all bodily actions are psychological phenomena in his book (1980: II. 195ff.). However, it is difficult to distinguish his final view, as formulated, from a form of (Davidsonian) token-identity theory.

[11] Susan Hurley (2002) and Andrew Clark (2008).

[12] There are also major differences between these accounts and Aristotle's understanding of the relevant bodily states. In Aristotle's view they are, as I have emphasized, defined as inextricably psycho-physical, not as purely physical.

[13] I am indebted to Jonathan Westphal for discussion of this issue. He defends a form of neutral monism in his book (2016) and assesses earlier versions proposed by Bertrand Russell, Ernst Mach, and David Chalmers.

that the purely physical and the purely psychological do not exhaust the range of states and properties relevant to an understanding of humans and other sentient animals, it is in substantial agreement with Aristotle's proposals. However, since many psychological and physical phenomena are, in his view, inextricably psycho-physical, he could not accept the further, positive, neutral-monist thesis: that both types of phenomena are grounded (in some way) in a further distinctive type of stuff that is neither physical nor psychological. There is no need, from his viewpoint, to postulate, in a quasi-scientific theory, a wholly new type of stuff to play this grounding role and then try to explain how the purely physical and the purely psychological are grounded in it.

8.2 The first inextricability thesis: the search for the purely psychological

Many are convinced that in perceiving, desiring, and being angry, there must be an essential purely psychological, or phenomenal, feature, defined without explicit reference to any internal physical feature or component. Some also believe that there is a purely psychological subject distinct from and definable independently of any physical, or bodily, features. One can separate in definition a purely psychological self or a purely psychological feature essential to anger or perception that, together with a definitionally separate physical part (or aspect), forms a complex union of physical and psychological components.

These views are inconsistent with Aristotle's. They treat phenomena such as anger as decomposable into two separately definable components: a desire for revenge defined independently of any specific internal physical components, and a distinctive physical feature (such as an adrenalin rush), defined independently of the psychological. From their standpoint, the central, Cartesian, question is: how are these two definitionally separate components combined when we are angry?[14]

One argument in favour of this anti-Aristotelian viewpoint focuses on the self. It challenges the basis of the Aristotelian picture. Descartes himself deployed one form of it. It begins (in broadly Cartesian terms) as follows:

1. I clearly and distinctly and completely understand myself to be a thinking, non-extended thing (and nothing else). [premise]
2. My essence is to be a thinking, non-extended thing and nothing else. (from 1)

---

[14] This difficult and controversial issue is discussed in, for example, Sydney Shoemaker (2007).

3. I clearly and distinctly and completely understand the body to be a non-thinking, extended thing and nothing else. [premise][15]
4. The essence of a body is to be a non-thinking, extended thing and nothing else. (from 3)

In this argument, the moves from 1 to 2 and from 3 to 4 both argue from the possibility of (clearly and distinctly) understanding myself as a thinking, non-extended thing (and nothing else) to the conclusion that my essence is to be a thinking, non-extended thing (and nothing else). However, Aristotle developed the resources to challenge these moves. He distinguished various kinds of separability: separability in thought, separability in definition, and separability in existence.[16] He further distinguished two kinds of separability in thought:

(1) A is separable in thought from B if and only if one can think of A without thinking of B.
(2) A is legitimately separable in thought from B in scientific contexts if one can think of A without thinking of B and no errors arise in one's relevant reasoning if one thinks of A without thinking of B.

Mathematical form (in *Physics* 19b32) is legitimately separable from physical matter, because no errors in mathematical reasoning arise from doing so. This case is contrasted with that of physical form, which, like snubness, cannot be separated legitimately in thought from physical matter. If one does so, errors arise in one's reasoning. One will, for example, lose the causal explanatory power of the enmattered form. Or, perhaps, one will fail to distinguish the type of form possessed by natural objects from mathematical form.

Aristotle deployed two different notions of separability in thought: one consistent with error and another, legitimate thought, in which no error results from the separation. He also developed two further, quite distinct, notions of separability:

Separability in definition: A is separable in definition from B if and only if A can be defined without essential reference as part of the definition to B

---

[15] Descartes' argument, it should be noted, continues in an attempt to establish the real distinction between me and my body:

4. The essence of a body is to be a non-thinking, extended thing and nothing else. [from 3]
5. No one thing can have two inconsistent essences. [premise]
6. Anything whose essence is to be a thinking, non-extended thing must be distinct from anything whose essence is to be a non-thinking, extended thing. [from 2, 4, and 5]
7. I and my body are really distinct things. [from 5 and 6]

Several of these steps would require analysis in a proper study of Descartes' philosophy. This argument and several others are discussed by Margaret Wilson (1991) and Gonzalo Rodriguez-Pereyra (2008).

[16] For a full discussion of these distinctions, see Michail Peramatzis' analysis of types of separability (2011: 59–63).

and

Separability in existence: A is separable in existence from B if and only if A can exist without B existing.

In effect, he distinguishes four distinct kinds of separability. Separability in thought does not entail separability in legitimate thought. In *Metaphysics* Z.3 and 11, Aristotle carries out thought experiments, which result in error. Although we can in thought separate pure matter and pure form, in doing so we fall into error: we lose our grip on the phenomenon we need for metaphysical understanding. Further, while separability in legitimate thought may imply separability in definition, not all types of separability in thought do so. Nor does separability in definition imply separability in existence. There can be, in Aristotle's account, necessary entities that are separable in definition even though, as necessary entities, one cannot exist without the other.[17]

It may be helpful, in considering the 'Cartesian' argument just presented, to focus on separability in thought, separability in legitimate thought, and separability in definition. The first premise in this argument is:

1. I can completely understand myself as a thinking, non-extended thing.

In support of this claim, some argue that I can have a complete and clear idea of a distinct thing that thinks (as Descartes himself seems to do in *Meditations* 5: 1985 ii. 78), and can see that it is not an extended thing. In this way, I can conceive that I exist, but no bodies do. At this point, Aristotle's question is clear: do we form a *complete* and *legitimate* thought of ourselves as a thing that thinks as a distinct thing? Is this a proper thought of ourselves?

Consider the case of anger. Although one could, in Aristotle's view, think of anger as a type of desire for revenge defined without reference to bodily states, this would not be a complete, explanatorily adequate, definition of anger. Instead, it would be an incomplete abstraction from such a definition. In his view, anger is not merely a desire for revenge but a hot, pain-driven, adrenalin-involving, type of desire for revenge. One needs to refer to these bodily features of anger in the definition itself to account for the desire's impact on the body, its onset, and its role in the causation of behaviour. If one does not do so, the resulting attempt at a definition of anger will be unsuccessful: it will, in Aristotle's terms, be a dialectical definition, 'empty and vain' (*De Anima* 403a2).

---

[17] The circle, for example, may be prior to the semi-circle (*Metaphysics* Z.10, 1035b10ff.) or the line to the triangle (*Physics* B.9, 200a17ff.). For further discussion of this issue, see Michail Peramatzis (2011: 46ff.).

Consider a similar question: is the Cartesian idea I have of myself as a thing that thinks a *complete* idea of myself? Or do I need, to have a complete idea of myself, to think of myself as extended and bodily: not just as a thinker but also as one who moves, gets angry, sees and tastes, and feels hunger? If I do, my idea of myself as a purely thinking thing would be an incomplete thought. It would not be the basis of a definition of the self in question. One would have abstracted from the real notion of the self, which is psycho-physical, and formed a purely psychological abstraction, that does not constitute the basic definition of the self. What remains cannot, for example, play the causal role that needs to be captured in an adequate definitional account of the self. Since error results if I define myself in this way, this definition is to be rejected. (See *Physics* 193b34ff. on similarly 'separated' definitions.)

Aristotle's opponent has a reply: I can, and indeed do, they will say, completely understand myself as a thinking subject without any thoughts provided by perception or emotions! Indeed, they may add: it is an accidental feature of me that I taste things, get angry, feel pain, and hear sounds. I could exist without having (or ever having had) sensory inputs, pains, emotions, and desires or even being capable of having them. However, all that said, the Aristotelian question remains: does his opponent's thought experiment deliver a legitimate case of separation in thought? Aristotle might agree that I can form a determinate idea of what it would be to exist in a purely mental condition, without incoherence, as a non-extended thinking being. Perhaps I can do this by abstracting from myself as the subject of perceptions, emotions, sensations, and actions, and, in this way, arrive at an idea of a subject of thought. But his question persists: is the subject, arrived at by abstraction in this manner, *me*: the very same subject I now am? Even if there is no incoherence in what is envisaged, is what emerges a surrogate, an abstraction from me, a purely mental subject that is non-identical with me? Is it perhaps an angelic replacement for me, something quite distinct from me? If it is, what is imagined will not be the basis for a definition of the type of self I am: a nutritive-perceptive-thinking organism. It will be a failed thought experiment.

It may be helpful to re-consider, once again, Aristotle's favoured case of snubness. One can, in his view, form a conception of concavity abstracted from, and defined independently of, noses. On this basis, we may come to have a determinate and coherent idea of a purely mathematical property of concavity. This is what one arrives at through a complex process beginning with abstraction from snubness. However, none of this shows that snubness is itself identical with mathematical concavity. One cannot use the latter to define snubness, since it is only a mathematical abstraction from it. Nor can one define snubness as the type of mathematical concavity that is situated in the nose. This is because thinking in this way leads to error since concavity, as a mathematical feature, cannot play snubness' role as the unified per se cause of physical change (see *Physics* 194a7ff.).

According to Aristotle, I should think of myself as, *inter alia*, essentially capable of locomotion, perception, hunger, and fear. However, the self envisaged by his Cartesian interlocutor is not in itself capable of any of them. It is not a per se cause of bodily movement, nor the subject of taste or smell, hunger or fear. In effect, his interlocutor has replaced our intuitive notion of self, as the embodied subject of these states, with something akin to a mathematical form—an abstraction. The self we have arrived at is not the one with which we began, but a thought-based abstraction, just as concavity is a thought-based abstraction from snubness. It is not legitimate to claim, on this basis, that I am to be defined as an essentially thinking, non-extended being. Indeed, I, the subject that plays the role in the world I do, cannot be defined, or legitimately thought of, in this way.

The interlocutor's viewpoint generates, as we have noted, the illusion of contingency. I, the thinking self, could have existed and not been me, the embodied self. How, one might even ask, did I, the Cartesian self, turn out to be me, this physical union of mind and body? But, for Aristotle, it is a mistake to ask these questions: the thinking self (so understood) is best understood as an abstraction from the self who moves and gets angry. It is not what I essentially am. In a similar fashion: concavity is an abstraction from snubness, not what snubness essentially is.

Consider, in a similar way, the case of anger. One can, no doubt, abstract from anger to the idea of a non-hot, non-physically defined, desire to avenge wrongs done to one. Perhaps we can imagine creatures who—maybe like angels—never experience anger and only desire to avenge injustice. However, what we grasp in thinking about such cases is, at best, an abstraction from anger, not anger itself. We can, using this abstracted idea, seek to generate the illusion of contingency: the thought that I could have been angry without being 'hot and bothered', without the process being defined as embodied in the way anger is. However, to do so is, from an Aristotelian perspective, to confuse something abstracted from anger with anger itself. This is because the latter is defined as a distinctively physical form of desire, a hot, tense, bodily, desire for revenge. Indeed, it must be defined in this way to play the per se causal role required of it.

Or consider the case of pain. We are sometimes inclined to think of this as defined solely by its phenomenological features, such as its painfulness.[18] However, from Aristotle's viewpoint, to do so is, as we saw in Chapter 6, to abstract from its roles as the per se cause of aversive bodily behaviour and the bodily effect of certain bodily states. Pain, so understood, is not defined solely by its phenomenological features. To focus exclusively on those is to abstract from pain, with its role as a bodily cause and effect, to a purely psychological analogue, *pain*, something that lacks the causal powers pain essentially has. The resulting thought of *pain*

---

[18] Saul Kripke suggested this in (1980: 152).

will, of course, generate the illusion of contingency. One could have been in *pain* and not been embodied. But this illusion arises from confounding the *abstractum*, *pain*, with the real thing. In the thought experiment, one is confronted, from an Aristotelian perspective, with an abstracted phenomenon that one mistakenly takes to be identical with pain and, on this basis, concludes that the latter itself is to be defined exclusively by painfulness, understood as a purely phenomenological feature of *pain*. The person who undergoes *pain*, it should be ceded, may well be unable to distinguish *pain* from pain. They may indeed fail to separate pain from something, with different causal powers, abstracted from pain: *pain*. In their case, the illusion of contingency arises because the thinker confuses an abstracted object with the original. However, the abstracted object is not itself pain (or anger or the self).

The apparently purely psychological features, on which his critic relies, are, from an Aristotelian point of view, themselves abstracted from the genuine, definitionally inextricably psycho-physical phenomenon.[19] It is because pain is, in reality, of this type that we ourselves define types of painfulness in terms such as stabbing, burning, piercing, and gnawing: terms that refer to the way in which our flesh, hands, and feet are stabbed, burned, pierced, or gnawed by physical objects. Specific types of painfulness, so understood, are defined in part in terms of our sensitivity to parts of our bodies being affected in these, or similar, ways: to one's hand being stabbed by a knife, one's foot being scorched by boiling water, or one's stomach being burned by acidic food. One cannot define the type of sensitivity involved in experiencing them without essential reference to bodily conditions of this type. Further, the types of sensitivity will be, given Aristotle's causal principles, essentially bodily. Bodily causes of this type have bodily effects. While one cannot define pain without reference to painfulness, the latter cannot be defined without explicit reference in its definition to bodily forms of sensitivity states and the bodily states which cause them. It is because this is so that pain and painfulness have the per se causal roles they do.

In sum: the arguments considered in this section do not compel us to reject Aristotle's view of anger, pain, or the self as, in the way suggested, inextricably psycho-physical. If we are permitted to take his view as our default position, we have been given no reason to give it up.

8.3 The search for the purely psychological continued: subjectivity revisited

Some may agree that the considerations so far adduced are not sufficient to require us to reject Aristotle's account. But, they will still insist, there are clear

---

[19] Or, alternatively, there is no such abstracted feature and we are confronted with the inextricably psycho-physical phenomenon, feeling pain, the self being angry, seen in an abstracted way.

cases of the required type of purely psychological phenomena. Isn't consciousness itself, it will be said, just such an essential purely psychological feature? Don't we encounter similar features in, for example, colour experience: in how colours strike us? Sydney Shoemaker once commented:

> experience having...phenomenal character would itself have to be physically realised, and this poses what I shall call the subjective explanatory gap problem. How is conscious experience of colour realised by a physical feature?[20]

David Chalmers raises a similar concern when he writes:

> It is widely agreed that experience arises from a physical base, but we have no good explanation of why and how it arises. Why should physical processing give rise to a rich inner life?[21]

Did Aristotle have the resources to address their concerns? In his account, as I have suggested,[22] the world contains sounds and colours, which we are able to discriminate. These are the per se causes of our auditory and visual experiences. We do not project colours or sounds on to a colourless, soundless reality on the basis of our purely subjective, mind-dependent, experience of (mental) colours or (mental) sounds. While the latter perspective may have commended itself to Galileo or Boyle, it was not one that Aristotle shared. What it is like for us to see colours is determined by the colours we see when all is going well: by how they impact on our perceptual systems through the medium of light.

It will be said: these remarks cannot be sufficient to account for our awareness of colours. We still need to address the 'hard' question by showing how purely physical processing gives rise to a rich inner psychological, phenomenal, life of the kind involved in experiencing colours. However, from Aristotle's viewpoint, we have already made a mistake when we pose the question in this way. This is because we cannot, in his view, define the relevant visual experiences in purely psychological terms. Nor can we adequately define them in a neutral manner, consistent with their being pure, and then ask how they are connected to the physical. Visual experiences are, in his account, inextricably psycho-physical: they cannot be defined without referring explicitly to specific types of physical, and internal physiological, features. More specifically they are a light-sensitive activity, the last stage in the activity of the colours of the object impacting on us.[23] Aristotle did not begin with the assumption that we have a legitimate definition of visual experience consistent with its being a purely psychological (and internal) phenomenon which (as a further step) needs to be located in, or generated from,

---

[20] 'Content, Character and Colour' (2003: 254).
[21] 'Facing up to the Hard Problem of Consciousness' (1995: 200–19).
[22] In Chapters 4 and 5.   [23] As we saw in Chapter 5.

a world of purely physical events and bodies. Instead, the experiences essentially involved in our seeing something red are, in his account, our inextricably psycho-physical responses to the colours of the objects.[24] Something's looking red to us is not, in his view, to be defined in terms of an internal, purely phenomenal feature which, in some way, arises out of a set of independent physical features, bodies, or events. Instead, it is essentially an inextricably psycho-physical light-based, response to, and discrimination of, redness, understood as a feature of external, physical, objects. One cannot adequately define this type of activity without essential reference (in the definition) to the relevant physical features, external and internal.

But does this Aristotelian response merely push the 'real' question just one stage further back? Isn't there, despite all that has been said so far, a purely psychological feature essential to visual perception: what it is like for the perceiver to visually discriminate colours or hear sounds? Isn't this exactly what is missing in Aristotle's account, rendering his definition of perception incomplete? A definitionally distinct, purely psychological element must be added.

Aristotle's account suggests a way to reply to this concern: one cannot, if one follows his approach, assume that we can properly define 'what it is like to be a perceiver' without essential reference in our definition to what is perceived (what is given to the perceiver through the medium: the colour of the rose), to how it is perceived via the relevant receptors and to how the perceiver responds to what it perceives.[25] Indeed, what it is like to be a visual perceiver will be inseparable in definition from visually discriminating and responding to certain properties of objects, their colours, on the basis of a distinctive perceptual system. It cannot be defined except in terms that refer to a psycho-physical activity of this type, one with its own pleasures and pains. Consider, by way of analogy, what it is like to weave, defined as engaging in the activity of weaving by discriminating and responding to certain properties of the wool and the loom and acting accordingly. One cannot, the suggestion runs, define what it is like to be a weaver except in terms that refer to these psycho-physical activities, with their own pleasures and pains. There is no purely phenomenal feature, what it is like to weave, defined independently of, and without essential reference to, these activities, to be added (as a definitionally separate component) to the definition of what it is to weave. Similarly, too, for perceiving, understood—like weaving—as ongoing inextricably psycho-physical activity. (I shall return to this analogy below.)

We are, no doubt, incapable of experiencing the sonar properties to which dolphins have access, lacking as we do their echo-locating discriminatory system

---

[24] Contrast the suggestion that, for example, looking red to us is to be defined wholly in terms of internal, purely psychological, phenomena. This suggestion permeates much of the discussion of the predicament of Mary, the colour-blind scientist, initiated by Frank Jackson in his essay 'What Mary Didn't Know' (1986: 291–5).

[25] See Chapter 5, Section 10.

and distinctive way of responding to their input. Perhaps we cannot imagine what it is like for the dolphin to engage in a perceptual activity of its type. But nonetheless, what it is like to be a dolphin-perceiver will be similarly inseparable in definition from its ability to discriminate and respond to certain properties via its type of perceptual system: to engage in the activities characteristic of the dolphin. When we define what it is like to be a dolphin, we refer to the properties it perceives and its capacity to discriminate and respond to them, even though only dolphins are able to experience and respond to those properties in that way. There is no additional purely phenomenal feature, defined without reference to these activities, which is an essential ingredient to be added to our definition.

One can, consistently with Aristotle's general approach, make a further concession: it may be possible (although it is less clear exactly how) to abstract in thought an idea of 'what it is like to be a dolphin', defined independently of the external properties to which dolphins are sensitive and their psycho-physical capacity to discriminate and respond to them. Perhaps we can abstract out a purely psychological, phenomenal, feature that, like concavity, does not causally interact with the external properties of the environment. However, even if this could be done, it would not follow that this is a special subjective, definitionally purely phenomenal, component, essentially present in dolphin experience. Indeed, there will not be if what is isolated in this way is something abstracted in thought from, rather than a distinctive actual component of, the dolphin's perceptual discrimination of objects and their properties. The phenomenal feature abstracted in this way would resemble mathematical concavity in Aristotle's discussion of snubness. If so, there is no reason to believe that a dolphin's discrimination of objects and sounds has to be analysed in terms of two definitionally separate components: a discrimination of external sounds and objects via their perceptual system and a further definitionally distinguishable real and purely subjective act of awareness. Indeed, this will not be the case if dolphin perceptual experience cannot be defined without explicit reference to external physical features and its inextricably psycho-physical capacities to discriminate and respond to them.

In sum: Aristotle's account points to ways to address some of the challenges brought against his position. By distinguishing separability in thought from separability in legitimate thought, as he did, he can allow that we can form an abstracted notion of the self, visual perception, or anger while denying that the resulting separation is one in legitimate thought or in definition. Even if, in Aristotle's view, we can carry through the required thought experiments (concerning, for example, what it is like to be a dolphin), the results will not be the basis for, or a separate part of, a correct definition of the dolphin's perceptual awareness of its sonar world. Indeed, from his viewpoint, it is a mistake to suppose that there is a definitionally pure psychological, or phenomenal, component of this type that is an essential part of the relevant phenomena. To do so is to mistake something abstracted in thought for the basis for an independent ingredient in, or basis for, a definition of the phenomenon itself. (Remember the error attributed to Socrates the younger in *Metaphysics* Z.11, 1036b25ff.)

Aristotle's response depends on understanding perceptual experience as an essentially psycho-physical type of discrimination of external features of the environment. What makes certain experiences the ones they are is determined in part by what brings them about: colours and sounds existing in the world outside the observer. Indeed, in his view, we cannot define perceptual experiences, or types of perceptual experience, without essential reference to the external world, its colours, sounds, and tastes, and our psycho-physical responses to it.

Aristotle understands perceptual experience as a goal-directed (survival- or flourishing-directed) *activity* aimed at the discrimination of and reaction to external colours. Token instances of perceiving are essentially instances of this type. They are not defined basically as individual events, or sequences of such events, which are token identical with purely physical events. He does not focus on one such particular event (or sequence of events) of this type, seen in abstraction from the activity of visual experience, and ask: how does this physical event, taken by itself, ground what it is like for the dolphin subjectively to experience sounds? If we follow his approach, we will seek to understand 'what it is like for us to see red' by focusing on the ongoing psycho-physical *activities* in which we engage when we look for, discriminate, and track colours, including our pleasure- or pain-based responses to them. If we ask ourselves: what is it like to see North Wales from the top of Snowdon, we are imagining the activity of looking in many directions, turning round to do so, trying to see certain places with which we are familiar, noting how the colours of the landscape change as clouds gather and disperse or as evening draws on. We might imagine what it would be like to do so on a calm, warm summer's day or when the northwest wind blows so strongly from Ireland that we have to lean against it to stay upright!

It may be helpful, once again, to compare how we might answer this question (or, for that matter, what it would be like to see the Earth from Mars) with how we might attempt to say what it is like to weave. That question, Aristotle might suppose, cannot be answered without essential reference to one's hands, the loom, the wool, and one's skilled movements in turning the wool, looking for flaws in what has been woven, making sure that the stitches are even and the texture consistent. Answers to this 'what is it like?' question might include: it is stressful, exhausting, demanding, relaxing, requiring of concentration, enjoyable, repetitive, slightly boring. Aristotle's focus on activities suggests a distinctive way of defining 'what it is like for us to experience' sounds, colours, and objects. Using it, we can capture (what might be called) the flow of our consciousness as we engage with, for example, coloured objects in changing light and in differing contexts, depending on what they are next to or contrasted with. What it is like to see the redness of a Rothko picture or of a stained-glass window reflected on Cotswold stone at eventide is, after all, different from what it is like to see the redness of a fast-moving cricket ball coming towards us head high. Our experiences of their redness will differ because the objects seen are set in different visual contexts (against different backgrounds, in different light conditions) and we are looking for, and responding to, different things in the different situations. The experiences of redness differ because they are parts of fundamentally different activities: aesthetic or religious appreciation, batting to save one's life, etc. From the perspective Aristotle recommends, we can offer replies to the relevant 'what is it like?' questions that are dependent on the type of activity involved and the physical environment in which it falls: awe-inspiring, peaceful, terrifying, all-engrossing, requiring concentration, etc.

These replies are unavailable if we isolate a momentary token event (or sequence of such events), identify it with one in the brain, and then seek to explain, on this basis, what it is like to be the subject of the relevant momentary visual experience. To undertake this task is, from an Aristotelian perspective, to make the mistake of focusing on a moment (or sequence of moments) abstracted from the ongoing psycho-physical activities in which their subjects engage. This is a misstep because, in taking it, we surrender the resources we have to address the 'what is it like?' question when raised about the activities of seeing (or weaving), from which such 'momentaneous' events are abstracted. In effect, we replace readily answerable questions about ongoing activities with different ones about events (or sequences of events) which we have little, or no, idea how to answer. This is, in no small measure, because our perceptual experiencing of the world is, fundamentally, a type of activity, not a series of distinct moment-by-moment events. Indeed, this is why we should not begin our enquiry into what it is like to be a perceiver by isolating one such event and then asking: what is it like to experience it? We struggle to answer this question because our experience of the world is not of the type the question, so posed, assumes.[26]

8.4 Further arguments against essential embodiment

There is a further argument that is sometimes taken to show that the mind is essentially non-embodied. Descartes himself may have formulated a version of it in his Sixth Meditation when he wrote:

> There is a great difference between the mind and the body, inasmuch as the body is by its nature always divisible, while the mind is utterly indivisible.

---

[26] For a dissenting voice, see: Kevin O'Regan (2011: 108ff.).

8.4 FURTHER ARGUMENTS AGAINST ESSENTIAL EMBODIMENT

This remark, which he took to be conclusive, might be understood as follows:

1. Body is by its nature always, indeed necessarily, divisible and extended. [premise]
2. I—as a thinking thing—have no parts. I am indivisible by nature. [premise]
3. I cannot be identical with my body or any body, because a body is necessarily divisible and extended and I am necessarily non-extended. [from 1 and 2]

This argument would, if successful, establish that I am essentially a non-embodied subject. However, it too can be blocked using Aristotle's own resources. Consider the basis for 2. Descartes claims that the same subject is present, whole, and complete, in all cases of thinking, and indeed in willing and sensing and understanding. How are we to understand his claim? Here is one interpretation:

(A) The same power of thinking is present and used in each case of thinking or willing or sensing and I, the Cartesian self, am identical with this power.

Descartes once commented:

> No one before me has stated that the rational soul consists in thought alone—that is, the faculty or inner principle of thinking. (in his comment on Regius' Broadsheet)

From Aristotle's point of view, as we have noted, powers and capacities are, as are, as powers or capacities, spatially indivisible. This applies to the power to run or fall as well as to the power to think. But that which has this power may be divisible. Subjects with the power to run are spatially divisible, even though their power is not. The powers themselves may be material powers: ones whose activities are dependent on material laws and (or) require an enmattered subject. But this does not mean that the powers themselves are spatially divisible. Indeed, in *Metaphysics* Z.10 and 11, Aristotle was at pains to distinguish matter, understood as what is spatially divisible, from being a material or bodily principle, which is not spatially divisible. This was, I suggested, one of his major moves in those chapters.[27] The relevant principles were later identified either with material capacities or with being materially such as to be capable. But neither of these is divisible into spatial bits. To think otherwise is, it seems, to confuse, for example, being a horse (being capable of running etc.) with individual horses, made up of spatial parts. In so far as Descartes' arguments depend on the claim that I (as a subject) am identical

---

[27] See Chapter 3 for a fuller discussion of these texts.

with the power of thinking or a given way of being and so not spatially divisible, they should be rejected.

There is, however, an alternative way to understand Descartes' argument, that takes as its starting point:

(B)   I am that which has the power to think and nothing else.

But this, as is immediately clear, is precisely the premise we discussed above. What makes it true that I am to be identical with the subject that has the power to think and nothing else, but not identical with the subject that, at the same time, has the power to move, to taste, to move my body? As Princess Elizabeth pointed out: I am, it seems, more than just a thinker. She wrote:

> I am one who moves my body, and this power cannot be possessed by a non-extended thing, so there must be more to me than being a non-extended subject.

It is instructive to note Descartes' reply:

> One must separate the I which thinks (I*), from the I which moves. The mover I is the union of body and soul, and this is not identical with the I*, the thinker, although these are easily confused. What is capable of locomotion is the union of body and soul, but locomotion belongs to the union and not to me*, the thinker. Similarly, I am capable of perception, but that faculty does not belong to me but to my body or perhaps to the union of my mind and body. I have sensations of hunger and thirst and pain, but these are modes of thought produced by the body and its union with the mind.[28]

In his view, there are two distinct substances, I, the union, and I*, the thinker, that are both present and closely connected. The thinker is immediately aware of sensations or patterns of bodily response and in this differs from the captain of the ship who is not in the same way aware of the movements of the rowers or the sails in the wind. However, the thinker only has causal powers to move the body when it is part of the union, the body and soul.

Descartes' response to Elizabeth gave rise to well-known problems. Since he understood the self as a union of two definitionally separate components, he has to answer a further question: how does *my* thinking affect the other component in the union, the body? And here, as is well known, he ran into difficulties. The soul, he suggested, exercised its functions in the pineal gland (*Passions of the Soul* 132: 1984 i340). But how does it do it? How does something that is essentially

---

[28] For their correspondence, see Margaret Atherton (1994: 9–21).

non-physical exercise its powers by causing physical movements in the pineal gland? From Aristotle's point of view, it simply cannot do so. The self that thinks, understood as a pure, mathematical-style, form, cannot bring about physical change in the bodily member of the union. At this point, there is, from an Aristotelian viewpoint, an important misstep in Descartes' thinking. His thought experiment depends, as before, on abstracting from the I who moves and tastes and arriving at another *I*, understood as a pure thinker. From Aristotle's viewpoint, this is not, as we have noted, a case of legitimate separability in thought: error results precisely because the *I* which results is not capable of doing what I do. Descartes' experiment generated something by abstraction from the basic union (the I which moves and perceives) but what is thus abstracted (the thinking *I*) cannot play the required causal role.

In sum: Aristotle had, and deployed, the resources to challenge some of the arguments often taken to show that there is a purely psychological component involved in sensation, perception, emotion, and the self. Indeed, Aristotle's idea of the self, anger, and perception as inextricably psycho-physical is not seriously challenged by the famous thought experiments Descartes and others devised. From Aristotle's point of view, they encouraged a series of false turns precisely because they failed to distinguish clearly between separability in thought and separability in definition (or legitimate thought).

If these Aristotelian replies withstand criticism, there is no need to address Descartes' own mind–body problem: how can the purely psychological, or phenomenal, be embodied in, or arise from, the purely physical? The Cartesian thought experiments fail to establish that there is the essential purely psychological component envisaged in creating this problem. Indeed, from an Aristotelian point of view, the purely psychological, so constructed, is an illusion.[29] If Aristotle is entitled to take as his starting point definitionally inextricably psycho-physical activities, capacities, and subjects, he has the resources to block and defuse many of the arguments that generated Descartes' version of the mind–body problem.

8.5 The second inextricability thesis: the role of the purely physical

Is Aristotle entitled to his starting point? Can we today legitimately take it as ours? Before considering these questions, I shall examine another challenge to Aristotle's position. From a scientific perspective, it will be said, we now know that there are purely material or physical phenomena that underlie, and ground, all other phenomena. This way of thinking, which has origins among the ancient

---

[29] There may of course have been other reasons to invent the purely psychological, perhaps stemming from a concern with human freedom, but I shall leave those aside at present.

atomists, has become deeply entrenched in a generally shared picture of the world. If it is correct, has Aristotle done more than merely relocate the basic problem? Even if he can liberate us from the philosophical idea of the purely psychological, isn't there a new, equally pressing, question to address: how does the purely physical ground the inextricably psycho-physical? While this may not be exactly Descartes' own problem, it is one of a similar form. How is the psycho-physical grounded in the physical? How does the former arise out of the latter?

Many will wonder, once these questions have been raised, whether anything has been gained by studying the details of Aristotle's picture. It may seem to be, at best, a notational variant of a form of physicalism, in which the psycho-physical, and not the purely psychological, is grounded in the physical. Worse still, his account may seem to require us to abandon our hard-won scientific idea of a purely physical base, perhaps replacing it with a form of mysterious 'pan-psychism', in which the relevant matter is psycho-physical 'all the way' down to its basic constituents. There is, it might seem, no distinct viable Aristotelian option. At best, he offers a somewhat different way to raise a fundamental question, not a route to avoid it.

Aristotle's second inextricability thesis, as formulated above, states:

[B]   There are no purely physical features essential to being angry, perceiving, or desiring, defined independently of all the relevant psychological features.

The matter in question, in the case of anger, is the hot (or blood), defined as what is capable of being hot in the way appropriate for one desiring revenge. What happens is a determinate type of heating: a desire-for-revenge type of heating.

As we have seen, Aristotle did not accept the spiritualist view that the sense organs are (mysteriously) disposed to perceptual activity without any change in their matter.[30] The activities involved in anger or perception are, in his view, inextricably psycho-physical. He is further committed to the claim that an animal's sense organs, which are themselves material, have the capacity for psycho-physical activity. Indeed, it is because these capacities and activities are defined in this way that for Aristotle the actions of the angry are not over-determined by two independent sets of causes, one purely physical, the other psycho-physical. The relevant material causes are themselves essentially psycho-physical: defined in terms which refer explicitly to the psycho-physical goal of the agent (such as revenge if the agent is angry).[31]

---

[30] Compare the spiritualist interpretation.
[31] If there were processes which resembled those of the angry in certain respects (heat, etc.) but were not the realization of the same capacity (and so were for different goals), they would be processes of a different type.

How can this be? Isn't this just as mysterious as thinking of matter as simply disposed to psychological activity? Isn't Aristotle's view, *au fond*, a form of pan-psychism? Hasn't he paid too high a price in avoiding the threat of overdetermination: that of adopting what is today a frankly unbelievable view of the physical?[32]

Aristotle's initial reply is clear: the material organization of the sense organ, in the case of perception, is precisely the one required if it is to succeed in its characteristic activities and to achieve the goals that it has as part of its nature. Indeed, it is essentially matter organized in the way required for these goals. The matter of the sense organ is essentially capable of acting in the ways that the organisms require. The relevant process is the exercise of an inextricably embodied, goal-directed, capacity.

It is important to note that this response does not commit Aristotle to the view that the relevant matter is, as the pan-psychist suggests, at every 'downward' step capable (at that step) of life (or conscious activity). While 'proximate' Aristotelian matter is defined as matter organized in such a way as to be capable of conscious activity, the matter involved is (as was suggested in Chapter 2) a specific type of a more general type of matter which can (and will) be found in other non-sentient objects and is not itself defined in terms of its capacity for sentience. Further, while matter which is capable of being proximate matter is capable of being organized in such a way as to be capable of life, it is not—then and there—capable of it. It needs to be modified and altered so as to become capable of life.[33]

Aristotle (as was suggested in Chapter 2) regarded matter as a determinable made determinate by the relevant form so as to make the body or the material capacity in question. This is the view we saw him taking in *Metaphysics* Θ.7 and in Z.12, 1038a5ff. His account begins the upward ascent with basic elements, such as earth, from which comes first wood, then planks, and finally a house or a ship. At each upward stage, the initial matter is made determinate by being made progressively into wood or, if it is already wood, into a plank etc. until finally we arrive at matter for a ship. The plank which is made into a ship is not yet fully determinate: it is not yet determined which of its capacities will be realized—will it be part of a house or a ship? It is not, as we saw, that the particular plank disappears when it is made into part of a ship. Nor does it survive as a separate entity present 'underlying' the ship. It is rather that its capacity to be part of a ship has been realized.

---

[32] Some might make this point by suggesting that Aristotle's account of the '*physical*' is not an account of our notion of the physical. But the question remains: is his account of the *physical* one we can take seriously today?

[33] I leave aside a further issue: is there a determinate bottom level of matter in Aristotle's picture? Or does his account differ from that proposed by the atomists in taking matter to be always further divisible into ever smaller pieces? While this problem is of importance in considering the priority of form, it lies outside the scope of the present discussion.

In this picture, planks are determinate forms of wood and wood is a determinate form of still more basic matter. The latter has the potential to be wood, wood to be a plank, and the plank to be part of a ship. But it does not follow, in Aristotle's account, that the basic matter has the potential to be the part of a ship. Indeed, it will only have this potential after it has become a plank. More generally: if A has the potential for B and B has the potential for C, it does not follow that A has the potential for C. The notion of 'having the potential for' is, in Aristotle's view, not transitive. The basic matter does not have the potential to be part of a ship or, for that matter, part of a conscious substance. Matter, on this view, is not 'pregnant with consciousness' at each stage in the descending sequence. There is not pan-psychic matter at its base.[34]

Consider, once again, the case of weaving. Weaving is, as Aristotle emphasizes, the exercise of the weaver's skill in which the weaver pushes and pulls the loom and the wool in certain, inextricably psycho-physical, ways. Pushing and pulling are, in Aristotle's view, basic physical types of process that can be made determinate in varieties of ways. A tree can push against the house, the wind against the window, a weaver against their loom. These are distinct determinate ways or forms of pushing. What marks out the weaver's pushing is that it is governed by their skill: it is a distinctive type of goal-directed pushing and pulling. Since pushing and pulling are general types of physical processes, not all are goal-directed in the way weaving is. The general, determinable type (pushing) can be defined in terms independent of goal-directed activities of this type (let alone consciousness). Goal-directed pushing only emerges at the level of the specific or determinate form of the activity. The type of activity, so understood, is not pan-psychic 'all the way down'.

At this point, it is natural to ask: how can there be, as Aristotle requires, skill-based determinants of the physical in the way just assumed? Hasn't he simply smuggled in his crucial move in an ad hoc way, 'cobbling' together physical processes with psychological determining features? How can there be psychology-involving determinants for any kind of physical activity—or for that matter physical determinants of any determinable type of psychological activity?

Aristotle has a reply: since inextricably psycho-physical capacities are required to cause weaving, there must be skill-based determinants of the kinds of pulling and pushing involved in that activity. They are required as the unified per se causes of the unfolding activity of the weaver. Nor are the relevant capacities or resulting activities ad hoc unities. One cannot define, in his view, the capacity to weave without essential reference in the definition to bodily capacities of the

---

[34] Matter at the higher levels will, on this view, have at some time the potential to be the matter of living animals. But this need not require the matter itself, at that time, to be possessed of 'proto-life', 'proto-desire', or 'proto-consciousness'. All that is needed is that the matter has (at that time) the capacity to—under certain conditions—be the matter of, for example, a desiring, conscious, animal.

weaver (to move hands and arms, for example). Nor can one define the resulting movements without reference to the skill and goals that the weaver possesses. Given that there are inextricably psycho-physical capacities and activities of this type essentially involved in weaving, there are psychological determinants of the kinds of the required physical capacities and activities. More generally, the use of the determinable/determinant structure is underwritten by Aristotle's account of the emotions, desire, and perception as inextricably psycho-physical.[35] From his perspective, there is no need to address a further, apparently transcendental, question: how are psycho-physical capacities or activities of this kind possible? Since we know they occur, it is a mistake to trouble ourselves with the further question: how are they possible? We are, after all, not preoccupied with questions such as: how is weaving or anger possible—or, for that matter, as to how are cricket, rugby, and baseball possible. Nor should we be since we engage in and watch these psycho-physical activities as they unfold. (I shall return to this issue in Section 8.7 below.)

8.6 Isn't Aristotle's view a 'notational variant' of non-reductionist materialism?

It is natural for us to respond as follows: even if Aristotle regards particular cases of anger or weaving as inextricably psycho-physical processes (or activities), there must be some particular purely physical events, definable in physical terms alone, which co-occur with and ground them. If so, his account will seem to be an elaborated variant of a familiar non-reductionist materialist view and so face its problem: how do purely physical events ground emotional or perceptual awareness? From this perspective, his talk of processes, activities, skills, and capacities will only require us to phrase our own basic question in a slightly unusual form.

In addressing this concern, one should begin by making a concession. Consider once again the case of weaving, focusing on individual (or token) physical activities and processes. There is, one can agree, a purely physical description of what happens in any particular case simply in terms of the spatial position and movement of the weaver's arms, the loom, and the cotton. However, this description would be, from an Aristotelian viewpoint, a partial description of the particular inextricably psycho-physical action of weaving, omitting mention of the weaver's goals and skill-based responses to circumstance. It will not be a full

---

[35] Without this underpinning, it appears ad hoc to introduce the determinable/determinant structure to articulate the relations between the psychological and the physical. One needs, if this approach is to constitute more than a possible thought experiment, grounds for taking the psychological as a determinant of the physical (or the latter as a determinant of the former). The support offered by Aristotle's discussion of states 'common to body and soul' provides a way of underwriting aspects of Stephen Yablo's use of the determinable/determinant structure in 'Mental Causation' (1992: 245–80).

description of a separate physical process. A description of Penelope's movements in terms of spatial position, force, and velocity alone will be an incomplete description of the activity in which she is engaged. It is, in Aristotle's terms, an abstracted description of what she does—just as concavity is an abstracted description of the real-world feature: snubness.

Aristotle can make a further concession. He can agree (for the sake of argument) that whenever there is a particular psycho-physical *activity* of weaving, there is a sequence of purely physical *events* that actually occurs. However, this sequence of *events* will not be identical with the particular *activity* of weaving and cannot ground it in the way the materialist thinks it must. This very activity of weaving could, as we have noted, have continued for a longer period than it did or might have been interrupted. However, the sequence of physical events, considered purely as such a sequence, could not have done either. It lacks (what I have called) the 'modal depth' of the particular activity. If so, while the relevant sequence of events co-occurs with the activity of weaving, it does not ground it or determine its identity. Further, which sequence of events actually occurs depends on which psycho-physical activity unfolds, where the latter is the realization of the goal-directed capacity of the weaver. It is this which determines where the sequence of purely physical events begins and ends. It is not that there is a given sequence of purely physical events, with purely physical causes, which we describe in terms of weaving. The physical events that occur do so because of the skill of the weaver, which is the basic causal driver of what occurs. From an Aristotelian perspective, the psycho-physical activity of weaving is metaphysically basic: the physical events are what we see when we look at this activity in a given way, leaving out of the picture the goals and skill of the weaver. Such events might be thought of as derivative parts of the fundamentally psycho-physical activity that occurs. They are not the metaphysically basic components that ground that activity, the elements from which it is derived.[36]

Aristotle could, it should be noted, further accept that there will be a sequence of particular physical events present when the weaver weaves on a given occasion. He could also grant that, in the context of the activity of a skilled weaver, the psycho-physical properties of their activity supervene on the physical properties of the physical sequence. Perhaps he might take this to be a condition for arriving at a satisfactory, purely physical, account of what occurs.[37] However, both these

---

[36] This formulation is intended to be neutral between the two formulations of inextricabilism distinguished in Chapter 4, Section 8. The relevant [Type 1] material alterations may be seen either as accidental descriptions of essentially psycho-physical [Type 2] activities or as distinct changes, definitionally dependent on [Type 2] activities.

[37] If a given process of weaving is inextricably psycho-physical, it may turn out that there could not be two sequences of events which are identical in their physical features and unlike in their psychological features (if the physical and psychological features can be extricated). Indeed, it is because processes are essentially psycho-physical in the way suggested that relevant supervenience claims hold. More precisely it is because processes are psycho-physical and the activities of a fully functioning goal-directive

claims, if true, wll be grounded in the existence of the basic psycho-physical activity of weaving and the psycho-physical goal-directed capacity of the weaver. Aristotle's picture, so understood, need not reject the claim, sometimes taken as definitive of materialism: that the psychological, or the psycho-physical, 'supervenes' on the purely physical. However, from his perspective, this claim will be derivative from, and grounded in, the inextricably psycho-physical nature of activities such as weaving, being angry, perceiving, and desiring, and the capacities which generate them. From this viewpoint, we can understand why such supervenience conditionals are true (if they are) when we see them as concerning features satisfactorily isolated (or, in Aristotle's terms, abstracted) from fundamentally psycho-physical activities and capacities. However, it is the latter which are causally basic features of reality, the per se causes of what happens. If there are true supervenience conditionals linking the purely psychological and the purely physical (as in contemporary non-reductionist materialist theories), these will be true in virtue of the inextricably psycho-physical activities and capacities which he takes as his starting point.[38] Aristotle can, in this way, agree with the specific claims made by non-reductionist materialist philosophers but treat them as metaphysically derivative. If he is entitled to take these inextricably psycho-physical phenomena as the ontological basis of his account, nothing so far said need trouble him.

Aristotle can make yet another concession. It is fully consistent with our treating psycho-physical capacities, activities, and processes as metaphysically basic that we can isolate particular dated physical events and formulate laws governing them under their physical descriptions. Such laws will, of course, be incomplete by comparison with the principles which govern psycho-physical phenomena, just as laws governing heating and cooling or pushing and pulling are incomplete when compared with laws governing weaving or getting angry. But there can, in principle, be covering laws of a physical type that apply, albeit in a general and non-specific way, to all the phenomena at issue. Such laws will, of course, be consistent with the per se causal explanations Aristotle offers in terms of skill, capacities, and psycho-physical capacities. One can accept the existence of such laws, formulated in this way, while regarding psycho-physical capacities and activities as metaphysically basic.

Aristotle's critics will not be satisfied. In their view, since the underlying basic reality is constituted by purely physical events, states, and their properties, psycho-physical activities and capacities must be metaphysically grounded in

---

organism that one can project supervenience conditionals that will obtain in any world in which such creatures exist.

[38] See Chapter 7, Section 1.

them. This picture exercises a pervasive grip on their (and indeed all our) thinking. I shall consider two reasons why this is so. There may be others.

[1] Many suppose that there must be basic purely physical events present in these cases to accommodate their favoured 'physicalist' doctrine about the ontology of the world. They reason as follows: we should accept that, in the modern physicalist picture, the physical is a 'complete and closed system'. In their view:

[A] Every physical effect has a sufficient physical cause, and
[B] Nothing non-physical can causally impact on the physical.

However, Aristotle could readily accept both these principles. The psycho-physical is, in his account, a species of the physical. Every physical effect has a sufficient physical cause in that nothing wholly non-physical causally impacts on the physical. All the relevant causes are, as I have emphasized, inextricably psycho-physical. While [A] and [B] may lead us to reject a dualism, in which something purely psychological causes physical change, they do not—as stated—threaten Aristotle's position in which physical effects, such as the moving of the body, have sufficient physical causes, albeit psycho-physical ones. He can agree that nothing that is wholly non-physical (including within the physical the psycho-physical) can causally affect the physical. Indeed, this is fully consistent with his own positive position and his criticisms of Plato for presenting mathematical forms as efficient causes of bodily change.

What is controversial, from the Aristotelian point of view, is the next step: the 'physicalist' restriction of the principles governing the physical to ones defined in terms of a small number of basic physical forces. There are, in his picture, causal powers that are not reducible to, or fully comprehensible in terms of, a small number of basic physical forces. Indeed, in Aristotle's view, such psycho-physical powers are required to account for the role of desires and skills as per se causes of bodily movements. His alternative to physicalist reductionism is not Cartesian dualism. It is a view of the psychological as essentially psycho-physical, capable of causally interacting with the physical word in virtue of its being psycho-physical.

In Aristotle's account, as we saw in Chapter 2, pulling and pushing, heating and cooling are general and determinable types of physical interaction, some of which are made determinate in a psycho-physical way. If there are general physical processes like heating and cooling that are present in everything that occurs, these will be general and determinable features and regularities made determinate in some cases in the psycho-physical way he emphasized. It may even be, as suggested above, that everything that happens falls under basic physical laws governing the hot and the cold, pulling and pushing. But these laws will be made determinate and specific by biological and psychological phenomena. They will not be the specific basic purely physical laws the 'physicalist' requires.

[2] Some may agree that, if we are to make sense of the idea that a given sequence of bodily movements could have gone on longer or been interrupted, we need to refer to the skill of the weaver which could have guided it differently. However, they will add: what is now needed is a fuller account of their skill to be given in terms of the physical or physiological features that constitute it. Only if we can secure a purely physical account of this type will we have succeeded in properly understanding the relevant capacity and the activities that flow from it. If no such account can be found, our common-sense categories of skill and skilful activity are inadequate to the task of providing the level of understanding we need.

Aristotle has two responses. First, as already noted, he understood activities and processes as the realization of goal-directed capacities of the organism to which they belong. One can only define which activity it is if one sees it as one that manifests the weaver's skill and goals. There is no need, from his perspective, for there to be a further process or capacity defined solely in terms of physical theory that grounds the act of weaving. We can accommodate the causal role of the weaver's skill by regarding it, and the resulting action, as essentially and inextricably psycho-physical. While we can learn more about the physiological aspects of their skill and activities, these are to be understood as features of essentially psycho-physical phenomena. We are misled if we think that more is required.

Aristotle was, as I have noted, avowedly sceptical about the possibility of giving a reductive account, in purely physical terms, of the relevant skill. Many of his criticisms of his predecessors consist in his noting problems and difficulties in their attempts to carry through reductive accounts of this type. As he remarked: 'none of them penetrated below the surface or made a thorough examination of a single one of the problems; none made any definite statement about growth, except such as any amateur might have made' (*De Generatione et Corruptione* 314b1-3).[39] His doubts about their project would, I suspect, have been fortified by centuries of failure to reduce, for example, actions and perception to purely physical phenomena. Take, once again, the case of weaving: how, he asked, can one define the relevant activity without reference to the teleological goals of the weaver or their skill at weaving? It is not enough to say the latter activity is caused by the weaver's skill: it needs to be caused in a way that manifests their ability and know-how as a weaver. Recent experience, in detailed discussion of deviant causal chains, has suggested that we are still unable to define what 'the right way' is without reference to the weaver's skills and goals, features that outrun the

---

[39] On this occasion Democritus is exempted from criticism. Elsewhere, Aristotle criticizes his predecessors for beginning their theories 'at too great a distance from what has to be explained' (765b1-7) and for not giving specific per se causes of the effects they wish to explain (743a21-4, *De Partibus Animalium* 641b27-30), in terms which apply to them all. I discuss these arguments in my essay (1988: 22-4).

resources of basic physical theory. The best explanation of this long history of failure is, Aristotle might conclude, that the reductive project cannot be successfully completed.[40]

Reflection on Aristotle's view suggests a diagnosis of the reductionist project. From his standpoint, in our search of a better understanding of our inextricably psycho-physical activities we isolate and focus on (in his terms 'abstract') what we take to be their purely physical aspects and to seek to understand all their other features, such as their goal-directedness or perceptual know-how, in terms of them. But why believe, one might ask, that what is abstracted in this way is a definitionally separate feature of reality, not something isolated in thought alone? Further, what type of understanding is it that requires us to attempt to explain all psycho-physical features in terms of a set of basic physical ones, isolated in this way? What sets the standards for an adequate understanding so high that they can only be met in this way? It is, after all, this view of understanding that has driven the reductive project despite its long history of failure. Perhaps we would be better advised to begin with a less demanding understanding of the definitionally inextricable psycho-physical activities in which we engage and the capacities which enable us to do so. Why require more at the outset?

8.7 Diagnosis, resolution, and remaining problems

In this chapter, I have suggested that our mind–body problem, as we have inherited it from Descartes, rests on assumptions that Aristotle would, with good reason, reject. They include:

[1] An abstracted view of the purely psychological: the myth of a purely psychological component essentially present in cases of perceiving, desiring, and being angry. It was argued above that there are no such purely psychological features in these cases. What is at stake are essentially psycho-physical features and processes, not purely psychological ones. (Nor can these features and processes be adequately defined in ways that are neutral as to whether they are purely psychological.)

[2] An abstracted ontology that focuses on events, whether types or particulars, considered in abstraction from the processes and activities that generate them and from the capacities that are realized in those processes. In this section, I have

---

[40] Consider an analogy: Timothy Williamson's argument (2000) against reductive accounts of knowledge in terms of true justified belief based on their failure to block Gettier-style counter-examples. The failure of psycho-physical reduction has a far longer, and even more distinguished, history, extending back before the origins of analytic philosophy to Democritus and the early atomists.

emphasized that Aristotle's ontology is one of goal-directed processes, capacities, and activities, not of events as understood by modern theorists.[41]

In the grip of these two assumptions, we ask: how can we account for the purely psychological features abstracted in [1] on the basis of the purely physical events, isolated as in [2] and their physical properties? Once we have raised this question—how does something as remarkable as a state of consciousness, when understood as in [1], emerge from physical events in our brain, understood as in [2]—the phenomenon itself can still seem (as Thomas Huxley once remarked) as 'unaccountable as the appearance of the djinn when Aladdin rubbed his lamp'.[42] As Huxley predicted, we are confronted with a major explanatory gap between purely physical events, on the one hand, and purely psychological features, on the other, that we do not see how to bridge. Perhaps the best we can do, once trapped in this predicament, is to posit that the physical events with their purely physical properties necessitate in some brute, unintelligible, way the presence (or emergence) of the relevant pure psychological features (just as, in the myth, the djinn inexplicably emerged from the lamp!).

Aristotle's perspective is fundamentally different: in his simple theory, desiring and perceiving are defined as inextricably psycho-physical activities, not in the two-component way in terms of some purely psychological event (or feature) and some purely physical event (or feature). Indeed, they must be defined in his way if one is to account for their distinctive causal roles (efficient and teleological). We are misled when we mistake the two abstractions, captured by [1] and [2], for basic features of reality. While they may be determinate instances of a general, determinable, type of activity (or process) that can be defined without reference to sentience, there need be no determinate type of physical process (or activity) which grounds the relevant psycho-physical type. Nor need there be a determinate particular physical process that grounds the particular psycho-physical one. There may, of course, be incomplete physical descriptions of the type of psycho-physical process. There may also be a complete series of determinate particular physical *events* generated on the basis of the particular psycho-physical activity. But it is not the case that there is a physical event (or series of such events) that is the basis for, or grounds, the relevant psycho-physical process or activity.

The mind–body problem, as we conceive it today, rests on a further philosophical claim:

[3] What is physically basic, the basic components of reality, is what is metaphysically basic.

---

[41] For further discussion of this issue, see the essays collected by Rowland Stout (2018).
[42] T.H. Huxley (1886: 193).

If we can locate in any psycho-physical process or capacity some purely physical event, property or constituent, these provide the metaphysical basis of our account. But this is precisely what Aristotle rejected. In his view, metaphysical understanding depends on taking starting points which are fully intelligible and detecting, on their basis, explicable connections between the phenomena in question. Our enquiry, in his view, should begin with processes, activities, and capacities that we fully understand and from which we can abstract or otherwise generate, by intelligible means, further purely physical and purely psychological phenomena.[43] On the basis of our simple, defensible, and intuitively appealing theories of, for example, desiring and perceiving we can move towards an intelligible overview of the whole, seeing the purely psychological and the purely physical as abstractions from our starting point.[44] To postulate brute necessities linking the psychological and physical is, from his viewpoint, anathema to a proper metaphysical understanding. To achieve the latter, we need to understand how the physical, so understood, gives rise to the psychological. But this cannot be achieved by simply pointing to a series of irreducibly distinct types or levels of co-occurring phenomena (such purely physical events, structure, purely psychological activities) and claiming that one supervenes on another. We need to understand how the purely physical, defined in the way it is, can ground the psychological. Without this, our theories seem to resemble what Aristotle described as 'badly constructed tragedies', in which no one can understand how the early scenes give rise to the later ones.

The assumption that metaphysical explanation is a species of physical explanation was *de rigueur* when reductionist thinking held sway. In that milieu, the search for what is physically basic was seen as the same as that for what is metaphysically basic. The latter claim, however, is not itself a claim made in physics or any empirical science. It expresses a philosophical assumption that Aristotle did not share. Further, there is some reason not to embrace it when investigation based on it leads us to postulate 'brute', inexplicable, connections between the physical and the psychological. By contrast, an adequate metaphysical explanation of the relevant phenomena will, as in Aristotle's picture, present a thoroughly intelligible picture

---

[43] For some further defence of this view of Aristotle's project, see my earlier discussion (2000a: 357–62). He is, I suggested, committed to taking as basic the kinds and colours with which we engage in craft or in perception. There are limits to the extent to which we can travel from our original starting point while retaining our grasp on what is to be explained. The examination of these suggestions (both exegetical and philosophical) lies far beyond the scope of the present study.

[44] Aristotle's account involves, from the outset, teleological as well as efficient causal explanation. However, the basis for his view was, it seems, his willingness to take as basic psycho-physical activities and capacities for activity, individuated as they standardly are in terms of goals, and our ordinary ways of understanding them. His view, so understood, is not *based* on a general theoretical commitment (such as a scientific realist might entertain) to teleological principles as part of the best scientific theory of changes, substances, etc. Although he did hold the latter to be the case, this was the result of his taking as his starting point our ordinary understanding of the goal-directed essentially enmattered capacities and activities we engage and observe.

of perception, emotion, and desire as distinctive, inextricably psycho-physical, activities, our ways of causally interacting with a material world. His account, so understood, escapes the danger of presenting our bodily actions as overdetermined by distinct psychological and physical causes (without embracing epiphenomenalism or reductionism). It is, at the same time, an attempt to maintain the non-accidental unity of the causal agent, the inextricably psycho-physical subject of experience, thought, and action. Satisfying this latter metaphysical requirement is a further, driving, motivation for his account.

Aristotle, I have suggested, escapes the Cartesian mind–body problem because he was attracted to four ideas:

(1) A view of the psychological as, in the way explained, essentially and inextricably psycho-physical.
(2) An insistence that the ontology should be specified in terms of processes and activities, with events as derivative and secondary.
(3) The assumption that there can be general or determinable types of physical phenomena made determinate in psycho-physical ways.
(4) The contention that metaphysical explanation is not reducible to explanation in terms of basic physical components. There are other requirements, such as concern unity and intelligibility, to be met.

If we are entitled to accept Aristotle's starting point, as expressed in his inextricabilist theory of perception, desire, and the rest, we can address, and begin to defuse, some of the arguments that have been taken to undermine his picture. Or so I have suggested.

But are we entitled to begin where he did? His simple theory offers an intuitively attractive picture of our causal interactions in perception and action with the material world. It also maintains our standing as non-accidental unities, inextricably psycho-physical subjects of experience and action. At the same time, it avoids the apparently insoluble problems generated by our Cartesian mind–body problem while offering a diagnosis of the assumptions that produced it. It does not, or so I have suggested, require commitment to any form of pan-psychism. Still less does it require the denial of theses such as 'the supervenience of the psychological on the physical' with which we are now familiar. In effect, apart from its rejection of the purely psychological, it leaves nearly everything as it is, re-orientating our philosophical perspective on what is metaphysically basic in the interest of gaining an intelligible picture of the relevant whole. Isn't this success enough? What more should we legitimately require?

Aristotle's approach does not, it is important to note, free us from all problems. Many remain. I shall mention just two.

One arises naturally from the discussion at the end of Section 8.5: how did goal-directed organisms with their inextricably psycho-physical capacities for anger and weaving develop? How did psycho-physical processes, or activities, of the type we engage in come into being in a world like ours? These questions are particularly pressing for us since, unlike Aristotle, we approach these issues from an evolutionary perspective.

From an Aristotelian viewpoint, these questions are best seen as scientific problems about how living organisms capable of weaving developed from more primitive living organisms. As such, they are topics for palaeontologists, evolutionary biologists, and psychologists. We do not seem to be concerned about the intelligibility of the relevant transitions: just with how they actually occurred. There is not a further, distinctively philosophical, question to be addressed.

There is, of course, a further question: how did the simplest living organisms develop from non-living entities? Isn't this life–body problem, *au fond*, similar to the mind–body problem? What, if anything, has been gained by replacing the latter with the former?

It is tempting to reply: it is the task of biochemists and molecular biologists to address the life–body problem. There seems to be no conceptual difficulty in making sense of the transition from non-living to living phenomena. We do not sense an unbridgeable gap between the simplest living organisms (such as viruses, endoparasites, or the simplest bacteria) and the non-living bodies from which they emerged. Many are inclined to think that there is, as Aristotle himself thought, a continuum of living organisms between animals and plants (with some genuinely borderline cases).[45] Perhaps something similar is the case on the boundary between living and non-living phenomena. If so, there will be no further purely philosophical life–body problem: how are living organisms possible? There is no conceptual chasm, comparable to that between self-conscious thought and matter, conceived in terms of extension alone, which Descartes used to frame his mind–body problem.

However, if there is a remaining philosophical life–body question of this type at this point, it will need to be set up, and motivated, in terms fundamentally different from those used to formulate the Cartesian mind–body problem. A great deal of argument will be needed to establish that there is, at this point, a conceptually perplexing gap of the type Descartes (and others) took themselves to have established. We are, after all, accustomed to think of the simplest living organisms (such as bacteria or viruses) in 'bio-physical' (or bio-chemical) terms. The transition to such organisms from non-living phenomena may not strike us as mysterious. We may think that the latter simply have the capacity, in certain

---

[45] For a study of these, see Geoffrey Lloyd's essay (1996: 76–92).

conditions, to become living organisms. Further, it should be noted that the life–body problem, as I have introduced it, focuses on the way in which unified psycho-physical organisms originally emerged. It does not require us to define these organisms, once they have emerged, in terms of distinct purely physical sets of events or properties which ground co-occurring, definitionally distinct, 'living' or 'psychological' phenomena. Once formed, their natures may be (in the way explained) inextricably psycho-physical. If so, there is no need to address the question: how do the underlying purely physical states and properties, present in such organisms, ground, their co-occurring psychological states or properties? From the Aristotelian viewpoint, as understood here, this question does not arise.

A second major problem remains: how best to define the specific inextricably psycho-physical activities that constitute, for example, being depressed, angry, afraid, or sad. If Aristotle is correct, our investigation into, for example, mood or emotion should not be compartmentalized into a search for two definitionally separate components, one purely psychological (or functional), the other purely physical, and a further enquiry into how they can be intelligibly combined. An adequate taxonomy and proper understanding of these phenomena should define them as essentially and inextricably psycho-physical. Indeed, some have already begun to work on this project, taking as their starting points phenomena such as excitement, stress, anxiety, or disgust, which appear to resist analysis in terms of traditional two-component accounts.[46] Others have suggested that it is only by rejecting the latter style of account that we can explain why certain forms of clinical depression are equally well addressed by Cognitive Behavioural and drug-based treatments.[47] However, much is yet to be done.[48] There are many substantial questions to be addressed independently of the assumptions that have generated our Cartesian mind–body problem.

In conclusion: the study of Aristotle's simple and intuitive account of the emotions, desire, and perception offers a way to liberate us from the seemingly insoluble mind–body problem we have inherited from Descartes. It may allow us finally to replace this problem, and the unsatisfactory conventional orthodoxies it has generated, with a series of genuine problems for which we can reasonably hope—in time—to find illuminating solutions.

---

[46] For examples of steps towards such a theory, see Antonio Damasio (2000: Chapters 2 and 9) and Matthew Ratcliffe (2007).

[47] See the discussion in P.M. Nathan and J.M. Gorman (2002: 315–16).

[48] For an example of dissatisfaction with two-component theories of some psychiatric disorders, see Eric Matthews (2017: 345–57).

Bibliography

Aristotle: Texts, Critical Editions, and Translations

Beare, J.L. (1908), Aristotle: *The Parva Naturalia*, Oxford.
Corcilius, K. (2017), *Aristoteles: über die Seele: De Anima*, Hamburg.
Frede, M. and Patzig, G. (1988), *Aristoteles 'Metaphysik Z': Text, Übersetzung und Kommentar* (2 vols.), Munich.
Gallop, D. (1990), *Aristotle on Sleep and Dreams*, Peterborough.
Hamlyn, D.W. (1968), *Aristotle: De Anima II and III*, Oxford.
Hicks, R.D. (1907), *Aristotle: De Anima*, Cambridge.
Lennox, J.G. (2001), *Aristotle on Parts of Animals I–IV*, Oxford.
Morel, P.M. (2015), *Aristote* Métaphysique *livre Èta*, Paris.
Nussbaum, M. (1978), *Aristotle's* De Motu Animalium, Princeton.
Peck, A.L. (1937), *Aristotle: Parts of Animals, Movement of Animals, Progression of Animals*, Cambridge, Mass.
Peck, A.L. (1942), Aristotle: *Generation of Animals*, Cambridge, Mass.
Primavesi, O. and Corcilius, K. (2018), *Aristoteles* De motu animalium, Hamburg.
Rodier, G. (1900), *Aristote: Traité de l'âme*, Paris.
Ross, G.R.T. (1906), *Aristotle:* De Sensu *and* De Memoria, Cambridge.
Ross, W.D. (1924), *Aristotle's* Metaphysics (2 vols.), Oxford.
Ross, W.D. (1955), *Aristotle:* Parva Naturalia, Oxford.
Ross, W.D. (1961), *Aristotle:* De Anima, Oxford.
Shields, C. (2016), *Aristotle,* De Anima, Oxford.
Sorabji, R. (1972), *Aristotle on Memory*, London.
Torstrik, A. (1862), *Aristotelis De anima libri III*, Berlin.
Van Der Eyck, P.J. (1994), *Aristoteles: De Insomniis, De Divinatione per Somnum*, Berlin.

Secondary Literature

Ackrill, J.L. (1972–73), 'Aristotle's Definition of *Psuche*', *Proceedings of the Aristotelian Society* 73: 119–33.
Allen, K. (2016), *A Naïve Realist Theory of Colour*, Oxford.
Anagnostopoulos, A. (2010), 'Change in Aristotle's *Physics* 3,' *Oxford Studies in Ancient Philosophy* 40: 33–79.
Atherton, M. (1994), *Women Philosophers of the Early Modern Period*, Indianapolis.
Balme, D. (1987), 'The Snub', in A. Gotthelf and J. Lennox (eds), *Philosophical Issues in Aristotle's Biology*, Cambridge, 306–12.
Beare, J.L. (1906), *Greek Theories of Elementary Cognition from Alcmaeon to Aristotle*, Oxford.
Beere, J. (2009), *Doing and Being: An Interpretation of Aristotle's* Metaphysics Theta, Oxford.
Berman, B. (2017), 'Why Can't Geometers Cut Themselves on the Acutely Angled Objects of their Proofs? Aristotle on Shape as an Impure Power', *Methexis* 29: 89–106.

Berryman, S. (2009), *The Mechanical Hypothesis in Ancient Greek Natural Philosophy*, Cambridge.
Bodnár, I. (2004), 'The Mechanical Principles of Animal Motion', in A. Laks and M. Rashed (eds) *Aristote et le mouvement des animaux*, Lille, 37–47.
Bolton, R. (2005), 'Perception Naturalized in Aristotle's *De Anima*', in R. Salles (ed.) *Metaphysics, Soul and Ethics*, Oxford, 209–44.
Bostock, D. (2001[2006]), 'Aristotle's Theory of Matter', in his *Space, Time, Matter, and Form*, Oxford, 30–47.
Bowin, J. (2011), 'Aristotle on Various Types of Alteration in *De Anima* II.5', *Phronesis* 56: 138–61.
Bowin, J. (2012a), 'Aristotle on First Transitions', *Apeiron* 45: 262–82.
Bowin, J. (2012b), '*De Anima* ii.5 on the Activation of the Senses', *Ancient Philosophy* 32: 87–104.
Brewer, B. (2011), *Perception and its Objects*, Oxford.
Broackes, J. (1992), 'The Autonomy of Colour', in K. Lennon and D. Charles (eds) *Reduction, Explanation, and Realism*, Oxford, 421–65.
Brunschwig, J. (1979), 'La forme, prédicat de la matière?', in P. Aubenque (ed.) *Études sur la Métaphysique d'Aristote*, Paris, 131–58.
Burnyeat, M. (1992), 'Is an Aristotelian Philosophy of Mind Still Credible? A Draft', in M.C. Nussbaum and A.O. Rorty (eds) *Essays on* De Anima, Oxford, 15–26.
Burnyeat, M. (1995), 'How Much Happens When Aristotle Sees Red and Hears Middle C? Remarks on *De Anima* II, 7–8,' in M. Nussbaum and A. Rorty (eds) *Essays on* De Anima, Oxford, 422–34.
Burnyeat, M. (2001), 'Aquinas on "Spiritual Change" in Perception', in D. Perler (ed.) *Ancient and Medieval Theories of Intentionality*, Leiden, 129–53.
Burnyeat, M. (2002), '*De Anima* II.5', *Phronesis* 47: 28–90.
Campbell, J. (1987), 'Is Sense Transparent?', *Proceedings of the Aristotelian Society* 88: 273–92.
Campbell, J. (1993), 'A Simple Theory of Colour', in J. Haldane and C. Wright (eds) *Reality: Representation and Projection*, Oxford, 257–68.
Campbell, J. and Cassam, Q. (2014), *Berkeley's Puzzle*, Oxford.
Campbell, K. (1984), *Body and Mind*, New York.
Caston, V. (1993), 'Aristotle on Supervenience', *Southern Journal of Philosophy* 31: 107–35.
Caston, V. (2002), 'Aristotle on Consciousness', *Mind* 111: 751–815.
Caston, V. (2005), 'The Spirit and the Letter: Aristotle on Perception', in R. Salles (ed.) *Metaphysics, Soul, and Ethics in Ancient Thought*, Oxford: 245–320.
Caston, V. (2008), 'Commentary on Charles', *Proceedings of the Boston Area Colloquium of Ancient Philosophy* 24(1): 30–49.
Chalmers, D. (1995), 'Facing up to the Hard Problem of Consciousness', *Journal of Consciousness Studies* 2: 200–19.
Chalmers, D. (1996), *The Conscious Mind*, Oxford.
Charles, D. (1984), *Aristotle's Philosophy of Action*, London.
Charles, D. (1986), 'Aristotle's Ontology and Moral Reasoning', *Oxford Studies in Ancient Philosophy* 4: 119–44.
Charles, D. (1988), 'Aristotle on Hypothetical Necessity and Irreducibility', *Pacific Philosophical Quarterly* 69: 1–53.
Charles, D. (1992), 'Supervenience, Composition and Physicalism', in D. Charles and K. Lennon (eds) *Reduction, Explanation and Realism*, Oxford, 265–96.
Charles, D. (2000a), *Aristotle on Meaning and Essence*, Oxford.

Charles, D. (2000b), 'Aristotle on Matter and Change: A Study of *Lambda 2*', in M. Frede and D. Charles (eds) *Aristotle's* Metaphysics Lambda, Oxford, 89–110.
Charles, D. (2004), 'Simple Genesis and Prime Matter', in F. de Haas and J. Mansfeld (eds) *Aristotle: On Generation and Corruption 1*, Oxford, 151–69.
Charles, D. (2006), 'Aristotle's Desire', in V. Hirvonen, T. Holopainen, and M. Tuominen (eds) *Mind and Modality, Essays in Honour of Simo Knuuttila*, Leiden, 19–40.
Charles, D. (2008), 'Aristotle's Psychological Theory', *Proceedings of the Boston Area Colloquium of Ancient Philosophy* 24(1): 1–29.
Charles, D. (2009), 'Aristotle on Desire and Action', in D. Frede and B. Reis (eds) *Body and Soul in Ancient Philosophy*, Berlin, 291–308.
Charles, D. (2010), '*Metaphysics Θ.7* and 8: Some Issues Concerning Actuality and Potentiality', in J.G. Lennox and R.Bolton (eds) *Being, Nature and Life in Aristotle*, 168–97.
Charles, D. (2012), 'Teleological Causation', in C. Shields (ed.) *Oxford Handbook of Aristotle*, Oxford, 227–66.
Charles, D. (2015), 'Aristotle's Processes', in M. Leunissen (ed.) *Essays on Aristotle's Physics*, Cambridge, 186–205.
Charles, D. (2018), 'Physics 1.7', in D. Quarantotto (ed.) *Aristotle's Physics 1*, Cambridge, 178–205.
Charles, D. (2018), 'Comments on Aryeh Kosman's *The Activity of Being*', *European Journal of Philosophy* 26(2): 860–71.
Charles, D. (2020), 'Aristotle on the Perception of Objects', in G. Guyomarc'h, C. Louguet, and C. Murgier (eds) *Aristote et l'âme humaine, Lectures de* De Anima *III offertes à Michel Crubellier*, Louvain-la-Neuve.
Charles, D. (forthcoming), *The History of Hylomorphism: Aristotle to Boyle*, Oxford.
Chiaradonna, R. (2014), 'La chair et le bronze. Remarques sur *Métaphysique* Z, 11 et l'interprétation de M. Frede et G. Patzig', *Les Études philosophiques* 110(3): 375–88.
Child, T.W. (1994), *Causality, Interpretation, and the Mind*, Oxford.
Clark, A. (2008), *Supersizing the Mind: Embodiment, Action, and Cognitive Extension*, Oxford.
Code, A. (2010a), 'An Aristotelian Puzzle about Definition: *Metaphysics Z.12*', in J.G. Lennox (ed.) *Being, Nature, and Life in Aristotle: Essays in Honor of Allan Gotthelf*, Cambridge, 78–96.
Code, A. (2010b), 'Commentary on Devereux', *Proceedings of the Boston Area Colloquium of Ancient Philosophy* 26(1): 197–209.
Coope, U. (2009), 'Change and its Relation to Actuality and Potentiality', in G. Anagnostopoulos (ed.) *A Companion to Aristotle*, Oxford, 277–91.
Coope, U. (2012), 'Commentary on *Physics* 246a10–b3', in S. Maso, C. Natali, and G. Seel (eds) *Reading Physics VII.3*, Las Vegas, 57–72.
Coope, U. (2020), 'Animal and Celestial Motion: The Role of an External Springboard: DM 2 and 3', in C. Rapp and O. Primavesi (eds) *De Motu Animalium*, Oxford.
Corcilius, K. and Gregoric, P. (2013), 'Aristotle's Model of Animal Motion', *Phronesis* 58: 52–97.
Crane, T. and Patterson, S. (2000), *The History of the Mind-Body Problem*, London.
Damasio, A. (1994), *Descartes' Error*, New York.
Damasio, A. (2000), *The Feeling of What Happens: Body and Emotion in the Making of Consciousness*, London.
Davidson, D. (1980), *Essays on Actions and Events*, Oxford.
Dennett, D. (1993), *Consciousness Explained*, London.
Denniston, J.D. (1966), *The Greek Particles*, London (2nd edition).
Descartes, R. (1984), *The Philosophical Works*, in J. Cottingham, R. Stoothoff, and D. Murdoch, trs., vol. 2, Cambridge.

Descartes, R. (1985), *The Philosophical Works,* in J. Cottingham, R. Stoothoff, and D. Murdoch, trs., vol. 1, Cambridge.
Devereux, D. (2003), 'The Relationship between Books Eta and Zeta of Aristotle's *Metaphysics*', *Oxford Studies in Ancient Philosophy* 25: 159–211.
Devereux, D. (2010), 'Aristotle on the Form and Definition of a Human Being: Definitions and their Parts in *Metaphysics* Z.10 and 11', *Proceedings of the Boston Area Colloquium of Ancient Philosophy* 26(1): 167–96.
Distelzweig, P. (2013), 'The Intersection of the Mathematical and Natural Sciences: The Subordinate Sciences in Aristotle', *Apeiron* 46(2): 85–105.
Everson, S. (1997), *Aristotle on Perception*, Oxford.
Ferejohn, M. (2013), *Formal Causes: Definition, Explanation, and Primacy in Socratic and Aristotelian Thought*, Oxford.
Fine, K. (1992), 'Aristotle on Matter', *Mind* 101(401): 35–58.
Fine, K. (1999), 'Things and their Parts', *Midwest Studies in Philosophy* 23: 61–74.
Frede, M. (1990), 'The Definition of Sensible Substances in *Met. Z*', in D. Devereux and P. Pellegrin (eds) *Biologie, Logique et Métaphysique chez Aristote*, Paris, 113–29.
Frede, M. (1992), 'On Aristotle's Conception of the Soul', in M. Nussbaum and A. Rorty (eds) *Essays on* De Anima, Oxford, 93–109.
Frede, M. and Charles, D. (2000), *Aristotle's Metaphysics Lambda*, Oxford.
Freudenthal, G. (1995), *Aristotle's Theory of Material Substance*, Oxford.
Funkhouser, E. (2006), 'The Determinable-Determinate Relation', *Nous* 40(3): 548–69.
Furth, M. (1988), *Substance, Form, and Psyche: An Aristotelean Metaphysics*, Cambridge.
Gill, M.L. (1989), *Aristotle on Substance*, Princeton.
Gill, M.L. (2006), 'First Philosophy in Aristotle', in M.L. Gill and P. Pellegrin (eds) *A Companion to Ancient Philosophy*, Oxford, 347–73.
Gotthelf, A. (1999), 'A Biological Provenance', *Philosophical Studies* 94: 35–56.
Gotthelf, A. (2012), *Teleology, First Principles, and Scientific Method in Aristotle's Biology*, Oxford.
Gregoric, P. (2007), *Aristotle on the Common Sense*, Oxford.
Gregoric, P. and Kuhar, M. (2014), 'Aristotle's Physiology of Animal Motion: *Neura* and Muscles', *Apeiron* 47(1): 94–115.
Haas, F. de and Mansfeld, J. (2004), *Aristotle's Generation and Corruption 1*, Oxford.
Haslanger, S. (1994), 'Parts, Compounds, and Substantial Unity', in T. Scaltsas, D. Charles, and M.L. Gill (eds) *Unity, Identity, and Explanation in Aristotle's Metaphysics*, Oxford, 129–70.
Heinaman, R. (1990), 'Aristotle and the Mind-Body Problem', *Phronesis* 35: 83–102.
Heinaman, R. (1997), 'Frede and Patzig on Definition in *Metaphysics* Z.10–11', *Phronesis* 42(3): 283–98.
Heinaman, R. (2007), 'Actuality, Potentiality and *De Anima* II.5', *Phronesis* 52: 139–87.
Henry, D. (2019), *Aristotle on Matter, Form and Moving Causes*, Cambridge.
Hurley, S. (2002), *Consciousness in Action*, Cambridge, Mass.
Huxley, T.H. (1886), *Lessons in Elementary Physiology*, London.
Jackson, F. (1986), 'What Mary Didn't Know', *Journal of Philosophy* 83: 291–5.
Jaworski, W. (2016), *Structure and the Metaphysics of Mind*, Oxford.
Johansen, T. (1998), *Aristotle on Sense Organs*, Cambridge.
Johansen, T. (2012), *The Powers of the Aristotelian Soul*, Oxford.
Johnson, W.E. (1921), *Logic*, Cambridge.
Johnston, M. (2006), 'Hylomorphism', *The Journal of Philosophy* 103: 652–98.
Johnstone, M. (2012), 'Aristotle on Odour and Smell', *Oxford Studies in Ancient Philosophy* 43: 143–83.

Johnstone, M. (2013), 'Aristotle on Sounds', *British Journal for the History of Philosophy* 21(4): 631–48.
Judson, L. (2015), 'Aristotle's Astrophysics', *Oxford Studies in Ancient Philosophy* 49: 151–92.
Kalderon, M.E. (2015), *Form without Matter*, Oxford.
Katz, E. (2019), 'Geometrical Objects as Properties of Sensibles: Aristotle's Philosophy of Geometry', *Phronesis* 64(4): 465–513.
Kim, J. (1989), 'The Myth of Non-reductive Materialism', *Proceedings of the American Philosophical Association* 3: 31–47.
Kim, J. (1996), *Philosophy of Mind*, New York.
Koons, R. (2014), 'Staunch vs Faint-hearted Hylomorphism: Towards an Aristotelian Account of Composition', *Res Philosophica* 91: 151–78.
Koslicki, K. (2006), 'Aristotle's Mereology and the Status of Form', *The Journal of Philosophy* 103: 715–36.
Koslicki, K. (2007), 'Towards a Neo-Aristotelian Mereology', *Dialectica* 61(1), Special Issue: *The Philosophy of Kit Fine*, 127–59.
Koslicki, K. (2008), *The Structure of Objects*, Oxford.
Koslicki, K. (2014), 'The Causal Priority of Form in Aristotle', *Studia Philosophica Estonica* 7(2): 113–41.
Koslicki, K. (2018), *Form, Matter, and Substance*, Oxford.
Kosman, A. (1969), 'Aristotle's Definition of Motion', *Phronesis* 14: 41–62.
Kosman, A. (1987), 'Animals and Other Beings in Aristotle', in A. Gotthelf and J.G. Lennox (eds) *Philosophical Issues in Aristotle's Biology*, Cambridge, 360–91.
Kosman, A. (2013), *The Activity of Being*, Cambridge, Mass.
Kraut, R. (ed.) (2006), *Aristotle's Nicomachean Ethics*, Oxford.
Kripke, S. (1980), *Naming and Necessity*, Oxford.
Langton, R. (2000), 'The Musical, the Magical and the Mathematical Soul', in T. Crane and S. Patterson (eds) *The History of the Mind-Body Problem*, London, 13–33.
Lear, G.R. (2006), 'Aristotle on Moral Virtue and the Fine', in R. Kraut (ed.) *Aristotle's Nicomachean Ethics*, Oxford, 116–36.
Lennon, K. and Charles, D. (eds) (1992), *Reduction, Explanation, and Realism*, Oxford.
Lennox, J.G. (1980), 'Aristotle on Genera, Species and the More and the Less', *Journal of the History of Biology* 13(2): 321–46.
Lennox, J.G. (2008), ' "As if We Were Investigating Snubness": Aristotle on the Prospects for a Single Science of Nature', *Oxford Studies in Ancient Philosophy* 35(1): 149–86.
Leunissen, M. (2017), *From Natural Character to Moral Virtue in Aristotle*, Oxford.
Lewis, F. (1994), 'Aristotle on the Relation between a Thing and its Matter', in T. Scaltsas, D. Charles, and M.L. Gill (eds) *Unity, Identity, and Explanation in Aristotle's Metaphysics*, Oxford, 247–77.
Lloyd, G. (1996), 'Fuzzy Natures', in G.E.R. Lloyd (ed.) *Aristotelian Explorations*, Cambridge, 76–82.
Lorenz, H. (2007), 'The Assimilation of Sense to Sense-Object in Aristotle', *Oxford Studies in Ancient Philosophy* 33: 179–220.
Makin, S. (2006), *Aristotle Metaphysics Book* Θ, Oxford.
Malink, M. (2013), 'Essence and Being', *Oxford Studies in Ancient Philosophy* 45(1): 341–62.
Marmodoro, A. (2007), 'The Union of Cause and Effect in Aristotle: *Physics* III 3', *Oxford Studies in Ancient Philosophy* (32): 205–32.
Marmodoro, A. (2013), 'Aristotelian Hylomorphism without Reconditioning', *Philosophical Inquiry*, 36: 5–22.
Marmodoro, A. (2014), *Aristotle on Perceiving Objects*, Oxford.
Martin, C.B. (1994), 'Dispositions and Conditionals', *Philosophical Quarterly* 44: 1–8.

Maso, S., Natali, C., and Seel, G. (2012), *Reading Aristotle's* Physics *VII.3. What is Alteration?* Las Vegas.
Matthews, E. (2017), 'Mind-Body Dualism and its Place in Mental Health Care', in T. Schrame and S. Edwards (eds) *Handbook of the Philosophy of Medicine*, Dordrecht.
Matson, W.I. (1966), 'Why Isn't the Mind-Body Problem Ancient?', in P. Feyerabend and G. Maxwell (eds) *Mind, Matter and Method, Essays in Honour of Hebert Feigl*, Minneapolis, 92–102.
McDowell, J. (1998), 'Having the World in View: Sellars, Kant, and Intentionality', *Journal of Philosophy* 95: 431–91.
McGinn, C. (1990), *The Problem of Consciousness*, Oxford.
Menn, S. (1994), 'The Origins of Aristotle's Concept of Energeia: *energeia* and *dunamis*', *Ancient Philosophy* 14: 73–114.
Menn, S. (2001), '*Metaphysics Z* 10–16 and the Argument-Structure of *Metaphysics Z*', *Oxford Studies in Ancient Philosophy* 21: 83–134.
Menn, S. (2002), 'Aristotle's Definition of the Soul and the Programme of the *De Anima*', *Oxford Studies in Ancient Philosophy* 22: 83–109.
Meyer, S. Sauvé (1992), 'Aristotle, Teleology, and Reduction', *Philosophical Review* 101: 791–825.
Mingucci, G. (2019), 'Aristotle and the "Cartesians" Error', in D. Zucca and R. Medda (eds) *The Soul/Body Problem in Plato and Aristotle*, Sankt Augustin, 159–76.
Modrak, D. (1987), *Aristotle: The Power of Perception*, Chicago.
Modrak, D. (1989), 'Aristotle on the Difference between Mathematics and Physics and First Philosophy', *Apeiron* 22(4): 121–39.
Modrak, D. (2001), *Aristotle's Theory of Language and Meaning*, Cambridge.
Morison, B. (2020), '*De Motu Animalium* 4 and 5: Completing the Argument That Locomotion Requires an External and Unmoved Mover', in C. Rapp and O. Primavesi (eds) *De Motu Animalium*, Oxford.
Morrison, D. (1990), 'Some Remarks on Definition in *Metaphysics Z*', in D. Devereux and P. Pellegrin (eds) *Biologie, Logique et Métaphysique chez Aristote*, Paris, 131–44.
Nathan, P.M. and Gorman, J.M. (2002), *A Guide to Treatments That Work*, Oxford.
Nussbaum, M. and Rorty, A. (1992), *Essays on Aristotle's* De Anima, Oxford [revised edition: 1995].
O'Regan, K. (2011), *Why Red Doesn't Sound Like a Bell*, Oxford.
O'Shaughnessy, B. (1980), *The Will: A Dual Aspect Theory*, Cambridge.
Owens, J. (1982), 'Aristotle on Common Sensibles and Incidental Perception', *Phoenix* 3: 215–36.
Passnau, R. (2011), *Metaphysical Themes 1274–1671*, Oxford.
Pears, D. (1975), 'Ifs and Cans', *Some Questions in the Philosophy of Mind*, London.
Peramatzis, M. (2008), 'Aristotle's Notion of Priority in Nature and Substance', *Oxford Studies in Ancient Philosophy* 35: 187–247.
Peramatzis, M. (2011), *Priority in Aristotle's Metaphysics*, Oxford.
Peramatzis, M. (2014), 'Matter in Scientific Definitions in Aristotle', *Oxford Handbooks Online*.
Peramatzis, M. (2015), 'What Is a Form in Aristotle's Hylomorphism?', *History of Philosophy Quarterly* 32(3): 194–216.
Peramatzis, M. (2018), 'Aristotle's Hylomorphism: The Causal-Explanatory Model', *Metaphysics* 11: 12–32.
Peramatzis, M. (2019), 'Review of Kathrin Koslicki's *Form, Matter and Substance*', *Mind* 129: 235–45.

Peramatzis, M. and Charles, D. (forthcoming), *Aristotle's Metaphysics: The Philosophical Project of the Central Books*.
Perenboom, D. (2011), *Consciousness and the Prospects of Physicalism*, Oxford.
Pfeiffer, C. (2018), *Aristotle's Theory of Bodies*, Oxford.
Philoponus, (1909), *Commentary on Analytica Posteriora*, ed. M. Wallies, Berlin.
Prior, A. (1949), 'Determinables, Determinates and Determinants', *Mind* 58: 1–18.
Putnam, H. (1975), 'Minds and Machines,' in his *Collected Papers*, vol. 2, Cambridge, 362–85.
Putnam, H. and Nussbaum, M.C. (1995), 'Changing Aristotle's Mind', in M. Nussbaum and A. Rorty (eds) *Essays on De Anima*, Oxford, 27–76.
Quarantotto, D. (2018), *Aristotle's Physics Book 1: A Systematic Exploration*, Cambridge.
Quarantotto, D. (2019), 'Aristotle on the Differences in Material Organisation between Spoken and Written Language: An Inquiry into Part-Whole Relations', *Elenchos* 40: 333–62.
Quarantotto, D. (forthcoming), 'Aristotle on the Order of Embryonic Development and the Homonymy Principle', in S. Föllinger (ed.) *Aristotle's Generation of Animals: A Comprehensive Approach*, Berlin.
Rapp, C. (2006), 'Interaction of Body and Soul: What the Hellenistic Philosophers Saw and Aristotle Avoided', in R. King (ed.) *Common to Body and Soul*, Berlin: 187–208.
Rapp, C. (2020), 'Joints and Movers in the Cliffhanger Passage at the End of Aristotle, *De Anima* III.10', in G. Guyomarc'h and C. Louguet (eds) *Aristote et l'âme humaine, Lectures de* De Anima *III offertes à Michel Crubellier*, Louvain-la-Neuve.
Rapp, C. and Primavesi, O. (eds) (2020), *De Motu Animalium*, Oxford.
Rashed, M. (2017), 'A Latent Difficulty in Aristotle's Theory of Semen', in A. Falcon and D. Lefebvre (eds) *Aristotle's Theory of Generation*, Cambridge, 108–29.
Ratcliffe, M. (2007), *Feelings of Being*, Oxford.
Rea, M. (2011), 'Hylomorphism Reconditioned', *Philosophical Perspectives* 25: 241–58.
Robinson, H. (2014), 'Modern Hylomorphism and the Reality of Causal Structure: A Skeptical Investigation', *Res Philosophica* 91: 203–14.
Rodriguez-Pereyra, G. (2008), 'Descartes's Substance Dualism and his Independence Conception of Substance', *Journal of the History of Philosophy* 46(1): 69–89.
Rorty, R. (1973), 'Genus as Matter: A Reading of *Metaphysics* Z-H', *Phronesis*, Supplementary Volume I: 393–420.
Rorty, R. (1974), 'Matter as Goo: Comments on Grene's Paper', *Synthese* 28(1): 71–7.
Russell, B. (1921), *The Analysis of Mind*, London.
Scaltsas, T., Charles, D., and Gill, M.L. (eds) (1994), *Unity, Identity, and Explanation in Aristotle's Metaphysics*, Oxford.
Searle, J. (1959), 'On Determinables and Resemblance', *Proceedings of the Aristotelian Society*, Supplementary Volume 33: 141–58.
Sellars, W. (1967), 'Aristotle's Metaphysics: An Interpretation', in his *Philosophical Perspectives*, Springfield, 73–124.
Shields, C. (1990), 'The First Functionalist', in J. Smith (ed.) *Historical Foundations of Cognitive Science*, Dordrecht, 19–33.
Shields, C. (1998), *Order in Multiplicity: Homonymy in the Philosophy of Aristotle*, Oxford.
Shoemaker, S. (2003), 'Content, Character and Colour', *Philosophical Issues* 13(1): 253–78.
Shoemaker, S. (2007), *Physical Realization*, Oxford.
Skrzypek, J. (2017), 'Three Concerns for Structural Hylomorphism', *Analytic Philosophy* 58: 360–408.
Slakey, T.J. (1961), 'Aristotle on Sense Perception', *Philosophical Review* 70: 470–84.
Sorabji, R. (1974), 'Body and Soul in Aristotle', *Philosophy* 49: 63–89.

Sorabji, R. (2001), 'Aristotle on Sensory Processes and Intentionality', in D. Perler (ed.) *Ancient and Medieval Theories of Intentionality*, Leiden, 49–61.
Stout, R. (2018), *Process, Action, and Experience*, Oxford.
Strawson, G. (2006), *Consciousness and its Place in Nature: Does Physicalism Entail Pan-psychism?* London.
Strawson, P. (1959), *Individuals*, London.
Tuozzo, T. (2014), 'Aristotle on the Discovery of Efficient Causation', in T. Schmaltz (ed.) *Efficient Causation*, Oxford, 23–47.
Wedin, M. (1988), *Mind and Imagination in Aristotle*, New Haven.
Wedin, M. (1993), 'Content and Cause in the Aristotelian Mind', *Southern Journal of Philosophy* 31: 49–105.
Wedin, M. (2000), *Aristotle's Theory of Substance*, Oxford.
Westphal, J. (2016), *The Mind-Body Problem*, Boston, Mass.
Whiting, J. (1986), 'Form and Individuation in Aristotle', *History of Philosophy Quarterly* 3(4): 359–77.
Whiting, J. (1991), 'Meta-Substance: Critical Notice of Frede-Patzig and Furth', *Philosophical Review* 100(4): 607–39.
Whiting, J. (1995), 'Living Bodies', in M. Nussbaum and A. Rorty (eds) *Essays on Aristotle's De Anima*, Oxford, 75–92.
Wiggins, D. (2001), *Sameness and Substance Renewed*, Cambridge.
Williams, B. (1986), 'Hylomorphism', *Oxford Studies in Ancient Philosophy* 4: 189–99.
Williamson, T. (2000), *Knowledge and its Limits*, Oxford.
Wilson, M. (1991), *Descartes*, London.
Witt, C. (2003), *Ways of Being in Aristotle's Metaphysics*, New York.
Yablo, S. (1992), 'Mental Causation', *Philosophical Review* 101: 245–80.
Zucca, D. and Medda, R. (eds) (2019), *The Soul/Body Problem in Plato and Aristotle*, Berlin.

Index Locorum

For the benefit of digital users, indexed terms that span two pages (e.g., 52–3) may, on occasion, appear on only one of those pages

Posterior Analytics
A
73a10ff: 49
87b37ff: 199
B
90a14–15: 249
91b35ff: 91
Topics
103b32: 199
120b25: 199
Sophistici Elenchi
181b34–35: 47
181b35–37: 47
181b37–182a2: 47–8
182a2–6: 47–8
Physics
A
184b2–3: 128–9
190b17–18: 44
B
193b4ff: 44
193b31–194a7: 26–7, 43–4, 73–4, 101, 262
194a7ff: 262
194a12–15: 43–4, 46, 101, 178–9, 213–14
194b12–13: 44
194b14–15: 44–5
194b25–27: 44
198a23–25: 44
198a36: 72
198b1–3: 44
198b26–199a3: 240–1
200a17ff: 261
200b4–8: 44, 77
Γ
202a9ff: 70, 140
202b12–22: 140, 169
205a6: 126
E
224b29: 126
225b10ff: 130
H
243a35ff: 121
245b15: 130

246a5–8: 145–6
246a10–11: 130–1
246a15: 130–1
246a19: 130
246b13–15: 146
246b18–20: 127, 145
246b21–247a19: 145–6
De Caelo
299a18–19: 74–5
305a28ff: 77
307a17–26: 74
De Generatione et Corruptione
310a25: 126
314b1–3: 280–1
335b18ff: 69
Meteorologica
384b22–23: 83–4
384b30ff: 145
388b11ff: 66
390b11–14: 106–7
De Anima
A
402b1–403a2: 23, 29, 31–2, 40–1, 91
403a3–10: 18, 21, 23
403a10–16: 30
403a16–22: 23, 30–1
403a22–24: 32
403a24–28: 18, 20, 22, 30–2, 35, 119
403a29–b2: 21, 23, 30–1, 38–9
403b2–7: 23–4, 61–2
403b7–16: 30–4, 43, 221
403b17–19: 18, 26–7, 31
404b31–405a7: 96
405a7ff: 237
406b20–25: 100
407b15–26: 40–1, 91, 99–100, 236
407b30–33: 251–2
408a1ff: 99
408a15ff: 99, 145–6
408b1–18: 36, 106–7, 220
B
412a20–24: 213–14, 216
412b6–9: 156

De Anima (cont.)
412b10–17: 239
413a8–10: 116
413b23–24: 213
413b24–25: 31–2
414b13: 213
414b28–31: 214
415a18–21: 138–9, 168, 170, 181–2
416a5–10: 99
416b6–7: 131–2
416b16–20: 132
417a18–20: 129
417a21–28: 122, 127
417a29–417b1: 121–4
417b2–5: 120, 122–3, 177
417b5–9: 121–3, 125, 127, 129
417b9–16: 114, 121–5, 127, 160, 177–8
417b16–19: 120, 125, 128
417b19–27: 199
418a9–16: 197
418a16–20: 197, 199, 203
418a20–25: 196–7, 199–200
418a28–31: 172, 175, 179, 198
418a31–b4: 172, 175, 184
418b4–9: 172, 174–5, 179
418b11–17: 177, 180, 182–3
418b20–26: 197–8
418b26–29: 176
419a1–6: 175, 198
419a9–11: 172
419b3–11: 168, 179
419b21–25: 165–6
419b25–27: 165–6
419b27–33: 178–9
420a2–5: 153, 163
420a5–7: 153, 155
420a7–11: 153, 155
420a15–19: 163
420a19–21: 168
420a23–26: 163, 166
420a26–29: 169
421b9–13: 139
422a2–3: 161
422a5–7: 141
422a7–10: 198
422a15–17: 139
422a17–19: 140–1
422a31–34: 198
422a34–b5: 137
422b5–6: 136, 213
422b6–10: 137, 186
422b15–16: 144–5
423b15–17: 153, 164
423b27–29: 153

424a5–10: 155, 157
424a17–21: 155–6
424a21–24: 158
424a24–28: 101–2, 110, 136, 158
424a28–b3: 136, 153, 159–60, 163
424b10–12: 169
424b12–18: 161
Γ
425a14–b3: 199–203
425b17–25: 176, 198
425b26–426a1: 164
426a11–15: 140–1, 168, 179
426a15–19: 168, 187
426a20–26: 169, 183, 185
426a27–30: 167–8
426b2–7: 163
426b8–13: 155
426b29–427a1: 203
428b10–12: 210
429a4–9: 210
429a23–26: 221
429b1–3: 221
429b21–22: 140, 170, 221–2
431a8–14: 209, 217–18
431b2–10: 217–18
431b17–19: 222
432a2–6: 220
433a14–25: 219
433b13–26: 94–6, 114–15
434a9–10: 211
434a14–21: 219
435b22–25: 213

De Sensu
436a1–4: 138
436a6–10: 29, 95, 146, 209–10
438a9–10: 178–9, 185
438a16–21: 185
438b4–5: 177
438b12–22: 180, 185
439a6–12: 138–9
439a15–21: 180
439a21–25: 179–80, 182–3
439a28: 180
439b1: 180
439b8–10: 179
439b11–12: 179
439b15–18: 179–80, 182
440a13–15: 181
440a19–26: 49, 177
440b15–25: 182
441b18–20: 139
441b20–24: 128
441b24–442a2: 132, 207–8
442a16–17: 178

442a19–22: 137
442a30ff: 149–50
442b28–29: 139
443a1–9: 139
443b6–16: 139
443b17–18: 206
443a8–19: 206
444a28–31: 207
444a31–33: 141
444b28–34: 207
445a14–15: 139–40
445a20–21: 132
446b30ff: 165–6
447a3–6: 177, 184–5
448a18f: 167

De Memoria
450a8–10: 63
450a25–27: 211–12
450a27–30: 211
450b9–11: 212
451b4–5: 212
452b7–11: 203–4
453a9–15: 212–13, 218
453b11: 218

De Partibus Animalium
640a10–14: 77–8
640b1–3: 107
640b27–30: 280–1

De Generatione Animalium
734b11–18: 107
734b32ff: 107–8
735a2ff: 193
736b22ff: 53–4
740b27–36: 107
743a21–24: 280–1
743a33–36: 117
744b32ff: 106
765b1–7: 280–1
779b31ff: 184
780a2–7: 184–6
780a10–16: 184, 186
780a27ff: 186

De Motu Animalium
701a3–5: 205
701a14–25: 104–5, 113
701a28–36: 103–5, 111, 210
701a36–b3: 104–5
701b2–4: 106
701b4–16: 102–4, 106
701b12–22: 103–4, 143, 205, 207, 210
701b22–28: 109
701b33–702a1: 102, 104–6
702a2–7: 105–6

702a7–14: 104–5, 109–10
702a15–21: 110
702a21–32: 110–11
702a32–b11: 105–6, 110
702b20–703a3: 103, 110–12
703a4–18: 103, 111–15
703a19–29: 72, 102–3, 109, 114–15
703a29–b2: 99

De Incessu Animalium
704b15f: 72

Metaphysics
A
992a25–31: 69
Γ
1003b22–25: 142
Z
1032b21ff: 69
1035a1–4: 56
1035a4–6: 49, 55
1035a11–17: 57
1035a17–25: 56–7
1035a25–31: 56, 58
1035a31–35: 58
1035b11–14: 59
1035b14–25: 59, 63, 239
1035b25–27: 85
1035b27–1036a2: 61
1036a27–31: 53–4
1036b7–17: 53–4
1036b21–28: 53–4
1036b28–32: 61–4, 73–4, 79
1036b32ff: 55
1037a10–13: 92
1037a13–20: 77
1037a21–34: 49, 60–1, 91–2
1038a5ff: 81, 90
1038b5ff: 81
1041a29–31: 90–1
1041b5–7: 90
1041b8–10: 66–9
1041b19ff: 251–2
H
1043a1–4: 67–8
1043a6–14: 65, 171, 244
1043a14–22: 65, 67–8
1043b2–4: 56
1044a15–25: 244
1044a29–34: 67, 80
1044b1–2: 80
1044b8–16: 66–7
Θ
1046a4–21: 73–4, 78, 99
1048a16–20: 72–3, 126

Metaphysics (cont.)
1048b7–10: 253
1049a27–36: 81–2, 244
1050a8–12: 72, 86
1050a34–b1: 215–16
I
1055b14–15: 124–5
K
1061a27ff: 24–5
Λ
1069b14–20: 79, 247

Nicomachean Ethics
1098b14: 196
1119a23ff: 209–10
1150a24: 209–10
1153a12: 147
1157a31: 196
1173b7ff: 29, 209–10

Politics
1340a7–28: 208–9
1340a33–b10: 208–9

Rhetoric
1370b35ff: 209–10
1390a15ff: 29

Problemata
vii: 167
xi: 29, 167, 209–10
xix: 167

General Index

For the benefit of digital users, indexed terms that span two pages (e.g., 52–3) may, on occasion, appear on only one of those pages.

Abstraction 15, 24–6, 28, 74–5, 261–3
Actions 26, 86, 99, 147–8, 219–20, 226–7, 230, 236, 257–8
  See processes and events
Anger 6–8, 18–21, 26–7, 83–4, 104, 119, 233–4

Capacities
  capacities and being capable 8–9, 122, 215–16, 250–2
  enmattered 73–4, 85, 163, 194, 225–6, 233, 255
  mathematical 73–4, 233
Causes
  efficient 11, 69–71, 99, 163, 194, 212, 246
  final 44, 65, 74 (*See also* teleology)
  formal 240, 246 (*See also* definitions, forms)
  material 235, 245–6, 273
  per se 8, 11, 70–1, 84, 116, 119–20, 194, 223, 229, 237, 263, 275–6
  efficient causes and effects 140–2, 206, 222–3, 230–1, 275–6
  efficient causes of material change 13, 70, 73–5, 95, 104
Changes
  bodily changes 26–7, 30, 78–9, 89, 97, 106, 209–10, 232–3
  mere Cambridge changes 130–1, 173, 177
  types of change 120–31, 133–4, 146
  See also processes, events
Colour
  colour of the object 128, 130, 157–8, 172–3, 179
  colour in the medium 172–85, 187
  colour in the eye 173, 185–8, 191–2
  colour and coloured objects 196–7, 204–5
  experience of colour 265–8
Completions 127, 130–2, 145, 163–4, 194
Cross-modal properties 195, 197, 199, 201–3

Definitions
  Analytics-style definitions 29, 66–8, 91, 237
  dialectical 23–4, 261

See also Unity, Priority
Desire
  definition of 37–8, 84, 95, 108–10, 258
  desire and perception 103–4, 227
  desire as a per se cause 11, 13–14, 96, 107–9, 116, 194–5, 226–7, 238
  varieties of desire 1, 10, 19, 217, 219
Determinables, determinants, determinates 50–2, 82–4, 89–92, 243–4, 274–5, 284
  See Snubness and S-structures

Emotions 5, 16, 26, 31–2, 39–40, 64, 97, 117, 119–20, 163, 172, 225, 232–3
Enmattered forms 10, 142, 163, 178–9, 225–6, 255
  definition of 51–2, 55
  causal role of 11, 42, 68–88, 97, 163, 174
  of natural substances 42, 88
  ontology of, *see* capacities, activities
Essences
  and forms 6, 29, 46, 84, 88, 91–2, 216
  See also definition
Eye 4, 161, 173–4, 180, 185–6, 189, 207–8, 213, 216

Fear 6, 18–21, 24–6, 31, 68, 95, 102–6, 109, 205
Flavour 76, 136–45, 148–52, 157–8, 161–2, 168, 206.
Food 117, 131–2, 206–8
Forms
  forms as activities 251–3
  forms as causes 69–74, 78, 85, 140, 194, 223, 232, 246
  pure forms 27, 30, 70, 85
  impure forms 11, 30, 45, 51–2, 247
  forms as capacities, *see* capacities and being capable
Functionalism
  role functionalism 234–6
  state functionalism 235, 237
Functionalist interpretation 3, 37–8, 96, 234–8

300 GENERAL INDEX

Harmonics 75–6, 167, 178–9
Harmony 65–6, 98, 159, 167
Harmony theory 11, 97–102, 251–2
Hearing 163–72, 185, 189, 192, 197–8, 208–9
  See also sounds
Hylomorphism
  history of hylomorphism 46, 257
  neo-Aristotelian hylomorphism 12, 246–52
  varieties of hylomorphism 221–2

Illuminable (*diaphanes*) 174–86, 192, 198
Imagination
  enmattered 105–6, 212
  imagination and desire 102–4, 194–5, 205,
    210–12, 217–19, 221–2, 225
Impure Form interpretation 22–3, 51–2, 62, 65,
    75–6, 88
  See also impure forms
Inextricability theses 34, 225, 254–9
  [A] psychological as inextricably physical 34,
    225–8, 259–72
  [B] physical as inextricably psychological 34,
    227–9, 233, 272–6

Light 11, 75–6, 154, 172–3, 175–93,
    204, 265–6

Materialism
  non-reductionist materialism 2–3, 35, 96,
    229–34, 253–4, 276–81
  reductionist 1–2, 16, 182, 228, 254,
    281, 283–4
Modal-specific properties 195–7, 199
Monism, neutral 2, 254, 258–9

Necessity, hypothetical 40–1, 45, 62–3, 66, 77–8,
    91, 101, 149, 236
Nutrition 5, 30–1, 131–3, 135, 207–8, 213–14,
    222–3, 251
Non-reductionist materialist interpretation 4,
    21, 37–8, 97–100, 116, 118–19, 144–51,
    171, 174, 190

Odour 138–9, 142, 207
Optics 75, 178–9
Over-determination 23–4, 85, 227–8, 233–4,
    242–3, 255–6

Pain
  experience of pain 2–3, 12, 263–4, 266
  pain and anger 24, 235–6, 261
  pain as bodily 29, 52, 104, 146, 195
  role of pain in action 102–6, 209–10

Pan-psychism 2–3, 244, n. 35, 274, 284
Passions, common to body and soul 6, 10, 85,
    92–5, 114, 194–5, 204–5, 213, 245–6,
    254–5
Pleasure 102, 146–8, 206, 208 10, 217, 268
Pneuma, connate 72, 102–3, 105–15
Priority
  priority condition 88, 234, 238–9,
    243, 246
  priority in being 87–8, 234
  priority in definition 168, 183, 213–14,
    238–9, 247
  priority in existence 234, 251–2
  priority of form 86, 88, 233, 241–2, 246
Processes (*kinēseis*)
  causes of 13–14, 70, 73–4, 223, 246
  identity of 34, 95, 106–7, 142, 257
  processes and events 230, 276–8,
    281–2, 284
  See also changes, types of and completions
Pure Form Interpretation 21–2, 27, 60–4, 149
  See also pure forms

Realism, direct 190–3
Realization, variable 83, 237

Sense, common 195–6, 198, 218
  special 195–7, 199–202
Separability
  in thought 37–9, 259–60, 262
  in definition 26–7, 42, 260, 266–8
  in existence 26, 261
Snubness 7, 43–5, 47–52, 55–6, 60–2, 75–6, 139,
    213–14, 237, 262–3, 276–7
Spiritualism 2–3, 273
Spiritualist interpretation 3–6, 36–9, 96, 131,
    133–4, 138–43, 165–8, 172–9, 186, 190
S-structures 49–51, 83, 244
Seeing 103, 127, 173–4, 189
  seeing as pleasant 114–15
  seeing colours 189, 195–6
  seeing objects 197–205
Soul, human 59–60, 110–11, 213–16, 222–3,
    250, 271–2
Sound
  sound in the medium 165–8, 171–2
  sound and hearing 169–72

Taking on the form without the
    matter 137, 155–61
Taste 118, 136–41, 144–5, 152, 198, 207–9
Thought 18, 30
  human thought 221–3

practical thought 103, 111, 217, 219–20, 225
  varieties of thought 170
Touch 153–5, 160, 164, 197, 202
Transparent (*diaphanes*), *see* Illuminable
Two-component accounts 2–3, 20, 38, 42, 78, 95, 117, 119–20, 135, 188, 194, 225, 254, 259

Unity
  condition 88, 233, 238, 243, 246, 251
  essential vs. accidental unity 85, 91, 234, 241, 245–6, 283–4
  unity of form 88
  unity of soul 213–15

Index Nominum

For the benefit of digital users, indexed terms that span two pages (e.g., 52–3) may, on occasion, appear on only one of those pages.

Ackrill, J. 239–40, 243–6
Anagnostopoulos, A. 122

Beare, J.L. 180
Beere, J. 126–8
Berman, B. 196
Berryman, S. 112
Bodnár, I. 112
Bolton, R. 137
Bowin, J. 123, 127
Broackes, J. 180, 184
Burnyeat, M. 2–5, 119, 122–3, 125, 131, 133, 137, 144, 160

Campbell, K. 255
Caston, V. 3–4, 40–1, 46–8, 51, 83, 89, 133–4, 145, 150, 158
Chalmers, D. 3, 20, 254–5, 258–9, 265
Charles, D. 21, 44, 46, 82, 96, 103, 127–8, 161, 209, 226, 235, 242, 247, 280–1
Chiaradonna, R. 58–9, 62
Child, T.W. 229
Clark, A. 258
Code, A. 46, 91–2
Coope, U. 109–10, 127–8, 130, 142
Corcilius, K. 109–10, 205
Crivelli, P. 156

Damasio, A. 12, 19–20, 29–30, 206, 286
Davidson, D. 3, 19–20, 120, 229–31, 258
Descartes, R. 1, 14–15, 24, 232, 241, 254, 259–61, 269–72, 281, 286
Devereux, D. 46, 53–4, 58–9, 80–1
Distelzweig, P. 75

Elizabeth, Princess of Bohemia 271–2
Everson, S. 4, 24, 89, 160

Fine, K. 247
Frede, M. 46, 55, 57, 63–4
Freudenthal, G. 109
Funkhouser, E. 50

Gasser-Wingate, M. 51–2
Gill, M.L. 46, 60, 90, 122, 128–9
Gregoric, P. 109–10, 112, 198

Heinaman, R. 3, 60, 90, 122–3, 125, 127
Harte, V. 217–18
Henry, D. 72
Hicks, R.D. 121, 124–7, 202–3
Hurley, S. 258
Hussey, E. 24–5
Huxley, T.H. 282

Inwood, B. 63

Jackson, F. 265–6
Jaworski, W. 240–1, 250
Johansen, T. 3–4, 36–7, 40–1, 132–4, 137–8, 149, 216
Johnson, W.E. 50
Johnston, M. 247
Johnstone, M. 133, 144, 165–6
Judson, L. 183

Kalderon, M. 179
Katz, E. 63, 74–5
Kim, J. 37–8, 230–2
Koons, R. 250
Koslicki, K. 243, 247, 250–2
Kosman, A. 127–8, 252–3
Kress, E. 70–1
Kripke, S. 263–4
Kuhar, M. 109–10

Labarrière, J.-L. 104–5
Langton, R. 37–8
Lear, G.R. 104–5
Lennox, J. 44–6, 51
Leunissen, M. 216
Lorenz, H. 122, 133–5, 161

Malink, M. 85
Marmodoro, A. 142, 195–7, 242

Martin, C.B. 207
Matthews, E. 219
McDowell, J. 118
McGinn, C. 2, 254–5
Meister, S. 57
Menn, S. 46, 116–17, 253
Meyer, S. Sauvé 70–1
Miller, F. 49
Modrak, D. 191
Morison, B. 109–10

Nussbaum, M. 3, 38–9, 96, 98, 134

O'Regan, K. 269
O'Shaughnessy, B. 257–8
Owens, J. 199–200

Pears, D. 126
Peck, A.L. 72
Peramatzis, M. 44–9, 53–5, 57, 61–2, 243, 251–2, 260–1
Piñeros, J. 200
Primavesi, O. 205
Prior, A. 50
Putnam, H. 1, 37–8, 40–1, 96, 98, 234

Quarantotto, D. 44, 72–3

Ratcliffe, M. 286
Rapp, C. 112
Rashed, M. 72

Rea, M. 250
Robinson, H. 232
Rodriguez-Pereyra, G. 260
Ross, D. 18, 27, 124–5, 130, 142, 176, 202
Rowett, C. 51–2
Russell, B. 120, 254–5, 258–9

Searle, J. 50
Shields, C. 3, 134, 199–200, 234, 240
Shoemaker, S. 259, 264–5
Skrzypek, J. 242–3, 247
Slakey, T.J. 134
Sorabji, R. 4, 134
Stout, R. 281–2
Strawson, P. 257–8
Strawson, G. 3, 231, 254–5
Suarez, F. 70–1, 90, 117, 215

Tuozzo, T. 70

Wedin, M. 58–9, 145
Westphal, J. 255, 258–9
Whiting, J. 53–4, 62, 240
Wiggins, D. 239
Williams, B. 232
Williamson, T. 48, 280–1
Wilson, J. Cook 50, 139
Wilson, M. 260
Witt, C. 253

Yablo, S. 275–6